Boatbuilding
Manual

The Beach Pea, a lapstrake-plywood boat. (*Doug Hylan*)

Boatbuilding
Manual

FIFTH EDITION

Robert M. Steward
with Carl Cramer

International Marine / McGraw-Hill

Camden, Maine • New York • Chicago • San Francisco • Lisbon • London • Madrid
Mexico City • Milan • New Delhi • San Juan • Seoul • Singapore • Sydney • Toronto

The **McGraw·Hill** Companies

1 2 3 4 5 6 7 8 9 10 11 12 13 14 15 DOC/DOC 1 9 8 7 6 5 4 3 2 1 0
Copyright © 1970, 1980, 1987, 1994, 2011 by International Marine/The McGraw-Hill Companies.

ISBN 978-0-07-162834-1
MHID 0-07-162834-7
eBook ISBN 0-07-174463-0

This publication is designed to provide accurate and authoritative information in regard to the
subject matter covered. It is sold with the understanding that neither the author nor the publisher
is engaged in rendering legal, accounting, securities trading, or other professional services. If legal
advice or other expert assistance is required, the services of a competent professional person should
be sought.
—*From a Declaration of Principles Jointly Adopted by a Committee of the American Bar
Association and a Committee of Publishers and Associations*

Library of Congress Cataloging-in-Publication Data is available.

Questions regarding the content of this book should be addressed to www.internationalmarine.com

Line art created by Bob Steward. Photos on pages xi and xiii by Molly Mulhern. The appendix on
page 416 originally appeared in *WoodenBoat* magazine.

McGraw-Hill books are available at special quantity discounts to use as premiums and sales
promotions or for use in training programs. To contact a representative, please e-mail us
at bulksales@mcgraw-hill.com.

This book is printed on acid-free paper.

Contents

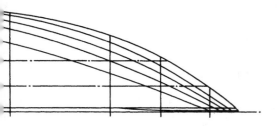

PREFACE TO THE FIFTH EDITION

INTERNATIONAL MARINE PUBLISHED the first edition of Bob Steward's seminal *Boatbuilding Manual* in 1970. At that time, I was an avid reader of anything to do with boats, especially yacht design. Skene, Chapelle, L. Francis Herreshoff, *The Rudder,* and *Yachting* were my primary sources of inspiration, until that first edition of the *Boatbuilding Manual* appeared.

International Marine and Bob Steward continued this proud legacy through four editions, with the fourth edition being published in 1994. More than 75,000 copies have been purchased to date, making it the most popular and invaluable contribution to boatbuilders to date. Sadly, Bob died in 1996.

The genesis for this particular edition came from a simple question I asked Jon Eaton, editor at International Marine, in 2009: "Jon, will you have a new edition of Bob Steward's book any time soon?" Jon replied that there were no plans to, although there was a definite need for it. At some point in our conversation, I vaguely remember Jon asking if I'd like to take on this task.

I've never been particularly good at saying "no" when asked, and I did feel the update was and is past due.

I consider this contribution of Bob's to be "Boatbuilding 101–110," and seldom have such golden words (his) about this topic been in print. Please view it in that perspective. It's not going to teach you everything you need to know about boatbuilding, but it will teach you all the rudiments, both historical and—to a degree—current practices. Much is evolving right now. If you want to outfit a state-of-the-art, systems-heavy boat, you will need other, more-current sources. And evolution is what we must recognize, if not necessarily adopt for our own boats. That is our choice, and this is yours as well. More to the point, you just need to decide to do it. Roll up your sleeves and get to work. Build the boat of your dreams, and learn from and enjoy your accomplishments! And then build another, putting your experience to work for you. Now, you are a "boatbuilder"—congratulations to you, and welcome to the family.

Bob, I hoist a glass to you—for all your knowledge, inspiration, and passion. I've tried to keep your spirit intact wherever I can. And to my wife Laura, for her forbearance throughout this ordeal of editing and updating. And to my extensive family: we devote major parts of our lives to boating, and to the enjoyment of what I consider an important endeavor. And, without fail, to my other family, WoodenBoat Publications, Inc. for their tolerance of me. They haven't caught me yet, even after 22-plus years of employment and fulfillment. (As I'm fond of saying, "Jon Wilson picked me up out of the gutter and gave me a career.") It's become much more than that, and I am eternally grateful.

Bob set me on the path that became my career, and I am so thankful for that. I suspect there are many others on whom he had the same effect. May Bob rest in peace, knowing that he has inspired so many of us. Thank you for all that you've done, now and in the future.

Let's just boat, and build boats. I hope to see you out there, using the boats we build from this tome. I will be, and I look forward to seeing you there.

FOREWORD TO THE SECOND EDITION

THE LIGHTS OFTEN SHOWED BRIGHT late in the evening at the Mizzentop in Huntington, New York, and continue to do so at Anchordown here in Darien. I have enjoyed a lifetime influenced by the talk of small boats—their design, their building, and their use. Most rewarding of all aspects, perhaps, are the letters that come along—letters extolling the grand experience encountered in the building of a boat!

There has always been great satisfaction—a justified feeling of accomplishment—related to making things with one's own hands. In this age of specialization I believe boatbuilding can offer even more satisfaction—as well as relaxation and a challenge to individual ability and ingenuity. Few things involve the many skills required in building a boat, each essential for its successful completion. Possibly nothing else is as rewarding.

Further, nicely fashioned, well-built boats are growing more and more expensive. To build your own may well be a practical solution—as well as rewarding. Surely the joys of being afloat are manifold, and those experienced aboard a boat you have built with your own hands are immeasurable.

Bob Steward, being exceptionally well qualified by his long experience in the "world of small ships," has produced a clearly written text of merit and great worth. After years as an apprentice he worked in several small boatyards before joining the highly respected office of naval architect Philip L. Rhodes, where he spent many years engaged in designing and planning numerous power and sailing yachts, as well as commercial boats. The period of World War II found him in an engineering capacity working between various yards and design offices. Far more pleasant work was resumed at war's end involving yachts—and Bob accepted a position with a West Coast firm as superintendent of yacht repair and construction. Some time later he returned to the East Coast where a number of yacht designs were produced, ranging from 22 to 86 feet, which required his experienced supervision of lofting and construction. The warmer clime beckoned, with its slower pace and easier living, and Bob moved to Florida to continue his work involving the designing and supervision of numerous yachts. Presently he is semiretired, but is still called upon to design small boats or to make half models.

Bob Steward's classic work has been heartily received from the time it was first published in 1950. In this latest edition, Bob has made numerous revisions relating to new materials and present regulations and standards in addition to providing more of his wonderfully clear drawings. Surely this comprehensive and practical material, so well presented, will provide the amateur boatbuilder and the professional with a world of valued and valid information. Indeed, scarcely a week passes when, in writing letters to boatbuilders all over the world, I do not suggest *Boatbuilding Manual* as a source of knowledge.

JOHN ATKIN, S.N.A. & M.E.
Anchordown
Darien, Connecticut

PREFACE TO THE SECOND EDITION

IT IS INDEED DIFFICULT TO REALIZE that 23 years have passed since International Marine Publishing Company went into business and acquired the copyright to *Boatbuilding Manual,* which was to become the first IM publication. It has been a happy marriage, but there have been two sad occurrences during that time: Boris Lauer-Leonardi, the small boatbuilder's staunch friend and longtime editor of *The Rudder* magazine when it was beloved and respected by true boatlovers worldwide, and Phil Rhodes, one of the greatest and most versatile naval architects, have both sailed over the horizon and are missed by countless friends.

I have met many more readers since the 1987 revision of *Boatbuilding Manual,* and it has been gratifying to hear from so many who have learned from the book. In addition, the Westlawn School of Yacht Design, located in Stamford, Connecticut, reprints portions of the book as two of its course lessons.

Throughout this book, and in the Appendix, you will find the names and addresses of firms that carry tools and materials or firms that provide services of value to boatbuilders. Such mention is not to be construed as advertising for the products or services offered. Rather, I believe that the reader will benefit from my research of the sources, possibly saving time in finding suitable boatbuilding materials. Contact the firms directly and tell them what you need.

In addition to the photo and illustration credits given in the earlier edition, I wish to thank the numerous individuals and firms that have furnished photos or drawings as illustrations in this expanded edition.

I cannot close without mentioning the small-craft designers and both amateur and professional boatbuilders for the enthusiasm that encourages me to continue extending the scope of this book. Thank you all, near and overseas.

ROBERT M. STEWARD
Jacksonville, Florida

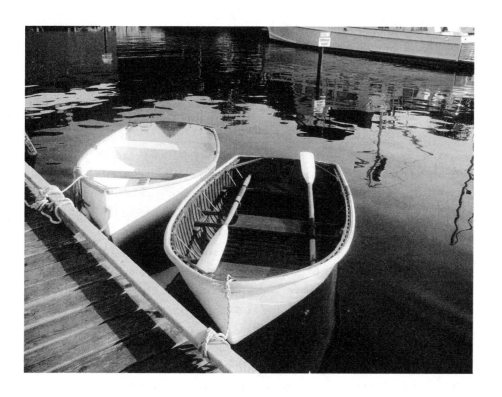

PREFACE TO THE FIRST EDITION

DURING A MEETING A NUMBER OF YEARS AGO with Boris Lauer-Leonardi and the late Andy Patterson, Editor and Business Manager, respectively, of the fine old *The Rudder* magazine, it was decided that I should write some articles about boat construction aimed at the amateur and, hopefully, of some value to the beginning professional. This decision resulted in a series of 20 consecutive monthly pieces that were so well received they were made into a book. The reception of this, too, was enthusiastic, and soon after it was introduced, the book was published abroad in French. Letters of approval were received from afar. One that lingers in my mind was from a Turkish naval officer who not only bought the book, but also built a boat from my plans. Then again Olin Stephens, famed yacht designer, told me how the French edition was of value to him on an inspection trip in Europe when the book illustrations served to break a language barrier between him and a builder. Things like this are heartfelt, because in so small a field the monetary reward must, unfortunately, be secondary.

As time went on, the number of requests for the book showed that a revision was in order. So now we have *Boatbuilding Manual,* again done with the enthusiasm of Boris as a prime mover, although there have been times, when the midnight oil was burning low, that I was not so happy with his prodding, since he charmed me with his silver tongue to sandwich a number of how-to-build plans and articles into the program at the same time. The new book has been rewritten, but includes a little of the old, as well as techniques I have picked up in the interim and new materials that have been accepted.

Do not think that this or any other book can teach all there is to know about boatbuilding. The best I can hope for is to give some guidance to those with the urge to build a boat—an urge that usually is very rewarding. I trust that this book, plus a good set of plans from an understanding and experienced designer, will lead to the realization of a dream for many who otherwise could not enjoy boating and the sea.

Assuming he has the ability with woodworking tools and is armed with plans and the elements of boatbuilding set forth in this book, there is no reason why an amateur cannot turn out a creditable boat, but he is cautioned not to be too pretentious at first. Better to start with something small, like a dinghy, to acquire the feel of boat construction, and then go on to a larger craft.

The author wishes to thank Philip L. Rhodes for the use of some photographs; Fred Bates for telling of his experience with strip planking; Joe Schabo of Fort Lauderdale for tracking down the remarkable photo of the Gulfstream 42 in frame; William G. Hobbs for the use of the same photo; and my family for patience on days when I was drawing or writing when we should have been fishing or sailing.

ROBERT M. STEWARD
Jacksonville, Florida

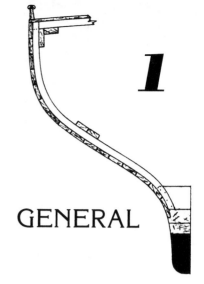

GENERAL

DURING THE PAST SEVERAL DECADES, more and more people have learned how to skillfully use both hand and power tools for household chores and improvements, making furniture, outbuildings, and the like, and they often turn out very creditable jobs. Such people are good candidates for boatbuilding. Yet many are intimidated by the thought of making something that is not all square corners; bending wood or other flat material to form curved shapes discourages them. And when they look into boatbuilding and see that it usually starts with a lines plan and the attendant table of offsets that dimensions the curves—well, that's *that*. But these people are unnecessarily depriving themselves of a very fascinating and satisfying pastime. It is true that many types of craft do require coping with the basics of traditional boatbuilding, but this can be learned to the necessary degree, and studying this book is a good start.

On the other hand, many people are happy with the kinds of boats that can be built using waterproof marine plywood. Some of these are virtually frameless. But more about this when you dig into the following chapters.

Constructing the first boat, however small, is an unforgettable experience. Watching a hull grow from flat paper drawings and flat material into a shapely form provides hours of fun and is excellent therapy after a stressful day. When the job is done carefully, the finished vessel is a source of great pride to the builder. And unlike a piece of furniture, which is often put in a corner and soon forgotten, a boat is used over and over for pleasure through the years.

A number of lucky people with the desire to learn boatbuilding have been able to take courses in various parts of the United States and the world. Currently, there are a number of good schools for boatbuilding in almost every country. But there will always be legions of aspiring boatbuilders who lack the money, the scheduling flexibility, or the proximity to attend one of these schools, which means there will always be ample reason for books like this one.

The purpose of this book is to introduce boat construction by explaining the elementary problems involved from starting the hull until water first laps at the keel. I don't purport to teach all the skills of an expert boatbuilder.

It is impossible to cover briefly all the information needed to build every type of boat, especially in view of new methods being developed. If you are fortunate enough to live in a boatbuilding area, you can learn a great deal from observation. When it comes down to building the kind of boat you want, you should bear in mind that a good set of plans is not only insurance against disappointment, but is also a source of construction details. In this book, I assume that you have acquired the ability to use ordinary carpentry tools—not much more is needed to build some boats— and, of equal importance, that you know how to keep your tools sharp. Nothing is worse or more discouraging than trying to make progress by hacking away with dull tools; there is no excuse for doing so. If you are a victim of dull edges, better take a week off in order to learn how to sharpen tools. A great reference is *Sharpening Basics,* written by Patrick Spielman. Another is *Fine Woodworking on Planes and Chisels.* You'll find complete publishing information on these and other books in the Appendix.

Along with the many modern products imported from Japan has come an increasing number of hand tools that are anything but modern, and made with steel that really sharpens well. In one mail-order catalog there is a story, told by an American tool buyer, of a Japanese woodworking shop in which the apprentices do nothing but sharpen tools for six months. So don't fret when you have to spend a few minutes bringing the edge of a chisel up to grade. Incidentally, I can attest to the effectiveness of Japanese water stones for honing, but to each his own.

The main thrust of this book is toward wooden construction, but the basics also apply to the layout and building of molds and templates for non-wooden hulls and to the finishing off of boats with non-wooden hulls.

If the project is to build a boat of a material other than wood or fiberglass, then another field has always been open, namely the cutting, shaping, and welding of metal. Builders of metal boats utilize many of the basic wood boatbuilding techniques, but for book-learning about metal hull construction, refer to the Appendix.

A person considering the building of a boat very likely has been exposed to boats and boating, either for pleasure or for commercial purposes, and may have a pretty good idea of what he/she wants—sail, sail and power, oars or paddles, or pure power. Yet I have received mail about boatbuilding over the years from people with no boating experience and nothing more to go on than a hope of being waterborne in the future. Somewhere along the line they must choose a certain type of hull after deciding what their requirements are.

There are three basic hull types: flat-bottomed, v-bottomed, and round-bottomed. Sawn in two at mid-length, sections through these hulls appear as shown in Figure 1-1.

The flat-bottomed hull in cross section consists of straight lines running across from side to side. The bottom may also be a straight line when

FIGURE 1-1.
Sections at mid-length of typical flat-, v-, and round-bottomed hulls.

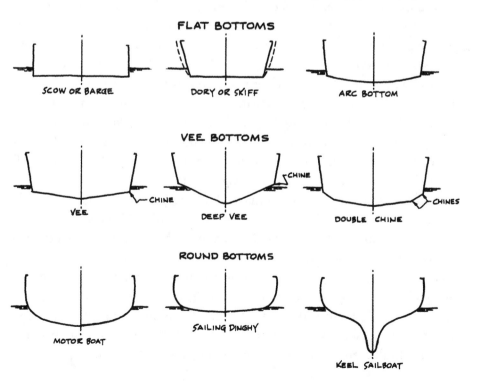

viewed from the side (such as in a scow or barge), or the profile of the bottom may be curved, or "rockered." In any event, the flat-bottomed hull is the easiest to build, has a minimum of beveled or twisted parts, and, if properly designed, can be a useful craft. Flat-bottomed skiffs are found the world over; flat-bottomed dories have a long heritage. Then there are pram dinghies, garveys, etc., which all have their places. In general, though, boats with flat bottoms are best used on sheltered waters. A lines drawing for a flat-bottomed skiff is shown in Figure 7-4 (page 145).

The arc-bottomed boat is a variation of the flat bottom and a close cousin to the v-bottom. Probably the best known arc-bottomed design is the Star class sloop. These 22-footers are still sailed worldwide, though they were designed in 1911. Both the flat and the arc-bottomed hulls require the minimum of layout work prior to building, as will be seen later.

The frames for a v-bottomed boat are made from a full-size drawing of the hull sections and then set up and left in the hull as permanent members of the structure. While this involves less work and less money for materials than framing a round-bottomed hull, it still calls for careful fitting. The chine pieces (corners in the sections of a v-bottomed hull) must be carefully worked to achieve bevels that continually change from bow to stern. The frames, too, are all beveled, and each is made up of as many as seven carefully fitted and securely fastened parts.

A round-bottomed hull has curved transverse frames that are sometimes called ribs. These are shaped by steaming or soaking them in boiling water until they are supple enough to be bent either directly on the hull framework or over forms in the shop, and then located in the hull after they have cooled and set. Most boats of the size a beginner would build have frames bent right in the hull; the bevel necessary to have them conform to the hull shape is twisted in during the bending process. Do not let this scare you. When working with relatively light material, the bending is not unduly difficult and can be mastered after a few attempts. In fact it can be a great deal of fun. The process will be described in more detail further along, during a discussion of framing.

An alternative to bending frames of one piece is laminating them of glued strips thin enough to take the necessary bend without treatment.

Bending wood by steaming or boiling is not restricted to round-bottomed construction alone, as it is entirely possible that certain parts of v-bottomed boats, such as the forward ends of bottom planks, will not bend on the boat cold and must be made limber for them to fit the shape of the hull.

Figure 1-2 is a lines drawing for a small round-bottomed hull. Lines drawings are discussed in detail in the chapter on lofting, which is the making of full-size hull drawings and templates for the various parts.

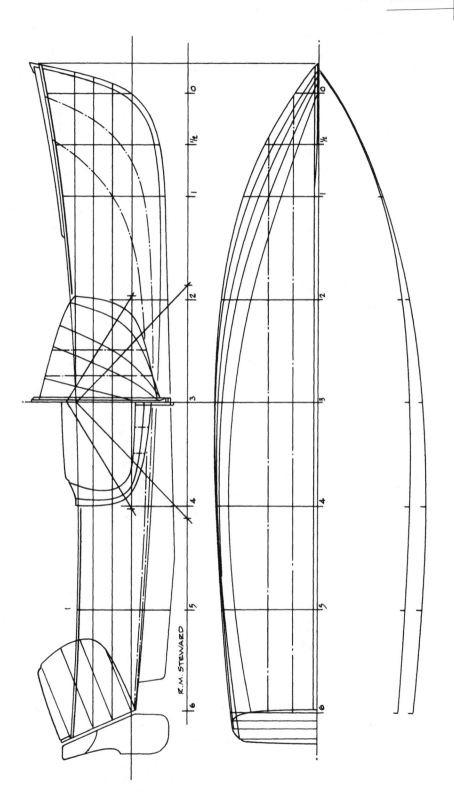

FIGURE 1-2.
A 17'7" round-bottomed wooden launch that has been built by numerous backyard and professional builders. This how-to-build design drawn by the author for *The Rudder* magazine in 1953 is the predecessor to the Barbara Anne launch design shown in Chapter 2.

The relative merits of the hull types are argued far and wide, but just about everyone will admit that there will never be a v-bottomed hull as handsome as a well-designed round-bottomed boat, especially for a sailing craft. I am probably prejudiced, so argue away!

Figures 1-3 and 1-4 show the essential differences between the framing of flat-, v-, arc-, and round-bottomed hulls. Although the lower ends of the frames in the round-bottomed boat are shown butted against the keel, it is sometimes possible, depending on the hull shape, to install them in one piece, extending from the deck on one side to the deck on the other side. In contrast, note the number of pieces that make up a frame for a v-bottomed boat. On the other hand, frames are spaced farther apart than in a round-bottomed boat, so the frames are fewer in number.

Figure 1-5 is a section through a rather normal sailboat of the cruising or classic ocean racing type. The construction is typical of either the so-called deep-keel or combination keel-and-centerboard type boats, the latter being

FIGURE 1-3.
Typical construction sections through v- and flat-bottomed boats.

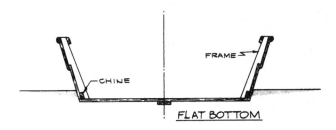

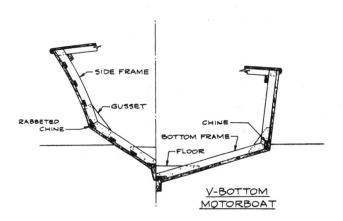

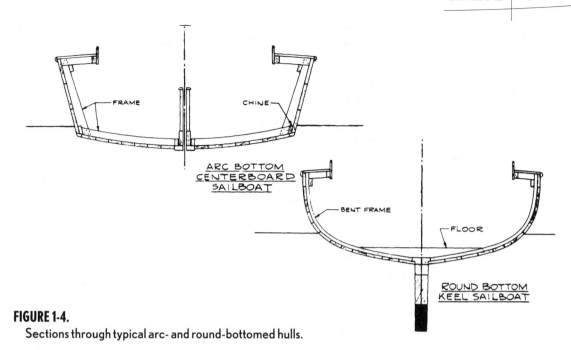

FIGURE 1-4.
Sections through typical arc- and round-bottomed hulls.

of moderately shallow draft, greater than an unballasted centerboarder but less than the deep-keel type. This type of boat is not recommended for the amateur's first attempt at boatbuilding unless he/she has helped on a similar job or has watched enough of this kind of construction that he will not become discouraged when on his own. The framing is more difficult due to

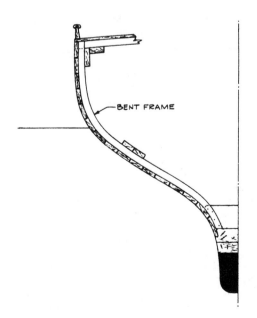

FIGURE 1-5.
The midship section of an auxiliary sailboat showing bent frame with reverse curve.

reverse (S) curves in many of the frames, the planking is a tougher job than on a simpler hull, and there is a lot of heavy work getting out the backbone and deadwood.

The time needed to build a hull can be reduced if the hull shape is such that it can be covered with large pieces of flat material such as plywood. If a hull shape does not have compound curvature it is called "developable" and can be formed from flat sheets. There are ways of designing a hull with developable surfaces, either graphically on the drawing board or with a computer program. The surfaces are cylindrical, conical, or a combination of both, and the designer must be content with the limitations of these curves, but there are a good number of choices. More about this in Chapter 7.

Figure 1-6 shows the lines for a 52-foot hull that was designed with the aid of a computer. This boat was built of large fiberglass sheets: one for each side, one for each half of the bottom, one for the transom, and a number of joined strips for the wide chine surface on each side. To my knowledge, this was an unusual method of construction at the time (1969). On the other hand, the v-bottomed hull in Figure 1-7 cannot be built in this manner, for there are concave sections in both the sides and the bottom. Flat sheets cannot successfully be bent in two directions at the same time.

FIGURE 1-6.
A 52-foot fiberglass commercial fishing boat hull having developable surfaces.

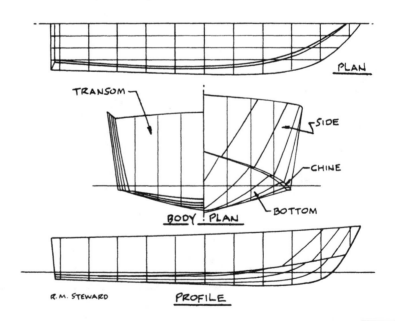

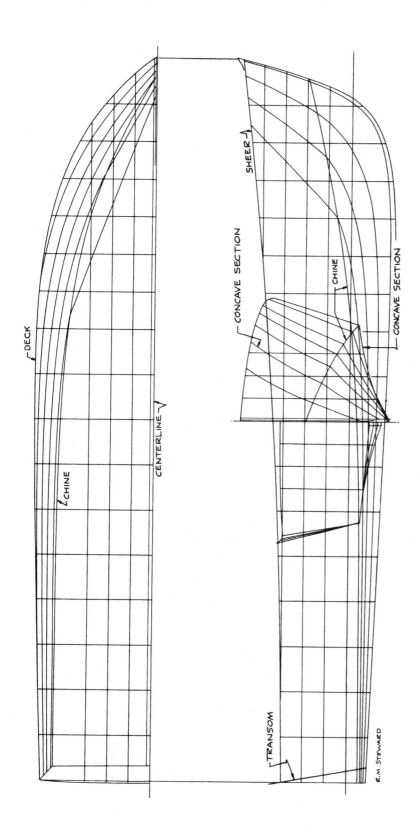

FIGURE 1-7.
A 32-foot wooden v-bottomed powerboat designed by the author and used as a specimen-collecting boat by the University of Florida.

Most of the figures in this chapter have been labeled with the names of some of the principal hull lines, and the beginner must become familiar with this nomenclature. For instance, the top edge of the hull viewed in profile is the sheerline, while the same line viewed in plan is the deck line, or deck at side. A chine is obviously the intersection between the side and bottom of a v-bottomed hull. Other lines in the surface of a hull will be explained later. Since both sides of a boat are usually the same, a designer draws the lines for only one side of a hull.

For hundreds of years, wood was the primary material used for building hulls, but matters are different now. As this is written, boats of fiber-reinforced plastic have been manufactured for more than 50 years; fiberglass boats dominate the standardized boat market, with hulls and other parts produced in volume from expensive molds and tooling.

But research never stops; resins have been improved, and there is a larger choice of reinforcements, some of them currently expensive but enormously strong. As of 2010, skilled amateurs as well as professional builders are building fast, strong racing boats from foam and carbon fiber, but this technology is not yet sufficiently well-established or user-friendly to be covered in this book. Look for that to change in the future.

Nor is wood dead. Both pleasure and commercial boats are still built of wood. Wood is being used in hulls in the conventional manner, some are built with plywood planking, and other hulls are made with multiple layers of relatively thin wood glued together and then often covered with a resin reinforced with a synthetic fabric.

The techniques of wooden boatbuilding are extensively employed in the construction of tooling for fiberglass boats and parts. Wood is used for the interior joinerwork in the better-quality fiberglass boats to avoid the cold, antiseptic appearance of the molded plastic and "mica" finishes that have become a logical extension of molded fiberglass hulls and cabins.

When demand is limited, such as for yachts 65 feet and longer, cold-molded composite (wood and epoxy) construction has become increasingly popular. True, welded aluminum alloy construction or a welded steel hull with superstructure built of the light alloy is still the choice of many of the larger builders. But here again, wood is usually chosen for the finish in the quarters because it provides a feeling of warmth that can never be achieved by the synthetics.

It is possible to gain an introduction to boatbuilding by purchasing and assembling a "kit" boat. There are a number of kits for v-bottomed motorboats, sailboats, canoes, and kayaks, usually with plywood planking. And there

FIGURE 1-8.
Susan, a flat-bottomed rowing skiff designed by the original author of this book in 1952.
Over 100 had been built by 1970. It was a great beginner's project at that time, and is still built in apprenticeshops around the world. (*Missy Hatch*)

FIGURE 1-9.
The Chester Yawl, a 15' Whitehall-type boat. This one was built from a kit manufactured by Chesapeake Light Craft and might be a reasonable project for an ambitious 21st-century first-timer. (*Chesapeake Light Craft*)

has been a proliferation of kayaks and canoes from a number of vendors. Most of these kits are furnished with beveled parts that require only reasonable care to set up the frames accurately to form the hull. Then there are firms that supply a bare fiberglass hull as part of a kit. Here is where an amateur must be careful to be sure that guidance is provided or available to locate components such as engines and fuel and water tanks. The weights of such items can be quite large, and the amateur should not bite off more than he/she can chew.

Making a kit boat does not give the same sense of accomplishment as building a boat from scratch, but the scheme does make sense for those with limited spare time or for those who want a particular model of boat that is available in kit form. And building a kit is a great introduction for the first-time boatbuilder. Shown here are photos of some of the many types of boats that can be built from kits (see Appendix). Except as noted, all these boats were constructed entirely from kits by amateur builders.

FIGURE 1-10.
The 16' Malahini is one of several outboard runabouts in the Glen-L catalog, which offers hundreds of kits of all types of boats. (*Glen-L*)

FIGURE 1-11.
The Swifty 11, a glued plywood lapstrake version of the Norwegian holmsbupram, is manufactured by Shell Boats. A sailing rig is available. (*Shell Boats*)

FIGURE 1-12.
The frame of this 23' cruiser was supplied as a kit by Clark Craft, another kit manufacturer with an extensive catalog. (*Clark Craft*)

FIGURE 1-13.
An 18' cedar strip–built King kayak from Redfish kayaks, which sells kits, like the one pictured, and finished kayaks. (*Redfish Kayaks*)

FIGURE 1-14.
The Penobscot 14 is a glued lapstrake kit from Arch Davis Design. (*Arch Davis Design*)

FIGURE 1-15.
Arrowhead Custom Boats and Canoes makes the kit for this 16' glued lapstrake canoe they call The Flyfisher.
(*Arrowhead Custom Boats and Canoes*)

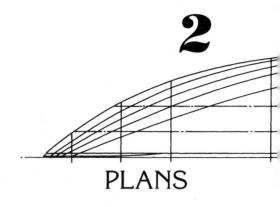

2

PLANS

THERE ARE SEVERAL WAYS TO GO once you have decided to build a boat. You can build from scratch using plans from one of the many sources available nowadays, buy a boat kit, or buy full-size paper patterns for hull parts. Refer to a current boating magazine or use online search for plans.

The boat of your dreams may be a simple rowboat, a boat for both rowing and sailing, a daysailer or cruiser, a power craft for waterskiing or fishing or both; or you may set your sights higher, and be satisfied only by a larger powerboat for cruising. Whatever the type and size, take your time selecting plans. Remember, it takes only a second to decide to build your own boat, but it might take years to complete it.

There is a wealth of plans for plywood composite construction methods such as the stitch-and-tape method, sometimes called stitch-and-glue or taped-seam. This method is discussed in Chapter 11. Some designers offer full-size patterns for the hull parts to be made from flat sheets; others furnish thoroughly dimensioned scale drawings for the parts.

Lofting, discussed at length in Chapter 7, is the process of drawing hull lines full size, working from the designer's scale drawing. Much, if not all, of this work is eliminated when building a hull by the stitch-and-tape method, but such hulls are limited to the shapes that can be formed from flat panels.

There are also designs available for a number of other construction techniques including lapstrake plywood, strip construction, and traditional wooden construction, as well as for other methods and materials covered by this book.

Regardless of their source, try to determine whether the plans that interest you are sufficiently detailed for you to completely understand the vessel's construction. It cannot be emphasized too strongly that good plans are well worth their price, because their cost is but a fraction of the total cost of the boat. The cost of the plans might be considered as insurance that the finished boat will be a success. When designers do not draw the profusion of details that the novice builder would like to have, this book should be very helpful in filling in some of the missing information.

I would warn you against making changes in the hull lines, heights of superstructures, or locations of major weights. Such procedures can result in unsatisfactory performance at the least, or even downright reduction of seaworthiness. Consult the designer before making any major changes, and if he advises against them, you will be better off using plans that will give you what you want without departing from the drawings.

EXAMPLES OF PLANS

I am using plans I drew over the years as examples of adequately detailed drawings. *The Rudder* magazine, which unfortunately disappeared many years ago, was once known far and wide for its down-to-earth practical content and "how-to-build" small craft plans. I was fortunate enough to be selected to do a number of these. In fact, in 1950 *The Rudder* collected

FIGURE 2-1.
Plans for this Herreshoff descendant, the Somes Sound 12½, by Brooks Boats Designs, run to 16 large sheets. (*Brooks Boats Designs*)

a series of my monthly boatbuilding articles and published them as *Small Boat Construction,* which was actually the first edition of this book. The majority of the illustrations from that first edition, drawn in 1949–1950, still appear in the edition of *Boatbuilding Manual* you are reading now. When it comes to building wooden boats, the old expression really is true: The more things change, the more they stay the same.

Figures 2-2, 2-3, and 2-4 are plans for a 19-foot arc-bottom daysailer I did in 1948 for *The Rudder* to the general specifications of the magazine's editor. I named this boat "Triton" (a name I do not think had been used for a class of boats at that time). Over the years I have heard good things about the design from as far away as England (where the builder obtained the framing lumber from an obsolete British army truck), Brazil, and Cuba, just prior to the Castro revolution.

Figures 2-5, 2-6, and 2-7 are for a 1984 design for an 18'7" inboard-powered launch I christened *Barbara Anne.* Respectively, the figures are a combination outboard profile and arrangement plan; the lines plan; and the construction plan. A separate written specification for the various parts on the construction plan is keyed to the circled numbers to avoid cluttering up the drawing any further. Running to three or four dense pages of scantlings and hardware, the specifications should of course be included in the plans package you purchase for a boat.

Over the last several years there has been a proliferation of small design firms focused on the amateur boatbuilding market. The tendency has been for these designers to develop and refine their plans packages to make them much more understandable and user-friendly than they were years ago, even to the point of providing fairly detailed written step-by-step instructions. Take some time to identify and compare some of these designers, and remember that the quality of the plans and the support available from the designer may end up being as important to you as the size, construction type, and general configuration of the boat itself. Lots of them have websites nowadays, and those who do not may be happy to talk to you on the telephone. If they don't have time for you before you become a customer, they probably won't later on!

The plans package for a Somes Sound 12½, a plywood lapstrake design by Brooks Boats Designs, for example, includes seventeen plan sheets, a thirty-two-page specifications manual, and twenty-seven pages of lists as well as seven full-size pattern sheets covering dozens of individual parts. Brooks, like many contemporary designers, has free study plans available online. Figures 2-8, 2-9, and 2-10 show details from the full-size pattern sheets for this boat.

Another approach to plywood boatbuilding that has gained considerable prominence over the last few decades is the stitch-and-glue method,

(*continued on page 28*)

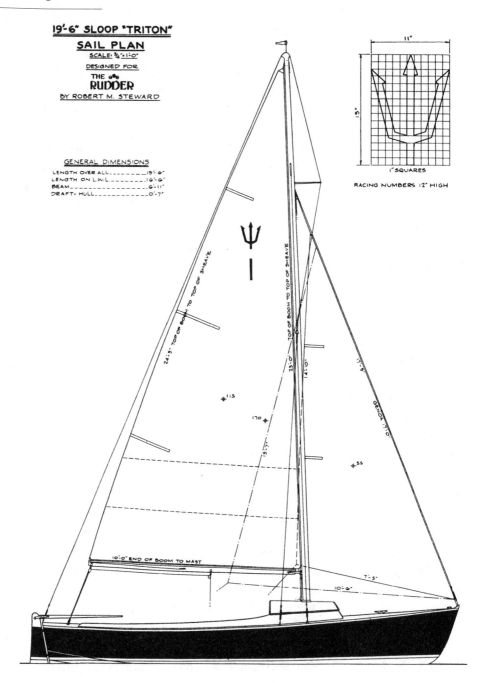

19'-6" SLOOP "TRITON"

SAIL PLAN
SCALE: ¾"=1'-0"

DESIGNED FOR

THE
RUDDER
BY ROBERT M. STEWARD

GENERAL DIMENSIONS

LENGTH OVER ALL_____19'-6"
LENGTH ON L.W.L._____16'-6"
BEAM_____6'-11"
DRAFT - HULL_____0'-7"

RACING NUMBERS 12" HIGH

1" SQUARES

FIGURES 2-2, 2-3, 2-4.
These plans were drawn by the author as part of *The Rudder's* "How-to-Build" series and appeared in the February 1948 issue of that publication. Large-scale blueprints were offered by *The Rudder* for use by home builders. The arc-bottomed form makes this a relatively simple boat to build.
(The Rudder, *reprinted with permission*)

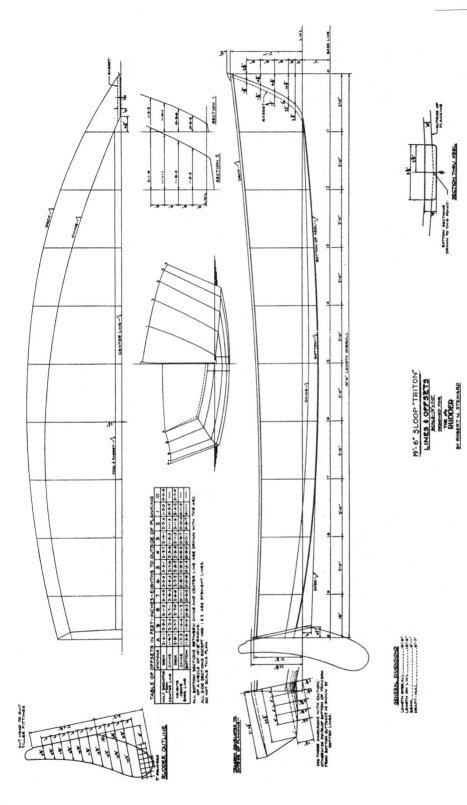

19'-6" SLOOP "TRITON"
LINES & OFFSETS
SCALE 1/2"=1'-0"
DESIGNED FOR
THE
RUDDER
BY ROBERT M. STEWARD

FIGURE 2-3

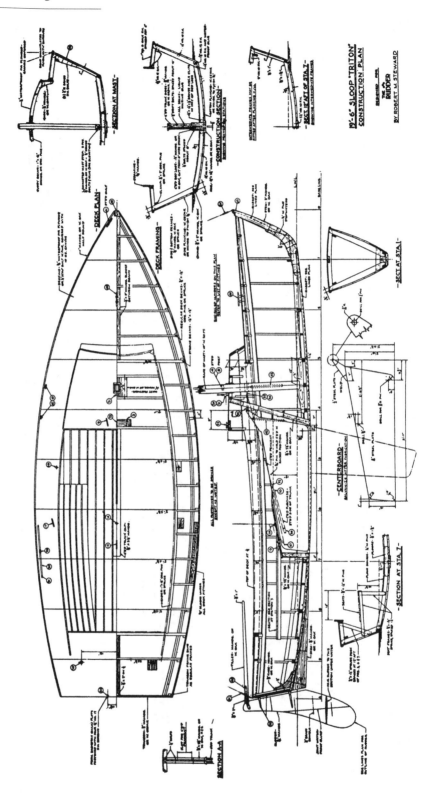

FIGURE 2-4

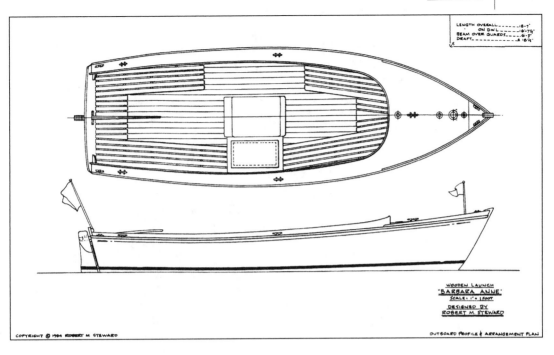

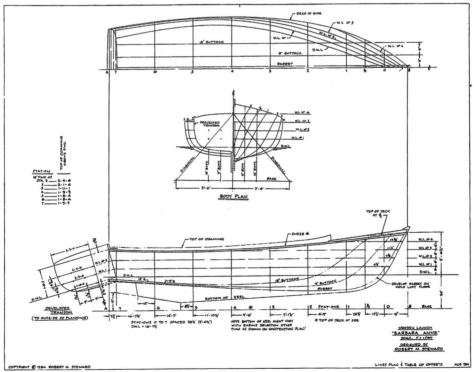

FIGURES 2-5, 2-6, AND 2-7.

Outboard profile and arrangement plan, lines plan (including the offsets), and the construction plan for the 18'7" inboard-powered launch Barbara Anne.

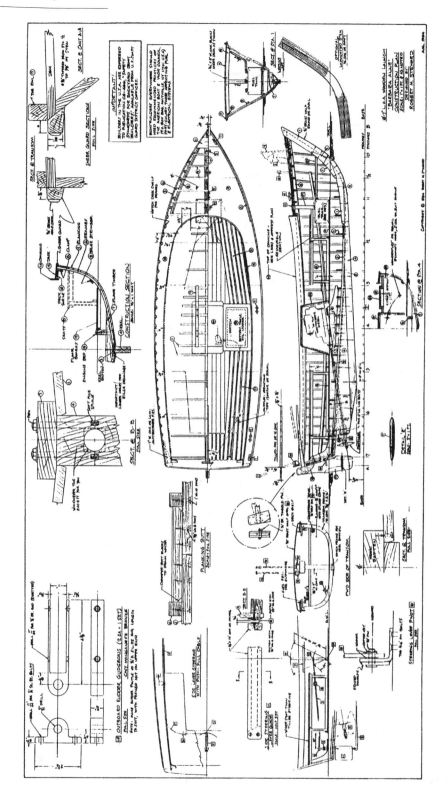

FIGURE 2-7

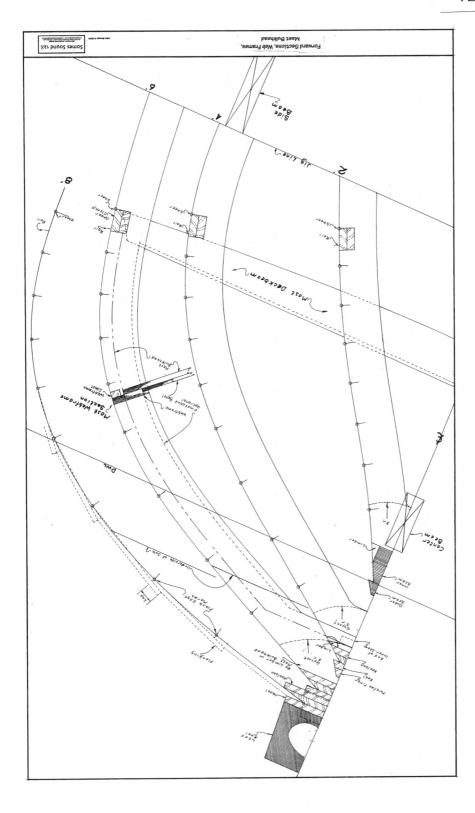

FIGURE 2-8.

Forward sections, web frames, and mast bulkhead—full size in the original—for the glued-lapstrake Somes Sound 12½ design from Brooks Boats Designs. (*Brooks Boats Designs*)

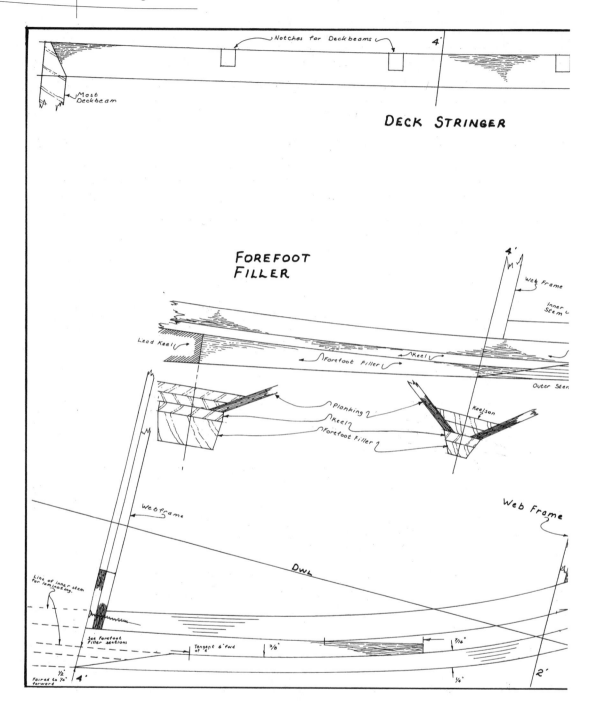

FIGURE 2-9.
Details of the stem profile, forefoot filler, and deck stringer from the full-size plan sheets for the Brooks Boats Designs Somes Sound 12½. (*Brooks Boats Designs*)

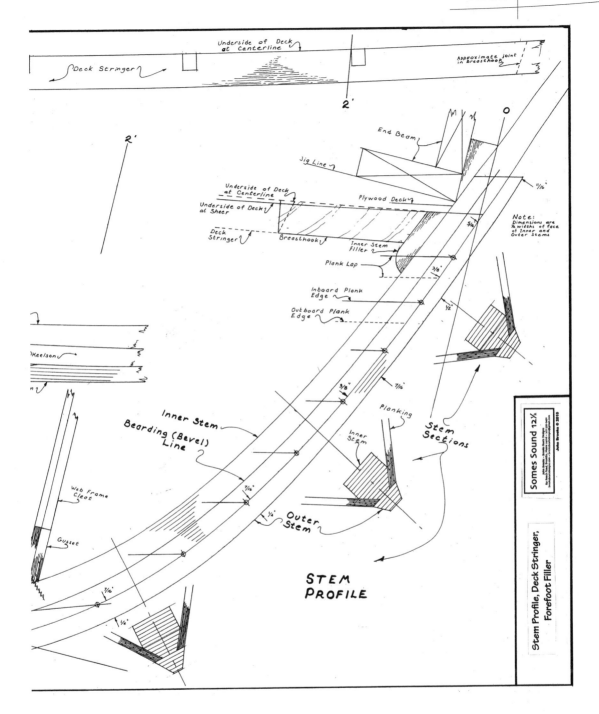

Underside of Deck at Centerline

Deck Stringer

Approximate joint in Breasthook

2'

2'

End Beam

Jig Line

Underside of Deck at Centerline

Plywood Deck

Underside of Deck at Sheer

Deck Stringer

Breasthook

Inner Stem Filler

Plank Lap

Inboard Plank Edge

Outboard Plank Edge

0

11/16

5/8

Note:
Dimensions are
½ widths of face
of Inner and
Outer Stems

3/8

½

3/8"

7/16

Keelson

Inner Stem

Bearding (Bevel) Line

Planking

Inner Stem

Stem Sections

Web Frame Cleat

7/16"

Outer Stem

¼"

Gusset

7/16"

¼"

STEM PROFILE

Somes Sound 12½

John Brooks © 2010

Stem Profile, Deck Stringer,
Forefoot Filler

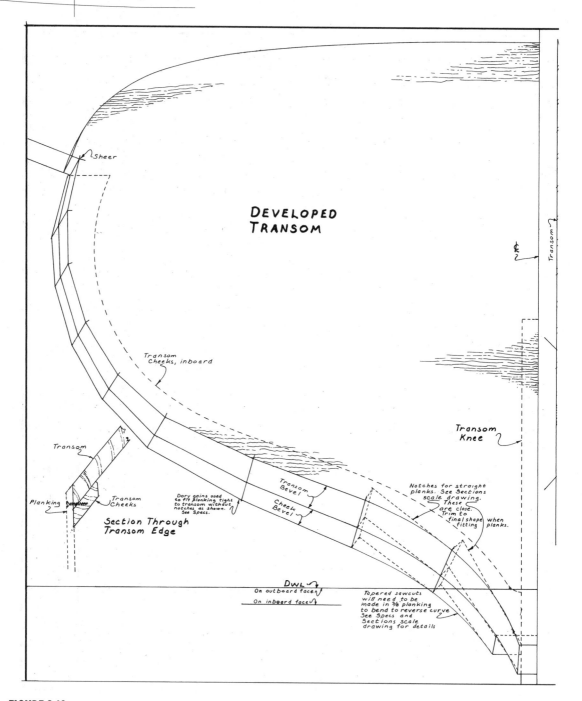

Sheer

DEVELOPED
TRANSOM

Transom
Cheeks, inboard

Transom

Planking

Transom
Cheeks

Section Through
Transom Edge

Transom
Bevel

Cheek
Bevel

Dory gains used
to fit planking tight
to transom without
notches as shown.
See Specs.

DWL

On outboard face
On inboard face

Transom
Knee

Notches for straight
planks. See Sections
scale drawing.
These
are close.
Trim to
final shape when
fitting planks.

Tapered sawcuts
will need to be
made in ⅜ planking
to bend to reverse curve
See Specs and
Sections scale
drawing for details

Transom

FIGURE 2-10.
The transom knee, transom profile, and other details from the full-size plan sheets for the Brooks Boats Designs Somes Sound 12½. (*Brooks Boats Designs*)

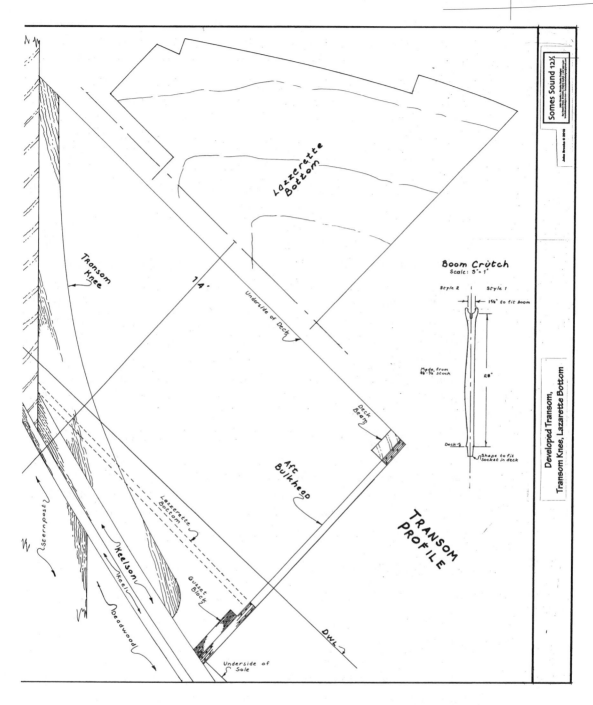

Somes Sound 12½

John Brooks © 2010

Developed Transom,
Transom Knee, Lazzarette Bottom

Lazzerette
Bottom

Transom
Knee

14.

Underside of Deck

Deck
Beam

Aft
Bulkhead

Lazzerette
Bottom

TRANSOM
PROFILE

Sternpost

Keelson

Keel

Deadwood

Gusset
Block

DWL

Underside of
Sole

Boom Crutch
Scale: 3"=1'

Style 2   Style 1

1⅝" to fit boom

28"

Made from
⅝"-¾" stock

Deck

Shape to fit
socket in deck

described in greater detail in Chapter 11. Sam Devlin is a West Coast designer who has refined and developed this method and has even written a book on it. His plans, or study plans, for the 22-foot powerboat he calls the Surfscoter can be purchased at his website, devlinboat.com. Figures 2-11 and 2-12 show a few details from those plans demonstrating the attention he gives to the specifics of construction and the needs of the amateur boatbuilder.

PLANS FOR BOATS CARRYING PASSENGERS FOR HIRE

Every year there is a great number of boats built to carry six or more fare-paying passengers, whether it be for sightseeing, dinner and dancing, or, more likely, fishing. If you are contemplating building such a craft, you should be aware that, in the interest of safety, the construction and equipment of passenger-carrying boats are regulated by the U.S. Coast Guard. The regulations are not unduly strict, but you should not start construction without at least obtaining approval of the hull construction. The routine is fairly simple if you take the time to consult with the closest office of the U.S. Coast Guard. In general, an application is made for the inspection of the boat, specifying the service, the route, and the number of passengers to be carried. If there is a complete set of plans, it should be submitted; otherwise, if construction is to be started quickly, general arrangement drawings are necessary and also details of the hull construction. The Coast Guard has a book of regulations that spells out the design and equipment requirements and lists the plans that must be submitted for approval. They no longer offer the book for free, but they can tell you the location of a government bookstore that stocks the publication. The regulations are also available online. You will find a great deal of guidance at the Coast Guard's website. Vessel construction and inspection information can be found at the "Passenger Vessel Safety Program" page.

RESTORATION

Restoring old wooden boats and even early fiberglass boats has gained considerable popularity. This is easy to understand since many of the older designs have more appeal than the look-alike plans turned out today. Much restoration is done by amateurs, but a good many professional shops are kept busy catering to those who prefer the older, sometimes classic boats, both sail and power, and can afford to have others do the restoration.

An amateur planning to restore a boat that has caught his eye should be wary of one that has deteriorated beyond his ability to repair it, or one that will require too much time and money—even if money is not important, an excessive amount of time can destroy his enthusiasm before the job has been completed.

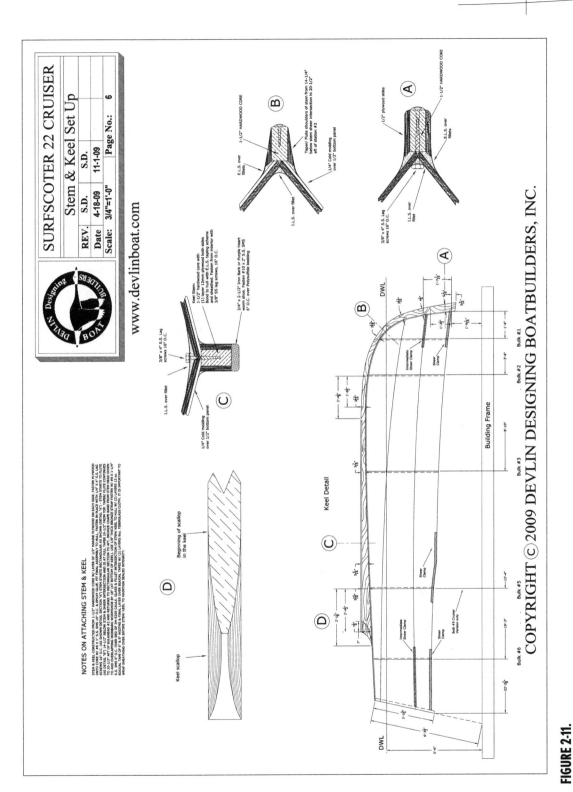

FIGURE 2-11.

Detail from Sam Devlin's plans for the Surfscoter 22 showing connection between hull and keel/stem. (*Sam Devlin*)

FIGURE 2-12.

This detail from the General Details sheet of the Surfscoter 22 plans might help the first-time builder evade a major pitfall of stitch-and-glue construction. (*Sam Devlin*)

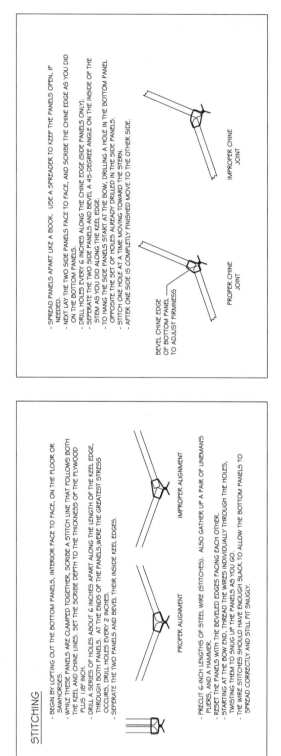

Hardly a month goes by in which a boating magazine does not carry a classified ad reading "1945 classic mahogany runabout, partially restored. . . ."

In any event, the situation is not unlike choosing plans from which to build your dream boat—first be absolutely certain the design is exactly what you want, and then, if you are not personally capable of making an accurate judgment of the boat's condition, hire a surveyor for the job. And don't use just any surveyor: get one that is unquestionably familiar with the type of construction employed in the craft being considered.

BOATS BUILT FROM PLANS AND KITS

Building a boat from readily available plans is one tried-and-true approach. Shown here are several boats for which plans and/or a kit is available.

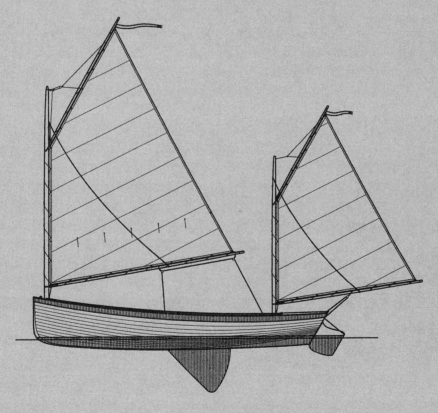

An elegant line drawing of the Coquina, a traditional plank-on-frame interpretation of a classic Herreshoff design available from D. N. Hylan & Associates. (*Doug Hylan*)

(continued)

Over the years, thousands of junior racers have trained on the Blue Jay, a 14-footer designed in 1947 by the venerable design firm of Sparkman and Stephens. (*Sparkman and Stephens*)

For modest ambitions, here is a trailerable 25-footer, a Roberts design. (*Bruce Roberts*)

This Dix 43, built in aluminum, is shown at anchor in Antarctica. (*Franz Joho*)

The Paper Jet is a hot little number—on a reasonable scale—from Dudley Dix. (*Billy Black*)

This interpretation of the traditional Nova Scotia Tancook Whaler was designed by George Stadel and built by Bill Rogers of Woods Hole, Massachusetts. This photograph was taken before the internal ballast was installed. (*Bill Rogers*)

The Norse-inspired designs of Iain Oughtred have a dedicated following on both sides of the Atlantic. This is Oughtred's Ness Yawl. (*Kathy Mansfield*)

The Surfscoter 26 is typical of the wide range of boat plans using the stitch-and-glue method available from Devlin Design Boatbuilders. (*Sam Devlin*)

Thousands of builder/sailors have lived the tropical dreams on the innovative catamarans of James Wharram. This is his Tiki model. (*James Wharram*)

BUILDING SEA KNIGHT

Glen-L sells a variety of plans and other materials to support home boatbuilding. Bill White purchased Glen-L's plans for Sea Knight, set up his shop, started building, and launched the boat sixteen months later. (*Photos and captions courtesy Bill White.*)

Building the form.

The framing is white oak; holes were drilled on the frame uprights before assembly.

The plywood for the hull was scarphed on the floor into 18-foot lengths and installed as single sections. No fiberglass was used on the boat.

Polyurethane enamel was applied over resin-based epoxy primer. No antifouling paint was needed.

Once the hull was turned upright, epoxy was applied to the bilge. From this point on in the construction process, attention was paid to the placement of fixed weight to achieve proper fore/aft and port/starboard balance.

Building the cabin.

The cabin was built, and a flexible texture finish was applied to all exterior surfaces above the bumper rail.

White polyurethane enamel was applied to the topsides.

Sea Knight after launching.

3

TOOLS

THE SELECTION OF TOOLS NEEDED to build a boat depends upon the type of project being undertaken. Generally it is best to start with a small craft to get the feel of the work—that is, to appreciate the difference between boatbuilding and common carpentry. A beginner's first choice will often be a plywood-planked open small boat. Such a hull requires a minimum of tools, most of which are usually found in a homeowner's tool chest—hammers, handsaws, planes, chisels, screwdrivers, a brace and auger bits, an "egg-beater" hand drill and twist bits, etc. There very likely is a corded or cordless electric drill in the kit as well.

Other hand tools such as a drawknife, spokeshave, bull-nose plane, rabbet plane, and round-bottom plane are out of the ordinary and can be added as the need arises.

One hand tool that is unmatched for planing end grain or plywood edges is a low-angle (12 degrees) block plane with a well-sharpened blade. Once you have become familiar with one of these, you'll put aside for good the regular block plane.

In addition, let's not overlook wood rasps—flat and oval—or metal files—flat, square, and round.

LAYOUT TOOLS

Essential tools for layout work—and useful from start to finish—are a 24" carpenter's framing square, a level at least 24" long, a pair of dividers, a chalk line, a carpenter's pencil compass, a 6-foot folding rule or a small retractable metal measuring tape, and, for larger craft, a 25- or 50-foot measuring tape of steel or fiberglass.

A tool that should be classed as an aid to layout is a sliding T-bevel such as the Stanley No. 18, if you can find one, used for transferring bevels from the drawings to the lumber and for picking up bevels in many ways. Garrett-Wade carries an "improved Japanese" T-bevel that may be worth considering.

Another type of bevel, almost indispensable, is a small one shown being used in Figure 8-10. I have one made with wooden cheeks and a brass blade, very old and source unknown. I once asked a tool company if it would make some, sending my bevel for examination, but it was not interested. However, Walter Simmons makes and sells at a reasonable price an all-brass "boatbuilder's bevel," $\frac{3}{16}$" thick × $\frac{1}{2}$" wide × 3" closed length. There is no substitute for this tool in tight quarters. (Addresses of this and other sources, including current Internet addresses where available, are listed in the Appendix.)

FIGURE 3-1.
There is still a place in the boatbuilder's tool chest for an old-fashioned "egg-beater" hand drill.

FIGURE 3-2.
The indispensable low-angle (12°) block plane.

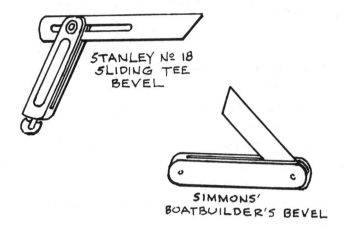

FIGURE 3-3.
Bevels are extremely handy for layout work.

CLAMPS

One might have a C-clamp or two in his kit, but when building a boat this is merely a start. There never seem to be enough clamps of the C-type.

The shorter versions of the bar-type clamps do much the same job as the C-clamps and also have a place of their own in the longer lengths. Jorgensen bar clamps have a unique "clutch" to regulate the clamping length; Wetzler bar clamps, on the other hand, have a more conventional method of adjustment. I would not turn down a gift of either kind.

I have a number of Pony spring clamps that are useful at times. In the larger sizes it takes a strong squeeze to open these, but the pressure is in proportion. I have tried lower-priced spring clamps made in the Far East that have very weak springs. Cheap, but no good!

Handscrew clamps, as illustrated, are handy at times too, and a few of the woodworker's tool shops sell the steel parts so you can make your own clamps using a hardwood like maple.

Figure 17-4 (page 355), shows bar clamps and hand screws being used to apply pressure to the glued joints of a hollow wooden spar under construction. Note the number of clamps employed!

Lapstrake or clinker planking of hulls is discussed in Chapter 11. Should you ever get to building one of the beautiful small craft possible with this type of construction, then very likely you will appreciate the custom lap or planking clamps made by Walter Simmons. I know of no other source for these specialized clamps at this time.

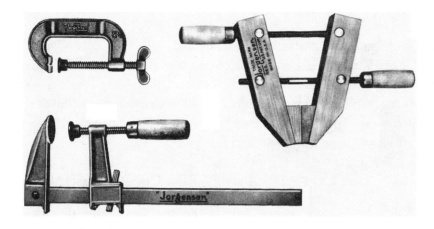

FIGURE 3-4A.
Top: A C-clamp, the most useful all-around clamp, and a handscrew clamp shown holding tapered pieces.
Bottom: Bar clamps are made with capacities of 12" to 36".

If you will be doing carvel (smooth) planking, you might want to have a look at the Conant Planking Clamps (see photo). These have one clamp screw that attaches to a frame and another, more or less at right angles, that pushes the plank you are fitting up against the adjacent plank for "tight seams with no hassles."

CIRCULAR TABLE SAW

There are many choices in both bench and free-standing types. Buy the best tilting-arbor saw you can afford—8", 9", or 10", with a rip fence that adjusts along a tube or bar, if you can find one (not just a shape integral with the table edge)—and fit it out with carbide-tipped blades.

With the rip fence out of the way and the blade raised just slightly more than the stock thickness, long and gentle curves can be cut using this tool.

FIGURE 3-4B.
Conant Planking Clamp. (*Rick Conant*)

BAND SAW

My shop has a 12" Craftsman (Sears) band saw, but I wish I had a 14" Delta, and not only for the extra depth of throat. The Delta table tilts in two directions, 45° right, 3° left.

Walter Simmons recommended Olson-brand band saw blades to me some time ago, and I have been using them happily ever since. They can be bought direct from the Olson Saw Company.

PORTABLE CIRCULAR SAW

This is the next best thing to a table saw and can perform a variety of tasks. It can be used for crosscutting, straight-line ripping (with a strip of wood tacked in place as a guide), and also for cutting easy curves, as described previously for the bench saw. There are numerous makes on the market, from Makita, Milwaukee, Craftsman, DeWalt, Ryobi, and many others. Skil, which still makes them, was one of the earliest manufacturers of this type of saw. Lots of old hands still refer to portable circular saws generically as "skillsaws"! There is a wide range of quality, features, power, and price among these saws. Woodworkers often accumulate two or three of them over the years, in which case it's convenient to keep a different blade (or even an abrasive wheel for cutting metal) on each.

PORTABLE SABER SAW

Again, there are many choices. A variable-speed model is good for cutting either wood or metal with the appropriate blade. This

FIGURE 3-5.
A 14" Delta band saw. (*Courtesy Delta Machinery*)

type of tool is used for curved cuts in plywood panels, for cutting away a plywood deck in the way of hatch openings, and for cutouts such as portholes, sink openings in galley counters, and the like.

TOOLS FOR MAKING HOLES

A great many holes have to be made during the construction of a boat— small holes for hundreds of fasteners, larger holes for through-hull and deck fittings. Most will be made with twist drill bits driven by rotary devices ranging from the small cordless drill for small jobs to $\frac{1}{4}$"-, $\frac{3}{8}$"-, and $\frac{1}{2}$"-capacity corded drills, preferably of variable speed.

In days past, one bought high-speed drill bits because they outlasted ordinary carbon steel bits, which tended to burn when drilling hardwoods and metals. Today bits are made that are even better than high-speed steel, and they are readily available. Some of the tough new bits are made of cobalt steel, and one of the best drill bits for wood, the brad-point bit, is now available with a carbide tip.

Extra-long twist bits, often called "electrician's" or "aircraft" bits, are sometimes necessary for the job at hand. You can find them in mail-order tool catalogs, or try looking in your hardware store.

I have seen old-hand boatbuilders grind twist drills to a tapered point, the profile becoming similar to that of a wood screw. The resulting hole gives the screw good holding power, and it is faster than having to drill first a tight hole for the screw shank and then a second, smaller one for the threaded length. There is much more about tapered drills and holes for fasteners in Chapter 6.

Incidentally, the experienced hands mentioned above were planking plywood lapstrake hulls and had to drill holes either through two layers of plywood planking along the laps between the frames, or through two layers of plywood plus the steam-bent oak frames, in both cases for copper rivets. They claimed a tapered bit tore only minimal wood fibers when it pierced, so they did not have to be concerned about the seating of the burr when driven over the rivet. Try it—it's true.

If your kit includes a traditional hand-operated ratchet brace and a set of Jennings- or Irwin-brand auger bits, these work nicely in boatbuilding.

In anything but the smallest hulls, there will be long holes to be bored, such as for floor timber fastenings, and others that will be discussed later on. These can be made with long twist drills or augers, lengthened if necessary by welding on an extension. Boatbuilders prefer the "barefoot" type of auger, which is easier to keep on a straight course and also is easier to withdraw for clearing away chips than a conventional auger having a threaded lead screw. Augers should be driven by hand or by a powerful, slow-turning electric drill, preferably reversible.

Hole saws are made in sizes ranging from ⁹⁄₁₆" through 6" in diameter, but their short length limits the thickness of the material they can cut and generally dictates that they be used for openings sized to suit through-hull fittings for water inlets, toilet and engine exhaust discharge fittings, and similar purposes. A size can be found to come very close to the outside diameter of pipes, but sometimes a rasp must be used to get the hole just right. Figure 3-6 shows an arbor that mates with and drives the saw using a power drill. A single arbor will not accept all sizes of saws. In the Morse-brand line, for instance, three sizes of arbors are needed to use the full range of saws. The arbor pilot bits are replaceable. Morse also makes a 12" extension.

Although small craft can be built in a shop without a drill press, there are times when this tool is very helpful. Chuck capacity should be ½", the minimum being ⅜". A press is particularly valuable when holes must be plumb to the surface. A drill press is surprisingly versatile, with the appropriate attachments and some imagination. With a set of drum sanders, for example, it can be used as a fixed sander. People have even been known to set up a drill press as a wood lathe, not as good as the real thing of course, but probably adequate to turn out the odd tool handle in a pinch.

FIGURE 3-6.
Hole saws and the old "barefoot" auger for long holes. (*W. L. Fuller, Inc.*)

JOINTER

This tool is used for edging and for making panels out of edge-glued solid boards. This process can be done as effectively with a well-set-up table saw or even, with practice, using hand planes. A power jointer, 4" or wider, is a useful tool but is not essential for the small-boat builder.

SPECIAL HAND PLANES

Pictured in Figure 3-7 are two planes seldom found in tool chests.

The Stanley No. 75 bull-nose rabbet plane is a short tool useful for cleaning up a rabbet, in a curved stem (see Figure 8-5 in Chapter 8) and elsewhere, when it has been cut too shallow for the plank thickness.

FIGURE 3-7A.
Stanley No. 75 bull-nose rabbet plane. (*Stanley Tools*)

FIGURE 3-7B.
Stanley No. 78 rabbet plane. (*Stanley Tools*)

In fact, a shy rabbet is not a bad idea—it can be finished off accurately after setting up. (More about this in Chapter 9.)

The Stanley No. 78 rabbet plane has a fence that is adjustable across the sole and slides on a rod to adjust the width of cut. The plane body is tapped for the rod on both sides, and there is a gauge to regulate depth of cut; thus this tool can be used with the right or the left hand. When the iron is moved to the forward seat, the plane becomes a bull-nose, but it is too long to get into tight places like the No. 75 does. With both the depth gauge and the fence removed, the plane will cut into corners or up against perpendicular surfaces.

Both of these planes were in Stanley's 1892 catalog, priced at $.50 and $1.50, respectively. The better-quality woodworkers' tool catalogs carry the modern equivalent by Stanley (see their new #90 bull-nose plane in Figure 3-8) and by others, including Lie-Nielsen. The classic models mentioned above, and others, are generally available on the used market.

FIGURE 3-8.
Stanley #90 bull-nose plane. (*Stanley Tools*)

FIGURE 3-9.
Makita KP 0810 electric plane. (*Makita Tools*)

ELECTRIC PLANE

I resisted buying a power plane for a long time, although I knew from boat-yard experience that it saves much labor when properly handled. Now I have one with a $3\frac{1}{2}$"-wide blade and have found it increasingly helpful. In one yard we had repairs to make on an Alden schooner that had tangled with a stone jetty in a fog at night. A lightweight 3" electric plane was used to smooth jagged gouges in the lead ballast keel at the cost of breaking the toothed drive belt a few times over a period of six hours. It was the perfect tool for the job. Makita and Porter Cable make great units.

CORDLESS TOOLS

Anyone having a passing familiarity with developments in woodworking over the last few years is aware of the extent to which battery-powered tools (and tool systems) have worked their way into almost every phase of craftsmanship, both amateur and professional. Over the years battery voltage, along with tool power, has steadily grown, and the marketing trend has been to sell these tools as combination packages, typically with a charger, two batteries, two to five tools, always including a drill and often a flashlight, all contained in a suitcase-size carrying case. It's tempting to buy the sets, of course, but in my opinion the drills are the only really essential part of the sets. All the tools can be bought individually of course. Generally these tools are not as powerful as their most powerful corded counterparts, but they are surprisingly often the right tool for the job. And the advantages of cordlessness are obvious. The drills, usually with variable speed, reversibility, and adjustable-torque clutches, work very well as electric screwdrivers. The circular saws tend to be smaller and lighter and have thinner blades than corded ones; they are great for cutting thin paneling and solid lumber up to about an inch thick. The most recent, highest-voltage models are able to handle ordinary two-by construction lumber and are pretty much indistinguishable from corded models. The chargers and batteries are one more thing to keep track of, of course, but the advantages of these systems seem to have won them a permanent place in the shop. All the manufacturers of corded power tools mentioned so far have cordless lines as well.

FIGURE 3-10.
Boatbuilding, despite all the changes in tools, still involves the forming and fastening of materials into the shape of a boat. In addition to the electric drills and screwdrivers visible here, there are nine C-clamps keeping the plank in place for fastening to the frames. Note that the hull has been tilted to make the bottom more accessible.

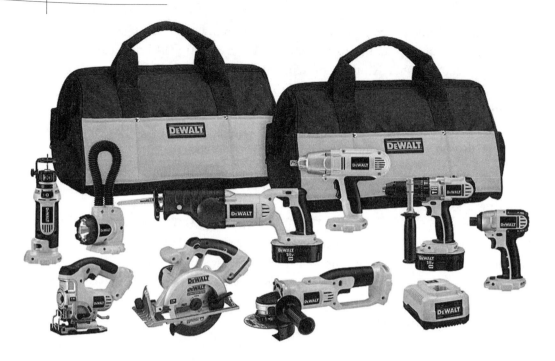

FIGURE 3-11.
A cordless tool combination set from DeWalt. (*DeWalt Tools*)

THICKNESS PLANER

This machine has always been the most costly piece of equipment in a small shop. But the story has changed in recent years, and some planers of limited capacity have become comparatively affordable. A planer is not essential, in that milling can always be done off-site, but it really is a nice machine to have in the shop. One example of the small planers now on the market is the Makita Model 2012 NB, which will handle stock up to 12" wide and 6" thick but will of course perform better on smaller-dimensioned stock. Its current consumption of 15 amps at 115 volts AC requires no special wiring. Sears, Ryobi, Delta Machinery (see their 13" planer in Figure 3-12), DeWalt, and others all have thickness planers in this size and price range.

MACHINE TOOL "CENTERS"

I have never been enthusiastic about the "smith"-type compact combinations of lathe, band saw, circular saw, etc., because by observing a friend

FIGURE 3-12.
Delta 13" thickness planer. (*Courtesy Delta Machinery*)

operate his conglomerate of machine tools I concluded too much time was wasted changing from one function to another, and impatience is one of my weak points.

But technology has improved, and now there are a number of multifunction machines that are highly useful in a professional boat shop for turning out interior joinerwork pieces, prefabricated interior furniture units, and related tasks.

One such machine, the Robland HX310 from Laguna Tools (Figure 3-13), includes a table saw, a thickness planer (the maximum width of which is sufficient for planing planking stock up to 6" wide), a jointer, a spindle shaper, and a mortiser, all usable without wasting time. Accessories (and there are many) include one for handling full-size plywood panels with the table saw.

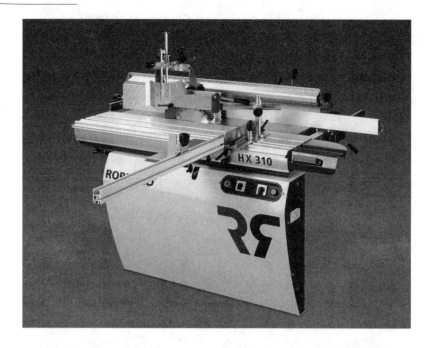

FIGURE 3-13.
The Robland HX 310 combination woodworking machine. (*Laguna Tools*)

ROUTERS

A router, which is used mostly when shaping the edges of boards, is not really necessary in boatbuilding, but it can be helpful. There are plain routers; laminate trimmers, which do just that (trimming the edges of "mica"-type wood overlays); and plunge routers, which will start a cut in the middle of a board without a starting hole.

A further step is to acquire a router table. The tool clamps to the underside of the table with the bit projecting above the table surface. Adjustable fences permit edging like a jointer, but not as wide a cut as can be done with a jointer; cutting board edges to ogee, radius, chamfered shapes, etc., is also possible.

There are many makes of routers on the market: Black & Decker (Delta Machinery), Skil, Craftsman, Porter-Cable, Makita, Bosch, Ryobi, and others. One way of judging the capacity of a particular router is by the amperage of the motor; the higher the amperage, the more power.

If you have no experience with routers, it would be prudent to study safe router operation, starting with the basics, such as not using it in the wrong direction. Router operators should definitely wear eye protection and, to reduce the volume of the whine made by a router, hearing protection.

Patrick Spielman has written two excellent books on router use: *Router Basics* and *Router Handbook*. You might also consider Bill Hylton's more recent books (find them and others on Amazon). The use of a router when building a lightweight hull with glued lapstrake construction is discussed in Chapter 11 and by Thomas Hill in his book *Ultralight Boatbuilding*. (See Appendix for complete listings.)

SANDERS

There are a number of stationary and portable sanders available. The most common stationary type is one with a vertical disc and adjustable tilting table, as well as a belt that pivots from horizontal to vertical. This tool is ideal for sanding small parts, if you can afford one and have the shop space.

A portable disc sander is great provided you learn how to control one. This tool can easily spoil any workpiece with unwanted gouges. Practice on something other than your hull!

A portable belt sander is used for smoothing planks or any long stock. This tool too can damage your work, but is easier to master than a disc sander. Keep the belt moving to avoid cutting a valley.

Another option is the random-orbit palm sander (Figure 3-13A). The most popular size for small craft takes a quarter sheet of standard 9" × 11" abrasive paper and is easy to control. I have used mine with paper from 40 grit (be careful!) to 220 grit for an acceptably smooth surface and the latter grit for the rapid sanding of varnish between coats.

The larger, more powerful right-angle random-orbit sanders, like the Porter-Cable 7345 shown in Figure 3-13B, are real workhorses around the boatshop. Always remember to have the abrasive surface touching the work

FIGURE 3-13A.
The Makita BO 4556 palm sander.
(*Makita Tools*)

FIGURE 3-13B.
The Porter-Cable 7345 random-orbit sander. (*Porter-Cable*)

surface when you turn these babies on; when they are running free they are basically high-RPM disc sanders, and they can gouge your work in a fraction of a second. The work surface will prevent the disc from spinning and convert the motion of the disc into a random orbit if you start the sander correctly—in firm contact with the work.

Another type of portable sander, one especially useful for corners and edges, is made in Germany by Fein Power Tools (similar products have appeared from other manufacturers, but the Fein still sets the standard). The sanding pads on these units are triangular with curved edges that permit sanding inside corners where other types cannot reach. The pad oscillates one degree side to side 20,000 times a minute. A perforated pad that enables it to be used as a dust extractor is offered as an accessory. Lately Fein has developed this tool into a multipurpose oscillating detail sander, scraper, saw, and chisel system (Figure 3-14) that is finding its way into many boatshops and yards. It is probably more useful in repairs and refitting than in new construction, but it is an impressive tool. It may be the best tool for the difficult problem of making clean flush cuts:

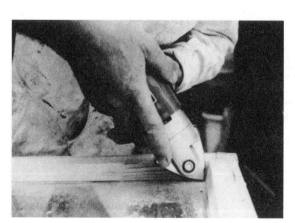

FIGURE 3-14A.
An oscillating sander simplifies working in corners and on edges.

FIGURE 3-14B.
The Fein MultiMaster oscillating tool system (detail sander). (*Fein Power Tools*)

for example, cutting out a section of cabin sole right up to the edge of an exist-ing furniture panel or bulkhead.

In Chapter 16 there is a discussion of abrasive papers and some sanding aids. Note that during most sanding operations it is prudent to wear a dust mask. This is a particular concern in boatbuilding because the more rot-resistant a wood is, the more toxic its sawdust is to people.

"STRUCTURED CARBIDE" ABRASIVE TOOLS

In the tool world something new is always being introduced despite the endless number of tools and accessories already available. Recently an inventor devised a way, to put it simply, to fuse patented "structured car-bide" teeth to a variety of tools (files, rotary burrs and router bits, sanding drums and discs, and even hole saws and circular saw blades), and they are reputed to outcut and outlast any other abrasive. The tools, made by L. R. Oliver & Company, are called "Karbide Kutzall," and there are two grades—silver for fast cutting, and gold for a finer finish. The teeth don't heat up or clog with use. They cut wood, laminates (including those of fiberglass), plastics, and rubber, but they have not been designed for cut-ting metal. These tools are available from Woodcraft Supply and directly (online) from the manufacturer.

I did not know these tools existed when ordering what a woodcarver's supply house catalog described as a "wood pulverizer." Now, a year later, I know that it is a silver donut wheel. When I used it with my 4" angle

FIGURE 3-15.
An assortment of Karbide Kutzall Tools. (*L. R. Oliver & Company*)

grinder (another very useful tool to have around the shop, by the way), I was amazed at how easily and quickly wood was cut away from a block glued up for a sailboat half-hull model.

JAPANESE HAND TOOLS

Let me lead into the subject of Japanese-made hand tools by admitting that I own one, a saw similar to the longer one in Figure 3-16. Do I like it? Yes! But one warning for starters, and I hope one is enough: That saw can cut hardwood, softwood, and human flesh just as easily as butter and makes an extremely thin cut on the *pull* stroke, which is Japanese standard procedure and makes for better control. When the extremely fine-toothed blades get dull they are replaced, not sharpened.

Builders form passionate attachments to their Japanese tools. One day I noticed a freelance boat carpenter using a Duzuki handsaw for a repair.

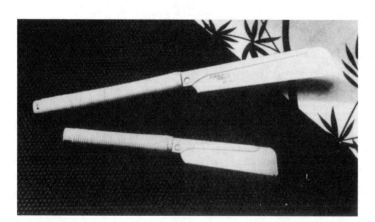

FIGURE 3-16.
Japanese saws, which are extremely sharp, cut on the pull stroke. (*Woodcraft, Inc.*)

When I asked him if he used the saw often, the reply was *"All* the time." On another occasion I visited a friend at a small one-off furniture-making shop, where I had my first exposure to a Japanese-made laminated-steel chisel. It was truly an experience to use that chisel.

Japanese tools have a lot going for them; otherwise they would not have been around so long. The Japanese have perfected flat laminated steel, backing up a very hard steel with a softer material that reinforces the steel doing the cutting. I would hazard a guess that this is why the gouges of various shapes one sees in catalogs under the general heading of "carving tools" always seem to be Japanese-made. Some of us cannot do without a variety of these for sculpting work, as in some kinds of boat modeling.

PORTABLE LUMBER SUPPORT ROLLERS

If you normally work alone, another person must be called to help when sawing long stock unless the shop has portable supports adjustable to the heights of the saw tables. There are many varieties of these to be seen in boatbuilding shops, most of them homemade. In my case the shop area calls for equipment that occupies a minimum of space when not needed. Figure 3-17 shows supports I built and named "My Wife," because she no longer had to be called upon to help me.

For the rollers I used hardwood rolling pins with free-turning handles having plastic bearings; the rest of the support parts are plywood and a few scraps of lumber. The roller unit is slipped over the crossbar of a sawhorse. The upper set of holes sets the roller at the height of my band saw table while the lower set suits the height of the bench saw table. If the shop floor is uneven, the plywood roller cheeks can be held at the desired height using clamps rather than the carriage bolts with wing nuts as shown.

Since making my supports, I came upon a substitute for the rolling pins— so-called infeed and outfeed rollers, 14" long with steel rods protruding from the ends. These are pictured in the Woodworker's Supply catalog.

Some of the tool houses now sell lumber supports through their catalogs. Beware of the cheap versions sold, as a rule, in warehouse-type home improvement stores; one unit I saw was so light it required ballasting at its base.

The more I work alone in a rather cramped area, the more conscious I become of space-saving equipment. Figure 3-18 is of a lumber rest that can be folded and stowed out of the way when not in use. A rest like this can be nailed together of 1"-thick boards about 3½" wide; plus feed rollers, as mentioned above, or improvised rollers; plus a pair of spacers, pivoted or not, to adjust the height of the roller to suit your machine tools.

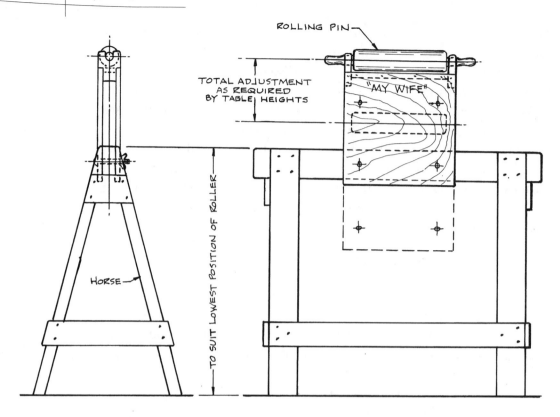

ROLLING PIN

TOTAL ADJUSTMENT
AS REQUIRED
BY TABLE HEIGHTS

"MY WIFE"

TO SUIT LOWEST POSITION OF ROLLER

HORSE

FIGURE 3-17.
Homemade portable lumber support.

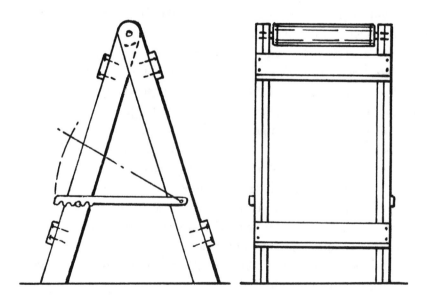

FIGURE 3-18.
Folding lumber rest.

THE ADZE

The boatshop that hired me as a late-teenaged helper had a number of Scandinavian boatbuilders. Occasionally an adze was brought out and used for a short odd job, but the kind of boats being built did not call for the extensive use of the tool, which is obviously best suited to trimming and shaping heavy timbers. Since then, I have never seen an adze in use. Due to my lack of experience, I cannot say more, but it will not do to overlook this traditional tool. Woodcraft is now carrying a line of adzes similar to traditional boatbuilders' adzes made by a Swiss firm called Pfeil. No doubt the old-style tools are available used if you really want to have them.

A unique short-handled version of a shipbuilder's adze is an *enxó* (pronounced *en-shaw*), a tool much used in Portugal by boatbuilders and other woodworkers. The design has been handed down since the Stone Age. The radius of the blade, which is about 4½" wide and 5" long, is similar to the length of your arm from hand to elbow. This makes it more natural to learn and faster to master than one of the long-handled two-handed adzes of the type usually associated with shipbuilding.

FIGURE 3-19.
Three adze heads. (A) is a straight adze 3¼" across, used to flatten stock. (B) is 2¼" across and curved to a 3" circle, obviously used for scooping. (C), a lip adze used by wooden-ship builders for shaping spars and fairing planking, is slightly curved and more man-sized at 5¼" across. Its handle would be about 32" long. *(Woodcraft Supply)*

FIGURE 3-20.
An *enxó* hand adze.

The *enxó* hand adze is imported and sold in the United States by boat-builder-designer Simon Watts. Sources for other types of adze include Woodcraft Supply, Garrett Wade, and Wood Carver's Supply.

PARTING WORD

Descriptions of desirable tools, both hand and power, could go on for many pages. Acquisition of tools beyond the absolute basics depends on three things: enthusiasm, shop space, and money. If you are lucky enough to live in an area where a lot of boatbuilding is going on, you may find it possible to borrow tools, especially if you are willing to lend them too. You have to think twice of course about buying a tool that would be extremely useful for only one job that you are not likely to repeat. Nowadays, though, with eBay and Craigslist as well as the many specialized boatbuilding and woodworking forums on the Web, it's much easier to buy used tools and sell them when they become superfluous. There's no doubt that having the right tools makes the whole job a lot more pleasant and leads to better results. Maybe it is not so important for the amateur when the issue is only speed, but there are definitely cases where the right specialized tool is much more likely to lead to a professional result. On the other hand, if you lean toward a minimalist approach, don't be discouraged, because in years past small wooden craft—and some not so small—were built only with unpowered hand tools. In fact, even today, boatbuilder Winer Malone of Hopetown, Abaco, Bahamas, builds his famous round-bottomed sawn-frame sailing dinghies in a shop that has no electricity.

A small number of power tools, however, can make life easier, for instance, as a minimum, a variable-speed, ⅜"-capacity electric drill, corded or cordless or both, that can also be used for driving screws. Also a good portable jigsaw or saber saw. A step up would be a 10" table saw and a portable circular saw (with the knowledge to use them safely). A giant step up would be a 12" or 14" band saw (preferably the latter).

One does not need a thickness planer, because this can be done for you by others; neither does one need a portable electric plane. But one indispensable operation one must master is the skill to keep all your tools *sharp*. Dull tools can ruin your day, as the saying goes, if not cause the abandonment of your boatbuilding project or any other woodworking job. Have patience; learn how to sharpen and hone to a razor-sharp edge. (This book's Appendix will get you started.) This is part of making woodworking a pleasure rather than a chore.

Professional shops generally have compressed air and the associated tools. If you already have a compressor and some tools, you may find lots of uses for them in boatbuilding. They would not be high on my priority list for a start-up home boatbuilding shop, however.

If you have a few of the catalogs (companies will keep sending them once you order something) and read the boatbuilding magazines, it won't be a problem for you to keep up with this rapidly developing area as your boatbuilding interests and abilities evolve.

An afterthought: I frequently use a wet-or-dry shop-type vacuum cleaner that can be converted into a blower. Many times, though, when I have managed to clog the suction, I have wished the hose was more than 1¼" inside diameter. Bigger is better, if you can afford it.

CODA—THE INTERNET

Perhaps the most significant technological development affecting the boatbuilder (and just about everyone else) since the last edition of *Boatbuilding Manual* is the Internet. Information about products and methods that not so long ago were, if not actually secret, at least very hard to obtain unless you had access to cooperative professional boatbuilders is now instantly available day and night anywhere in the world. If you are not already proficient at Internet research, here are a few suggestions for getting the best results from this wonderful resource. Your overriding mantra should be "consider the source" because there is a tremendous range of quality in the information on the Web, from unimpeachable to intentionally false. If you get to know a few particularly useful sites (the WoodenBoat Forum might be a good place to start, or the Glen-L site), you will soon see that there are ways to evaluate the various sources. At those sites, you will find newbies asking questions, a few opinionated but poorly informed sources giving answers, and a number of experienced and thoughtful people who have fielded hundreds if not thousands of inquiries. Often there are schools of thought on various issues, sometimes with tedious repetitive discussions. But with careful searching and scanning, it is usually possible to learn the facts and principles that will allow you to handle your issue more confidently. Use Google and other search engines to find discussions and sources, and bookmark sites where you have found useful information.

Many amateur builders keep blogs (WoodenBoatBlog.com has a collection of these). Bloggers often highlight their mistakes as well as their triumphs, and you are often likely to avoid a major pitfall by encountering it first on someone else's blog. If you keep a blog of your building project, you might occasionally find that some kind soul will give you a heads-up on a method or problem you are considering that will save you some wasted effort.

Perhaps most important, especially if you live in a less nautical part of the country, you are likely to gain a great deal of support and confidence from becoming part of a virtual community of people who are involved in projects much like yours. As with any tool, the more you use the Internet, the more helpful it will be as you become more proficient and discerning. And very likely after a while you will find yourself helping others in their projects and deriving a whole new set of satisfactions from that. This edition contains many Internet references, but addresses change and companies and other sources come and go. Don't fret, just Web-search it!

4

WOODS

WOOD IS ONE OF THE EASIEST MATERIALS out of which the amateur can build a boat, and it remains a favorite of many professionals, despite the great growth in popularity of synthetic materials. Not all woods are suitable for boatbuilding, however, so as we go along, there will be comments on those kinds that have proved durable—one of the most desirable qualities sought—and have the necessary strength.

It is beyond the scope of this book to more than scratch the surface on the subject of wood, even when limited to the trees found in the United States, so I will limit our discussions to the small number of commonly accepted boatbuilding woods and how the lumber is manufactured from logs. A few reasons for the elimination of certain woods from boatbuilding are brittleness, softness, weakness, susceptibility to decay, and shortness of growth. On the other hand, there are time-tested woods available that have the necessary qualities, but these types can seldom be found in an ordinary lumberyard. Fortunately almost every area where boats are built has a yard that fully understands the needs of the boatbuilder, and the amateur is advised to seek the aid of such a supplier to obtain the high-grade lumber needed for long hull life. There should be no compromise in the matter of lumber quality, for when the labor of the builder is considered, the extra cost and trouble of good material is of little consequence. (Sometimes beginners find this difficult to believe.)

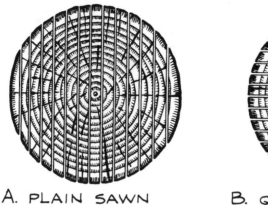

A. PLAIN SAWN   B. QUARTER SAWN

FIGURE 4-1.
Plain-sawn (not generally desirable for boatbuilding) and quarter-sawn boards.

SAWING OF LUMBER

Grain is formed by the angle of the annual rings with the face of a board, and its orientation has much to do with the suitability of the lumber for use in boats. The grain's orientation in boards depends upon how the lumber is cut from logs. After a tree has been felled and trimmed, it is easy for the lumber worker to run the log through a saw and cut it into boards, as shown in A in Figure 4-1. This is called plain sawing, and all but one or two of the boards sawn from the log in this manner are called slash grain or flat grain. A more expensive and more wasteful method of cutting up the log,

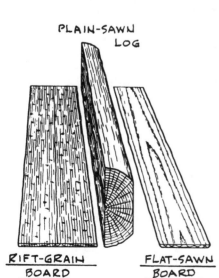

PLAIN-SAWN LOG

RIFT-GRAIN BOARD   FLAT-SAWN BOARD

shown in B in Figure 4-1, is called quarter sawing, and the resulting boards are known as rift, vertical, or edge-grain boards.

It can be seen from Figure 4-2 that a few boards from the middle of a plain-sawn log have rift grain just like quarter-sawn lumber, but the majority of the plain-sawn boards are not desirable for boatbuilding, as will be shown.

FIGURE 4-2.
When boards are plain sawn, a few of them wind up rift-grain; the greater majority are not. (*Courtesy Forest Products Laboratory, USDA Forest Service.*)

SEASONING

Wood for almost any purpose at all must be dried or seasoned to reduce the moisture content present when the tree is cut, at which time the content may be as much as half or more the weight of the log. There are two ways that wood contains moisture: absorption by the cell walls and absorption into the cell cavities themselves. When the wood has taken on as much as the cell will hold, the wood is said to be at the fiber saturation point. In this condition the moisture content of the wood averages about 25 percent, and no shrinkage takes place until this percentage is reduced. Seasoning is the process of reducing the moisture content to about 15 percent, an acceptable level for boatbuilding material, and this is when the wood shrinks. After it seasons to whatever level is wanted, wood shrinks further if more moisture is removed and swells if more moisture is taken on. Shrinking or swelling is greatest in the direction of the annual rings (tangential), about one-half as much as across the rings (radial), and only a little in the length of a board. Distortion from shrinkage is shown in Figure 4-3, and it can be seen that slash-grain boards cup more than rift-sawn. Shrinkage of rift-sawn lumber tends more toward reducing thickness than width, producing boards with greater dimensional stability than flat-grain ones, and for this reason rift-sawn lumber is desirable for planking, decking, and other boat parts.

The tendency to cup should be considered when planking. For example, when planking the bottom of a simple boat like a skiff, the annual rings should curve against the chine (see A in Figure 4-3). The cupping tendency shows up in time when planks are wide.

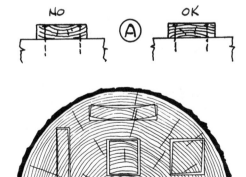

FIGURE 4-3.

Characteristic shrinkage during seasoning of pieces sawn from a log. Logs that are rift-grain suffer less distortion from shrinkage. When planking, consider the tendency of certain planks to cup, so make sure the annual rings curve against the chine, as shown in A. (*Forest Products Laboratory, USDA Forest Service*)

There are two methods used for seasoning wood, and the mention of the merits of one versus the other just might start up an argument in the local boatshop. There are those who will accept only air-dried lumber, a process that can take several years, depending upon the thickness of the pieces. It is generally accepted that air-dried wood is the best for boatbuilding, and on numerous occasions I have seen this being done right in boatyards. On the other hand, modern production cannot wait too long for material, so the lumber is placed in a kiln to be dried in a number of days. Drying boat lumber by this method must be done with care, because the normal product of the kiln will have a moisture content as low as 8 percent, whereas time has shown that regardless of the drying method, the moisture content of boat material should be between 12 and 16 percent, with many accepting 15 percent as ideal. Moisture content, incidentally, is expressed as a percentage of the lumber weight when oven dry. More about this in *Wood Handbook*, published by Forest Products Laboratory, U.S. Department of Agriculture and available free online. (See Appendix.)

Drying in a kiln speeds up the evaporation of moisture, causing fast drying on the surface and slow drying inside, and is said to affect both the strength and elasticity of the wood. Lumber for boats must not be too green or it will shrink and check excessively during the building period, nor must it be too dry or it will absorb moisture and swell unduly. With some types of planking the latter condition could be very serious.

The best procedure for the amateur is to leave the selection of the wood to the experts who understand the requirements of boatbuilding. These people also know that boat lumber should not have large knots and checks, decay, or nondurable sapwood.

On the other hand, and particularly for the lucky person who has everything, there are meters made for determining the moisture content of wood. They must be used properly for correct results.

If you get deep enough into boatbuilding you may just decide to cope with seasoning wood yourself. I never meant to, but one day I passed an operating sawmill adjacent to a road, made a one-eighty turn to see what the workers were up to, and found they were plain sawing a cypress log. The boards were clear and were rough-sawn 1" thick, had bark edges, and would net out about 10" wide; also they were a bargain, so, naturally, they wound up drying in my yard. I inserted crosswise "stickers" between layers of boards to allow air to circulate, as shown in Figure 4-4. You can use scrap wood for stickers, but it must be free of rot and other diseases. You can monitor the drying progress with a borrowed moisture meter.

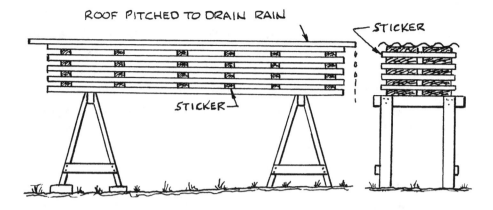

ROOF PITCHED TO DRAIN RAIN

STICKER

STICKER

FIGURE 4-4.

One arrangement for air-drying a small quantity of boards. Ground blocks must be large enough to maintain sufficient bearing throughout the time the pile is being seasoned. Small blocks will "bury" in areas where the ground freezes and thaws with seasonal changes. The "roof" consists of corrugated roofing panel.

If you want to try kiln drying, Nyle Dry Kiln Systems makes drying kilns with a capacity of as little as 500 board feet.

KINDS OF WOOD

In the northeastern part of the United States, where many like to think boatbuilding in this country was born, the practice of using certain available native woods was established long ago, and time has proved its worth. Through the years, lumber from other parts of the country, as well as material from foreign lands, has been added to the list of suitable woods, with substitutions of local products being made in certain areas as a result of satisfactory experience with these woods for boatbuilding. As a typical example, frames would be of oak in most localities, but keel, deadwood, and other backbone members might be yellow pine in the South, white oak in the Northeast, or Alaska cedar or Douglas fir on the West Coast. As long as it is proven, the choice of wood makes little difference, but a boat involves too much work to gamble with untried materials that may rot in a short time or be brittle or not hold fastenings.

As a guide, I give here a list of good woods, together with principal properties and approximate weights per board foot (one foot square by one inch thick) at 12 percent moisture content.

I have heard (though never firsthand) that in sections of the United States where black locust and sassafras trees are native, these woods have been used for frames and planking, respectively. Therefore, these woods are described in the following.

White Oak

Weight about 4.2 pounds per board foot (heavy). Durable, stiff, strong, and holds fastenings exceptionally well. Easily steam-bent, thus excellent for frames, but for this purpose the oak should be green, not seasoned. Also used extensively for all backbone members such as keel, stem, deadwood, etc. Good white oak grows in New England southward through the Appalachian area. It has been axiomatic among traditional boatbuilders that the most durable oak is from trees felled during the winter when the sap is not flowing. This does not seem to be supported by the research (see "Winter Cutting vs. Summer Cutting" later in this chapter), but woodcutters' still prefer to cut in the cooler months. When white oak is wanted for bent frames, explain to your prospective supplier that you want straight-grained material from butt logs. White oak parts that are normally submerged, such as a keel, can be green and will shrink and swell less. Attempting to dry hefty pieces will very likely twist them out of shape.

Douglas Fir

Weight about 2.9 pounds (medium). Strong and straight-grained, useful for stringers, clamps, sometimes for spars as a substitute for Sitka spruce when light weight is not of utmost importance, and for planking when rift-sawn. Grows in Oregon, Washington, and California. Logs are large, from which veneer is peeled for manufacture into plywood panels. Douglas fir is often called Oregon pine, and it is available—as are Western red cedar, Sitka spruce, and meranti (a mahogany-like wood)—as ⅛" veneers for cold-molded hull construction.

Yellow Pine (Longleaf)

Weight about 3.4 pounds (heavy). Strong, very durable, and straight-grained. Used for stringers, clamps, and for planking if weight is not a factor, also as a substitute for white oak keels, deadwood, etc. May be available in good long lengths in some localities. Has been reported as not durable in fresh water, but I cannot substantiate this. Grows in southern United States in Atlantic and Gulf states.

White Pine

Weight about 2.1 pounds (light). Genuine northern white pine, enormous quantities of which were used in the construction of sailing ships years ago and for spars in the British Navy's sailing warships, and often later for laid decks in yacht building, is seldom seen nowadays. White pine is mentioned here because the wide, clear boards available make it a tempting material for the amateur, but the dubious durability of many varieties makes this wood undesirable for boat construction, except for interior joinerwork.

White Cedar, Northern and Atlantic

Weight about 1.9 pounds (light). Northern white cedar grows from Maine southward along the Appalachian Mountain range. Atlantic white cedar, which grows near the Atlantic coast from Maine to northern Florida and westward along the Gulf Coast to Louisiana, is also known as juniper, southern white cedar, swamp cedar, and boat cedar. It is not strong, but its uniformity and resistance to rot make it excellent for planking. Soaks up moisture rapidly, but shrinkage is low, both of which qualities are especially good for light lapstrake-planked boats that are alternately in and out of the water. Sapwood layer is usually thin. Almost always supplied as "flitches," that is, plain-sawn boards with or without bark on the edges. These "boat boards" (or "round edge" or "live edge" boards) taper in width just as the tree trunk does and can be advantageously used for hull planking.

Port Orford Cedar

Weight about 2.4 pounds (light). Moderately strong, clear, and straight-grained. Heartwood very resistant to rot. Used for planking and bright finished decks. Grows in southern Oregon and northern California and is a material familiar to the layman as the wood from which vast numbers of venetian blind slats used to be made. Has a distinctive spicy odor.

Western Red Cedar

Weight about 1.9 pounds (light). Highly resistant to rot and available in good widths and lengths for planking. This wood, however, is soft and weak, thus not the best material for this purpose, except for certain hull types that will be revealed as we go along. The dust of Western red cedar is said to be toxic, so be sure to wear a respirator when cutting or sanding this material.

Cypress

Weight about 2.8 pounds (medium). Moderately strong, heartwood very resistant to rot. Used for planking where weight is not a factor because it soaks up water to a great extent, making for a heavy boat after a short time in the water. Grows in southern low swamplands of the United States. If you want to use cypress in a boat, find a supplier who understands this material, because I have been told that the supply of stock of boatbuilding quality is "sorry."

Sitka Spruce

Weight about 2.4 pounds (light). Moderate shrinkage, high strength for its weight, and availability in long, clear lengths make it ideal for spars. Grows on Pacific Coast in a narrow strip from northern California to Alaska. Not particularly resistant to rot, but this is not detrimental when spars have proper care. Still available in aircraft quality because, believe it or not, there are always plenty of amateur-built wooden aircraft under construction. In 2010 Sitka spruce is available from several of the suppliers (see Appendix) in one-inch thickness with lengths up to 20 feet and widths up to 9 inches.

Spruce (Northern White)

Weight about 2.4 pounds (light). High strength for weight, not very resistant to rot. Used for deck and interior joinerwork framing where weight-saving is the primary consideration. Grows in New England.

Philippine "Mahogany"

Weight about 3.0 pounds (medium). This is the market name for woods known in the Philippine islands as *luan* and *tangile*. It is decay-resistant and an excellent material for planking; it is used by the finest builders for this purpose. When selected for color and grain it is attractive for cabin sides and trim. Somewhat more difficult to finish than true mahoganies. Hardness and color vary considerably. Holds fastenings well and is relatively inexpensive considering its qualities. According to one large importer, the best grade is known as "firsts and seconds," and the better boatbuilders prefer the more expensive, darker red variety.

Other Mahoganies

Weights vary from medium to heavy. Honduras, Mexican, and African mahoganies have all been used for planking, exterior finish, and interior joinerwork of fine yachts. They are heavier than the so-called Philippine mahoganies and are better looking, easier to finish, and more expensive. Honduras or Mexican mahogany is a favored first-quality planking and finish material. According to Abeking and Rasmussen of Lemwerder, Germany, builders of some of the finest yachts in the world, suitable African mahoganies are *Khaya ivorensis, Sipo utile, Sapeli aboudikro,* and *Niangon nyanko,* and if this firm uses these kinds they should be acceptable to anyone. Abeking and Rasmussen has stated that there are other kinds of African mahoganies that are not suitable, so here again it is a case of dealing with a reliable supplier of woods.

Teak

Weight about 3.5 pounds (heavy). Not as strong as people think, but extremely durable. Has a natural oil that excludes moisture and thus has minimum shrinkage. The acceptable kind is grown in Burma or Thailand and is so expensive in the United States that its use is reserved for decks and trim. Teak decks are not coated, as a rule; they are scrubbed periodically to a whitish finish that, in the opinion of many, has no equal, or treated periodically with one of the dozen or more "teak oil" finishes on the market. Varnished teak trim has a rich appearance. Worms are not fond of teak, so this wood is often used to sheath the bottom of a keel as protection in case some of the toxic antifouling bottom paint is rubbed off. Teak also contains a gritty substance that dulls tools quickly, adding somewhat to the cost of working it.

Teak has been planted in Costa Rica, and in 2010 is being marketed as a sustainable product, mainly in the form of outdoor furniture and architectural flooring and decking. But a specialist in teak deck installation told me the rapid-growth Central American teak will never compare to the old-growth trees of Burma. See the section on sustainability later in this chapter and the Appendix for sources.

White Ash

Weight about 3.4 pounds (heavy). Straight-grained, strong for its weight, and very durable. Used for deck beams as a substitute for oak where reduction in weight is desirable. Suitable for steam-bending and used for small boat frames; also a favorite for sailboat tillers and an old standby for oars.

Hackmatack

Weight about 3.1 pounds (medium). Also called *larch* or *tamarack*. Tough and durable. Apparently only the roots, from which natural crooks are made, are used for boatbuilding. Stems for small boats and knees are cut from these crooks. On the other hand, Abeking and Rasmussen once told me that larch was their second choice (behind African mahogany) for single-planked hulls.

Figure 4-5 is a snapshot I took of a rough 2"-thick knee and a sketch of the shape it will be cut to make a stem for a dinghy. After planing to finished thickness, the knee will be rabbeted to take the hood ends of the planks.

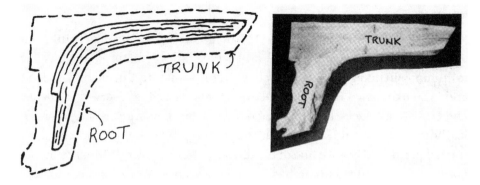

FIGURE 4-5.
The rough and the eventual shape of a hackmatack knee.

Alaska Cedar

Weight about 2.6 pounds (medium). Straight-grained, moderately strong, heartwood very resistant to decay. Minimum shrinkage when seasoned. Good for planking and used for keels in areas where it is grown, southeastern Alaska to southern Oregon. Heartwood is bright yellow, sapwood usually narrow.

Black Locust

Weight about 3.6 pounds (heavy). Hard and high in strength and stiffness. Moderate shrinkage. Heartwood highly resistant to decay. In the distant past locust was used for "treenails" in wooden ship construction. Locust grows in the Appalachian Mountain range from New England to northern Georgia. This wood seems to be increasing in popularity for many uses and has recently been referred to as "New Hampshire teak" and "the new oak." Maybe it's an exaggeration, but Yankee farmers have been known to say that it "lasts only about as long as granite" when used as a fence post.

Sassafras

Weight about 2.4 pounds (light). Moderately hard, moderately weak in bending, highly resistant to decay. Grows eastward from southeastern Iowa and eastern Texas. Freshly cut boards are said to have a sassafras odor, if you know what that is like!

It is recommended that those who want to learn more about wood acquire the *Wood Handbook* mentioned earlier in this chapter.

WINTER CUTTING VS. SUMMER CUTTING

In the remarks about white oak, it was noted that the old hands in boatbuilding generally agreed that the most durable wood comes from trees felled in the winter; therefore, it was something of a jolt to come across the following paragraphs in *Wood: A Manual for Its Use as a Shipbuilding Material:*

"An old belief still given wide currency is that winter-cut lumber is more durable than summer-cut lumber. The belief is based on the erroneous assumption that in winter, 'the sap is down,' while in the summer, 'the sap is up,' in the living tree. Actually, tests have demonstrated conclusively that standing trees contain about as much sap in winter as in summer.

The only sound objection to summer-cut lumber is that logs are more likely to deteriorate if left exposed to high summer temperatures that may accelerate checking and attack by insects and decay fungi. Reasonable precautions, particularly prompt sawing after felling, and good piling and seasoning methods, remove the danger of such damage to summer-cut material."

STRENGTH VS. WEIGHT

Because a comparison of strengths is of interest, the woods mentioned earlier are listed below in order of strength, with the weight per board foot again shown.

Species	Pounds	Species	Pounds
White ash	3.4	Cypress	2.8
White oak	4.2	Sitka spruce	2.4
Yellow pine	3.4	Northern white spruce	2.4
Douglas fir	2.9	Port Orford cedar	2.4
Teak	3.5	Alaska cedar	2.6
Hackmatack	3.1	White cedar	1.9
Honduras mahogany	2.9	White pine	2.1
Philippine "mahogany"	3.0	Western red cedar	1.9

ABS DESIGN STRESSES FOR WOOD

The strengths of a few of the foregoing woods are listed in the *Rules for Building and Classing Reinforced Plastic Vessels,* a 1978 publication of the American Bureau of Shipping (still current in 2010), the American counterpart of Lloyd's Register of Shipping, which is available for download free online at the ABS site. ABS specifies that the wood be of best quality, well seasoned, clear, free of defects adversely affecting its strength, and with grain suitable for the purpose intended, and lists *allowable design stresses* in pounds per square inch (psi) as follows:

Species	Extreme Fiber in Bending	Compression Parallel to Grain
Ash, white	1,866	1,466
Cedar, Alaska	1,466	1,066
Fir, Douglas	2,000	1,466
Mahogany*	2,330	1,333
Oak, white	1,866	1,333
Pine, longleaf yellow	2,000	1,466
Spruce, Sitka	1,466	1,066
Teak	1,500	1,200

*35 pounds per cubic foot minimum weight

PREVENTION OF WOOD DECAY

The first step in the prevention of decay is to select woods that have proved durable in boats, and it should be remembered that the heartwood of a log is the most resistant to rot. Decay is caused by fungi that feed on the cellulose between the cell walls of wood. For the fungi to grow, certain conditions of moisture, temperature, and air must be present. The moisture content must be on the order of 25–30 percent, the temperature 75–90 degrees F, and the air stagnant. Wood that is always dry does not rot because of the lack of moisture, and wood that is continuously wet does not rot because there is no air present.

This is backed up by a discussion of decay in *Wood: A Manual for Its Use as a Shipbuilding Material*, in which the following two statements are made:

1. No decay can occur in any wood species if the moisture content is below 20 percent.
2. No decay can occur in totally submerged lumber.

There will be more later on the importance of building to avoid leaks in deck and cabin, where water can enter and be trapped, just waiting for the right temperature for the fungi to grow.

In addition to the natural decay resistance of some woods and the precautions against leaks that can be taken by the builder, chemicals can be used that are toxic to fungi and marine borers. These preparations are cheap and easy to apply, and they reduce the chances of decay.

Copper naphthenate has been used by boatbuilders as a wood preservative for many years. Be sure to read and heed the instructions printed on the containers. At this writing (2010), the standby Cuprinol Green #10 seems to be off the market, but similar formulations are available at hardware and paint supply stores—for example, Jasco Copper Green Wood Preservative. As with many hazardous chemicals used in boatbuilding, availability and restrictions on the use of these preservatives cannot be predicted.

The preservatives are easy to apply by brushing or dipping, the larger parts being brushed and smaller pieces, such as planking butt blocks, short deck beams, and the like, being dipped in a container of the preparation. Be aware that naphthenate preservatives can take weeks to dry to a ready-to-paint state.

There are some other fairly inexpensive chemical approaches to rot prevention, including ethylene glycol (preferably the pure stuff, but some people have used plain old antifreeze) and borate preparations, which you can buy in liquid and powder form. In accessible interior spaces, paint, varnish, and keeping things reasonably dry are probably adequate precautions, especially when combined with the judicious selection of rot-resistant materials. In recent years many boatbuilders, particularly amateurs, have gotten into the habit of sealing much, most, or even essentially all of the wood on their boats with epoxy, a practice that is certainly encouraged by the epoxy manufacturers. Sealing everything with epoxy adds dramatically to the cost of construction (and adds a certain amount of weight too). There certainly may be advantages to the practice, which, if done properly, stabilizes the treated wood from dimensional changes and associated problems, as well as preventing rot. Traditionalists will point out that boats have been built successfully for centuries without epoxy. But it is undeniable that traditionally built boats were subject to damage and destruction by rot. A modern wooden-boat builder might like the prospect that the boat could last longer or be more free of maintenance headaches if he or she includes epoxy sealing in the construction process.

Epoxy coatings break down in sunlight, like most things, so they need to be protected by paint or UV blocking varnish to really stand up.

A judicious partial use of epoxy sealing with a focus on the elements of the boat that are exposed to rainwater and the elements that will become more or less inaccessible as the boat is completed might constitute a reasonable compromise between cost and protection. An additional consideration in the rot-prevention strategy you decide on is safety. Chemical preservatives may remain in the air of the boat you build for quite some time, and no one really knows what their effect may be on human health. Epoxy, in contrast, once it is fully cured, is generally thought to be a relatively inert and benign presence on the boat. As a basic rule of thumb, it's probably good to remember that if you can smell a chemical, you are taking it into your body. The reverse is not true, however; just because something is odorless does not mean it is not present, whether or not it is harmful.

The previously mentioned *Wood Handbook* classifies the decay resistance of woods, both native to the United States and imported, said to be suitable for boatbuilding. Some builders—including those who have used the vulnerable sapwood by mistake—may not agree with all of these. In general, the handbook makes the following recommendations: use only heartwood of a *durable* species, free of infection, preferably below 20 percent moisture content; provide and *maintain* ventilation in the hull compartments; and exclude fresh water. The specific classifications follow.

Resistant or very resistant: cedars (including junipers), white oak, redwood, sassafras, Caribbean pine, greenheart, iroko, kapur, lignum vitae, American mahogany, meranti, Spanish cedar, teak. (Black locust for some reason is not on this list, despite its excellent rot resistance.)

Moderately resistant: bald cypress (young growth), Douglas fir, western larch, eastern white pine, longleaf yellow pine, slash southern yellow pine, tamarack (hackmatack), khaya (an African mahogany), Philippine "mahogany" (red luan and tangile), sapele.

Slightly resistant or nonresistant: ashes, basswood, birches, butternut, red and black oak, pines (other than longleaf, slash, and eastern pine), poplars, spruces, balsa, Philippine "mahogany" (white luan and mayapis), Parana pine.

The handbook notes that the southern and eastern pines and bald cypress are now largely second growth with a large proportion of sapwood; therefore substantial quantities of heartwood lumber of these species are seldom available.

There was undoubtedly good reason to list all these woods in the handbook, although many of them the reader will never have heard of and will never come across. For instance, I have never seen a piece of lignum vitae large enough for anything but belaying pins, block shells, and the like, but it is nice to know these parts would not rot!

PLYWOOD PANELS

Panels composed of layers of wood veneers glued together were used for many years for items that were to be protected from the weather, but their use for marine purposes awaited the development and application of completely waterproof adhesives since World War II. This touched off a boom of plywood hull building. Plywood is still used for this purpose, but mostly by amateurs on a one-off basis, because the stock boat manufacturers have gone almost totally to production-line building of fiberglass hulls. Nevertheless, there are still some production shops in the United States specializing in plywood hulls—some using panels, others using glued lapstrake construction. Plywood is also used for such parts as decks and superstructures for limited-production fiberglass boats, and it is used extensively for structural bulkheads and interior joinerwork in hulls of all construction types.

Being made of thin layers of wood securely bonded to each other, plywood panels are stiffer than boards of equal thickness and have advantages over regular lumber, even for some parts of boats made completely of wood. Due to the stiffness of plywood panels, weight can be saved—a matter that can be of importance in both powerboats and sailboats—and working with panels instead of a number of small pieces can save a lot of time.

Although there are exceptions, it is not theoretically possible to plank a hull with plywood panels unless the designer has specially shaped the hull for such construction. As mentioned in Chapter 1, plywood cannot be bent in two directions at once to fit on a surface that has compound curvature. However, in reference to the exceptions mentioned above, it has been found that the bottom planking of certain arc-bottomed hulls can be made of plywood with the use of strategically located clamps and fastenings. Only experience can help you with this.

If you should happen to have a set of plans for the boat you want and get the notion that it should be planked with plywood in large pieces (rather than in narrow strips, as in glued lapstrake construction), even though the designer has specified otherwise, check with him first to see whether it is feasible. This procedure may save you a major heartbreak.

Plywood is made by laying up thin layers of wood with the grain of adjacent layers usually at right angles to each other. The number of layers is always odd so that the grain of the face plies is always parallel. The number of plies and their thickness is important. Cheap ⅜" plywood, for instance, might have two thin faces and a relatively thicker inner ply, whereas a better grade will have five plies of wood, each of about equal thickness. It can readily be understood that with right-angle-grain construction, the three-ply panel will be relatively weak when bent parallel to the grain of the inner ply.

The most common and inexpensive kind of plywood usually has been made of Douglas fir. To obtain the veneer for making plywood panels, the logs are placed in a lathe and turned against a knife edge that peels the veneer at its desired thickness; thus most of the grain is flat grain, called *wild grain,* and in fir it is indeed difficult to tame sufficiently for a smooth paint finish. Fir also checks badly, so that a paint finish develops hairline cracks that become greater in number as time goes on. This situation is at its worst when the plywood is exposed to the elements, but even when the plywood is used in interior joinerwork, checking can make it difficult to achieve a first-class paint job. Such checking can be substantially reduced by coating the fir with a sealer before painting, using a plywood sealer such as Interlux 1026 Interprime or clear epoxy. Fir plywood is acceptable for interior work that is to be covered with either one of the modern vinyl wall coverings or with one of the durable high-pressure laminates such as the Formica brand. It can also be used for planking and decking that is to be covered with a synthetic cloth, such as Dynel, or ordinary fiberglass and either polyester or epoxy resin, in which case you would *not* seal the surfaces to be covered.

Plywood Grading

Previous editions of this book carried data furnished by a large marine plywood manufacturer that has since closed its mill. For this edition I am indebted to Harbor Sales Company of Baltimore, Maryland, and the American Plywood Association for the updated plywood information.

Marine and exterior grades of plywood are both laminated with phenolic waterproof glue (with resorcinol glue also used for gluing edges), the difference being in the quality of the veneers. Marine-grade panels made in the United States are, in my opinion, *not* what they used to be from post–World War II through the early 1950s. Current grading is to U.S. Product Standard PS 1-95. At one time marine-grade panels were always made with both faces of A-grade veneer; however, PS 1-95 shows marine grades A-A, A-B, and B-B and high- and medium-density overlay grades. Grades other than A-A and the overlay grades may be hard to come by.

PS 1-95 calls for the use of only Douglas fir or Western larch in marine panels. The marine-grade-A faces are limited to a total of nine repairs in a 4-foot × 8-foot panel, with inner plies of B-grade or better veneers. The specification for the B-grade is stated, and if you are sufficiently interested I suggest you obtain a copy of PS 1-95 from your dealer or from the American Plywood Association, or you can download it from the APA site.

The PS 1-95 standard spells out the tests the finished panels must withstand, but it permits ⅛" gaps between the crossbanding (the plies of veneers between the face of a panel) and limits the number of gaps or edge splits to four in 8 feet of crossband veneer, while edge splits or gaps on either end of a panel are limited to an aggregate width of ⅛". In view of the boatbuilding labor involved, whether amateur or professional, in my estimation gaps cannot be tolerated. I have samples of marine plywood from a well-known manufacturer that do not have gaps between the crossbanding veneers. Obviously, unless proved otherwise, these samples do not represent the actual 4-foot × 8-foot or larger panel for sale at the lumberyard.

The wild grain of Douglas fir that makes panels almost impossible to paint without hairline cracks developing later resulted in the introduction of Medium Density Overlay (MDO) and High Density Overlay (HDO) panels. Dealers including local lumberyards stock these panels in a good variety of sizes. They are exterior grade with medium-density resin-impregnated fiber fused to one or both sides of the panel. The wood in the panel faces is B-grade veneer, with C-grade inner plies. Used for interior joinerwork, MDO and HDO panels are ideal for a first-class paint finish. The high or medium designation refers to the density of the surface layers only. High density is preferred for reusable concrete forms—the biggest market—but medium density will provide the durable, easily painted surface we are looking for in boat interiors at a slightly lower cost.

Plywood Panel Sizes

Harbor Sales, Boulter, and Maurice L Condon Company (see Appendix) sell the best of the domestic Douglas fir plywood panels. They also carry the superior plywood made overseas that is discussed below.

Sizes of domestic marine plywood up to 8 feet long are stocked by most suppliers, whereas you must go to specialty suppliers for longer lengths, which they make by scarphing (or you can do this yourself). Some can make panels up to 30 feet long. Here are the thicknesses and lengths of marine-grade A-A sheets:

- ¼" × 3 ply; ⅜" and ½" × 5 ply; ⅝" and ¾" × 7 ply; 1", 1⅛", and 1¼" × 9 ply; and 1½" × 11 ply—all in 4-foot × 8-foot sheets.
- ¼" through 1" in 4-foot × 10-foot sheets, and ½" and ¾" in 5-foot × 10-foot sheets. All thicknesses from ¼" through 1⅛" are available in 4-foot wide sheets and in lengths up to 30 feet.

The MDO panels are available overlaid one or both sides in most of these sizes:

- ⁵⁄₁₆", ⅜", ½", ⅝", ¾", 1", 1⅛", and 1¼" thick × 48" and 60" wide × 8 to 10 feet long.

Do not use MDO panels for hull construction unless they are made to PS 1-95.

Marine-grade Douglas fir plywood made to equal or exceed PS 1-95 is still available at Harbor Sales and other suppliers that cater to the amateur boatbuilder (see Appendix).

Foreign Marine Plywood Panels

I believe that specifications for marine panels manufactured in Europe are higher than for those manufactured in the United States; due to increased demand, these European panels are now stocked in the United States. All of the imported panels appear to be of hardwood and are thus much easier to finish than domestic fir panels.

Foreign-made plywood panels are laminated to metric thicknesses. Listed below are the equivalents to U.S. measurements:

Inch	mm	Inch	mm
⅛	3	½	12
⁵⁄₃₂	4	⅝	15
³⁄₁₆	5	¾	18
¼	6	1	25
⅜	9	1⅛	29

Here are some examples of imported marine-grade plywood that can be obtained, usually to British Standard BSS 1088 WBP:

AA-grade rotary-cut or ribbon-sliced luan (Philippine "mahogany") or meranti, a similar wood; also rotary-cut khaya, a durable African hardwood,

¼ through ¾ inch thick × 4 feet wide × 4 through 24 feet in length. (When panels are to have a clear finish bear in mind that there is a difference in grain between rotary-cut—the way Douglas fir veneers are made—and sliced, which means the veneers are slice-cut from a fixed rather than a spinning log.)

The Dutch have been making really fine marine-grade panels for some time under the brand name of Bruynzeel. Although the company was recently sold and has moved some of its operations to France, it is still producing plywood of high quality that remains available in the United States from Condon and others. The same species of wood is used throughout the panels, and two kinds of wood are offered. One, the heavier, is of African Regina mahogany; the other, lighter by about 30 percent, is of okoume, sometimes called gaboon, an African hardwood not as durable as the Regina but used by those seeking to save weight wherever possible.

For the teak lovers there are many choices of teak-faced panels, most with very thin face veneers (1.0 mm, or only a fat ¹⁄₃₂ inch!).

There are also panels faced with teak strips about 2½ inches wide separated by narrow strips of very light wood to simulate laid decking. These are used for cabin soles. For exterior use as, for example, a fiberglass deck overlay, there are panels made in which the teak strips are separated by inlaid black silicone rubber "caulking."

Readers are aware that in the twenty-first century, more and more attention is being paid to the environmental aspects of all human activities. Woodworking and boatbuilding of course have no exemption from this development. There are a number of ethical questions involved in the use of first-growth woods, particularly hardwoods, and especially tropical hardwoods. These issues relate to deforestation, carbon footprint, sustainability, Third World exploitation, and more. While it is certainly not the role of a manual of this sort to give a full analysis of these issues, much less offer resolutions, it does seem appropriate to remind readers—potential wood consumers—that the issues exist. Boatbuilders who wish to incorporate these issues into their thinking about the design of their projects, particularly about materials choices, will find plenty of guidance and advice out there. An international organization called the Forestry Stewardship Council (www.fsc.org) provides a great deal of information on this question as well as a sustainability certification process for manufacturers and suppliers involved in woodworking industries. Look for FSC designations on wood products you are considering. A paper called "Guidelines for

Avoiding Wood from Endangered Forests," available at www.rainforestrelief. org, makes a disturbing case, in particular, against the use of our standby, Burmese teak. Food for thought. Needless to say, this discussion applies equally to plywood products and solid lumber.

Cutting Plywood

Due to the thin veneers that make up a panel, plywood tends to splinter on its underside when sawed, and fir is one of the worst in this respect. A piece of solid lumber clamped on the underside of the panel will eliminate this splintering. Cuts should always be made by a fine-toothed crosscut saw with the face side of the plywood up. Lightweight portable circular saws are handy when much plywood is to be cut, and there are blades with fine teeth made for just this purpose. The edges of plywood panels are best smoothed with a low-angle, sharp block plane set for a fine cut and held at an angle to the edge rather than parallel to it.

Bending Plywood

Plywood can be bent to curvature either dry or after it has been steamed. If the latter method is used, the panel must be dried before another part can be laminated to it. Sometimes it is advantageous to dry-bend two panels each of half the desired finished thickness. The following chart is a guide (not the gospel) to the minimum radius around which a dry panel should be bent. Panel thicknesses and bending radii are in inches.

Panel Thickness	Axis of Bend across Grain	Axis of Bend Parallel to Grain
$1/4$	24	60
$5/16$	24	72
$3/8$	36	96
$1/2$	72	144
$5/8$	96	192
$3/4$	144	240

BALSA CORE PANELS

Flat, stiff panels of end-grain balsa wood faced with a variety of materials are suitable structurally as bulkheads, but they are so well suited to cabinetry that they are described in Chapter 15, "Interior Joinerwork."

VENEER

Builders who wish to build a cold-molded wooden hull (more about this method later) are fortunate to have suppliers of 1/8"-thick veneers of different kinds of suitable wood. Some of these woods are vertical-grain Western red cedar, vertical-grain Douglas fir, vertical-grain Sitka spruce, and vertical-grain red meranti, which is similar to Philippine mahogany.

LAMINATING WOOD

Glued parts of laminated solid wood or plywood can be used in boat construction because of the availability of waterproof adhesives that cure at room temperature. Lamination often allows curved parts to be made with minimum waste of material and means that large parts can be made of small pieces of wood readily obtained and easily handled. Cold-molding and strip planking, as described later, are both forms of wood laminating, as are hollow spars. Laminated parts are not necessarily cheap due to the time that must be taken to prepare the form and the material, but the parts are strong, particularly laminated solid wood assemblies of parallel grain construction, such as deck beams, that would have cross grain in them if sawn from solid stock. Laminations are much less likely to check and split than nonlaminated parts, and although laminating does not increase the strength of the wood itself, the strength of an assembly such as the stem shown in A in Figure 4-6 is greater than if it were made of solid pieces jointed in the conventional manner.

Builders with an interest in laminating become quite ingenious at concocting forms for laminating parts that, if built from one piece or from jointed pieces, would be less strong or less durable.

The lamination of a tiller is shown in B in Figure 4-6. A part like this would have cross grain if sawn from one piece of wood. A form for a part such as a tiller can be made either by steam bending a strip of wood and fastening it to cleats secured to the bench or floor to the designated shape of the tiller, or the form can be sawn from a board about 1½" thick. Clamps to hold the shape of the lamination must be spaced closely to prevent voids in the lamination.

Another type of form is shown in C, and it can be used for laminating either solid stock or plywood. Fir plywood 1/8" thick can be bent quite sharply to laminate such parts as deckhouse roof corners, cockpit coaming corners, and the like. D in Figure 4-6 is a sketch of a form used to glue up right- and left-hand parts with twist, such as the bulwark rails at the bow of a boat.

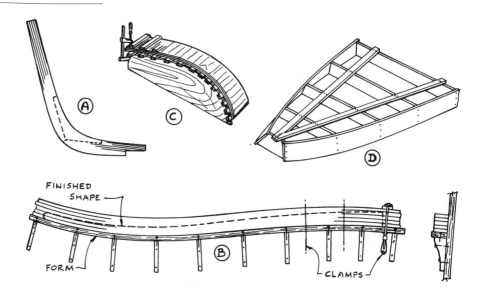

FIGURE 4-6.
Examples of forms used for laminating: stem (A), tiller (B), cockpit coaming (C), and bulwark rail at the bow (D).

No matter how the form is constructed, there is one thing that must be remembered: the form must be covered with waxed paper to prevent it from becoming glued to the part being laminated.

There is no rule for the thickness of the lamination strips except that they must be thin enough to take the required shape easily. If they are not sufficiently thin, you will have a hard time holding them in place while clamping.

Builder Robert G. Leahy of Easton, Maryland, sent me a snapshot showing the process he used when he made the transom knee for the 18'7" utility launch he built from the plans for my Barbara Anne design. The picture would not reproduce satisfactorily, so I laid tracing vellum over it and uncorked the ink bottle to draw Figure 4-7, in which A is his pattern for the knee, B is the shape over which he bent and glued the strips of wood (C), and D is the finished knee.

SCARPHING LUMBER AND PLYWOOD

When lumber is not obtainable in long-enough lengths for the job at hand, shorter lengths can be joined with glued flat-scarphs having a length-to-thickness ratio of 8 or 10 to 1. Boards can be tapered by a hand or an electric plane using a rig as shown in Figure 4-8, and a similar rig can be devised

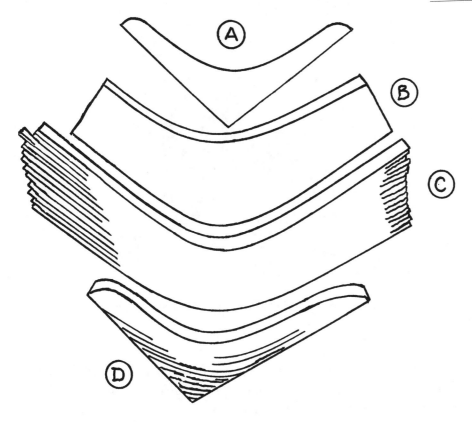

FIGURE 4-7.
A laminated knee substituted for a natural crook. Pattern (A), form (B), glued-up strips of wood (C), and finished knee (D). (*Robert G. Leahy*)

to do the planing with a router. However, scarphing a wide plywood panel this way takes a lot of patience, especially if you have to set up the rig for just one or two scarphs. Consequently a tool called the "Scarfer," put out by the Gougeon Brothers, is indeed of interest to the amateur and professional alike. As shown in Figure 4-9, the Scarffer is an attachment for a portable circular saw. A sharp 7¼" carbide-tip saw blade is strongly recommended

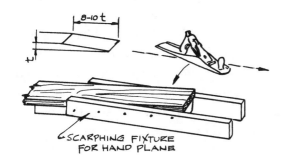

SCARPHING FIXTURE
FOR HAND PLANE

FIGURE 4-8.
Boards joined by gluing can be hand-planed.

FIGURE 4-9.
The Scarffer, put out by the Gougeon Brothers firm, simplifies cutting scarph joints in plywood sheets.

because of abrasive wear from cutting the glue lines. A well-written instruction manual is included with the tool. There is also a scarphing attachment made by John Henry, Inc., for use with an electric planer that will work on panels up to ½" thick. If you have just a few scarph joints to make, or if you are scarphing very thick panels, you might want to consider the following "manual" scarphing method.

THE PAYSON PLYWOOD BUTT JOINT

H. H. "Dynamite" Payson has built dozens of plywood hulls, some of which required 15-foot-long panels made of two commonly available 8-foot panels joined by a butt strap, which caused an unfair "hard spot" in the plank when bent to a curve. Dissatisfied with this, and being unafraid to try something different, he experimented with an idea that works, a simple end-to-end butt joint reinforced with fiberglass. Needed are two pieces of 3" to 4" fiberglass tape a bit longer than the width of the butt; a bit of mat (1½-ounce split to half thickness is good); polyester or epoxy resin; and a broad putty knife or plastic spreader. Start by laying a piece of tape on a smooth, flat surface and saturating the glass and 2" each side of it with resin; then apply resin to the plywood and turn it over, as shown in A in Figure 4-10. Carefully align the panels and weight them or otherwise prevent movement.

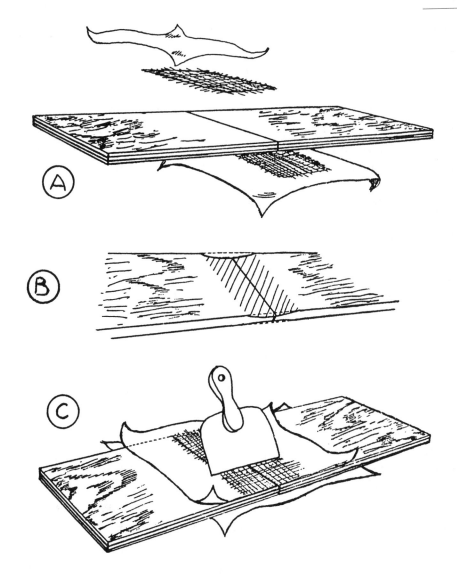

FIGURE 4-10.
The Payson Plywood Butt Joint: apply resin to plywood (A), scoop a hollow and then fill (B), draw the putty knife across the joint (C). (*Tim Payson*)

Now for the upper side. Scoop a hollow (B in the figure) using a disc sander, fill the hollow with a piece of mat and lots of resin, lay the second piece of saturated tape on top, cover with waxed paper or light polyethylene film (not that clingy stuff used in the galley), and then draw the putty knife across the joint (C in the figure) a number of times. With pressure this feathers the joint, so little, if any, sanding is needed after the cure.

Working with plywood ⅜" or more I would scoop the hollow on both sides of the joint.

During a visit, Dynamite had me test—by breaking it over a knee—a joint he had made of ¼" plywood. I brought one for him to test, too. Both broke in the wood, not in the joint. There was one difference in the samples, mine being made with epoxy resin instead of polyester, and Orcon unidirectional fiberglass strands instead of tape. I have so much faith in properly used epoxy I would always use it in such a joint.

LUMBER BILL OF MATERIAL

Due to competition to sell boatbuilding plans, those for the smaller hulls planked with plywood often list the number, dimensions, and type of ply panels needed. If the list of solid lumber needed is included, consider yourself fortunate, for otherwise the builder must figure out the quantities himself. If one is located close to a source with a complete stock of boatbuilding woods, the material takeoff can be done piecemeal; otherwise there is homework to be done to pick up the material from the designer's drawings and specifications.

When one is planning to build a larger boat, the chances are good that a lumber list will not be part of the plans; the designer's drawings and specs usually show net dimensions.

This brings up terminology peculiar to the lumber trade—for instance, the use of "quarter" when buying rough lumber: 1" thickness is called "four quarter," 1¼" is "five quarter," and so on, and these are the rough-sawn thicknesses as they come from the sawmill. Boards planed smooth as found in a typical lumberyard and called "one by" will be found to measure anywhere from ¹¹⁄₁₆" to ¹³⁄₁₆" in thickness, and when the width is said to be 6" one cannot figure on any more than 5½" in width. These boards are surfaced four sides (S4S) and may be priced by the piece or by the linear foot (LF).

Other terms are "random width and length" (RWL), meaning just that, and "board foot" (or feet, as the case may be). Rough-sawn lumber such as Philippine mahogany planking stock is priced by the board foot, which is a piece of wood 1" thick, 12" wide, and 12" long (or, put another way, 144 cubic inches); thus a piece 1" thick, 6" wide, and 12" long is half a board foot.

If you plan to buy boatbuilding lumber from a remote supplier, ordering online or by telephone and having the lumber shipped, you may not have the opportunity to hand-select the pieces that will serve your needs most effectively. The suppliers mentioned in this book understand the needs of the boatbuilder and will make an effort to send you what you need, but that's no substitute for your being on the spot. There are two things you can do to minimize this concern. One of them is simply to travel to the supplier's site and, assuming it is permitted, do the hand selection. (You might pay for the trip by bringing the material home with you—a good-size boat trailer can be modified easily to carry a whole lot of lumber.) The other is to allow a little more for "waste" than you might if you had hand selected. Most woodworkers agree that good material is never really wasted—it always gets used eventually. The worst scenario is ending up with just a little less wood than you need for a particular project and then finding out that the supplier is sold out, requiring a substitution that may not be quite right.

A term that could baffle a beginner is "round edge" (also known as "bark edge" or "flitch sawn"). These boards taper in width the same as the diameter of the tree trunk (see Figure 4-1 and Figure 4-2), and if curved the shape can reduce waste when planking a hull. This is how "boat boards" of white cedar (in the northeastern United States) and juniper, a close cousin (in the southeastern United States) are usually cut as planking stock.

SCANTLINGS

The dimensions of the hull timbers in wooden boatbuilding are called scantlings. For instance, a list of scantlings includes the size and spacing of frames, planking thickness, keel depth and width, stem width, and sizes of clamps, stringers, deck beams, etc. The actual dimensions may be given as the "siding," generally the smaller dimension, and the "molding," usually a vertical dimension. As an example of this, referring to Figure 4-11, a deck beam would be sided 1½" and molded 2½", while a clamp would be sided 1½" and molded 4". The dimensions of frames are an exception to the above, because the fore-and-aft dimension is the siding, and the athwartship dimension is the molded size. The terminology is peculiar to boatbuilding, and the builder quickly becomes adjusted to its usage.

It has been noted that quite a few designers, apparently tiring over the years of hand lettering the words "sided" and "molded" on their drawings, simply abbreviate these words to S and M. This could be very confusing to the first-timer, but now you know.

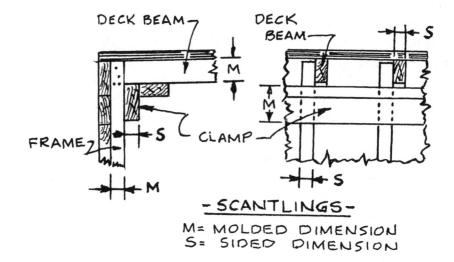

- SCANTLINGS -
M = MOLDED DIMENSION
S = SIDED DIMENSION

FIGURE 4-11.
The dimensions (breadth and thickness) of the hull timbers in boatbuilding are known as scantlings. When describing frames (left), the molded dimension is the athwartship dimension and the siding dimension is the fore-and-aft measure. In other parts of the scantling list, the siding is generally the smaller dimension and the molding the vertical dimension.

METRIC LUMBER MEASUREMENT

I scoured my hundred-book reference library and found that although there are discussions of foreign woods for boatbuilding, there is no mention of how lumber is measured in countries using the metric system. I am indebted to Iain Oughtred, talented small-craft designer and builder, for his contribution to my search based on his own experience.

Iain has added metric dimensions to his plans to help European builders, but in his opinion only a small percentage of British builders use metric. On the other hand, he has found that British lumber suppliers use English and metric measurements indiscriminately. The copies of stock lists he sent me featuring English oak give all measurements in metric; thickness and widths are given in millimeters, lengths in meters, and there is not one hint of how to convert to English. Then, oddly enough, prices are stated in pounds sterling per *cubic foot* and per *cubic meter*.

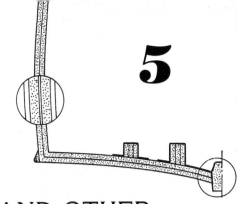

FIBERGLASS AND OTHER HULL MATERIALS

WOOD HAS BEEN THE TRADITIONAL MATERIAL for boatbuilding, and it remains so because of the relative ease with which it can be worked. However, depending upon the skill and ingenuity of the builder, there are other materials to be considered, sometimes in combination with wood.

WOOD AND FIBERGLASS

When the type of wood hull construction is suitable, there is much to recommend sheathing the wood with resin and fiberglass or other synthetic fabric. The hull planking should preferably be of a stable type, such as strip planking, double or triple diagonal planking, or plywood. Normal carvel planking swells and shrinks with moisture changes, and this might cause the covering to crack. However, there are those who do not hesitate to cover old carvel-planked hulls with fiberglass, but the covering is made quite thick and is mechanically fastened to the hull.

The late Allan H. Vaitses was one of the advocates of mechanically fastened, relatively heavy fiberglass sheathing, and his book *Covering Wooden Boats with Fiberglass* (out of print, but available used online) tells how to do it and proves the value with many examples of his work in this field. Another well-known book on the subject of sheathing, which includes Vectra polypropylene and Dynel modacrylic fabrics as alternates to fiberglass, is *How to Fiberglass Boats*, by Ken Hankinson.

When the hull is suitable, the use of covering adds strength, prevents rot, minimizes leaks and weight gain from absorption of water, and protects against the attack of worms and borers. The latter by itself is a great advantage, for it reduces the worries that can be brought on by delays in hauling out a wooden hull for bottom cleaning. The weight of the covering, if properly proportioned, does not add much to the overall weight of the boat, and when it is planned for in the design, the wooden structures can be reduced in size to compensate for the weight of the covering. In anything but very fast boats the added weight does not count for much anyway.

The fabric is usually fiberglass cloth, but polypropylene and Dynel are also used (more about these later), as are such "miracle fibers" as Kevlar and carbon fiber. (Reuel Parker, boatbuilder and author of *The New Cold-Molded Boatbuilding: From Lofting to Launching*, cannot understand why anyone would sheathe wood with glass when Xynole-polyester fabric is available.) When fiberglass is used, hulls are typically covered with cloth weighing (without resin) between 6 and 20 ounces per square yard, depending on size and service, and often doubled in areas of strain such as at the chines of v-bottomed boats. Ten-ounce cloth is about right for covering vertical cabin sides made of plywood. The accompanying table (Figure 5-1) indicates approximately how much weight is added by covering a surface with fiberglass cloth and polyester resin; common fiberglass reinforcements besides cloth are included. Since weights are in direct proportion to thickness, materials other than those shown are easily interpolated.

FIGURE 5-1.
Sheathing a hull (or decks, or any part of a boat) with fiberglass or other reinforcement adds weight; thicker materials are heavier.

APPROX. WEIGHTS PER SQ.FT. OF FIBERGLASS REINFORCEMENTS INCLUDING POLYESTER RESIN			
	DESIGNATION	WT. OZ./ SQ.FT.	THICK-NESS (INCH)
CHOPPED STRAND MAT	¾ OZ. / SQ. FT. 1 1½ 2	3 4 6 8	.028 .033 .050 .067
GLASS CLOTH	6 OZ./ SQ. YARD 8 10	1.33 1.8 2.25	.011 .016 .018
WOVEN ROVING	14 16 18 24	3 3.5 4 5.25	.022 .025 .028 .038

Courtesy of Torin, Inc.

Covering is recommended for plywood decks, cabintops, and the like, and the covering of joints in cabin sides, etc., to prevent leaks is a genuine boon to the builder when the joined work is to be painted rather than varnished. Taped joints can be sanded to feather edges and made invisible under a paint finish.

The resin for sheathing wood with fabrics can be epoxy, polyester, or vinylester. Epoxy is superior in strength and adhesion, costs more, is more toxic, and is more time-consuming due to a slower cure at room temperature than the esters.

The polyester resin traditionally used for laying up production fiberglass boats is known as laminating resin; it wets out fast and does not need sanding between coats. However, when you are building up multiple layers of fabric, it is not the best type for sheathing. This application requires a finish resin, which has wax added and can be sanded. This type of resin is sold in small containers, probably a gallon maximum, in marine supply stores. It can also be found in the automotive sections of department stores, along with the equally small packages of fiberglass mat, cloth, and tape used for patching rusted autobody parts. Finish resin is satisfactory for sheathing decks, cabin sides, and the like where it is desirable to sand smooth between coats. If the resin sags when sheathing nonhorizontal surfaces, a thickening agent must be added. A number of these are described in Chapter 6.

Vinylester laminating resin has come to the fore only in recent years—although it was developed during the 1950s—because of the widespread incidence of gelcoat blistering on production fiberglass hulls laminated with the old standby polyester resins. Vinylesters are a bit more expensive, but they are tougher and resist the passage of moisture, which eventually causes blistering. Typically, modern production builders incorporate a layer or two of fabric laminated with vinylester resin immediately under the gelcoat (which is the material applied by spray to the female mold as the initial step in hull layup) while using the less expensive polyester resins in more interior layers. Some builders of high-quality yachts use vinylester resin, and even epoxy resin, throughout the layup, and presumably other builders will follow suit. Vinylesters weigh about a pound less per gallon than polyesters.

MOLDED FIBERGLASS HULLS

The shiny, commercially produced fiberglass hulls are usually made from a female mold. This requires that a wooden male plug be made, just as though you were building a wooden hull, using strip planking or plywood, whichever is suitable for the hull shape. The plug is then covered with glass cloth and resin and is worked to an extremely smooth finish, for every blemish will be reproduced when the female mold is made. When the plug is finished as desired, a release agent is applied so that the female mold will not stick to it. Then glass cloth and mat and polyester resin are laid up successively until a strong, rigid mold has been made. Rather than rely entirely upon shell thickness to hold the mold's shape, the shell is reinforced on the outside with a network of rough wood and sometimes steel. If a particular hull shape is such that it cannot be withdrawn vertically, the mold is made to split on the centerline.

Some builders decrease the time needed to build stiffness into the mold by using sandwich construction. After a portion of the fiberglass laminate has been laid up against the plug, they use a core material followed by more fiberglass. The mold stiffness is thus increased greatly by spreading the glass skins apart, the core material acting in much the same manner as the web of an I-beam that separates the flanges.

Suitable core materials are cellular foams and end-grain balsa. If the plug from which the female hull mold will be made is not constructed to be later used as a boat, then price dictates the choice of core material for the plug.

When the female mold for the production of a hull has been removed from the plug, it is polished to a mirror-like finish and waxed, and any blemishes are repaired. It is then ready for laying up a hull. Sometimes a partial disc of wood or steel, larger in diameter than the beam of the boat, is added to the outside of the mold near each end so the mold can be rolled from side to side while laying up the fiberglass and resin. When the hull is anything larger than dinghy size, this minimizes the amount of time the builders must spend actually working in the hull while laying up and makes the work mostly downhand. The more you can stay out of the sticky resin the less distasteful the job will be. This presumes that the hull will be made by laying up the laminates by hand and applying the resin with roller and brush. When hulls are produced in large quantity, resin and chopped glass fibers can be applied with specialized spray equipment, but these hulls are not as strong as those laminated with fiberglass cloth.

The high-gloss finish on the outside of molded hulls or other similarly constructed parts of the boat results from first spraying a gelcoat of resin on the surface of the mold, as has been mentioned earlier. The gelcoat can be of any color desired, and contrasting stripes at the waterline and other accent stripes can be sprayed as well when you know what it is all about.

After the gelcoat has been applied, the hull is laid up with fiberglass fabrics (usually cloth, woven roving, and chopped strand mat) until the necessary thickness has been reached.

How does one make a mold and lay up a fiberglass hull if detailed instructions are not available? Watching others do these things is the best way, but if this is not possible, there are books that spell out the techniques. The laminate schedule—information detailing the composition of the fiberglass hull laminate, such as the weight and type of glass reinforcement, number of layers, etc.—should be outlined in the plans of the boat. As experience is gained, the builder may develop his own ideas about laminates, but guidance is needed for the first attempt at this type of boatbuilding.

A book from which much can be learned is *Fiberglass Boat Building for Amateurs,* by Ken Hankinson. (Do not be fooled by the title.) In the realm of fiberglass hull repairs, another excellent book is Allan Vaitses's *The Fiberglass Boat Repair Manual,* which deals with both cosmetic and structural repairs to fiberglass hulls.

FIBERGLASS HULL BLISTERS

Owners of fiberglass hulls were perplexed—beginning in the late 1970s—when blisters began appearing on hull bottoms. It was and is disconcerting to stick blisters with an ice pick and see water smelling of styrene trickle out. Boats built prior to 1973 have not blistered as badly or at all, perhaps because heavier laminates were used. Boats built in the late 1970s and early 1980s have proved most susceptible.

I know one sailboat owner who lost the use of his boat for a year because he thought it necessary to wait that long for the hull to dry out after the gelcoat had been removed by much sanding. This is not the book to discuss a proper cure for blisters—information on the subject is accumulating rapidly, and a mini industry has grown up around the prevention or cure of blistering on production fiberglass hulls. For our purposes in this book, the specter of "boat pox" is another reason to consider building a wood or wood-epoxy boat.

"ONE-OFF" FIBERGLASS HULLS

It was inevitable that builders would figure out a way to build a fiberglass hull without having to spend the time and money to construct a female mold. Seemann Fiberglass (now "Seemann Composites") not only devised a method but also invented and patented C-Flex "planking," which consists of parallel rods made of fiberglass-reinforced polyester alternating with bundles of continuous roving, with each "plank" being held together by a webbing of two layers of lightweight, open-weave fiberglass cloth.

The construction method is fairly simple. A hull form is framed with sectional molds and sometimes stiffened with longitudinal strips let into the molds. Smaller hulls are most conveniently built upside down, as shown in Figure 5-2, but the larger sizes are best built right side up. The molds must be spaced so that the C-Flex "planking" will not sag between them, the spacing varying with the weight of the C-Flex. The C-Flex, which bends longitudinally and sideways, is then laid over the molds and conforms to the hull shape with little fitting. On the framework for a round-bottomed hull, one edge of the planking is usually shaped to the sheerline and secured; then each additional "plank" is carefully butted to the adjacent width (Figure 5-2). For a v-bottomed hull, the C-Flex is applied to the chine, and the covering is continued to the sheer and, on the bottom,

FIGURE 5-2.
A roll of C-Flex being laid down. Note that the widths laid down earlier (being held in place by ice picks) are carefully butted against one another.

to the centerline. When the frame has been completely covered with the C-Flex planking, it is wet out with resin, either polyester or epoxy, and then lamination is continued with conventional fiberglass materials until the desired thickness has been reached.

By the nature of its construction, the C-Flex is very strong in the direction of the rods. It is made in two weights, 0.33 and 0.5 pound per square foot, is 12" wide, and comes in 100' and 250' rolls. Like any similar construction, the amount of finishing time depends upon the care taken to have a fair layup and the degree of smoothness desired. Seemann has patented a method of using C-Flex construction for sheathing to prolong the life of wooden hulls and will furnish detailed information to anyone interested in this approach.

One-off fiberglass boatbuilders frequently use a technique known as sandwich construction, where the laminate consists of a core between fiberglass skins. This type of construction has several advantages over single-skin construction. Probably the biggest advantage is its favorable stiffness/weight ratio. A sandwich laminate is significantly stiffer than a single skin of the same number of laminations, and with a lightweight core such as balsa or foam, the weight of the sandwich is not much greater than the single skin. This fact presents the designer using sandwich construction with options: he can keep the same thickness and weight laminate as for a similar single-skin hull and end up with a thicker, much stiffer hull; he can reduce the thickness and weight of the glass skins and have a cored laminate with strength equal to the single skin; or he can use a sandwich laminate designed both to save weight and increase stiffness.

Other than stiffness and light weight, sandwich construction offers additional benefits. The interior sweating for which single-skin fiberglass hulls are notorious is minimized or nonexistent in a sandwich hull. Noise and vibration are also reduced, and the absence of the transverse framing sometimes used in single-skin fiberglass hulls gives more usable space inside the hull.

Another comparison that should be made between single-skin and sandwich construction is what happens in the event that the hull is punctured, particularly under the waterline. In such circumstances, the single-skin hull will admit water, but this is not true of a sandwich hull unless both skins and the core are punctured—something that advocates of sandwich construction feel is unlikely during the normal life of a boat. It follows, of course, that if a cored laminate should be completely punctured the result of such an accident is no worse than for a single-skin hull. As a safeguard against impact, the outer skin of a sandwich is often made thicker than the inner skin, up to a ratio of 6:4. The repair of a sandwich laminate is no more difficult than for a single skin, unless the core material has been damaged, in which case a piece of the core will need to be inserted if the hull is to be repaired in the same way it was constructed. Otherwise, the damaged section of the outer skin is ground away with abrasive tools, feathered into the adjacent undamaged skin, and the void is filled with fiberglass and resin the same as for single-skin fiberglass repair.

To build a sandwich hull, a framework of transverse section molds and longitudinal strips (called *ribbands* or battens) is needed to define the shape of the hull, and it makes sense to build upside down. Figure 5-3 shows the forward end of a male mold for an 86-foot powerboat hull designed by the author.

Using foam core as an example of one-off construction, the sheets are fitted against the mold (using a heat lamp to make the foam pliable where necessary or using scored, or "contoured," core material instead) and held in place with nails driven through plywood scrap "washers" until the foam can be held in place with screws through the ribbands from

FIGURE 5-3.
The male mold for an Airex-cored 86-foot powerboat. Note the close ribband spacing.

ribbands

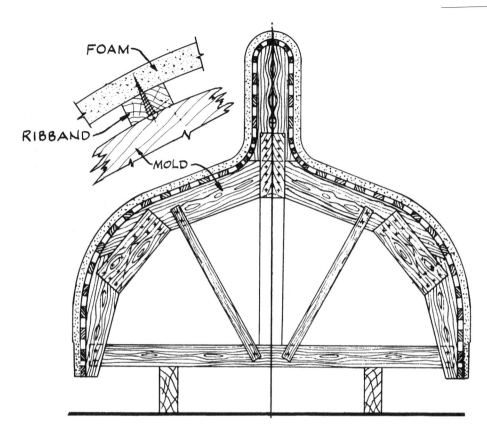

FIGURE 5-4.
The foam is held in place temporarily with screws through the ribbands.

inside the mold into the foam (Figure 5-4). (See "Temporary Fasteners" in Chapter 6 for another method of holding foam core in place.) The foam is then covered with the specified thickness of the fiberglass outside skin (Figure 5-5).

Careful workmanship is required to ensure a complete bond between the core material and the glass skins. Interruptions in the bond will hasten delamination of the sandwich when the lamination is loaded to deflect between supports, and this will weaken the affected part of the hull. When there is a good bond between the skins and the core, some of the burden of the laminate strength falls upon the core itself. For this reason the laminate designer must carefully investigate the available core materials for use in boat hulls. Obviously, a material that resists crumbling upon impact and does not absorb water is desirable.

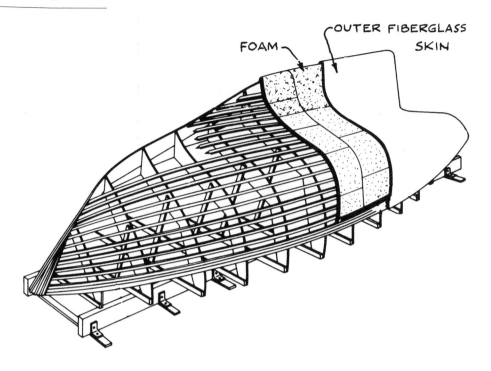

FIGURE 5-5.
The foam is covered with fiberglass.

Some of the most popular cores are:

Airex. Closed-cell thermoplastic structural foam, which has been used extensively in the United States and abroad. Used in boats as far ranging as those sailed by Russell Couts and megayachts.

Klegecell. Closed-cell PVC/polyurethane foam.

Divinycell. Closed-cell PVC/polyurethane foam.

ContourKore. End-grain balsa wood attached to a fiberglass scrim, which makes it a very conformable material.

DuraKore. A glued and hot-pressed sandwich, with presealed end-grain balsa inside and lauan mahogany veneers outside; sold in 8-foot finger-locking strips for hull "planking," and in sheets for such areas of gentle curvature as transom and decks.

Also: Corecell (SP/High Modulus), **Nidacore,** and **Trciel Honeycomb.**

I cannot go into all the construction details here; suffice it to say that while the hull is still upside down, the outside fiberglass skin should be smoothed to the extent desired while it is still possible to work downhand.

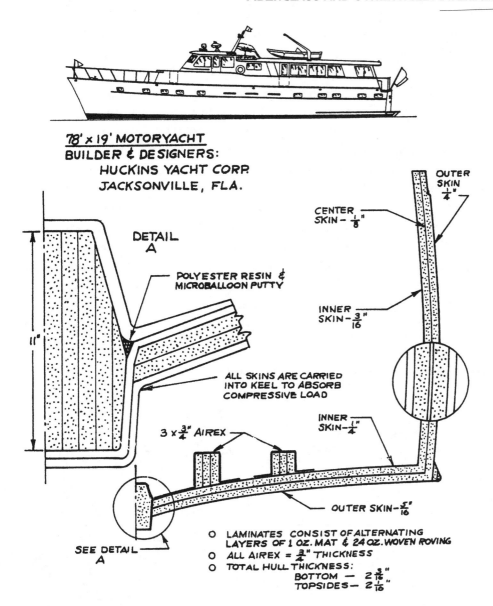

78' x 19' MOTORYACHT
BUILDER & DESIGNERS:
    HUCKINS YACHT CORP.
    JACKSONVILLE, FLA.

DETAIL A

POLYESTER RESIN & MICROBALLOON PUTTY

CENTER SKIN - $\frac{1}{8}$"

OUTER SKIN $\frac{1}{4}$"

INNER SKIN - $\frac{3}{16}$"

11"

ALL SKINS ARE CARRIED INTO KEEL TO ABSORB COMPRESSIVE LOAD

INNER SKIN - $\frac{1}{4}$"

3 x $\frac{3}{4}$" AIREX

OUTER SKIN - $\frac{5}{16}$"

SEE DETAIL A

O LAMINATES CONSIST OF ALTERNATING LAYERS OF 1 OZ. MAT & 24 OZ. WOVEN ROVING
O ALL AIREX = $\frac{3}{4}$" THICKNESS
O TOTAL HULL THICKNESS:
        BOTTOM — 2$\frac{3}{16}$"
        TOPSIDES — 2$\frac{1}{16}$"

FIGURE 5-6.

The 78-foot motoryacht *Deep Stuff*, designed by the author. The "club sandwich" Airex foam core/fiberglass hull was engineered by Thomas J. Johannsen. The cross section shows how the skins are carried down into the keel.

If you wish more information on sandwich construction, the core manufacturers can supply it.

The aforementioned book *Fiberglass Boat Building for Amateurs* includes details of cores and vacuum-bagging techniques for sandwich-core hulls, plus an enormous amount of valuable information about fiberglass boatbuilding.

Overturning a cored hull is a trying procedure because the shell is quite limber before the inner fiberglass skin is added to the laminate to complete the sandwich. One method used by several builders of hulls with Airex foam cores is shown in Figure 5-7. This involves the use of a holding cradle fitted to the upside-down hull to support the hull as it is overturned, and which the hull sits in while the construction of the boat is completed.

Although the aforesaid is a "one-off" method of hull construction, the mold can be used for additional hulls. It is a matter of economics to calculate how many hulls can be produced before the cost of a female mold is justified. Female molds that have been built for the production of single-skin fiberglass hulls can also be used for molding a sandwich hull. The laminate is simply changed to include a core.

FIGURE 5-7.
Constructing a holding cradle makes overturning a cored hull a tad easier.

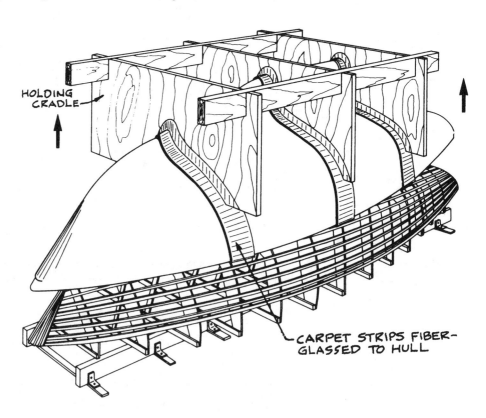

HOLDING CRADLE

CARPET STRIPS FIBER-GLASSED TO HULL

The use of an existing hull as a male mold—either with permission if necessary, or without conscience if plagiarized—is yet another method of making a hull shape.

STEEL

When you stop to think about it, steel is a remarkable material. It is strong, very inexpensive when compared with other metals, and with proper equipment, it can be worked to almost any shape desired. The relative ease of joining pieces by electric welding makes it a suitable material for small craft with a saving in weight over old-fashioned riveted construction. One disadvantage of steel is its low resistance to corrosion by seawater. Fortunately, the years have brought about improved coatings to protect steel against corrosion, but the coatings must be constantly maintained. An advantage of steel construction (and aluminum construction as well) is that inner bottom integral fuel and water tanks can be built in, using the hull for one to three sides, enabling larger capacities to be carried than in wooden hulls.

Steel is not a material for the average beginner by any means, but without reflecting for too long I can remember two good-sized auxiliary sailboats of steel built by people who had not built a boat before. However, they did have metalworking experience and the necessary equipment. The worst fault of these boats was the humps and hollows in the hull plating, and both builders said that they had gained experience so that if they did it again the hulls would not be so rough. This would reduce, if the vessel is a yacht, the time and material necessary to fair the hull.

Rough plating of steel hulls is often disguised by skillful application of trowel cement, probably because it is cheaper to do this than to expend the labor needed to smooth plating by heating and quenching. The roughness of the plating is caused by stresses set up when welding the plating to the frames and one plate to another. The sequence of welding is of importance in this respect.

Here in northern Florida there are several builders of full-bodied steel sailboat hulls using a system of framing and plating that results in better-than-average fairness.

Even though steel is an old material, research technicians have invented new alloys of higher strength so that steel hulls can be built lighter today than ever before, and somewhat more resistant to corrosion as well.

Bluewater cruising on your mind? This Roberts 392B, a radius chine steel sailboat, was built in England by Peter Boast. (*Bruce Roberts*)

ALUMINUM ALLOYS

A few of the many aluminum alloys, notably alloy 5086 in the United States, are satisfactory for boatbuilding. These alloys are relatively high in strength and corrosion resistance and can be satisfactorily welded. Standard practice calls for using alloys 5086-H116 or 5086-H32 in critical high-strength areas requiring welding. All bottom plating and fabricated structural framing should be 5086-H116; 5086-H32 may be used for hull sides. A fair amount of this metal is consumed by yacht builders, but by far the most of it has been used to build a large fleet of offshore oil field crew transports and platform supply vessels.

If the reader is capable of building a welded aluminum alloy hull, and the number of calls during recent years indicates there are a growing number around, be sure to use plans and specifications prepared by a designer familiar with this type of construction. As an example, at this time hull framing materials such as flat bars, angles, and channels are hard to find in the 5086 alloy; 6061-T6 is an acceptable substitute for structural shapes.

In general terms, alloys of aluminum reduce construction weight over that of steel. This permits the carrying of more deadweight or an increase in speed, or the possibility of achieving speed with less horsepower.

Several builders of pleasure boats either build only in aluminum or have a line of aluminum boats in addition to those of other materials. Small craft such as dinghies and runabouts of aluminum are made by stretch-forming sheets over male molds to produce a large part or an entire half out of one piece of metal, or by assembling precut parts using formed aluminum extrusions at the joints. Otherwise, regular transverse or longitudinal framing is used and covered with plating as in steel construction. Aluminum construction is more expensive than steel construction, for not only does the aluminum itself cost more per pound than steel, the actual welding also costs more. This more than makes up for the fact that the weight of aluminum involved in a particular project will always be less than the weight of the steel required. On the other hand, reduced maintenance costs of well-built aluminum hulls often make them cheaper to own over time.

Many builders of steel boats have converted to aluminum construction with little need to change equipment except for welding, but like steel, it is not a material for the beginner. One very important problem area encountered with aluminum construction is galvanic corrosion. This occurs between the aluminum hull and dissimilar metals found in such fittings as seacocks, propellers, shafts, rudders, etc., and it also occurs when the aluminum hull is exposed to stray electrical currents in anchorages. This can be prevented, and the methods for doing so should be spelled out in the plans and specifications for the boat. If you lack this information, the marine departments of the aluminum manufacturers can be consulted for help.

Welding and the preparation of the finished surface are also areas that require care. Welding aluminum is quite different from welding steel. It is imperative that weld areas be absolutely clean if good welds are to be made. If you are in need of information about welding, see *Boatbuilding with Aluminum*, by Stephen F. Pollard. When it comes to painting the surface, marine paint makers offer special systems for coating aluminum and steel, and instructions for cleaning them before coating. The highest-quality hull takes a lot of labor; a really smooth yacht finish on the topsides of a welded aluminum yacht hull requires smoothing of the surface with fairing compounds.

WEIGHT OF ALUMINUM STRUCTURE VS. STEEL AND WOOD

J. B. Hargrave of West Palm Beach, Florida, has designed a great many plea-sure craft from moderate to megayacht in size and has made a study of common full materials based on weight. During a design symposium he indicated that aluminum is one-third the weight of steel yet is nearly as strong and can be designed in structures that, with equal strength, weigh 45 percent as much as a comparable steel structure. Aluminum, compared to wood, produces boats of about equal weight and cost where an equal com-plexity of structure is accepted. Wood boats offer better inherent insulating qualities, both in thermal values and in the capacity to absorb noise.

FERROCEMENT

Some years back there was a wave of enthusiasm about constructing hulls of ferrocement. Essentially, the system consists of a framework of concrete reinforcing rod interlaced with wire, with cement applied to it so that the steelwork is completely embedded and not exposed to the atmosphere. It is understood that great care must be taken to eliminate voids in the cement, and that the basically heavy weight of the construc-tion makes it impractical for hulls under 30 feet in length. At this writ-ing interest in ferrocement construction seems to have declined, but the method continues to have adherents, and at least one designer is actively promoting it.

"GEODESIC AIROLITE" ULTRA-LIGHTWEIGHT HULLS

The late Platt Monfort of Monfort Associates developed a new way of build-ing very light small-craft hulls. Plans, and sometimes materials kits, are available. The hull is built of a simple wooden framework reinforced with triangulated tensile strands of DuPont Kevlar (a very strong material), then covered with heat-shrinkable Dacron cloth airplane wing-covering mate-rial. Also used are epoxy glue and a high-bond adhesive tape. At this writ-ing all of the boats in the line (more than a dozen of them) are of cartop size and weigh from 8 to 30 pounds.

The Classic 12 model, a 12-foot-long, 30-pound Whitehall-type boat for rowing or sailing, is shown in all the Geodesic Airolite construction pictures. The light diagonal lines in the hull are the Kevlar strands (see Figures 5-8 and 5-9).

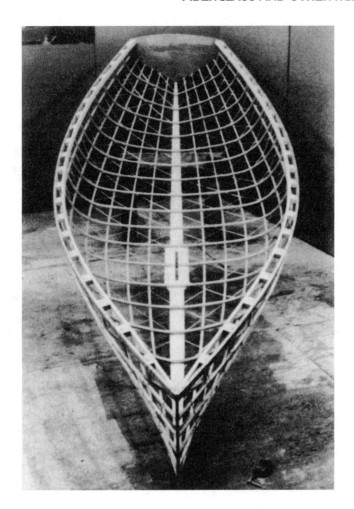

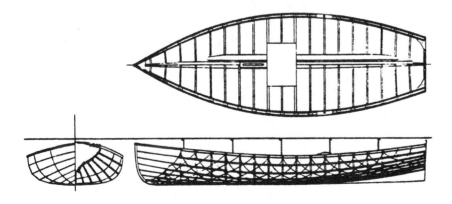

FIGURE 5-8.
Platt Monfort's Classic 12 model 30-pound boat of "Geodesic Airolite" construction. The diagonal thread-like reinforcements shown in the photo are Kevlar cords.

FIGURE 5-9.
Platt Monfort's Classic 12 under sail. The sail is made of Tyvek.

The sail is a do-it-yourself "Jiffy Sail" designed by Monfort to be made of Tyvek, a plastic material used in the house-construction industry and for mailing envelopes that cannot be torn; the seams of the sail are joined with a fiberglass-reinforced double-faced outdoor carpet tape called Turf Tape.

EXOTIC HULL MATERIALS

There have been a number of materials developed recently that have higher strengths and lower weights than wood and fiber-reinforced plastic, and development in this area is bound to continue. Carbon fiber has been used in super-lightweight fishing rods and in highly stressed areas of racing sailboat hulls. It is three times stronger and five times stiffer than steel. Likewise, S glass, which is twice as strong as the common E glass from which the standard boatbuilding glass fabrics are made, is much stronger and is stiffer for its weight than steel. Kevlar fabric, made from DuPont aramid fibers, is another lightweight, high-strength material.

Exotic materials have also found their way into bulkheads. Years ago, the introduction of relatively stiff marine plywood bulkheads was a giant step forward in strength as compared to the bulkheads made of vertical wood staving or decorative panels. Now, plywood as a bulkhead material has been surpassed by at least two other materials that are stiffer and much lighter. Panels of both these materials come with fiberglass skins, and they are used in large transport aircraft. One type of core is end-grain balsa, and the other is a honeycomb made of a DuPont material called Nomex, which is used in helicopter blades.

Although such exotic materials can work out well, especially where light weight is a consideration, there are other factors to consider. If they are to be used properly these materials require specialized techniques and knowledge. Another consideration is their high cost. For example, S glass is twice as expensive as E glass. As for Kevlar, a builder of high-speed powerboats who uses this material once told me that, pound for pound, a Kevlar/resin combination was as much as seven times more expensive than the standard mat/woven roving/resin combination. Since these exotic materials are not used throughout a hull, but only as a local substitute for strength-contributing laminate material, it is hard to make a general comment about the cost of building hulls using exotic fibers, for laminate designs differ from boat to boat. About all that can be said, then, is that the use of such exotic materials will certainly lead to an increase in cost.

The state of the art is constantly changing. New materials will always be developed, and there are always those who will try to apply them to boatbuilding, just as surely as there are always those who seem not to care about the cost of yachts that appeal to them. Various boatbuilding techniques and materials become popular or fall out of favor. But it remains safe to say that few amateurs—and certainly very few beginning boatbuilders— build using the methods above. Unless you are particularly experienced with an alternative material, you are well advised to build your first boat from wood. There are so many off-the-shelf designs available that, in most cases, you can find something close to what you want to build in a set of preexisting plans. There are many techniques of wooden boatbuilding to choose from, and there are many books, articles, and websites to help you every step of the way.

6

FASTENINGS

COMPARED WITH THE HEAVILY CONSTRUCTED wooden boats of the old days, almost all modern craft can be considered to be lightly built. Thus, the innumerable fastenings holding the parts together assume extra importance as a primary contribution to a tight, seaworthy boat. All fastenings should be sized according to their task and located with thought by the designer and builder. They should always be driven in carefully drilled holes of proper size to ensure maximum holding power.

MATERIALS FOR FASTENERS

Galvanized Iron
The builder of a wooden boat could theoretically save a considerable amount of money by using galvanized iron hull fastenings. Old-timers have passed down the word that galvanized-fastened boats will last a lifetime, and indeed there are hulls here and there that seem to prove this point. On the other hand, I examined a wrecked shrimp boat, beached about 10 years after it was built, that proved just the opposite.

Although the above would appear to offer contradictory evidence regarding the durability of galvanized fastenings, it doesn't. The galvanized fastenings of today simply are not the galvanized fastenings of yesterday. In the first place, the old-timers used galvanized iron, whereas the fastenings available today are most likely of mild steel. When bared of their protective coatings, fastenings of mild steel do not have nearly as much resistance to corrosion as do iron ones. Second, the old-time iron nails and rods were always coated by hot dipping in molten zinc. Many "galvanized" fasteners today are zinc coated by electroplating, which results in a relatively thin coating that cannot be compared to coating by hot dipping. In fact these "zinc-plated" fasteners have no place in a boat.

Here is what Independent Nail, Inc., a manufacturer of special-purpose nails, has to say about the zinc coating of fasteners:

> "Galvanized" has turned out to be generally a poorly understood adjective. The best type is a hot-dip, whose surface is, for practical purposes, pure zinc. Tumbler, hot-tumbler, hot-galvanized each refers to a tumbler process from which the coating may be contaminated with iron right on the surface. Electro and mechanical galvanizing each generally produce very thin zinc coatings serving for appearance more than for performance.

Galvanized boat nails and galvanized wood screws have often been used to fasten planking to frames. A frame should be at least 1½" thick if a nail is to be buried in it without going through the frame. With lighter frames, the nail goes through the frames and is clinched over on the inside. When poor nails are used, the zinc will separate from the nail where it is bent, exposing the bare metal. Many boats have had to be refastened because corrosion started at the end of such nails and progressed throughout the length of the fastening. Renailing is an expensive job, and the necessity to do so is a good sign that the fastenings were inferior or inadequate to start with.

In the case of the smaller-sized hot-dipped galvanized wood screws, the threads are frequently clogged with zinc when they are dipped, and when driven, they tear the wood around the hole, reducing holding power.

Even if he has had some good experiences in the past with galvanized fastenings, the builder is advised to be sure of his fastenings by using a better metal for fastenings that are to be constantly in water. Although more expensive initially, the best fastenings are cheap in the end.

BRASS

If a decision is made against using galvanized fastenings, it might seem that a good alternative would be brass fastenings, but the use of brass for fastenings exposed to salt water cannot be advised against too strongly. Brass as furnished for the manufacture of screws and bolts is very high in zinc content, perhaps as much as 30 percent, and in an electrolyte such as seawater, the zinc leaves the alloy. What remains is a spongy copper so reduced in strength that the fastening is practically useless. This is called dezincification and can be expected when a copper alloy is used that contains zinc in excess of 16 percent. There are mechanical disadvantages, too. The high-zinc brass alloys are not particularly strong; it is easy to break off screws being driven into hardwoods. Brass is all right for the fastening of interior parts such as joinerwork, but care should be taken not to use it in the hull.

SILICON BRONZE

For every structural fastening in a boat it is hard to beat a copper silicon alloy sometimes called Everdur. It is about 96 percent copper and is so strong that fastenings are seldom wrung off when being driven and, of major importance, it is highly resistant to corrosion from seawater. The use of this metal removes the risks involved with the brasses and galvanized steel fastenings and is well worth the difference in cost. A point to be remembered is the higher resale value of a bronze-fastened hull. It is best to shop around for the lowest prices on silicon bronze fasteners, particularly flathead wood screws.

MONEL

This nickel copper alloy ranks above silicon bronze in strength and corrosion resistance, but the cost of screws and bolts made from it is much too high for most people to afford. It can be used in conjunction with silicon bronze without fear of much galvanic action between the metals. For instance, Monel is often used for fastening bronze propeller shaft struts, and Monel shafts have bronze propellers in direct contact. The strength and stiffness of Monel make it very satisfactory for Anchorfast boat nails, a popular fastening for some purposes because of the labor saving it offers over driving screws (see "Threaded Nails"). Monel as a metal has many uses in boat construction and will be mentioned further.

COPPER

Copper has excellent corrosion resistance, but because of its softness it is suitable mostly for the flathead nails that are used as rivets or for the clout nails sometimes used in hulls with light lapstrake planking or with two layers of planking such as double diagonal (see Chapter 11).

STAINLESS STEEL

There are many alloys under this common heading. It is recommended that these metals not be considered for hull fastenings unless you are guided by someone who has vast experience and satisfactory proof of corrosion resistance and freedom from galvanic action with other materials being used in the same boat. Without such assurance, the use of stainless steel should be limited to applications above water. It is the best metal for fastening aluminum alloy deck hardware, stanchions, and aluminum alloy window frames, for it avoids corrosion of the alloy parts. Of the many stainless steels, the one known as Type 316 seems to be the most corrosion resistant in a salt atmosphere, but finding fastenings of this alloy may take some doing. One or two of the high-quality yacht builders have, in the past, special-ordered Type 316 wood screws to secure stainless steel half-oval rub strips to minimize "bleeding" of the screw heads. These builders might be happy to reduce their stock of such fastenings. There are now special stainless steel screwdriver bits available for driving stainless steel fasteners. Their manufacturer, Wera, claims that they will avoid bleeding from screws, which they say comes from contamination caused by ordinary steel tools.

Other than as a fastener material, stainless steel is being used more and more for boat parts, notably deck hardware, sailboat specialty hardware, stanchions and pulpits, engine exhaust system parts, and propeller shafting. Stainless is also used for wire rope rigging and rigging fittings on spars. As with many materials that might be used in a boat, it is best to leave experimentation to others, using it yourself only when you know the application has been proven.

Fasteners of 316L stainless steel are available off the shelf, with the best of 18–8 (18% chromium, 8% nickel) alloys. Types 316L and 304L (with a carbon content of less than .03%) were developed to provide austenitic steels with superior corrosion resistance. (The L stands for "low carbon.") I have used 316L in plate form for a number of years to make fabricated rudders for high-speed boats.

MIXTURE OF METALS

The loosely used term "electrolysis" is applied by the average boater to the corrosion and erosion of metals by electrolysis, cavitation, or galvanic action; usually the destruction of metals is blamed on electrolysis, due to lack of knowledge of the other causes. Except for discussing galvanic action between fastenings, the subject of electrolysis is beyond the scope of this work.

Seawater is an electrolyte that will cause an electric current to flow between dissimilar metals when in contact or close proximity to each other. When this occurs, current will flow from the anode to the cathode; that is, the anodic fitting or fastening will be attacked and gradually destroyed by what is properly termed galvanic corrosion. The intensity of the attack will vary according to the relative positions of the metals in the galvanic series and also the relative areas or masses of the metals. The positions in the galvanic series in seawater of some metals follow:

Anodic or Least Noble

Zinc

Galvanized steel or galvanized wrought iron

Aluminum alloy 5456

Aluminum alloy 5086

Aluminum alloy 5052

Aluminum alloy 356, 6061

Mild steel

Wrought iron

Cast iron

18–8 Stainless steel Type 304 (active)

18–8 Stainless steel Type 316, 3% molybdenum (active)

Lead

Tin

Manganese bronze

Naval brass (60% copper, 39% zinc)

Inconel (active)

Yellow brass (65% copper, 35% zinc)

Aluminum bronze

Red brass (85% copper, 15% zinc)

Copper

Silicon bronze (96% copper, 4% silicon)

Cupro-nickel (90% copper, 10% nickel)

Cupro-nickel (70% copper, 30% nickel)

Composition G bronze (88% copper, 2% zinc, 10% tin)

Composition M bronze (88% copper, 3% zinc, 6½" % silicon, 1½% lead)

Inconel (passive)

Monel

18–8 Stainless steel Type 304 (passive)

18–8 Stainless steel Type 316, 3% molybdenum (passive)

Titanium

Cathodic or Most Noble

It might be possible to use only one metal, notably silicon bronze, for all of the fastenings in a wooden hull, but where a mixture is the most practical, the metals used should be ones that are reasonably close together in the galvanic scale, such as copper, silicon bronze, and Monel. All of these metals are used to manufacture fasteners of one sort or another.

Note that stainless steels are shown in the series in two different positions. As I understand it, the surface of the steel is passivated by chemical treatment to hasten the formation of oxide. This can be done after all machining and working has been finished, and after the steel has been thoroughly cleaned and degreased. The passivated surface is more resistant to corrosion. Without passivation, the corrosion resistance is severely reduced, and it is best to avoid the use of these metals for underwater fastenings. If the surface has been treated, but the treatment has been destroyed or altered, the metal's corrosion resistance will be uncertain; it is best to treat such metals as if they were not passivated.

At one time I had a number of Type 316L powerboat rudders made by a fabricating shop working exclusively with stainless steel, which I learned automatically passivated the rudder as a final step.

I know of a case where, due to ignorance, a bronze stern bearing casting was fastened with galvanized iron lag screws—a perfect example of setting up galvanic corrosion. The dissimilar metals were in contact in seawater; first the zinc disappeared, and then the iron was attacked until the bearing finally came loose.

Many boats with bronze hull fastenings have been built with cast-iron ballast keels, but in this case the comparatively huge mass of anodic material, the iron keel, would show only slight signs of attack due to its bulk. The bolts securing the keel can be of hot-dipped galvanized wrought iron or Monel. The outside of the iron should have several coats of a marine vinyl-type anticorrosive paint to act as a nonmetallic barrier to galvanic action.

Needless to say, only the least expensive steel fasteners should be used in the construction of molds, jigs, plugs for fiberglass parts, bracing, etc., that will never be part of a boat. It may seem ridiculous to even mention something like this, but I have seen boatyard employees use bronze and Monel fasteners in throwaway work rather than visit the stockroom for steel nails and screws. (See "Temporary Fasteners" further on in this chapter.)

TYPES OF FASTENERS

Screw Bolts

These are ordinary machine bolts with square or hexagonal heads and nuts, and they are made in silicon bronze, stainless steel, Monel, and "galvanized" steel. Longer bolts can be homemade by threading a piece of rod on both ends, screwing a nut as a head on one end, and peening over the end of the rod to prevent the head nut from turning. Washers of the same material are used under the head and nut. Drilled holes should be the same diameter as the bolt. Screw bolts are used for fastening many backbone parts and have the advantage over drift bolts of being able to be tightened when the wood shrinks unduly.

Well-equipped professional builders sometimes head their own long nonferrous bolts. They have a die, usually for a flat head, and the end of the rod is heated and forged to shape.

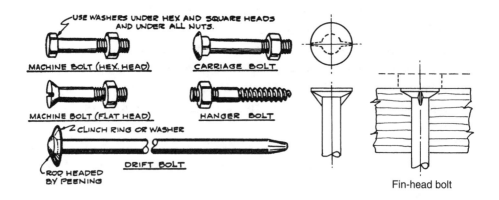

FIGURE 6-1.
(*Left*) Bolts commonly used in boatbuilding include machine bolts with hex and flat heads, drift bolts, carriage bolts, and hanger bolts. (*Right*) The fin-head bolt has many applications in wooden hull structure.

Drift Bolts

When bolts must be very long and a through-bolt is not practical or necessary, a drift bolt can be used. They are made from a piece of rod and driven like a large nail. One end is pointed slightly by hammering; the other has a washer or clinch ring under a driving head formed by riveting the end of the rod. The *clinch ring* (see Figure 6-1) is thick, flat on the underside, and has an edge rounded up to a countersunk hole as for a flathead wood screw. This takes the end of the rod peened to shape. The hole is bored between one and two diameters shorter than the bolt to be driven and should have smooth sides. The size of the hole must be less than the diameter of the bolt for a tight, driving fit. Be careful not to bend the bolt above the timber when driving it. When a pair or a series of drift bolts is called for, it is best to drive them at an angle (Figure 6-2) that locks the parts together and enables them to resist strains. Drift bolts are usually made of silicon bronze or galvanized steel.

Quite often drift bolts must be driven through narrow stock like floors, rudders, and centerboards, all of which will be discussed later, so keeping the hole on course is imperative. A homemade jig, Figure 6-3, is useful for this purpose.

Carriage Bolts

These are screw bolts with a round, shallow button head and a square neck on the shank just under the head that keeps the bolt from turning in the wood, provided the hole for the bolt is the same size as the shank and also smooth. There is a chance a carriage bolt head will spin in a rough-sided sloppy hole, thus defeating the purpose of using a carriage bolt in the first place. These bolts are used in many parts of the structure, such as to fasten

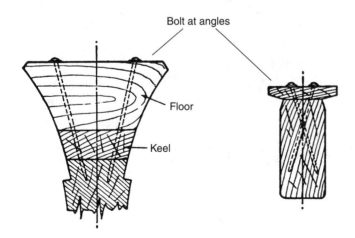

Bolt at angles

Floor

Keel

FIGURE 6-2.
When drift bolts are driven in pairs or a series, it is best to drive them at an angle to lock the parts together.

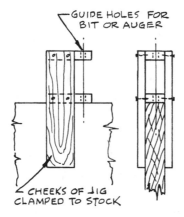

FIGURE 6-3.
A homemade jig helps drive drift bolts in narrow stock.

frames to floors, stringers to clamps, and frames and deck beams to clamps or shelves, and are made in silicon bronze, galvanized iron, and stainless steel.

Fin-Head Bolts

The best all-around type of bolt for wooden boatbuilding is the fin-head type shown at the right of Figure 6-1. Such a bolt can be hammered flush with the wood surface, or countersunk and plugged without leaving a cavity. I'll guarantee that the floors-to-frames fasteners in the Nevins-built auxiliary shown in Figure 6-4 were fin-head bolts, although the label indicates the more conventional carriage bolt.

FIGURE 6-4.
The frame of a Nevins-built auxiliary yacht, illustrating the uses of bolts mentioned in the text.

The noted designer L. Francis Herreshoff wrote about fin-head bolts that "pressure should be brought to bear on manufacturers to produce them. . . . With Everdur bronze or Monel this type could be cold-headed and I believe it would be one of the cheapest to produce for there is no slot to be cut." At least one supplier, CC Fasteners, seems to have paid attention, because assorted sizes of silicon bronze fin-head bolts are available from them.

Special Note on Bolt Threads

Fastenings are used to hold parts together and keep them from moving; therefore, they must be tight in their holes. This is not possible if the bolts have what are called *rolled threads*. Bolts of this type are common today because threads formed by rolling instead of cutting are cheaper to manufacture. The unthreaded shank of these bolts is smaller in diameter than the outside of the threads, so the shank cannot possibly be tight in the hole. Bolts of this type are all right when the fastening is in tension only, but this is seldom the case in the hull structure, so rolled-thread bolts should not be used.

Wood Screws

Flathead screws are used extensively in wooden boatbuilding for fastening planking and decking and many other parts. They are available from stock made of galvanized iron, brass, or silicon bronze, and are also produced of Monel and stainless steel. All are made with slotted heads, many

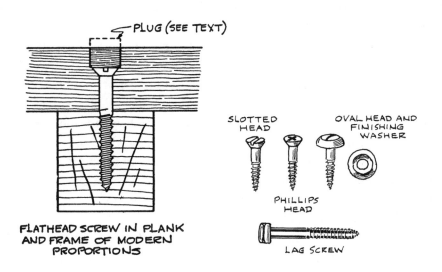

PLUG (SEE TEXT)

SLOTTED HEAD

OVAL HEAD AND FINISHING WASHER

PHILLIPS HEAD

FLATHEAD SCREW IN PLANK AND FRAME OF MODERN PROPORTIONS

LAG SCREW

FIGURE 6-5.
Wood screws come in a wide variety of heads, including Phillips, flat, and square drive (not shown). Holes left in planking by screws benefit from being plugged with circular discs of the same material (see text).

with the Phillips or similar type heads that some builders prefer in order to minimize screwdriver bit slippage and thus the possible scarring of the adjacent wood. Freason-head fasteners are often mistaken for Phillips head fasteners, but the cuts in the head (in the shape of an "x") are deeper and wider than on the Phillips—drivers are not interchangeable for these.

One would think the choice of screw heads was complete enough to suit anyone, but not so. Several years ago I was asked by a friend to remove window shade hardware and install new blinds. I took enough tools to take care of any situation but one: the shade brackets were secured by screws with square recess heads I had never seen before, so I had to shop around for a proper screwdriver. Hardware stores carry the square-end tips for power screwdrivers. I think this type of screw head may prove superior to the older types. I am told that these screws have become popular in Canada for many purposes.

Tests have shown that screws with sharp, thin threads develop the greatest holding power in tension. The threads of hot-galvanized wood screws in the smaller sizes are bad in this respect. However, withdrawal resistance of screws used as plank fastenings is theoretically not too critical; the most important function of fastenings is not to keep the planks from springing off, but to prevent them from "working" past their neighbors in a fore-and-aft direction when the hull is being driven through seas. (Such working is the cause of leaking seams in a conventional single-planked hull.) Indeed, the primary job of hull fastenings is to hold the parts in place. Here the area of the wood that bears against the fastenings is very important; a thick fastening puts more wood to work resisting stresses than a thin one. This is a strong argument for using screws instead of nails as planking fastenings, because for a given length, a screw can be used that is thicker than a nail. Figure 6-6 shows the screw sizes that have been accepted over the years for planking and decking, and if you compare the gauge of any one of the screws with an ordinary boat nail of the same length, the greater screw thickness will be obvious. You can still obtain bronze annular nails in thicknesses up to 4 gauge, which is nearly a quarter of an inch, from Jamestown Distributors.

Some will consider the screw sizes in Figure 6-6 to be on the heavy side, but the table is meant for hulls that will be subject to rigorous service, such as ocean cruising. The sizes may be reduced by a gauge or so for powerboats and other boats of light construction built for sheltered waters. When building from plans, be guided by the fastening sizes specified.

PLANK THICKNESS	SCREW LENGTH & GAUGE[1]	SCREW DIAM.	BODY DRILL	LEAD DRILL[2]	PLUG DIAM.
3/8"	3/4" No. 7	.150"	9/64"	No. 44	NONE
1/2"	1" No. 8	.163"	5/32"	No. 40	NONE
5/8"	1 1/4" No. 9	.176"	11/64"	No. 37	3/8"
3/4"	1 1/2" No. 10	.189"	3/16"	No. 33	1/2"
7/8"	1 3/4" No. 12	.216	13/64"	No. 30	1/2"
1"	2" No. 14	.242"	15/64"	No. 25	1/2"
1 1/8"	2 1/4" No. 16	.268"	17/64"	No. 18	5/8"
1 1/4"	2 1/2" No. 18	.294"	9/32"	No. 13	5/8"
1 1/2"	3" No. 20	.320"	5/16"	No. 4	3/4"

FLATHEAD WOOD SCREWS FOR PLANKING

[1] MAY BE REDUCED ONE GAUGE FOR DECKING.
[2] FOR HARDWOOD

FIGURE 6-6.
Body drill sizes for various plank thicknesses and the corresponding diameter of the plugs needed to fill the holes left by the screws.

The size of a drilled hole for a screw affects the screw's holding power to an appreciable extent. A general rule to follow for determining the lead hole size is 90 percent of the diameter at the root of the screw threads in hardwoods and 70 percent in softwoods. The lead hole drill sizes in the table are a guide for hardwood, such as oak, because the threaded part of a screw used for fastening planking is sunk into the frame, but it is best to check the table sizes by driving a few screws in samples of the wood to be used. Most builders use just one drill for screws in mahogany or white cedar planking and oak frames, and this is satisfactory if the plank does not split in the way of the unthreaded screw shank. If splitting does occur, you should drill through the *plank only* using a body drill that is *slightly* under the actual screw diameter. The sizes for these are also shown in Figure 6-6. It is recommended that either laundry soap or beeswax be rubbed in the threads of screws, especially when driving into hardwood. This acts as a lubricant, reducing the driving force, and does not affect holding power. More about drilling holes for wood screws further on.

In the best yacht practice, the screw holes in carvel planking (see Chapter 11) ⅝" thick and over are counterbored and plugged (Figure 6-5) with plugs of the same kind of wood as the planking, while the heads of screws in thinner planks are set slightly below the surface, with the heads puttied over to make the fastenings invisible on the finished hull. Marine hardware suppliers sell plugs of mahogany, teak, or oak, or you can buy a plug cutter for a drill press and make your own from scraps of the same kind of wood you will be plugging.

The depth of counterbore for the plugs should be about one-third of the plank thickness. The plugs are dipped in thick paint, waterproof glue, or varnish (the latter recommended for wood that is to have a natural finish), set in the counterbored holes with the grain parallel to that of the planking, and lightly tapped home with a hammer. If hit too hard, the plug may be crushed and it may swell later, possibly breaking the paint film or at least presenting an unsightly look. Give the bond a day or so to harden, then cut the plugs flush with the surface using a sharp chisel. Do not try to flush off the plug with one cut of the chisel. Rather, take light cuts to determine run of the grain; then you will not chip off the plug below the surface of the plank and have to start all over again.

Drilling proper holes for wood screws can be done with separate bits or with bits that combine the operations. There are patented countersinks that drill the lead hole followed by the countersink for the screw head and patented counterbores that drill the lead followed by the hole for the plug. The latter is used most because it is unnecessary to countersink for a flat-head screw that is to have a plug over it.

Plugs can sometimes become crowded where planking strakes are narrow, particularly near the strakes' ends, where the plank width is least. This can be overcome either by carefully staggering the holes if the width of the frame will permit it or by reducing the gauge of the screw just enough to use a plug of the next smaller size.

Some years ago I began to use tapered drills for wood screw holes. From a maximum diameter matching that of the screw body (which reduces the risk of splitting the plank), the drill is ground to taper to a point, thus conforming to the wood screw shape. The bit is used with a countersink that is adjustable for the length of the screw. This countersink drills for a flathead fastener; when an adjustable stop collar is used, it also counterbores for a plug to the depth desired. In addition the countersink can be used with an untapered drill bit to drill and counterbore for a machine-screw-type fastener. The diameter of the counterbore is proper for a plug larger in diameter than the screw head. Stock sizes of these countersinks are shown in Figure 6-7.

SIZE SCREW	DRILL DIAM. *	COUNTERBORE (PLUG. DIAM.)
NO. 6	9/64"	3/8"
8	11/64"	3/8"
10	13/64"	1/2"
12	7/32"	1/2"
14	1/4"	1/2"
16	1/4"	5/8"

* STRAIGHT OR TAPERED DRILL.

FIGURE 6-7.
Stock sizes of countersinks with counterbore for wood plug.

Much superior to a common twist drill for making clean holes in wood is the brad point bit. It is also easily centered for starting a hole where it belongs.

Shown in Figure 6-8—but not to relative scale—are a tapered drill with countersink and stop collar (positioned for a shallow plug), a brad point bit, and a plug cutter.

W. L. Fuller, Inc., has been supplying countersinks, counterbores, plug cutters, and tapered drills to the boatbuilding industry for many years. These items may be difficult to find locally, but they appear in many tool catalogs and can be purchased directly from Fuller.

During the late 1980s, power drill and screwdriver bits with hexagon shanks appeared in profusion to suit the quick-change chucks that were appearing at that time. These bits are also usable in the usual chucks for round bits. Fuller now makes their well-known tapered bits with hex shanks (Figure 6-9).

FIGURE 6-8.
From left to right: A tapered drill with countersink, a stop collar, a brad point bit, and a plug cutter.

FIGURE 6-9.
A tapered wood screw bit with a hexagon shank.

Since the 1980s a good number of suppliers have started to carry what I always thought of as exotic twist drill bits—carbide-tipped (*not* masonry bits), cobalt steel, and titanium nitrate. Describing the latter, one supplier's catalog read, "may last an incredible 12 times longer than any bit we sell." All bits of the above materials will outlast those of carbon and the so-called high-speed steel, are superior for drilling metal, and are much higher in price. You can get along without them, but they are worth considering. You may find them indispensable if you drill stainless steel frequently.

There are only a few places where roundhead screws are used in boats, but, for example, they are the logical fastening for securing rigging tangs to wooden masts, since the thin metal of which a tang is made will not permit a countersunk hole. Oval-head screws are only used in light joinerwork where fastenings must show and for securing panels that are removed from time to time for access to such things as steering gear and other items located behind joinerwork. In these places oval-head screws are used with finishing washers so that screw holes do not become too worn from repeated use.

Stainless steel screws labeled 18-8 have become easily available in the standard configurations of flat-, round-, and oval-head wood screws. It is possible that these will be sold for less than silicon bronze screws; therefore they should be considered for fastening joinerwork, but I am reluctant to use them below the waterline until I have greater experience with them. Stainless steel "tapping" type screws are also easy to find. These are basically sheet-metal fasteners but can be used in fiberglass parts. Normally they are threaded for the entire length of the shank, so they are best in tension rather than for bearing loads.

Lag Screws

Lag screws, sometimes called lag bolts, are large wood screws with a square head that are turned in with a wrench. Periodic tightening of a lag screw can wear the threads in the wood until the holding power of the screw is gradually lost; therefore lags are used only where through-bolts are not possible or practical. A hole of the same diameter as the lag screw is bored for the length of the unthreaded shank, and the hole for the thread should be sized the same as for a regular wood screw. Lag screws are made in galvanized steel, brass, stainless steel, and silicon bronze, the latter being preferred in boat construction. The smallest lag screw made is ¼" diameter.

Hanger Bolts

These are lag screws having the upper or head end of the shank threaded for a nut. They are used principally for fastening propeller shaft stuffing boxes and stern bearings and for holding down engines to beds. By backing off the hanger bolt nut, these parts may be removed for repair or replacement without disturbing the screw thread in the wood. Hanger bolts are turned in with a wrench applied either to a nut run down to the end of the threads or to two nuts locked together on the threads. They are usually made of brass and silicon bronze, the latter being preferred in boat construction.

Galvanized Boat Nails

Galvanized fasteners are the most inexpensive and normally will have a shorter life than those of more durable metals. The nails are forged, have a peculiar button head, rectangular shank, and either a blunt or a chisel point (Figure 6-10). In frames up to about 1¼" thick, chisel-pointed nails are driven so that the points project about ½" to ⅜" through the frames and are clinched against the frame with the grain. To prevent splitting the frame, the nail is driven with the chisel edge across the grain. A nail of acceptable quality will clinch without cracking either the nail or the zinc coating. Blunt-pointed nails are used in heavier frames and are buried entirely

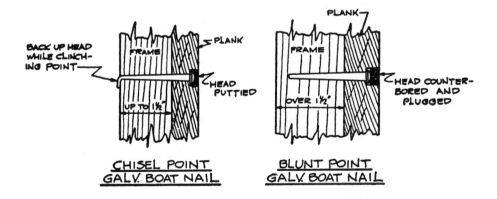

FIGURE 6-10.

Galvanized boat nails are available in chisel point and blunt point. Make sure to drive the nailhead below the wood surface.

within the frame. Whether or not the holes are counterbored for plugs, the heads of either type nail must be driven below the surface of the planking with a nail set, and an attempt must be made to prevent cutting the coating of zinc by using a set shaped to fit over the entire head of the nail. If a better grade of hull fasteners cannot be afforded for some reason, a few suppliers have catalogs as well as online stores and may stock hot-dipped galvanized boat fasteners: Anchor Staple & Nail Company, Chesapeake Marine Fasteners, Hamilton Marine, Jamestown Distributors, and Tremont Nail Company (see Appendix). All of them have a wide selection of the fasteners used in boatbuilding described in this chapter.

Copper Nails as Rivets

Copper nails are made in the form of common wire nails with flat heads. They are used almost exclusively as rivets for fastening frames to floors, stringers to frames, planking laps to one another in lapstrake construction, and planking to frames where both the planking and frames are light in size. The hole for the nail should be drilled as small as possible without it being so small that the parts split or the nail bends while being driven. Drive the nail all the way in to draw the parts together; then the head must be backed up with an iron while a copper burr is driven over the point of the nail (see Figure 6-11). A burr is simply a washer, and it is important that it be a driving fit over the nail or else it will dance all over the place when the rivet is being formed. The burr is driven up against the wood with a set, which is nothing but a length of steel rod with a hole in the end slightly larger than the diameter of the nail. With nippers, cut off the point of the nail so that a length equal to one to one-and-a-half times the diameter of the nail is left for riveting. Again with the head of the nail backed up with the iron, do the riveting with many light blows with the peen end of a machinist's hammer, gradually rounding the head of the nail. Heavy blows will bend the nail inside the wood. A bent rivet tends to straighten under stress, resulting in a weak, loose fastening. Light blows form the head and draw the wood together. It pays to make a few trials if you have never done riveting.

Copper rivets are excellent for light work but are rather soft. Screws should be used for fastening planking when the size of the frame will permit the screw to be completely buried. Nails are normally thinner than screws for the same job, a point discussed under "Wood Screws." Figure 6-12 shows the sizes of copper wire nails.

Copper wire nails are also made with larger-diameter heads, which some boatbuilders prefer. These are sold as "slating" nails.

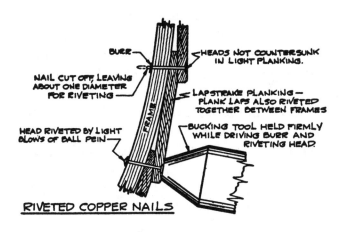

RIVETED COPPER NAILS

FIGURE 6-11.
Copper nails are riveted in many instances in wooden boatbuilding—the technique shown here is for lapstrake planking.

NONFERROUS NAIL SIZES

LENGTH	COPPER WIRE		ANCHORFAST & STRONGHOLD	
	SHANK DIAM.	APPROX. NUMBER PER LB.	SHANK DIAM.	APPROX. NUMBER PER LB.
5/8"	.065"	1380	.065"	
3/4"	.065"	1160	.065"	
	.072"	956	.109"	462
7/8"	.072"	808	.065"	825
			.109"	393
1"	.072"	704	.072"	775
			.109"	350
1 1/4"	.083"	424	.083"	525
			.109"	280
			.134"	
1 1/2"	.109"	208	.109"	210
			.134"	135
			.165"	90
1 3/4"	.109"	180	.134"	120
	.120"	144	.165"	76
2"	.134"	106	.134	105
	.120	130	.165"	68
2 1/4"			.165"	64
2 1/2"	.134"	86	.165"	58
2 3/4"			.165'	53
3"	.148"	56	.165"	48
3 1/2"	.165"	40	.165"	25

FIGURE 6-12.
Sizing table for copper wire nails as well as Monel Anchorfast and Stronghold silicon bronze nails usually found in the stocks of distributors.

Then there are square-cut copper nails. These have greater holding power in wood than the round wire nails, but inasmuch as the primary use of copper fasteners is as rivets, the holding power increase is quite unimportant. Traditionally, with square-cut nails a dish-shaped copper "rove" is used instead of a flat burr. Roves can also be used for making rivets of round wire nails. An advantage of a rove, which is driven over the shank of a nail with the hollow side toward the wood, is that the dished shape grips the wood and helps tension the rivet. The heads of the square-cut nails shown in Figure 6-13 may be left "proud" above the surface of the wood or countersunk into the plank as illustrated. In the latter case the bucking iron (also known as a bucking tool) must be suitably shaped, as shown.

Still another copper nail fastening is the square-cut "clout" nail shown in Figure 6-14. These are used in light construction for fastening planking to thin, flat frames as used in canoes; for fastening the laps of clinker planking up to about ½" in thickness; and for "quilt" fastening the layers of double diagonal planking between frames. In the case of the latter, where the layers of planking are glued together and the nails are used only to ensure a good bond, some builders drive the nails against a heavy iron

FIGURE 6-13.
The riveting process when traditional square-cut (also known as square-shank) boat nails are used in conjunction with dished "roves."

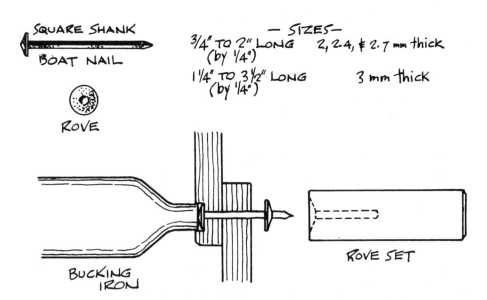

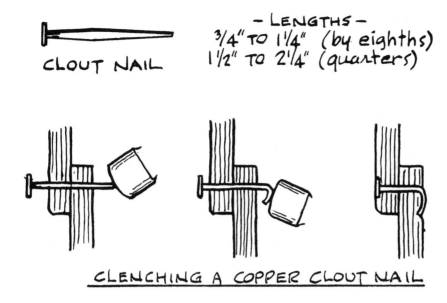

FIGURE 6-14.
Clenching a copper clout nail in lapstrake construction.

held against the inside of the planking by a helper. When the iron is used properly, the point of the nail turns 90 degrees and is flush with the wood. It takes teamwork to know where the next nail will be driven, but once the routine is established, the nails are clenched at a fast rate.

The point of the nail is turned back into the wood when clout nails are used as primary fasteners without adhesives. This works all right in the laps of softwood planking and with softwood frames like those of canoes, but when used with hardwoods, a rivet is more reliable than a clenched nail.

For clench-nailing, first drill a snug hole as described earlier for riveting copper wire nails. As the nail is driven through, the point is turned over by holding an iron against the point and forming it into a hook. When the point is about to enter the wood, the iron is held against the hook, and the worker outside completes driving the nail until the head is flush with the wood. This all takes practice and some trials to determine how much longer the length of the nail should be compared to the thickness of the parts being fastened together. Figure 6-14 shows the elements of the clenching process, using lapstrake planking for illustration.

Threaded Nails

Another type of fastening for a boat hull is a nail with a unique annular thread. As the nail is driven, the grooves on the shank shape the wood fibers into countless minute wedges that grip the shank to resist withdrawal

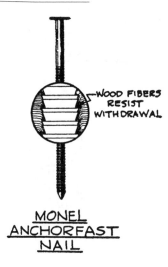

WOOD FIBERS
RESIST
WITHDRAWAL

MONEL
ANCHORFAST
NAIL

FIGURE 6-15.
Using threaded boat nails for planking can significantly reduce labor time and expense.

(see Figure 6-15). It is claimed that it takes 65 percent more force to pull this threaded nail than an unclinched galvanized boat nail, 31 percent more than a clinched boat nail, and 3 percent more than a wood screw. As these nails are available in nonferrous material, the objection to nails because of corrosion has been overcome. Some boatbuilders have used these nails for their planking, and figures show that some yards have reduced their plank-fastening labor by one quarter.

There are several kinds of threaded nails on the market, including some made abroad. Tests have shown the importance of the thread form, and one of the best is rolled on the nail. The Monel nails are stiffer than the silicon bronze, making them more resistant to bending when driven. If Monel nails cannot be found, it is recommended that the second choice be limited to those made of silicon bronze.

For fastening planking, nails should be the same diameter as the screws they replace, or else more of them should be used. Pilot holes as recommended by the manufacturer should be drilled for all but the smallest sizes. The pilot hole size recommended is 50 to 70 percent of the nail diameter, depending upon the hardness of the wood, and about 80 percent of the nail length.

Figure 6-12 (see page 123) shows the sizes of Monel Anchorfast and Stronghold silicon bronze nails usually found in the stocks of distributors. Figure 6-16 is a comparison of standard nail and screw gauges as a guide for those wishing to substitute nails for screws, and in Figure 6-17 nail sizes for various types of planking and decking are tabulated. These sizes, of course, must be used with discretion, as they do not necessarily apply to every case.

Temporary Fasteners

Another type of fastener is the so-called drywall screw made of steel (Figure 6-18). The bugle-shaped head usually sets without splitting the wood, and the shank with full-length threads is made with a point that

FIGURE 6-16.
Comparison of screw vs. nail diameter.

SCREW GAUGE VS. NAIL DIAMETER		
SCREW		NAIL
SHANK DIAM.	GAUGE Nº	WIRE DIAM.
.086"	2	.083"
		.095"
		.109"
.125"	5	.120"
.138"	6	.134"
.164"	8	.165"
		.180"
.190	10	
		.203"
.216	12	.220"
.242	14	.238"
		.265"
.268	16	
		.284"
.294	18	.300

eliminates drilling a pilot hole. Commonly available sizes are #6 × 1", 1¼", 1⅝", and 2" in length, and #8 × 3" long. The heads are recessed for a #2 Phillips screwdriver, and there are adapters for drywall screw bits for use in an electric drill. Drywall installers use special drivers, and magnetic bits are made, enabling one-hand screw driving, at times a great help.

Drywall screws can be used to advantage fastening the parts of molds (such as shown in Chapter 8, Figure 8-4), and they could not help but speed up the job of fastening foam core sheets to ribbands (as shown in Chapter 5, Figure 5-4) because pilot holes in the ribbands are not necessary (the foam *never* needs pilot holes!) and also because of the optional one-handed operation. But don't ever use the steel drywall screws where they would be left in the boat to rust.

Another type of steel fastener for strictly temporary use is a common nail with two heads, variously called a double-headed, scaffold, or staging nail. As shown in Figure 6-18, the use is obvious—they are driven until the first head makes contact, leaving a proper amount to remove the nail later with a claw hammer or pinch bar. I have seen 8-penny (2½") and 16-penny (3½") in stock in building supply stores, but never shorter lengths. It's too bad; I can think of uses for small double-headed nails as temporary fastenings in the construction of lightweight small craft.

Metric Fasteners

Because the metric system of measurement is standard almost worldwide, it is likely that even in the United States, where the system is sparsely used, a person will be faced with drilling holes for metric fasteners, the diameters of which are identified by the prefix M. An M8 bolt, for instance, has a diameter of 8mm (or 0.315 inch).

THREADED NAILS

PLANKING & DECKING (NOT PLYWOOD)

WOOD THICKNESS	NAIL SIZE LIGHT DUTY HULLS	NAIL SIZE HEAVY DUTY HULLS
1/2"	1 1/4" × .083"	
5/8"	1 1/2" × .134"	1 1/2" × .165"
3/4"	1 1/2" × .134"	1 1/2" × .180"
7/8"	1 3/4" × .165"	1 3/4" × .220"
1"	2" × .165"	2" × .238"

PLYWOOD PLANKING & DECKING

PLYWOOD THICKNESS	NAIL SIZE	NAIL SPACING	
		ALONG EDGES	PLANKING BATTENS & DECK BEAMS
1/4"	7/8" × .109"	1 1/2" – 1 3/4"	3" – 4"
3/8"	1 1/4" × .109"	2 1/2" – 3"	4" – 5"
1/2"	1 1/2" × .134"	3" – 4"	4" – 5"
5/8"	2" × .165"	4"	5"
3/4"	2 1/4" × .165"	4"	5"

STRIP PLANKING (SEE TEXT)

WOOD THICKNESS	NAIL DIAM.	APPROX. SPACING
5/8" – 3/4"	.083"	4"
7/8" – 1"	.109"	5"
1" – 1 1/4"	.134"	6"

FIGURE 6-17.
Nail sizes for various planking and decking.

FIGURE 6-18.
Two types of temporary fasteners: A bugle-head drywall screw (top) and a double-headed scaffold nail.

NOMINAL DIAM.		CLEARANCE
MM	INCH	DRILL (U.S.)
M 3	.118	NO. 31 OR 1/8"
M 3.5	.138	NO. 28 OR 9/64"
M 5	.197	NO. 8 OR 13/64"
M 6	.236	1/4"
M 8	.315	21/64"
M 10	.394	13/32"
M 12	.472	31/64"
M 14	.551	9/16"

FIGURE 6-19.
Drill sizes needed for metric fasteners.

Referring to the U.S. standard screw and bolt sizes given in Figure 6-20, Figure 6-19 is a brief guide to similar information for a few metric sizes. More complete details can be found in the catalogs of the suppliers mentioned below. Also see the Appendix for conversions from U.S. to metric measures.

One supplier of metric fasteners, Metric and Multistandard Components Corporation, carries an enormous selection of metric fasteners of every description as well as rules, including wooden folding rules, tapes, calipers, micrometers, and thickness gauges; it also has high-speed steel twist drill sets and taps and dies for cutting metric screw threads.

BODY & TAP DRILLS FOR U.S. STANDARD MACHINE SCREWS & BOLTS				
SIZE	DIAM. INS.	THREADS PER INCH	TAP DRILL	CLEARANCE DRILL
NO. 6	.138	32	NO. 36	NO. 28
NO. 8	.164	32	NO. 29	NO. 19
NO. 10	.190	24	NO. 25	NO. 11
NO. 10	.190	32	NO. 21	NO. 11
NO. 12	.216	24	NO. 16	NO. 2
NO. 12	.216	32	NO. 13	NO. 2
1/4"	.250	20	NO. 7	17/64" OR 9/32"
5/16"	.3125	18	F	21/64" OR 11/32"
3/8"	.375	16	5/16"	25/64" OR 13/32"
1/2"	.500	13	27/64"	33/64" OR 17/32"

FIGURE 6-20.
Drill sizes for machine screws and bolts.

Identifying metric fasteners for replacement is easy when you have suitable gauges. There is a metric version of the "Screw Chek'r," which has been around as long as I can remember for checking U.S. standard fastener sizes. In a pinch an identified die makes a great gauge for a bolt thread; a tap does the same for a nut.

MISCELLANEOUS FASTENERS

There are a few other types of fasteners that have some uses in boat construction when they are made of proper noncorrosive materials. Machine screws are bolts and are useful as through-fasteners for light work. Usual sizes are from Number 6 (a fat ⅛") up through ¼" in diameter. Figure 6-20 is a table showing hole sizes for clearance and for tap drills, etc.; there will be times when you will find this very handy. Machine screws are made with flat, round, and oval heads, and in brass, chrome-plated brass, bronze, and stainless steel.

Staples, applied with hand, electric, or air-operated guns, can be used to hold thin pieces of wood when laminating, securing cold-molded hull planking, positioning fiberglass or other woven materials, and for many other such jobs. If the staples are to be removed later, they can be of inexpensive steel; otherwise bronze, Monel, or stainless steel must be used. The ultimate staple that I have seen is a rather long Monel wire staple with coated legs that defy withdrawal. Driven with an air gun, the staple head will sink flush with the surface of fir plywood. These staples have been used to fasten plywood decking that is glued to beams and around the edges and many other similar plywood parts. Stapling is the fastest method of securing parts and is quite satisfactory when used in conjunction with an adhesive.

Now available are plastic staples, T-nails, and finish nails, all of which must be air-driven by a special stapler or nailer. I won't dwell on this, but the products are interesting for corrosion resistance if nothing else.

For many years riveting remained a method of fastening used only by professional metalworking shops, but due to the invention of "pop" rivets, minor riveting jobs can now be done by the amateur. Most hardware stores carry these rivets and hand-operated riveters. This kind of fastening is a one-person job, because pop rivets are inserted into a drilled hole and secured from the same side without the need for any backup. Pop rivets are extensively employed in production fiberglass boatbuilding. A typical application is in securing a molded deck that fits over the hull, the rivet holding together the deck, hull, and rub rail. The latter is usually an aluminum alloy extrusion, and the rivets are of a similar alloy. Their use should be limited to above the water, and generally for fastening thin parts, say an assembly having a total thickness of no greater than ½" (see table). Those who make their own metal enclosures, such as aluminum alloy cases for electrical switchboards, will find that pop rivets make the job go a lot easier and faster.

Pop Rivet Sizes and Grip Lengths

Rivet Diameter	No. of Sizes	Grip Range
5052 Aluminum Rivets		
⅛"	6	⅛"–½"
⁵⁄₃₂"	3	⅛"–⅜"
³⁄₁₆"	6	⅛"–¾"
305 Stainless Steel Rivets		
⅛"	5	⅛"–½"
⁵⁄₃₂"	2	⅛"–⅜"
³⁄₁₆"	4	⅛"–½"

18-8 Stainless Steel Rivets
(Check with your supplier.)

Pop rivets are made of both aluminum alloy and stainless steel and look like A in Figure 6-21. B shows how the body looks after it has been squeezed and the shank has broken off, and C shows a large-flange button-head rivet, best used when fastening soft materials or plastics for greater distribution of head-bearing load.

FIGURE 6-21.

Pop rivets, also known as blind rivets, come in a variety of sizes dependent on your desired diameter and grip length (A). After the body has been squeezed, the shank is broken off (B). Another variation is the large-flange button-head rivet (C).

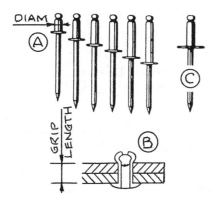

FASTENING METAL FITTINGS

To avoid galvanic corrosion, fasten bronze underwater parts such as shaft logs, stern bearings, rudderposts, seacocks, and propeller shaft struts with silicon bronze. On deck, fasten stainless steel trim and hardware with stainless steel, bronze fittings with silicon bronze, galvanized fittings with hot-dipped galvanized fastenings, Marinium fittings with stainless steel or Monel, and aluminum alloy fittings with stainless steel.

ADHESIVES

Adhesives, used either alone or in conjunction with mechanical fasteners, are some of the best fasteners. However, it must be remembered that an adhesive is not a cure-all and that for it to provide strength it must be used as directed, with attention to mixture (when the adhesive is two-part), temperature and working time, clamping pressure, and curing period.

Until World War II there were only *water-resistant* adhesives rather than *waterproof* ones. This fact notwithstanding, thousands of hollow masts and booms were glued up with what was called casein glue and protected from moisture by coats of varnish or paint. Water-resistant glue still has a place in boat construction for interior joinerwork that is not subject to wetting and that is protected with finish coating. After the war a number of waterproof glues were formulated and widely employed in boatbuilding, chiefly urea-resin, urea-formaldehyde, and resorcinol glues. These are still available, but they have largely been replaced in the boatshop by epoxy.

As discussed in detail later in the chapter, epoxy's advantages and disadvantages lie in the necessity for mixing. In some boatbuilding applications, more conventional glues are easier to use and completely effective, most notably the one-part aliphatic resin glues. These cream-colored glues are rated water-resistant. (It took a couple of weeks for the joint of a sample I made and immersed in water to fail easily.)

These are the glues generally used in small furniture and cabinetmaking shops and are fast-setting and well-suited to interior boat joinery. The two best-known glues of the type are Elmer's Carpenter's Glue and Titebond, the newest version of which, Titebond III, is actually rated waterproof. These glues are rendered useless if they are allowed to freeze, and they have a limited temperature range for application and curing, so let the gluer beware. Another type of glue you may have some use for in boatbuilding is contact cement, used for sticking Formica-type high-pressure laminates to wood and metal. Be aware that the fumes from contact cement are not only obnoxious, they are also very dangerous to health and highly flammable. In addition, unfortunately a surface coated with the cement must be allowed to dry to the touch before mating. (Worse still, in one shop in which I worked for years, the very experienced foreman insisted on two coats.)

Epoxy resins are among the best adhesives for use in building wooden boats and parts. They can even be used for joining wood and polyester fiberglass parts to polyester fiberglass, although care must be taken to ensure that the binder in the fiberglass is compatible with (will not dissolve in) epoxy. Epoxy is extremely strong, it does not require pressure to achieve a good bond, and it is gap-filling if used thick enough so that it does not run out of the joints. Not needing pressure to ensure a strong joint, epoxy is easier to use than resorcinol for laminations and hulls with multiple planking layers. Various additives such as microfibers, microballoons, and microspheres are used to modify the epoxy to the requirements of different applications, from bonding, which requires high strength, to surface fairing, which requires easy sanding characteristics. Another additive, colloidal silica ("angel dust"—Cab-O-Sil is a trade-name version of it) is added when a more thixotropic or non-sagging mixture is needed, as when applying to a vertical surface. There are also epoxies available in caulking-gun cartridges that are thick enough for use in certain applications.

The strength of epoxy when used as an adhesive, plus the advantage of not requiring high pressure on the mating surfaces, really makes it an ideal material for boatbuilding. Remember, though, that mixing epoxy with the *hardener* is not at all similar to adding the *catalyst* to polyester resin. The amount of the catalyst determines the speed at which polyester resin will set up at various temperatures, whereas an exact amount of epoxy hardener regulates the chemical reaction that results in the cured material performing as expected. Do not tamper with the epoxy manufacturer's stated proportions for this expensive material. If the instructions specify a 1:1 mixture of resin and hardener by *volume*, simply mix them this way. On the other hand, if the quality of the cured epoxy requires mixing the proportions by *weight*, take the trouble to do it right. Some makers of epoxy resins have devices such as pumps to help you mix the components so the finished product will have the strength expected.

The two brands of epoxy I have seen most while visiting yards are WEST System and System Three. The Gougeon brothers, makers of WEST, were pioneers in the use of epoxy in wooden boat construction. Over the years they have compiled a big, superbly illustrated book on boatbuilding with epoxy, *The Gougeon Brothers on Boat Construction*. Besides many, many construction details, the book explains WEST System hardeners and how they modify the curing of the popular WEST #101 epoxy resin. There are now four hardeners, each of which has specific properties relating to speed of cure, the specific application, and environmental conditions. All are mixed in a 5:1 ratio of resin to hardener by volume. To eliminate otherwise messy measuring, Gougeon sells plastic minipumps in pairs—one for resin, one for hardener. These pumps screw onto the containers in place of the cap and automatically dispense the resin and hardener in the proper ratio. Personally I have not had great luck with these pumps, especially when not using them on a daily basis. And they cannot be used for amounts less than one stroke of the pump, which is a fair amount. Frequent epoxy users will learn, though, that it is tricky to mix the small amounts that one usually needs for specific jobs (bearing in mind that once it is mixed it has a very short "pot life").

There are lots of tricks for measuring small amounts accurately, including disposable graduated cups, but nothing is better than a digital scale. WEST is now marketing a digital scale as part of its system, and I think it would likely pay for itself in otherwise wasted resin in a short time. A digital scale will work for all epoxy systems and allow you to be very precise with the ratio of the dry additives. The additives are usually added by feel and experience, but greater precision will allow you to repeat good results and avoid not-so-good ones. Add the fillers a little at a time—you can't get filler out once it's in.

System Three epoxy is mixed in the ration of 2:1, resin to hardener. One builder told me he liked the flexibility of this resin. This system offers three hardeners with pot lives of 15 minutes, 30 minutes, and 70 minutes, respectively (at 77 degrees F). Incidentally, System Three has published *The Epoxy Book,* which is a bible of sorts and well worth acquiring if you plan to use epoxies.

Five-Minute "Quick Cure" Epoxy Adhesive

Sooner or later we putterers find a need for a fast-cure adhesive. Even grocery stores nowadays sell a bubble-packed card containing two ½-ounce tubes of the necessary two parts, but this gets relatively expensive. Unlike System Three's standard adhesive, its "Quick Cure" is mixed 1:1 by volume and is packed in squeezable bottles with a dispenser top. WEST has a similar product, called G5. My own preference is to keep things simple and stick with the basic system (especially now that I have a digital scale), but this product could be useful in some situations.

Epoxy Additives

Epoxy resins used as adhesives or for fairing areas where buildup is needed must be thickened to prevent "starving" a joint from runout from too thin a mixture or sagging when used as a fairing. Fortunately, the major resin suppliers carry a variety of fillers, so one does not have to shop around. Following are a number of materials used as fillers:

Colloidal silica is an extremely fine white powder used to control the tendency of the mixture to flow. One brand name is Cab-O-Sil.

Phenolic microballoons are tiny hollow spheres used to make a putty or fairing compound. They are light in weight and brown-purple in color.

Quartz microspheres are hollow, lightweight glass spheres. They are harder to sand when cured than the phenolic. Neither quartz microspheres nor phenolic microballoons should be used when strength is sought. They are typically used for fairing.

Chopped glass strands, ½" long, add strength and viscosity.

Milled glass microfibers make a thick paste for filling large areas when maximum strength is desirable.

Among the various systems are a number of other additives—for improved anti-blister properties, for making fillets that will show, for friction reduction on bottoms and rudders, and for tinting. As I said, it's a pretty versatile product.

CAUTION TO EPOXY USERS

So much is written about epoxy resins, and the material is so valuable to boatbuilders, principally as an adhesive, that I would be remiss not to warn that epoxy resins, especially hardeners, must be used with caution. Avoid contact with unprotected skin and breathing the fumes released by epoxies as they cure. These words are to reinforce manufacturers' directions that are often taken lightly. I have never had a problem, but skin sensitization is a serious health hazard—and irreversible. Don't fail to wear protection.

If resin does get on hands and tools, how does one get rid of the partially cured goop? As a low-tech solution, I've noticed several letters to the editor of small-craft magazines suggesting the use of white vinegar to clean noncured epoxy resin (one of them also mentioned polyester resin) from tools, wood, brushes, and skin. The vinegar is used as one would a thinner, followed by a soap-and-water wash. A product called Bio-Solv has recently come out that may prove to be a boon to epoxy users. It is composed of ethyl lactate and said to be an entirely safe and effective replacement for traditional boatbuilding solvents such as acetone, MEK, and paint thinner. Worth looking into!

By far the best and safest way to go is to keep polyester or epoxy resins and other chemicals off the skin by wearing appropriate gloves and Tyvek gauntlets or sleeves. When working with epoxy, make sure the shop is well ventilated, because fumes alone can cause reactions in some people, and when coating large areas, get the work done quickly and leave the shop until fumes from the curing process have dissipated. And wear proper respiratory protection (see Chapter 22).

Sealer/Adhesives Other Than Resins

Although we normally think of materials packed in cartridges to be applied with a caulking gun as either sealers or bedding compounds for wood-to-wood joints and deck hardware, some of them have value as adhesives as well and are properly described by their manufacturers as sealer adhesives or adhesive sealants. A popular, very tenacious one is 3M 5200, a polyurethane adhesive sealant that often gets cussed when a deck fitting that has been bedded with it has to be removed. It just won't let go unless a hot putty knife is used, and maybe not even then. But for certain applications, notably the permanent bonding of a deck to a hull in fiberglass vessels, it can't be beat. There are a number of other types of sealing compounds, all less effective adhesives (thankfully) than 5200 and each with pros and cons in different applications (see the table below). In my experience the most versatile for routine installation of deck hardware, portholes, et cetera, is Boatlife's Life-Caulk, a polysulfide formulation. Life-Caulk cures by exposure to water.

Generic Types of Sealants and Adhesive Sealants

	Silicone	Polyurethane Adhesive Sealants	Polysulfide
Cure rate	Fast	Varies	Slow
Adhesion	Poor	Best	Fair
Paintability		Best[1]	Best
Sandability		Best[1]	Best
Wood to wood		Best	Good
Teak deck seams		Best[2]	
Bedding hardware (wood boat)		Best	Good
Bedding hardware (FRP boats)	Good	Best	Good
Bare wood to FRP	Good	Good	Best
Wooden hull seams		Best	Good
FRP deck to FRP hull	Good	Best	Good
Through-hull fittings (wood boats)		Good	Best

Follow instructions on package

1 = not polyurethane/silicone paint; 2 = with primer.

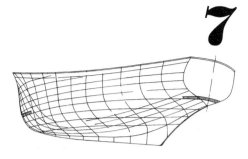

LINES AND LAYING DOWN

TO PROPERLY BUILD A BOAT FROM PLANS, the hull lines and part of the construction plan must be drawn full size. This fact has been repeated to the point of monotony in countless "how to build" articles, but the job is so important to the successful completion of a boat that instructions in boatbuilding would be incomplete without a description of the work involved.

A few firms offer full-size patterns for hull parts or completely dimensioned drawings so the shape of the parts can be drawn directly on the material. The purpose of this is to eliminate the work described in this chapter, but these services may not have a design to suit you in their selection.

The job of drawing full size is distasteful to some, even among professional boatbuilders, but others find it to be fascinating work. Either way, it is true that once the plans are on hand one becomes impatient, but be assured that no matter how many hours are used to properly prepare for the actual building it is time well spent and will never be regretted. The full-size drawings from which molds and templates are made are especially valuable when more than one boat is to be built from the same plans, or for the construction of a one-design class sailboat where the hull must conform to reasonably close dimensional tolerances.

One must trace the history of shipbuilding to discover why the full-size hull lines are "laid down" on the "mold loft" floor. The full-size drawing board, so to speak, in a shipyard almost always consisted of a floor above a workshop of some sort, thus it was a loft. Molds or templates were taken off the full-size drawings, hence the terms "mold lofting," "laying down," and "taking off." The roof above the mold loft was preferably trussed, so there were no columns to obstruct the work, and there were windows on all sides and overhead to provide maximum light. The wooden floor was level and smooth, sufficiently sacred so some yards prohibited the wearing of hard-soled shoes. The floor was painted flat white or light gray, sometimes dull black, and on one edge of the floor there was a permanently fixed batten having an absolutely straight edge that served as a baseline.

There are exceptions to the need for complete mold lofting before starting hull construction since the introduction of computers. First, consider a hull that can be built of sheet materials like plywood, aluminum, steel, or even sheet fiberglass. The surfaces of such a hull must be "developable" so a flat sheet can form a surface without buckling. Not too long ago there were several methods available to the boat designer to draw developable surfaces, but it was usually a long, drawn-out, tedious, cut-and-try affair. The sections through a hull (see Figure 7-5 on page 145) were formed by a long method. This steel hull has three developable surfaces—the upper hull sides, the surfaces between the chines, and the bottom. With a computer and appropriate program, such hull lines can be done in a matter of a few hours. In fact, a computer and plotter combination can draw full-size patterns for the surfaces.

The end result is the availability of plans, mostly for small craft, with fully dimensioned hull parts so the shapes can be laid on the sheets and cut to size. Others offer full-size patterns; and then there are the firms that sell kits of preshaped hull parts. Many of these hulls are planned to be built by the "stitch-and-glue" method, details of which are discussed in Chapter 11. See the Appendix for sources, but read the catalogs carefully so you don't buy something that is not exactly what you want.

On the design side, the computer can do an enormous number of tasks for the naval architect, but these are beyond the scope of this book. So is metal hull construction, for that matter (see the Appendix "Recommended Reading"), but lofting applies to hulls of all materials, so a few remarks are in order.

There are metal hulls that cannot be built of steel or aluminum applied in flat sheets. Steel plates that need shaping to conform to lines plans are "furnaced" by heating and beating them over a form while red-hot. This is not a task for an amateur, no matter how ambitious.

Equipment in a steel boatbuilding yard includes a set of rollers, some-what like old-fashioned washing machine rollers, that can form a plate into a cylinder—though seldom a complete cylinder, unless for making a tank. The roller operator must know his business; most often just a portion of a plate is rolled.

Aluminum hulls, on the other hand, often need plates shaped, and much can be done by "bumping" in a press with a variety of dies. Paul Luke, of East Boothbay, Maine, demonstrated this for me while building a 40-foot deep-keel sailboat, and I have nothing but admiration for a master of this technique.

The point is, there is no escaping complete lofting of metal hulls too shapely to be constructed of flat sheets of aluminum or steel.

HULL LINES

The work of enlarging the plans from the scale of the blueprints to full size is termed mold lofting, for it is from these drawings that molds are made for the shape of the hull and various other parts. It is imperative to understand the different lines drawn by the architect or designer to define the hull shape; as an aid to the beginner, Figure 7-1—in which we cut up a model to illustrate the terminology—has been prepared. Some of the lines are obvious, because from reading the design sections of yachting magazines and from prowling around hulls under construction or stored in boatyards most of you are familiar with the first three lines drawn by the designer that really characterize a hull. These are the sheerline or edge of deck as seen from the side, the profile (the outline of the bottom and ends as seen from the side at the same time the sheerline is viewed), and the deck line, a gull's-eye view of the outline of the hull as seen from above. Although these lines are important, they do not provide sufficient information from which to build a hull. Also needed is the shape of the boat between the three lines. To provide points to define the hull shape between these lines, the designer cuts the hull, so to speak, into pieces on planes that conveniently establish points for dimensions. These planes are called waterlines, buttocks, and diagonals.

If a hull could be lifted straight up out of the water without the resulting hole filling in with water, the shape of the edge of the hole would be the same as the shape of the boat at the surface of the water. On the boat, this line is called the load waterline, and it is one of the most important lines drawn by the designer. For further subdivision the designer then divides

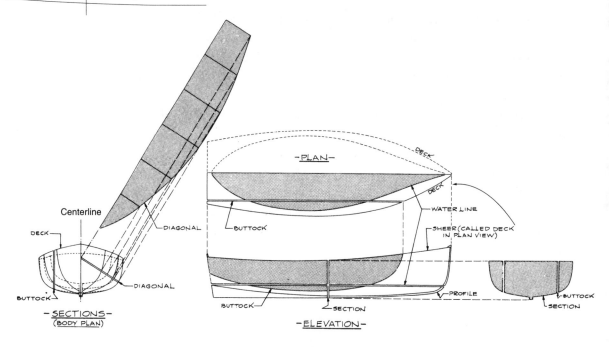

FIGURE 7-1.
A solid block half-model sawn (saw lines are the double lines) to pictorially show waterline, buttock, diagonal, and sectional planes. The shapes of the planes are shown by the shaded areas, and on the body plan it may be seen how a point on the hull is created wherever a buttock, diagonal, or waterline is intersected by an athwartship sectional plane.

the depth of the hull above and below the load waterline into convenient spaces, and draws the edges of additional horizontal planes, which, for the want of something better, are also called waterlines because they are parallel to the load waterline. Then there are vertical planes called buttocks, located parallel to the centerline of the boat and conveniently spaced outboard to each side of the centerline. Finally, the edges of inclined planes are drawn, and these are called *diagonals*, because they are drawn diagonal to the horizontal and vertical planes. These planes, like the others, are located to provide as many significant dimensioned points for the boatbuilder as is possible.

(Sometimes it is possible to define the shape of a hull without the use of diagonals, such as in Figure 1-7 in Chapter 1. In the case of a really simple hull with straight-line sections [see Figure 7-4], the sheer, deck line, chine, and/or profile provides a sufficient number of points from which to make the frames or molds. This eliminates the need for waterlines, buttocks, and diagonals, as explained a little further on.)

All of the aforesaid lines are fore-and-aft lines running the length of the hull, and although it has been mentioned above that these lines are drawn for the purpose of having points on the surface of the hull, actually no usable points are established until vertical planes *across* the hull have been drawn to intersect the fore-and-aft lines. The outlines or shapes formed by vertical transverse planes intersecting the horizontal, vertical, and diagonal fore-and-aft planes are called *sections*. A point on the hull is established wherever a section intersects one of the fore-and-aft lines, and by means of the many points of intersection it is possible for the builder to make molds for the exact shape of the hull as designed.

Sections may be compared to slices of bread. Just as is the case with the sections on a shapely boat, the slices through an old-fashioned rye loaf are all different, for the shape is ever-changing from end to end. A vessel's shape, then, can be transmitted into three-dimensional form by making full-size templates of the sections. When these are set up at each section's respective station the same as called for in the lines drawing, a vessel's shape in skeletal form has been established. The vessel's shape is represented in this manner just as a loaf of bread would be if every other slice was removed, while keeping the spacing of the remaining slices the same.

The various definitive lines in perspective. A rabbet line—indicating a slice or notch cut in a member to allow another piece to fit against it—is found usually in traditional wood construction (for example, the rabbet in the stem that the planking fits and is fastened to) but may or may not exist in other types of wood construction or in fiberglass or metal hulls. A bulwark is the cap on the sides of the hull, found mostly on large traditional wood boats.

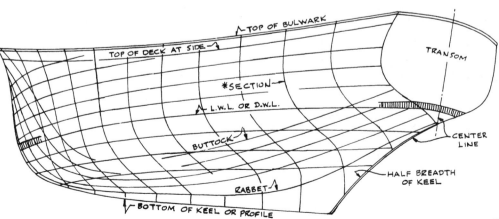

＊ SECTIONS SHOWN ARE LOCATED AT STATIONS.　　　　　　　　**FIGURE 7-2.**

FIGURE 7-3.

A typical lines plan (that is, the designer's drawing) and table of offsets for a round-bottomed boat, the same hull shown in Figure 7-1. On this plan are shown all the lines mentioned in the foregoing together with the necessary dimensions to reproduce them. (Incidentally, do not attempt to build a boat from these lines, as they are purely for illustration and have not been worked out for any specific purpose.) Note that spacing of waterlines, buttocks, and stations are indicated, as well as offsets for the profile of the stem, dimensions for the profile angle of the stern board (usually called a transom, although stern board is technically a more accurate description), and a table of dimensions for laying out all the fore-and-aft curved lines. Because of the nature of diagonals, their location can be indicated only in section—that is, on the body plan.

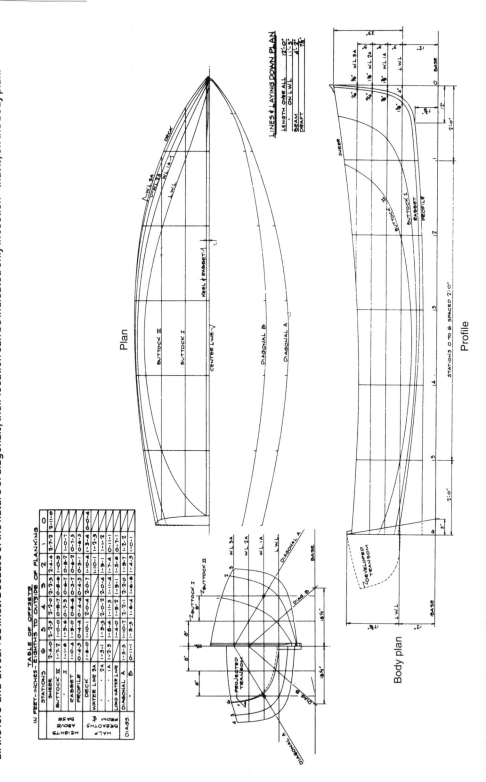

ABBREVIATIONS

Before we go any further, it should be pointed out that many sets of lines plans for hulls have abbreviations for words used thus far in this chapter, and it is a help for the reader to be familiar with them.

Centerline	C. L.
Waterline	W.L.
Load waterline	L.W.L.
Designed waterline	D.W.L.
Buttock	Butt. or Butt'k
Diagonal	Diag.
Baseline	B.L.
Station	Sta.
Frame	Fr.
Deck	Dk.
Length overall	L.O.A.
Section	Sect.
Displacement	Displ.
Salt water	S.W.
Fresh water	F.W.
Pounds	#
Longitudinal center of buoyancy	C.B. or L.C.B.
Center of gravity	C.G.
Longitudinal center of gravity	L.C.G.
Vertical center of gravity	V.C.G.

OFFSETS

An offset is simply another name for a dimension, and is always taken from a straight line of reference such as a baseline for the elevation drawing or the centerline in the case of the plan view of the lines. In other words, it is a dimension for a point that is *offset* from a straight line, the baseline or the centerline. Dimensions are tabulated, except for some very simple hulls. This convention was made standard in shipbuilding because it is obviously impossible to write out all the dimensions on a lines plan and not have them become confused.

To eliminate a multitude of fractional dimensions, it is customary to write offsets in feet-inches-eighths of inches. For example, 2-5-3 means two feet, five and three-eighths inches. (You will find that you will read them automatically once you have tried a few.) Some designers pride themselves on the accuracy of their lines and offsets and read some dimensions to one-sixteenth of an inch; this is shown in the offset table by a plus sign or ½ after the "eighth" numeral, thus we get 2-5-3+ or 2-5-$7/16$. One of these days metric offset tables will make life a lot simpler than struggling with feet, inches, and all those 64 fractions of an inch. Metric scales and full-size rules are easy to find.

The use of the offset table will be explained further along, but at this time it would be well to note that the lines for a vessel's hull are almost always drawn to the *outside* surface of the hull. Consequently, when molds are made, the thickness of the wood or fiberglass skin or the aluminum or steel plating must be deducted from the molds' lofted edges. The lines for metal ships or large wooden vessels with built-up sawn frames are often drawn to the *inside* of the plating or planking in order to save the mold loftsman from deducting the thickness from the full-size drawing of every frame, all of which must be drawn when sawn or metal frames are employed, for each frame is individually shaped before installation.

The hull lines discussed above are for a round-bottomed boat, the number of waterlines, buttocks, and diagonals involved depending upon the size of the boat. Other hull types have fewer lines. Figure 7-4 shows an ordinary, flat-bottomed rowboat (top illustration) having but four fore-and-aft lines (namely, the deck and sheer), and two views of the chine, which is the corner at the intersection of the side and bottom. Also shown are the lines for a v-bottomed boat (bottom illustration) having lines similar to a flattie except for the addition of a bottom profile. The sections of this particular boat consist of straight lines. If they were curved, other points would be needed to draw the sections, and these would be established by waterlines, buttocks, and diagonals.

There are also multi-chine hulls. A few traditional small craft built of wood were so shaped. Some steel hulls, generally workboats, may be multi-chine designs in order to dispense with the laborious shaping of hull plates. Figure 7-5 is the body plan for a multi-chine workboat hull.

THE MOLD LOFT

Although we have said that the builder's first step is lofting the hull, in reality the first thing is to find a place to do the job. At a minimum, the

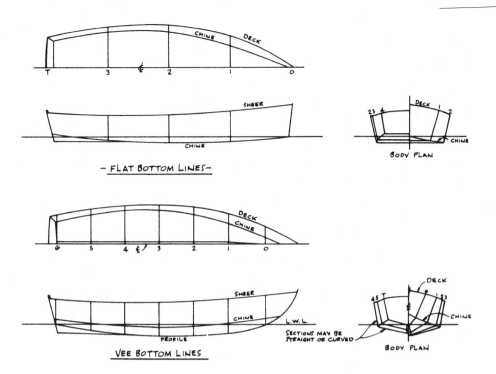

FIGURE 7-4.

Straight-sectioned hulls like the flat-bottomed skiff shown at the top have simple lines. Possible refinements, shown in the v-bottomed hull below, are curved sides above the chine and a curved stem profile.

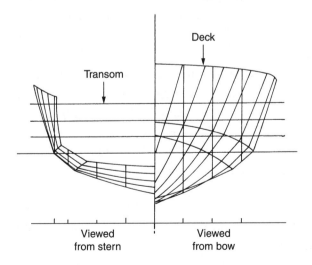

FIGURE 7-5.

Body plan for a multi-chine workboat hull. The left side of the plan is the view from aft; the right side shows the view from the bow.

space should be at least four or more feet longer than the boat in one direction, while in the other it must be equal to the distance from the baseline to the highest point of the sheer, or to the top of the cabin if its shape requires lofting, plus some space on all sides for working around the drawing. Well-equipped boatyards use a level wooden floor maintained for just this purpose that is sanded smooth and coated with flat light gray or white paint. It is too much to ask that an amateur have such facilities at his disposal, so the next best alternative would be a level space, such as a floor or platform, where paper or plywood may be used to lay down the lines.

If you can find it in a drafting room supply shop, the old-style buff detail paper (made up to 54" in width and in rolls 10, 20, and 50 yards long) is satisfactory for lofting small craft and is reasonably priced. Some of the paper-faced building panels are also all right, and so is plywood, as mentioned above, in standard-size panels that may be arranged edge to edge to make any size desired. Whatever the material, if several pieces are used to make up the required size, the pieces must be secured against movement.

LOFTING TOOLS

The tools for lofting are few and simple. To draw sharp lines, flat carpenter's pencils are used, sharpened to a chisel point so a thin line may be drawn for a long distance. Resharpen any kind of pencil in midstream to ensure fine lines. Colored pencils may also be used to advantage to make it easier to distinguish between different types of lines. For measuring, a steel or fiberglass tape longer than the boat is ideal, but an ordinary folding six-foot rule will do, and the rule can also be used to lay off many short dimensions. A large carpenter's square, either as manufactured or home-made out of ¼" or ⅜" wood, is needed for drawing lines perpendicular to other lines, such as for station lines in relation to the base and waterlines. You may also erect perpendiculars with a regular or improvised beam compass, as will be shown later. The adjustable bevel shown in Chapter 3, Figure 3-3, is a must; also needed is a straightedge 6 to 8 feet long, which you can make yourself from a piece of thin wood. For marking the really long, straight baselines and waterlines, you should use either a mason's chalk line, penciling the line on the floor before the chalk rubs off, or a length of light, strong fishing line stretched tightly between two nails, marking in points directly under the cord at intervals of about 3 feet, to be connected later with a straightedge.

BATTENS

Curves are said to be *fair* when they have no humps or bumps and are pleasing to the eye. To draw them, you must have a set of battens, which are nothing more than straight, square-edged pieces of clear white pine, basswood, mahogany, or other straight-grained wood. These should be at least two feet longer at each end than the line to be drawn. When the available stock isn't long enough for the job, battens can be made up of two pieces connected in the middle, where the curve is least, by making a long tapered glue splice of about 18" to 2 feet in length (a short splice will result in an unfair batten and therefore unfair curves). Or the line itself may be pieced if you make sure there is a fair overlap over the length of a couple of stations. For best results, you should use as stiff a batten as will go through all the points on the curve, for a stiff batten will tend to fair itself unless unduly forced, whereas a supple batten can be passed through all the points and not lie fair. It is difficult to say just what size battens should be used, as the correct size depends so much on the length of the line and the character of the curve.

A batten ½" to ¾" thick by 1½" to 2" wide, used on the flat, is suggested for relatively easy curves like the sheerline. For certain curves it may be necessary to taper the battens at the ends somewhat, with all the taper cut on one edge. For curves in the plan view, also known as the half-breadth plan, something like ½" × 1" or ½" × 1½" used on the flat, possibly tapered at the ends, or ¾" square and untapered might be tried. Like a lot of boatbuilding operations, accumulated experience will aid in the selection of batten sizes. If you have a table saw, start by making the battens on the heavy side until you get the hang of it, ripping the strips narrower as needed. Curves such as sections, the stem profile, and similar shapes will be drawn with shorter battens, probably ⅜" and ½" square, and inasmuch as these curves sometimes have harder bends in the middle than at the ends, such as around the turn of the bilge, they may have to be tapered in the middle in order to make a fair curve that touches all the points. These battens *must* be straight-grained material. A batten is held in place with finishing nails driven on both sides of it, not through it. Not necessary by any means, but very desirable from the standpoint of readily sighting the shape of a batten when sprung to a curve, is a coat of flat black paint. The contrast of the dark batten against the light-colored floor or paper will help detect a line that is not fair.

THE GRID

By examining the table of offsets in Figure 7-3, it will be seen that dimensions for the waterlines, buttocks, diagonals, sheer, and profile curves are laid out on the station lines and are measured above the baseline and out from the centerline. Therefore, it is the straight lines that must be laid down in the beginning. This group of lines, called the grid, is shown in Figure 7-6. You will note in Figure 7-7 that the grid is set up in a condensed form relative to the paper plans: the half-breadth plan is superimposed over the profile drawing to save space and to minimize the distances one must crawl on hands and knees when laying the lines down. (Some professionals save themselves from crawling around the loft floor by building a dolly of padded plywood mounted on low swivel casters.) Thus the grid is started by drawing a straight line that doubles both as the baseline for the profile view and the centerline for the half-breadth plan. The spacing of the stations is laid off along this line, and the stations are drawn in perpendicular to it.

The perpendiculars may be drawn either with a set of trammel points, a regular beam compass, or an improvised one, and is done as follows. Mark a point A (Station 2 has been used as a practical example in Figure 7-6); then using the compass with A as a center, strike an arc B equidistant to each side of point A. Lengthen the arm of the compass and, using each of the points B as a center, strike two intersecting arcs above the baseline. From the intersection C draw a straight line through A on the base. The line CA is perpendicular to the base. This method can be used at each station, or it can be used at only one, with the resulting right angle used to build a large square for drawing in the remainder of the stations perpendicular to the base. This is also shown in Figure 7-6.

The spacing of the waterline planes in profile relative to the baseline and that of the buttock planes in the half-breadth plan relative to the hull centerline are taken from the designer's lines plan.

As mentioned above, the offsets for the curves are dimensioned as heights above the baseline or distances out from the centerline as the case may be. Some of the dimensions will be long enough that you will not be able to tell readily whether the end of your rule is exactly on the line or not. To be sure of this and to save time, it makes sense to nail a batten against the underside of the baseline as shown in Figure 7-6. The end of the rule can then be butted against it when making measurements. Instead of a batten, a nail may be driven at each intersection of a station with the base. You will find either way to be very helpful and certainly easier on the knees. Using the rule can also then remain a one-person job.

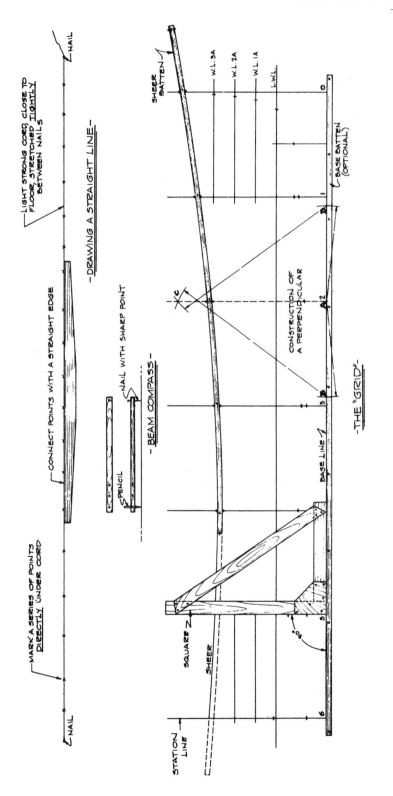

FIGURE 7-6.

The grid for full-size hull lines is made up of straight lines and is laid out on a suitable floor. In addition to the straight lines, this illustration shows the sheerline batten, which has been added by marking sheer measurements from the table of offsets, starting at station 0 (bow) and connecting those positions with a batten.

SHEERLINE AND DECK LINE

Either the sheerline or the deck line will be the first curved line to be drawn and faired. For the sake of argument we will select the sheerline, which the table of offsets, Figure 7-3, shows is dimensioned above the baseline. Starting at the bow, Station 0, the table reads 2-11-0 for the height of the sheer; so with the rule against the nail or batten measure up two feet, eleven inches above the base on Station 0 and make a mark. Move the rule over to Station 1, read 2-7-2 from the table and make a mark 2' 7¼" above the base. The process is repeated similarly at all of the stations.

With all the points marked, it is time to select a batten with which to draw the sheerline, placing it so that it extends beyond the length of the boat at each end. With one edge of the batten against the sheer point on a station amidships, Station 3 of the boat we are using as an example, drive a pair of finishing nails to hold the batten in place. Now fasten the batten at Station 2, then at Station 4, alternating toward the ends of the boat until the batten is sprung to and fastened at all the points. The batten's ends, which project beyond the boat, should be sprung to extend the curve fairly and then secured.

After the batten is secured for the entire length, sight along it to see whether there are any unfair or lumpy spots in the curve. If so, pull the nails at the stations adjacent to the unfairness and note the result. If the batten moves very far from one of the points and still does not appear to be fair, pull other nails and make adjustments, giving here and taking there until the resulting line is pleasing to the eye. You may expect points to be out of line occasionally because the designer has drawn the lines to a small scale compared to the full-size job; thus errors are bound to creep into the work. However, it must be remembered that the batten should be shifted as little as possible to obtain a sweet and true curve without hard spots.

The deck line is faired in the same manner after it has been laid down from offsets measured out from the centerline.

PROFILE AND RABBET

After the deck line has been drawn in and faired, you can continue working on the profile plan, drawing and fairing the profile (bottom of keel), the stem, and the rabbet. The rabbet line is normally found in traditional wooden construction, although it may or may not exist in other types of wooden hull construction, or in fiberglass or metal hulls. For these latter hulls, a similar line may be referred to by some other name. In any case, the lines plan will make all this clear.

The profile and rabbet must be faired in so that they will meet the relatively quick curves of the stem and stem rabbet. With these bow curves not yet drawn in, the best way to ensure that the two sets of curves will meet fairly is to extend the rabbet and profile forward beyond the point of tangency with the stem and its rabbet. You will note that this has been done in Figure 7-7, immediately to the left of the bold letter A.

The stem profile and the stem rabbet are drawn with a thin batten, as mentioned previously. When points for the stem curves have been marked in from the dimensions on the lines plan, a nail is driven at each spot, the batten is bent against the nails, and other nails are driven on the opposite side of the batten to hold it in place.

If your particular plans give a half-siding for the rabbet, this should be drawn in next before going on to the body plan. This also has been done in Figure 7-7.

BODY PLAN SECTIONS

It is strongly recommended that the body plan be drawn on a separate portable board called a *scrive* (pronounced screeve) *board.* Such a board is easy to move around to suit making molds, and it avoids confusion of lines on the floor. Referring to the body plan for the lines in Figure 7-3 (page 142), you can see that the board or paper used for the sections must be somewhat wider than the boat and at least as high as the distance from the baseline to the sheer at Station 0, the bow. Begin by drawing the baseline; then draw the centerline perpendicular to the base. The waterlines are drawn in parallel to the base, the buttocks parallel to the centerline, and the diagonals exactly as dimensioned on the lines plan. Trouble will result if the waterlines and the buttocks of the body plan are not spaced *exactly* the same as they were laid out on the half-breadth and profile plans.

Cut a few ¾" × ¾" wood strips and square the ends. The size of the hull being lofted dictates the length of the sticks, but generally the greatest length needed is the distance from the baseline to the highest point of the sheerline. These measuring sticks, useful on all four sides when made square instead of flat, are variously called "pick-up sticks" or "pick-up battens," or sometimes "story poles," and eliminate the necessity of accurately reading and recording numerous measurements from a rule. A stick in the pick-up position is shown at Station 4 in Figure 7-7.

To start the full-size body plan, the half-breadths of the deck line and the height of the sheer and rabbet are picked up and transferred to the scrive board (Figure 7-8). Align the end of a stick against the baseline and

FIGURE 7-7.

The lofted hull lines are arranged differently from those on a designer's plan to save space on the mold loft floor. The pick-up stick shown eliminates the need for repeatedly measuring from a ruler—see text.

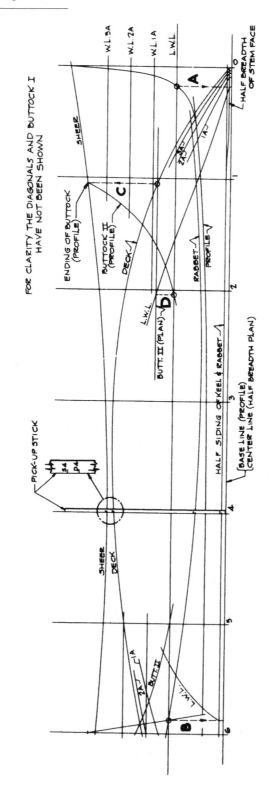

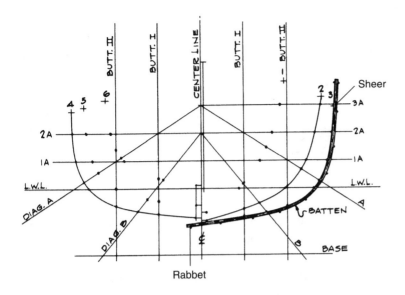

FIGURE 7-8.

The body plan is best drawn on a portable surface called a scrive board. Here a batten has been laid down at Station 3—note how the batten extends beyond the sheer and the rabbet.

mark the half-breadths and heights on a stick with a sharp pencil, being careful to identify each mark with a symbol and station number.

With the end of the pick-up stick at the baseline of your body plan, mark the heights of the sheer and rabbet on the centerline. Draw short horizontal lines at each rabbet point and draw in the width of the rabbet. Draw horizontal lines at each sheer height, and with the pick-up stick against the centerline of the body plan, mark the deck width corresponding to each station. At each intersection of sheer and deck draw a small cross and label it with the station number. Each section now has two definite points: the sheer height/ deck width intersection, and the intersection of the rabbet height and width.

Now to fill in some of the points in between. Nail a batten against one side of the centerline on the body plan, and with the rule laid on a waterline with its end against the centerline batten, mark points for all the waterline half-breadths from the offset table and label each one. For instance, lay the rule on waterline 2A to the right of the centerline and from the offset table under Station 1 mark off 1-1-2, put a little circle around it with a 1 next to it to show it is a point on the section at Station 1; then mark 1-9-1 for Station 2, and so on. Do the same with the offsets for the other waterlines. With the waterlines done, go on to the buttocks. Place the rule on Buttock I with the end of the rule at the base and mark all the heights for Buttock I from the offset table. Follow with Buttock II. Then lay the rule along the diagonal with the end of the rule again at the centerline and lay off all the diagonal offsets along the diagonal lines. Move the batten to the left side of the centerline and lay out all the waterline, buttock, and diagonal offsets for the sections in the stern half of the boat. All the layout and transfer of measurements should be done with utmost care and accuracy. In the end, the time spent to this end will speed the job to completion faster than if the work is done in a slipshod manner.

BODY PLAN BATTENS

Nails are driven at all the reference marks on each section. Then a batten is bent around the nails of each section, using a batten long enough to extend 6" or so above the sheer point and beyond the rabbet at the centerline, as shown in Figure 7-8. Holding the sheer and rabbet points as definitely fixed by the previous fairing of these lines, examine the batten carefully and shift it, if necessary, to get a smooth, true curve. Before doing any shifting, remember that points established by lines crossing other lines at right angles, or nearly so, are more accurate than those established by crossings at acute angles. When two lines intersect at an acute angle, it is difficult to tell precisely at which spot on a line the crossing occurs; consequently it is possible for the designer, working from his small-scale drawing, to misread offsets taken from such intersections (see Figure 7-9). With this fact in mind, it is readily seen that for the flat part of the bottom sections, the best points are given by the buttocks. The waterlines give the most unreliable points for the same parts of the sections, but on the other hand, they are the best for the topside sections. Points may also be out due to mistakes in the designer's scaling technique (although less so in the age of computers). As a result, all the points on one line, such as a diagonal, may appear to be out by the same amount. In such a situation these points may be ignored, the other points being held if they give a fair section or line.

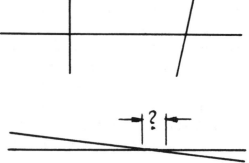

FIGURE 7-9.
When lines intersect acutely, it is difficult to determine the location of points, leading to the misreading of offsets. Strive instead to establish points where lines cross more at right angles: the best points are given by buttocks; waterlines provide the most unreliable points.

FAIRING DIAGONALS

Fair the diagonals first, because they are laid out to cross the majority of the sections at a good angle. Lay a pick-up stick along a diagonal in the body plan, and mark and identify all the points where it crosses the sections; then move the batten to the half-breadth plan and mark each diagonal half-breadth on its proper station. The diagonal is then faired, again proceeding as described for the sheerline. If the batten will not go through all the points and at the same time produce a fair line, the usual adjustments must be made. Bearing in mind not to make more changes than are necessary, the sections on the body plan are then corrected accordingly.

LONG LINE ENDINGS

When fairing the long fore-and-aft lines, it is necessary to terminate them correctly. The location of waterline endings is fairly simple. Considering the bow in Figure 7-7, the profile of the stem has been faired and drawn permanently. Each intersection of the stem profile with one of the waterlines is a definite point in the profile plan, and the corresponding point in the half-breadth plan is found simply by projecting the intersection in the profile down to the line representing the half siding of the stem face in the half-breadth plan as shown in A in Figure 7-7. The aft endings are done exactly the same way, as indicated at B in the stern end of the same figure. It is obvious that in this particular design only the L.W.L. ends within the boat at the stern, because the other waterlines cross the section at Station 6.

Buttock endings are also quite simple. A short length of a buttock is drawn in plan to cross the deck line, and then the point of crossing is projected to the sheer. The intersection with the sheer is the ending of the buttock in the profile view as shown at C in Figure 7-7. When drawing the waterlines and buttocks, fairing points in addition to those on stations are established wherever a waterline and a buttock cross. D in Figure 7-7 illustrates how the crossing of the L.W.L. and Buttock II in profile projected to Buttock II in plan gives another point on the L.W.L. in plan.

The determination of a diagonal ending at the stem is somewhat more difficult to understand; therefore the steps taken are shown in Figure 7-10, which should be self-explanatory.

The preceding explanation of lofting a round-bottomed boat is modified for other types such as v- and arc-bottomed hulls; generally speaking, the latter types are easier to loft. However, all boats except double-enders have

FIGURE 7-10.

Four steps in finding the correct ending of a diagonal that crosses the face of the stem. (1) Measure length diagonal 1 below waterline 2a from the body plan; (2) move to the profile plan and lay off diagonal 1 below waterline 2a; (3) project that point to the centerline of the half-breadth plan; and (4) using measurement of diagonal 2 from body plan, find the end of diagonal b at the intersection of line x and that added radius.

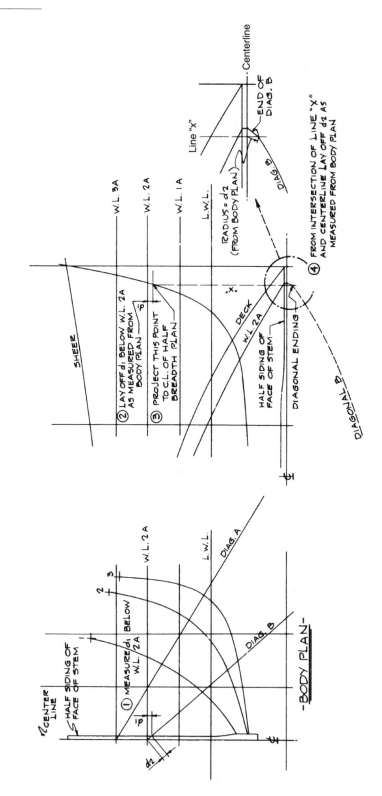

one additional lofting problem in common, and that is the development of the transom or stern board (unless it is flat across and vertically plumb).

Now that offsets and the grid have been explained, let's digress by going back to the little round-bottomed hull shown in Figure 7-3 and consider just one station, the one labeled Station 3. I will describe how each point on the section is established on the body plan grid, assuming that the grid (centerline, baseline, waterline planes, buttock and diagonal planes) has been accurately drawn full size using the dimensions on the designer's lines plan (for example, waterline plane spacing above baseline, buttock spacing from centerline and diagonal locations as dimensioned on the lines plan drawing; see Figure 7-11).

Incidentally, some naval architects do not like the lines drawing to be cluttered with dimensions, so they put these and the table of offsets on a separate drawing.

Returning to Figure 7-11, point A for the sheerline is made by picking up the *deck half-breadth* and the *sheer height above base* from the lines as you

FIGURE 7-11.

The origins of the many dimensions when lofting a section—here Station 3—from the round-bottomed skiff in Figure 7-3 (page 142).

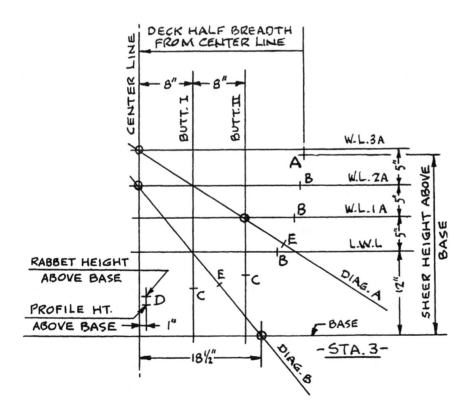

laid them down prior to working up the body plan—the full-size drawing shown in the making in Figure 7-7. To add a little emphasis, the body plan sections are *not* made from the numbers in the table of offsets.

The *waterline half-breadths*, B, are picked up likewise and laid off on the body plan grid, also the *buttock heights above base,* points C.

The profile and rabbet *half-breadths* are as dimensioned on the half-breadth plan and as laid down full size beforehand; the profile and rabbet *heights above base*, points D, are also picked up, but from the profile view of your full-size lines plan, like the one in Figure 7-7.

The points E for the diagonals are picked up and laid off on the full-size body plan, the one under discussion, along the diagonal lines dimensioned by the designer.

PROJECTED TRANSOM

After the sections (that is, the stations) have been faired satisfactorily, it is time to consider the development of the true shape of the transom or stern board of the boat. Sometimes, the transom is plumb vertical, in which case the section drawn at the transom station is actually the shape of the transom. More often, the transom is raked, with the result that its true shape does not appear in the body plan. This view is meaningless to the builder and need not be reproduced full size on the mold loft floor. The same is true of the plan view of the transom, although it may be useful for obtaining transom bevels.

The only way that a true view, and thus a pattern, of a raked transom can be gotten is if its shape is projected square off its centerline in the profile view.

FLAT TRANSOM DEVELOPMENT

Development of the shape of the transom is sometimes puzzling to the builder, but there is nothing really mysterious about the work. The 12-foot rowboat has a flat transom of the simplest type, and its transom shape development is shown in Figure 7-12 (page 160). The rake of the transom in profile has, of course, been previously drawn from dimensions given on the naval architect's lines plan. For ease of illustration, the centerline for the developed transom has been drawn at the stern end of the lines in Figure 7-12, but this is not necessary and it may be located on a separate board or piece of paper.

The transom is just the same as any section, except that it is located at an angle with the baseline instead of perpendicular to it. Points on the transom are taken from the waterlines and buttocks the same as ordinary sections: it is merely a matter of picking up the waterline half-breadths and buttock heights at the right places and transferring them to the development drawing.

If you have space for the transom drawing at the end of your lines, as shown in Figure 7-12, the development is exactly as indicated in the diagram. However, if you must locate the grid for the transom plan elsewhere, there is one important point to remember throughout the development, or you may end up with a stern board that will not fit as it should. On the profile drawing of the lines, the waterlines are spaced 5" apart above the L.W.L., but due to the profile angle of the transom, the distance between the waterlines drawn across the transom grid is obviously greater than 5". Therefore, when laying out the grid, the spacing must be carefully measured *along the centerline* of the transom.

In Figure 7-12 the centerline for the transom grid has been drawn parallel to the rake of the transom, and then the intersections of waterlines and the sheer with the transom in profile are projected across the centerline together with projections of the buttock and rabbet intersections with the transom's face. With a flat transom, as in the design for this rowboat, you can lay off the spacing of the buttocks the same as they are on the body and the half-breadth plans, and draw them in the grid parallel to the transom centerline. Two points, P, are established on the transom development where the buttocks thus drawn cross the lines projected from the buttocks in profile. Lay off d, the width of the rabbet, to locate another point, R.

Now project the intersections of the waterlines and buttocks with the transom profile down to the centerline of the half-breadth plan. The waterline half-breadths a, b, and c are picked up with a batten and laid off as points A, B, and C on the corresponding lines in the grid. With all the points spotted, draw in the transom with a batten the same as you did the regular sections.

If you must draw the transom on a separate sheet, very carefully pick up the spacing of the intersections along the profile of the transom on a batten, as shown in Figure 7-12, and complete location of points as described above.

The shape thus developed describes the transom's outside face; and for a metal transom this is all that has to be done. In a wooden hull, however, the transom consists of the planking and the frame, and professionals add the thickness of the parts together and develop another shape the resulting distance forward of the first. This gives the shape of the forward face of the transom frame and, consequently, the bevels. This will become clear when we discuss hull construction.

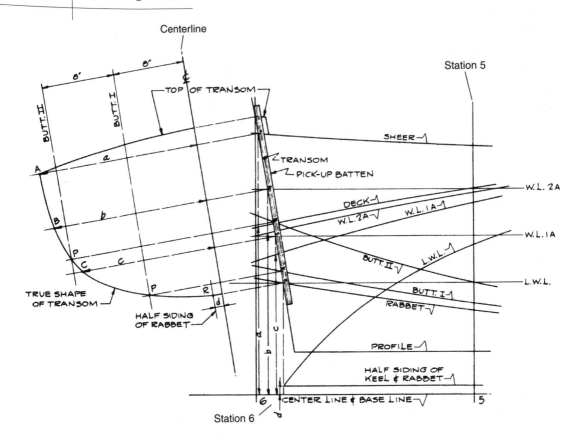

FIGURE 7-12.
Development of a flat transom drawing for a 12-foot rowboat. The centerline has been drawn parallel to the rake of the transom.

CURVED TRANSOM DEVELOPMENT

A curved transom on either a sailboat or powerboat is very handsome, and although the development is more involved than for the flat type, the extra work is worthwhile when the transom's finished appearance is considered. From the aesthetic viewpoint, a curved transom is not generally necessary on small craft up to 20 or 25 feet overall, but above this range the curved transom becomes a necessity, and for good looks it is an absolute must on a hull with an overhanging counter stern. This type is the most difficult to develop, due to the combination of the radius to which it is built and the angle of the transom in profile. The planks forming such a transom are bent to the arc of a circle with a radius perpendicular to the after side of the transom as seen in profile. A pattern for the shape must be made, and this is accomplished as though a cylinder were cut and rolled out flat.

A transom proportioned as shown in Figure 7-13 is developed principally with buttocks, because they cross the edges of the transom more nearly at right angles than do the waterlines, and thus are the most accurate. By this time you are familiar with buttocks and must realize that those on the naval architect's lines plan are not the only ones it is possible to have on a hull. There are an infinite number, and they may be spaced as closely as needed to help you make proper templates for parts. The stern in Figure 7-13 has been purposely drawn with enough buttocks to develop the transom accurately, but ordinarily, extra buttocks for development of the transom must be added between those shown on the lines plan.

Before the transom is attempted, the hull lines have been completely faired full size, usually to a station beyond the transom. To be sure of the shape of his hull, the naval architect designs to a vertical station at the extreme stern and then cuts it off at the desired angle in profile and in a radius in the plan view as mentioned above.

There are undoubtedly many methods of transom development in use and sworn to by their advocates. However, the system illustrated here will at least help the reader understand the principle. To avoid confusion, the profile and half-breadth plans of the stern in Figure 7-13 have been drawn separated and the transom radius made smaller than usual to clarify the drawing. Dashed lines show the projection of one view to another. After following the development of the flat transom in Figure 7-12, the use of the buttocks in Figure 7-13 is obvious, with the exception of their spacing in the grid for the expansion.

Extend the after side of the transom in profile up clear of other drawings, A in Figure 7-13, and draw a centerline perpendicular to it. Tangent to the intersection, swing an arc of radius as shown on the plans. This is the curve to which the transom planking will be bent when it is built. Draw the buttocks parallel to the centerline, spaced the same as in the half-breadth plan. Project the intersections of the buttocks with the arc down to cross the corresponding buttocks in the profile view. Now prepare the grid for the expanded transom, B in Figure 7-13, spacing the buttocks out from the centerline as measured *around the arc* instead of as laid out in the half-breadth plan. These measurements give the true distances between the buttocks when the cylindrical transom is rolled out flat. Project the buttocks in profile to the grid to obtain points on the edge of the transom as was done in the flat transom, Figure 7-12. For clarity only one buttock, Buttock II, has been used as an example in Figure 7-13.

FIGURE 7-13.

Steps in the development of a curved transom on the grid.

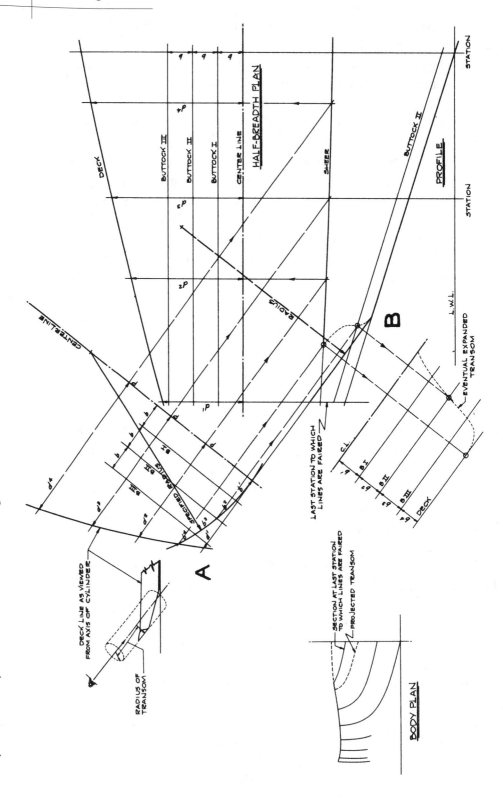

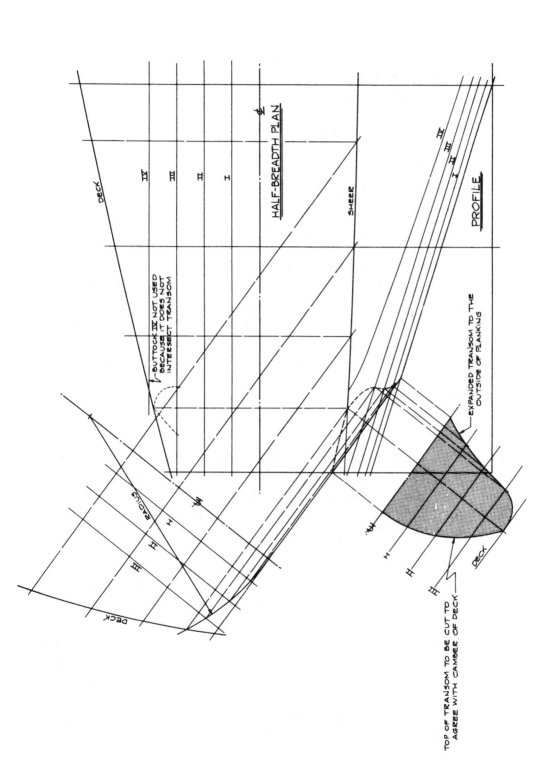

DECK

IV

III

II

I

HALF-BREADTH PLAN

SHEER

BUTTOCK IV NOT USED
BECAUSE IT DOES NOT
INTERSECT TRANSOM

IV
III
II
I

PROFILE

RADIUS

IV
III
II
I

DECK

EXPANDED TRANSOM TO THE
OUTSIDE OF PLANKING

II

III

DECK

TOP OF TRANSOM TO BE CUT TO
AGREE WITH CAMBER OF DECK

FIGURE 7-14.

The complete development of the curved transom started in Figure 7-13.

In order to find the point where the transom terminates at the sheerline, the deck line is drawn in the auxiliary projection shown in A in Figure 7-13. To draw the deck line in this view, select convenient points (P) along the projection's centerline; square them above the centerline and also down to cross the sheer on the profile; and then square the points of intersection with the sheer parallel to the stations to cross the deck line in the half-breadth plan. The widths of the deck at these points are lifted and transferred to the auxiliary projection, and a batten is run through them. The corner of the transom at the deck is located where the deck line intersects the arc of the transom. The half-breadth of the point is measured from the centerline around the arc and duly transferred to the grid.

ELLIPTICAL TRANSOM DEVELOPMENT

Curved transoms on "traditional" hull designs such as Grand Banks schooners and many yachts patterned after the type do not have a sharp corner at the intersection of deck and transom; the resulting shape is then elliptical when viewed from astern. This shape really blends well with a saucy sheerline and a spoon bow or a clipper bow. To prove that the development of an elliptical transom is not a recent problem, reproduced here is a development method drawn by naval architect R. B. Cook in 1913.

Mr. Cook's method has been redrawn in order to reproduce properly; the original handwritten instructions are best understood in print as follows:

1. Fair out lines completely before attempting development of transom.

2. Draw top of deck at centerline in profile, crossing transom face at A. Project this intersection to A′ and A″ as shown.

3. From A′ sweep desired arc representing deck ending, A′B. Project B′ and B″. B′ is the first point in the profile of the transom.

4. Using point B″ as a guide, sketch transom in body plan to conform in general to last station. Cross with closely spaced waterlines 1, 2, 3, et cetera, and project them to the sheer plan; project intersections with the transom face to half-breadth plan.

5. From B′ draw a line parallel to waterline, intersecting transom face at D. Project to centerline of half-breadth plan, point D′. Sweep arc D′B. With same radius sweep arcs from 1, 2, 3, et cetera, pick up half-breadths on body plan of 1, 2, 3, et cetera, and lay off on half-breadth plan as chords to arcs, resulting in points 1′, 2′, 3′, et cetera, giving shape of half-breadth projection of transom face.

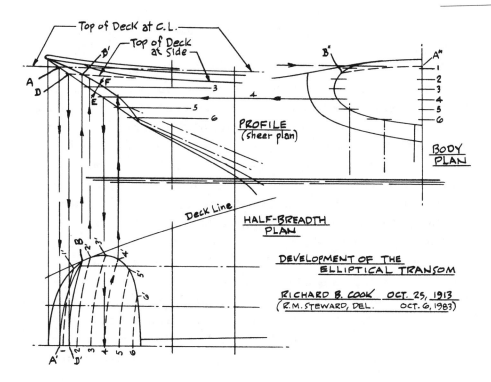

FIGURE 7-15.
Development of an elliptical transom as might be found on a Grand Banks schooner or yachts based on that type.

6. Project points 1', 2', 3', et cetera, to the profile to intersect the waterlines projected from the body plan, then draw the edge of the transom in profile.

Note: The arcs 1-1', 2-2', 3-3', et cetera, are sections through the transom face parallel to the waterline. The true amount of curvature is measured perpendicular to the face of the transom, as at E-F.

Although Mr. Cook showed on his drawing how buttocks can be used to generate additional points on the transom edge, he did not mention this in his instructions. Nevertheless, that procedure is presented (and repeated) elsewhere in this chapter.

POWERBOAT TRANSOMS

Sailboat transoms often have considerable rake, as shown in Figures 7-13 and 7-14, but there is usually little angle to those on modern power cruisers. A small amount of rake may be neglected in the development of the transom, and the radius can be drawn directly on the half-breadth plan, as will be explained.

Many powerboat transoms have "tumblehome"—that is, the deck half-breadth at the transom is less than the half-breadths of some of the waterlines between the L.W.L. and the deck. The transom in Figure 7-15 has tumblehome even though it is not a powerboat. Regardless of the type of hull, tumblehome causes waterlines to pile up on each other in the half-breadth plan, which can become very confusing. This is a good reason to use colored pencils to distinguish one waterline from another.

Draw the profile angle of the transom and project every intersection of it with the profile view of a waterline or buttock up to the centerline in the half-breadth plan. Holding the specified radius constant throughout, swing an arc from each of the projected points on the centerline (using the C.L. as center for the radius) until the arc crosses the line on the half-breadth plan corresponding to the line in profile. Project the half-breadth intersections with the arcs back down to the corresponding lines in profile and then across to the grid (A in Figure 7-16). Of course it is important that the buttocks on the grid are spaced as measured around the arc (B in Figure 7-16).

The development is the shape of the outside edge of the transom planking, but allowance must be made for the bevel on the edges, which causes the transom to be larger on the inside than on the outside face. When making the transom frame, the planking thickness must be deducted before the allowance for beveling can be made.

ADDITIONAL STUDY OF THE LOFTING PROCESS

Over the years many books have been published entirely devoted to lofting. In my library I have two old books, both for the most part done by naval architects, both principally about lofting for steel construction but also including lofting of wooden hulls. They are World War I vintage, when there must have been a shortage of people with lofting skills to keep up with the wartime demand for ships. These books are instructive, though in this age of computers they are not needed, at least not for professionally built and larger vessels. But I have no doubt there will always be a need for lofting the hulls for small craft, if for no other reason than to save cost for the builder of small boats, amateur or professional. I was indeed gratified to learn that the late John Gardner encouraged students at Mystic Seaport to read this chapter.

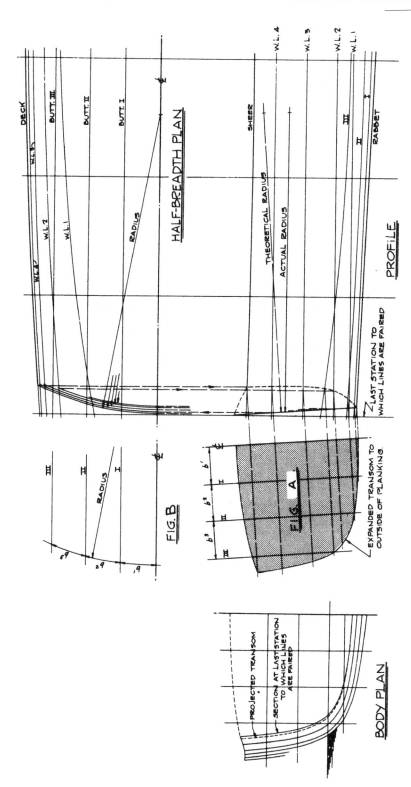

FIGURE 7-16.

The complete development of the grid lines of a curved transom having little rake.

For further information on lofting, the reader can refer to a variety of books (particularly Allan Vaitses's *Lofting*, still in print), magazine articles, DVDs, and websites. Many of the boatbuilding schools have modules on lofting—worth considering if you are thinking of taking on a biggish project as a first-timer.

COMPUTER LOFTING

The high-tech techniques of shipbuilding, where design and fabrication are integrated in CAD/CAM systems, are gradually making their way into boatbuilding, especially among professional builders. For these applications, hand drafting and the entire lofting process is a thing of the past. Even a small design shop nowadays is able to put out full-size patterns of molds and other parts, often produced in Mylar or other dimensionally stable and durable films. Many of the kit boats and semi-kits available nowadays use these methods and dispense with lofting altogether. But there is a certain magic to the process of converting a faceless table of offsets into the curves that will define your boat—a process that will inevitably involve the lofter's own artistry in the final adjustments. I encourage you to take on the challenge if you have the choice: you may find it to be one of the most satisfying aspects of the entire boatbuilding adventure.

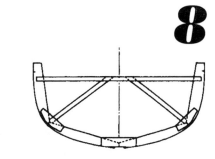

8

MOLDS, TEMPLATES, AND THE BACKBONE

UPON COMPLETION OF THE FULL-SIZE drawings of the lines for the hull, the builder is at last ready to start cutting wood—be it frames for a sawn-frame boat, molds for a round-bottomed hull, or a male plug for a fabric-reinforced resin or cold-molded wooden hull.

Molds are made from the body plan, and because they are only temporary, they are made from lower grade lumber than that used for the boat parts. Any lumber except hardwood is suitable, the thickness of the molds varying with the size of the boat. A rough guide is ¾" for boats to 16 feet, ⅞" for 16 to 24 feet, and 1" or 1⅛" for 30-footers. As you will see further along, the molds are set up on the backbone or keel of the boat, and strips of wood called ribbands are bent around the molds similar to planking, except that ribbands have spaces between them. The frames for a round-bottomed boat are bent to shape against the ribbands. There are two schools of thought as to whether the frames should be bent inside or outside of the ribbands, but it will be observed as experience is gained that setting up the frame for the boat is simplified when the frames are bent inside the ribbands. When a number of boats are to be built alike, it is advantageous to make a permanent mold, in which case the frames are bent outside and the mold is removed for further use when the hull has been planked. Also, when a round-bottomed hull is built upside down, the frames are bent on the outside.

The lines for the 12-footer in Figure 7-3, like those for all small boats, are drawn to the outside of planking, and the full-size lines are lofted accordingly. For setups where the frames are bent *inside* the ribbands, the molds for the sections are made only after the thickness of the planking has been deducted. Similarly, frames for conventional v-bottomed boats are made only after the thickness of planking has been deducted. It should be obvious after you have studied construction that to make a mold for a round-bottomed boat with the frames bent on the *outside* of the ribbands, the combined thickness of planking, framing, and ribbands must be deducted from the sections that are drawn to the outside of the planking.

FIGURE 8-1.

Planking thickness can be deducted simply by drawing a section that is parallel with and inside the true section, and separated from it at all points by the amount of the planking thickness. However, this is not the most accurate method. The shape of the section will be transferred to the mold stock by pressing the lumber down against the closely spaced tacks (see later in this chapter).

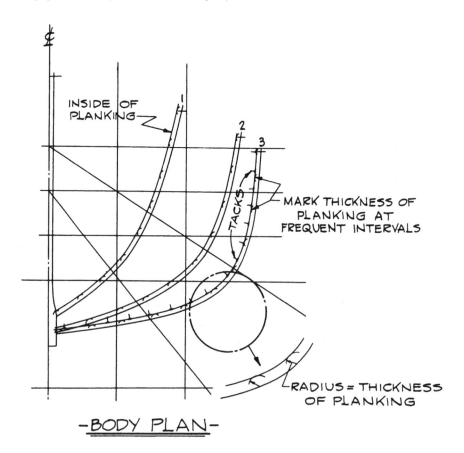

For methods other than conventional wooden construction, the ways of getting the deductions depend upon the peculiarities of each construction type. To make a male plug that will be used to form a female mold for a fiberglass hull, only the thickness of the plug planking or covering need be deducted. To make a male mold (or plug or jig—call it what you will) for a so-called one-off fiberglass sandwich hull as described in Chapter 5, "Fiberglass and Other Hull Materials," the deduction must be equal to the *outer* FRP skin thickness plus the core material thickness plus the ribband thickness. To make a male plug for a cold-molded hull, the deduction must be equal to the total thickness of the hull planking plus the thickness of the plug planking or ribbands.

Countless boats have been built from molds where planking thickness was deducted by simply drawing lines inside the sections by the amount of the planking thickness (Figure 8-1). *However, this method is acceptable only when the planking is thin.* Let me try to simplify this. If a hole was drilled through the planking, and the thickness of the planking was measured in the hole, the planking would measure correctly *only if the hole were at right angles (normal) to the surface of the hull.* (See Figure 8-2.) By the same token, such a hole would represent a truly accurate deduction only when *the hole itself* lies in the same athwartships plane as the stations. Thus, in a shapely hull, the deductions would be fairly accurate amidships, where the plan view waterlines run approximately parallel to the hull's centerline, but as the waterlines break away sharply toward the centerline as one progresses to the ends of the hull, the deductions would become increasingly inaccurate.

FIGURE 8-2.

Deductions for planking thickness are truly accurate only at right angles.

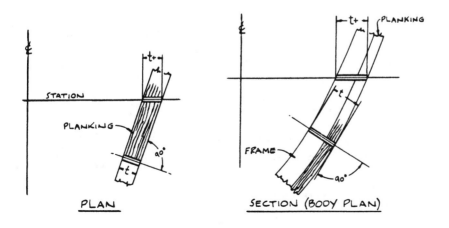

PLAN   SECTION (BODY PLAN)

Unless the planking is thin, it is best to take a little more time and make an effort to deduct planking thickness more accurately. To make the thickness deduction almost absolutely correct, it should be done on the diagonals, even to the extent of adding diagonals in addition to those shown on the lines plan, but this chore is not necessary in most cases. Rather than use this procedure, at each station lay off the planking thickness parallel to the waterlines in the plan view of the lines, then pick up this thickness along the station line and transfer it to the body plan, laying it off normal to the section. (See Figure 8-3.) When this has been done at each waterline, take a batten and draw through all the points to get the inside of planking. Once you have done this for a few points, the work will go quite rapidly.

When all the sections have been redrawn to the inside of planking, the molds for a round-bottomed boat can be made (unless additional deductions are required, depending on construction alternatives, as explained earlier in this chapter). Figure 8-4 shows typical mold construction, and Figure 8-1 shows how the shape of the section is transferred to the mold stock by pressing the lumber down against closely spaced tacks with their heads laid on the line to be reproduced. Turn the wood over, use a batten to connect the marks made by the tack heads, then work the board to the line. Do this for each station.

FIGURE 8-3.

Deducting planking thickness on the diagonals at each station on the waterline plan and transferring that measurement to the body plan is more accurate than marking planking thickness on the body plan (see Figure 8-1).

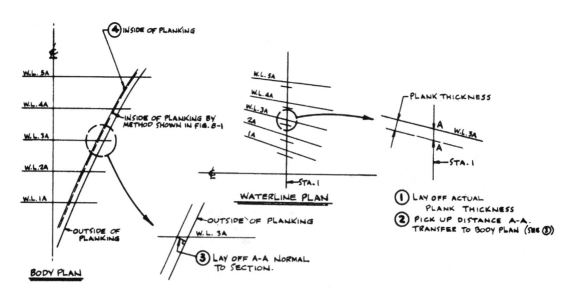

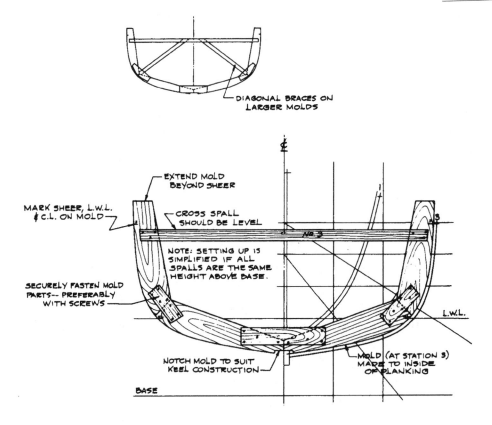

FIGURE 8-4.
Typical mold construction—this mold at Station 3 as seen in Figure 8-1. Molds must be well fastened and braced to retain their shape when set up.

It is not practical to use boards wide enough to get out an entire half mold all in one piece. Plywood of sufficient thickness would be too expensive compared to #2 or #3 solid lumber. Therefore, the mold is made in as many parts as necessary, and laid out in any convenient manner to suit the lumber stock. Just remember that the mold must not be too flimsy. Normally the mold should be extended a half foot or so above the sheerline, but if it is planned to build the boat upside down—a logical method for some small craft—the molds should be extended to a straight baseline above the sheer that represents the building floor. (See Figure 9-1 in Chapter 9.) Depending on the size of the boat, the inverted baseline is made parallel to the waterlines, and at a height enabling the greater part of the hull to be planked from a normal standing position.

Lay the mold parts on the sections of the body plan while carefully fastening them together with screws and butt blocks. Before the half mold is lifted from the plan, mark it at the deck line and L.W.L. for reference while setting up and building. Turn the first half of the mold over so that the butt blocks are down and make a second half to match it. When the mold is assembled, the butt blocks will then all be on the same side. Connect the two halves at the bottom with a block, which should be notched if required by the keel construction, and fasten a crosspiece, called a *spall*, at or near the deck line. Spalls on all molds should be level, and if they all are located at the same height above the waterline or base, the molds will be much easier to align when set up on the keel or floor.

STEM AND RABBET

The stem assembly is drawn on the full-size lines, either as dimensioned on the construction plan or, lacking dimensions, from widths scaled from the construction plan. In boatbuilding language the widths of the stem are the molded dimensions, whereas the thickness of the material for the stem is the sided dimension. Ideally, a stem for a small craft like a dinghy should be made from a natural hackmatack or oak crook as they were some years ago. This is still possible in New England—hackmatack knees are available (see Chapter 4). A template of the stem would be taken to the dealer in this material to select a crook with a shape similar to the stem. But it seems very few people bother with this method anymore.

Often the stem is too large to get out of a natural crook (a range of hackmatack knee sizes is described in Chapter 4), so an assembly of wood will be made up as illustrated in Figure 8-5 or the stem assembly will be laminated. For the amateur, who does not usually count labor, a lamination is often the best way. When an assembly of parts is used, templates of the parts are made, the lines being transferred with tacks as explained for the molds in Figure 8-1. Templates are made of easily worked softwood ⅛" to ⅜" thick; ⅛" or ¼" plywood; thin plywood "doorskin" veneers; ⅛" hardboard such as Masonite; or lofting paper (see "The Mold Loft," Chapter 7). Besides representing the shapes of the parts, the templates must also provide guidelines for rabbeting the stem assembly to receive the planking.

The profile of the rabbet line may or may not be dimensioned on the lines or construction plan, and even though it is shown, it should be checked *full size* for accuracy and fairness. The width or half-breadth of the rabbet line is generally the same as the siding of the stem (unless the hull is designed with a round-nosed flaring stem) and either retains a constant width throughout the length of the boat or swells in width toward amidships and then narrows again toward the stern. Bear in mind that the

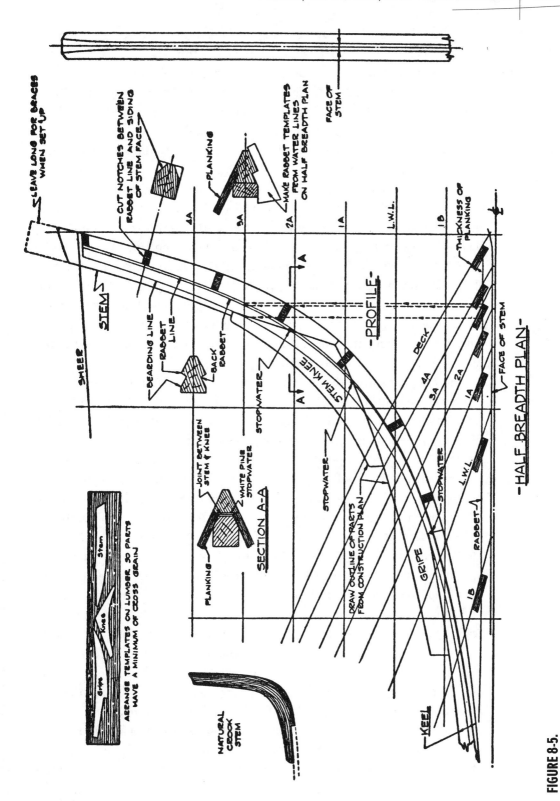

FIGURE 8-5.
Plotting the stem and rabbet lines.

rabbet for planking at the stem, along the keel or horn timber, etc., permits the edge or end of a plank to be square. Reasons for this—caulking, fastenings—will become obvious as you continue to learn how to build a boat.

It was mentioned before that countless boats have been built from molds made by deducting the thickness of planking by a less-than-precise method, and so it is with the stem rabbet. I will discuss this first and then explain how to lay out the rabbet by a more precise method that consumes but little more time.

Note in Figure 8-5 that the half-breadth of the stem (the half siding—or one-half the thickness) has been drawn as well as the half siding of the face of the stem, and on each waterline half-breadth the thickness of planking has been drawn to get the back rabbet and bearding lines to which the material must be cut. The nomenclature is shown on the section through the stem drawn on waterline 4A in the profile, Figure 8-5. Points to plot these lines on the profile are projected from the waterlines in the half-breadth plan to the waterlines in profile and connected with a batten. The lines for the rabbet and the outline of stem parts are all transferred to the template material at the same time.

The templates are laid out on the stem material and arranged so that there will be a minimum of cross grain in the finished part. Cut and plane the parts to shape (if too heavy for your equipment have a mill do this for you) and lay them out on the full-size lines to check the alignment of the joints in the assembled position. Mark the sheerline, all the waterlines, and the centerlines of the bolts; then bore the bolt holes and put the stem assembly together with an oil-based bedding compound (if you anticipate a day when you may wish to take the assembly apart again) or a polyurethane adhesive sealant such as 3M 5200, Sikaflex 231, or the brushable Sikaflex 251 (if you want a bulletproof joint that will never come apart) generously applied between the faying surfaces of the joints. (Faying surfaces are those in contact with each other.) Whether or not the bolt heads are countersunk and plugged, you should take an extra precaution to make the bolt holes watertight by using a grommet. This is a piece of cotton wicking caulking long enough to go around the bolt a couple of times. In some locales you may hunt in vain for the proper cotton wicking, which is not at all like kerosene lamp wicking. It is available from Jamestown Distributors and Hamilton Marine (see Appendix). Apply bedding generously to the wicking and wind it around the bolt beneath the head just before the bolt is driven all the way home. After assembly of the stem, mark the centerline of the boat on the stem and the width of the stem face on each side of the centerline.

Referring to the half-breadth plan in Figure 8-5, make a template of stiff cardboard or thin wood for the rabbet at each waterline. Use the templates to cut a short length of the rabbet at the waterlines, and then complete the rabbet by working away the material between the templated cuts on the waterline. The rabbet may be cut with confidence if the full-size drawing is *accurate* and complete. However, even some professionals leave the rabbet just a little shallow and complete it when fitting ribbands at the time the boat is set up. In many cases this is because they have learned from experience that their rabbet is not as accurate as it might be. Here is how you can make it more accurate.

In the beginning of Chapter 7 it was stated that vertical sections are drawn at intervals throughout the length of the boat to define the shape of the hull, but it should be realized that sections can be drawn through the hull at any angle, not only at the vertical planes of the stations and buttocks, the horizontal planes of the waterlines, or the diagonal planes. The designer often does this while drawing the construction plan to get the true, accurate sizes of parts such as the stem assembly; only when a section is drawn normal to the part is full accuracy assured. Since the waterlines and buttocks are the most out-of-normal to the hull surface at the bow (and at the stern of double-ended hulls), it certainly pays to draw auxiliary sections at right angles through the stem of the boat in order to more accurately cut the rabbet.

It is well to note here that for the same reasons of accuracy, bevels should be taken off lines that are normal to the hull surface, or nearly so.

Figure 8-6 has been prepared to show how easy it is to draw sections through the stem (or the sternpost of a double-ender). The sections should be spaced at intervals close enough so that there is no question about having enough of the plotted points for the rabbet, back rabbet, and bearding lines (see Figure 8-5) to ensure a fair line. To save time and effort, the sections should be drawn right on the lines profile, as in Section B-B of Figure 8-6, rather than apart as was done for clarity in Section A-A.

First a centerline is drawn normal to the face of the stem, long enough to cross enough buttocks and waterlines to give a number of points so a batten can be set up to draw a fair section. For instance, the centerline for Section A-A intersects two waterlines and a buttock. Then perpendiculars to this centerline are drawn at the waterline and buttock intersections and at the joints in the stem assembly. (For an illustration of how these perpendiculars can be laid off when the section is drawn directly on the lines profile, see Figure 8-7.) Next the half-breadths at these points of intersection are picked up as in the plan view and laid off on the perpendiculars

FIGURE 8-6.
A method of drawing sections through the stem.

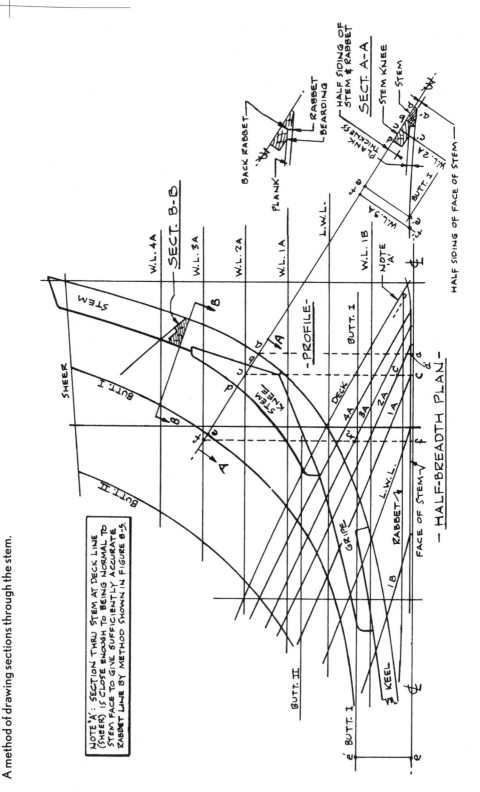

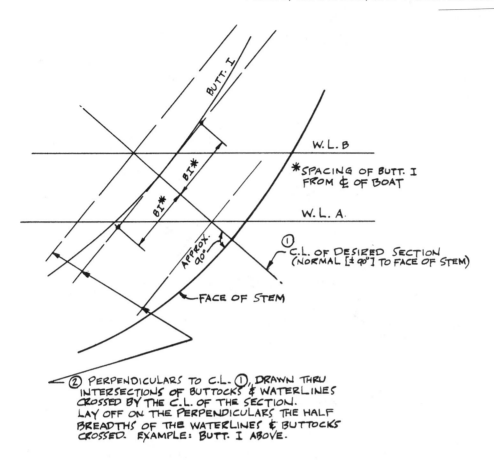

BUTT. I

W. L. B

*SPACING OF BUTT. I
FROM ₵ OF BOAT

BI*

BI*

W. L. A.

APPROX. 90°.

① C.L. OF DESIRED SECTION
(NORMAL [± 90°] TO FACE OF STEM)

FACE OF STEM

② PERPENDICULARS TO C.L. ①, DRAWN THRU
INTERSECTIONS OF BUTTOCKS & WATERLINES
CROSSED BY THE C.L. OF THE SECTION.
LAY OFF ON THE PERPENDICULARS THE HALF
BREADTHS OF THE WATERLINES & BUTTOCKS
CROSSED. EXAMPLE: BUTT. I ABOVE.

FIGURE 8-7.
Setting up the grid for drawing stem sections in place on the profile.

to establish the points for the section to the outside of planking (section A-A of Figure 8-6). After the section line has been drawn, the thickness of planking is set off, and this sets up the points for the rabbet, back rabbet, and the bearding line.

Instead of making templates for the rabbet from the half-breadth plan in the method shown by Figure 8-5, make them from the more accurate sections drawn on the profile as illustrated by Figure 8-6.

STOPWATERS

Softwood dowels called stopwaters are fitted in joints in the backbone to prevent water from leaking into the hull along the joints. The locations of stopwaters are important for full effectiveness; it is imperative that they

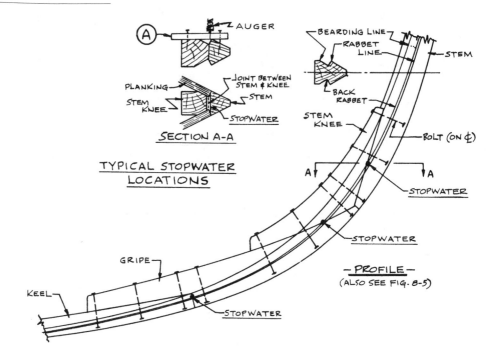

FIGURE 8-8.
Stopwaters are extremely important to prevent a leak into the hull wherever a joint in the stem, keel, et cetera, crosses the plank rabbet line.

be placed wherever the rabbet crosses a joint in the backbone. Any durable softwood such as white pine or cedar will do, and there are so few of them that they can be whittled out of scrap, but they must be as round as the bored hole and a snug fit. Stopwaters are indicated in Figure 8-5 and in larger detail in Figure 8-8. It is tricky to start a drill in the right direction on the surface of the rabbet, so try tacking a piece of softwood on the side of the joint to provide a flat surface (see A in Figure 8-8).

On the other hand, if you plan ahead it is obviously much easier to drill for stopwaters after the rabbet lines are drawn on pieces like the stem and gripe and *before* the rabbet is cut.

Stopwaters are recommended even when the joint bedding is one of the highly effective polyurethane adhesive sealants.

V-BOTTOMED HULL FRAMES

Temporary molds are not necessary for the construction of v-bottomed and arc-bottomed hulls. Instead, the body plan is used to make frames that become a permanent part of the structure. Typical v- and arc-bottomed hull frames are shown in Figures 1-3 and 1-4 in Chapter 1, but these sectional views do not reveal that the bottom and side pieces are beveled so the planking will bear against the entire siding of the frames (see Figure 8-9, A, and Figure 8-10). Note that the bevel—with rare exceptions—is *not* the same at the sheer as it is at the chine. This makes for more work, but this is the nature of boat hulls. The character, or curvature, of the deck line and chine, etc., determines the amount of bevel. At Section B-B in Figure 8-9, where the deck line and chine are approximately parallel to the centerline, it can be seen that there is practically no bevel needed. However, as the deck and chine curve in toward the centerline, forward and aft of B-B, the frames must be beveled.

For a simple boat with straight sections like that shown in Figure 8-9, the bevels can be measured as indicated—the side frame bevels at deck and chine

FIGURE 8-9.
Making frames for a v-bottomed hull.

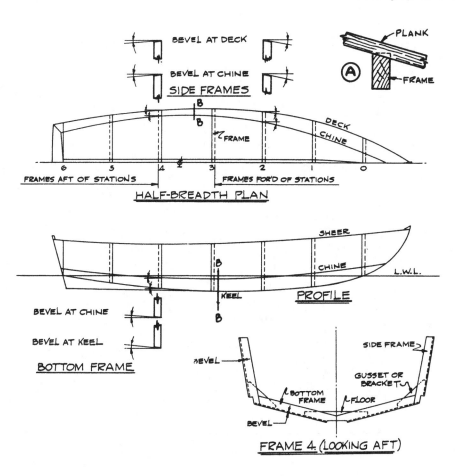

in the half-breadth plan, and those for the bottom frames at chine and keel in the profile. The bevels are cut in a straight line between deck and chine and between chine and keel, respectively. If the frames have some curve, the bevels at major points as described above are just the same, but those for the side frames at points between the deck and chine are taken from the waterlines in the half-breadth plan; those for the bottom frames at points between the chine and the keel are taken from the buttocks in the profile. Bevels for the notches in which the keel, chines, and clamps are fitted are taken off similarly or cut later when the boat is set up. At that time, battens for fairing the frames are run in and bevel adjustments are made by planing the frames.

To determine bevels with more accuracy, however (and this is very important to time saving in the larger hulls with a good number of frames), the bevels should be measured *normal* to the surface, much like the deduction for planking thickness previously discussed. This can be done by the method shown in Figure 8-10. The square can be made up by the builder

FIGURE 8-10.
Bevels should be measured normal to the surface to ensure accuracy, and marked on the body plan and on the actual frame material.

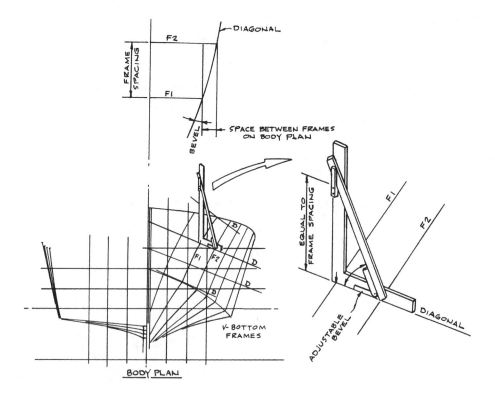

and applied as shown to measure the bevels. Once gotten, the bevels should be marked right on the body plan in degrees for reference and then marked on the actual frame material so that it can be sawn to shape with the proper bevel. The bevels should be taken along diagonals laid out to be as close to normal as possible to all the frames crossed.

BEVEL BOARD

Instead of using a protractor to measure a bevel each time you take one off, make yourself a simple bevel board as shown in Figure 8-11. Use a piece of plywood about 3½" wide and mark off angles from zero to about 30 degrees. Slide the adjustable bevel along the left edge of the bevel board until it lines up with one of the angles and read it off.

When a bevel is marked on a piece of stock to be sawn, it must be designated as either *under* or *standing,* marking the piece UB or SB. This is most important, and after you have ruined a few pieces, you will understand the principle.

LOFTING BY COMPUTER

Fairing hull lines with the aid of a computer was mentioned in the previous chapter, which dealt with enlarging to full size the designer's scale drawing of the set of lines defining the shape of the outside of the hull, whether it be wood, metal, fiberglass, or otherwise. Earlier in this chapter

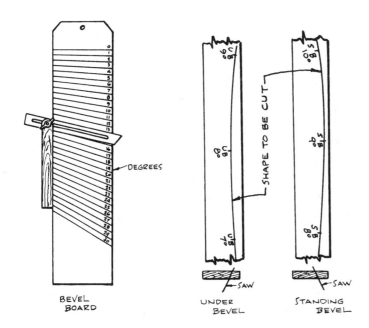

BEVEL BOARD

UNDER BEVEL

STANDING BEVEL

FIGURE 8-11.
Make a simple bevel board out of plywood—marking off angles from zero to 30 degrees.

it was explained that for round-bottomed hulls, molds are needed to make a male framework on which to shape the frames, and that for v-bottomed hulls frames are needed on which to build the boat. Here is where fairing by computer pays off if your project justifies the expense. A computer-guided plotter can draw full-size sections through the hull (spaced either equally or unequally) at any location desired, complete with deductions from the outside of the hull.

If lofting by computer is used, most of the lofting in the shop is avoided, but the bevels for the edges of the molds or frames will not be available to you. Therefore, you must order bevels from the computer people. Be certain that you understand how the bevels given by the computer should be applied to the section drawings. An explanation will be furnished, along with probably two or three times as many bevels as you really need. There's just no stopping that computer, but better too many bevels than too few!

The mold spacing for round-bottomed hulls and the frame spacing for v-bottomed hulls is usually at uniform intervals. Sometimes the location of joiner bulkheads, those partitions dividing the cabin accommodations, etc., are not located in the same place as molds or frames. If full-size bulkhead drawings are desired, these, too, can be supplied by the computer service, and once again you should ask for the edge bevels.

Many of the larger boats are built of welded steel or aluminum alloy framing, with a skin or shell plating of the same material. For this type of construction the computer service can supply full-size drawings, using your scale drawings, from which to cut the frames to shape from flat material, so the drawings should be ordered with the deduction for the thickness of the shell plating.

TRANSOM AND TRANSOM BEVELS

As will be seen later, the station molds, the stem, and the transom are needed before the boat can be set up. The molds and the stem have been explained, and the development of the transom shape has been illustrated. You also need the bevels on the transom edges. Remember that the developed shape of the transom is to the outside of the planking, and depending upon the type of construction, it may or may not represent the actual size of the finished transom. The simplest method is to let the side planking overlap the transom and to then cut it flush with the after side. In this case the plank thickness is subtracted from the edges of the transom. The best practice, however, is to make the transom to the outside of the planking and rabbet the edge for the planking. Both methods are shown in Figure 8-12.

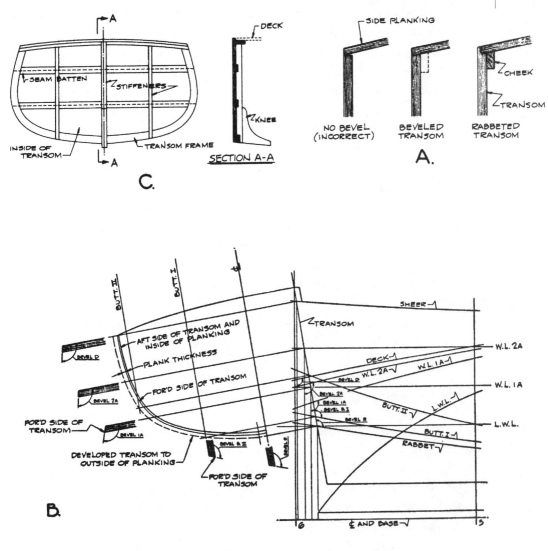

FIGURE 8-12.
Transom bevels and typical construction.

A in Figure 8-12 shows that the inside of the transom is larger than the outside, except at the top edge where the shape depends upon the construction details, because the boat narrows from amidships to the transom. Consequently, like the frames of a v-bottomed boat, the edges of the transom must be beveled to allow the planks to lie flat. The bevels are taken from the full-size lines as shown—those for the sides from the waterlines in the half-breadth plan and those for the bottom from the buttocks in the profile drawing. But once again it should be remembered that this is not the most accurate way to take the bevels off, because it has not been done normal to the surface of the hull by the method shown in Figure 8-10.

Small-boat transoms are generally made of wide boards whose edges are splined or doweled and waterproof glued. The boards should be sufficiently thick so that the hull planks can be properly fastened to the edge. Such transoms can also be made of marine plywood, with cheek pieces around the edges to take the plank fastenings. Larger transoms, like that shown in C in Figure 8-12, are made the same thickness as the hull planking or thicker and have a frame or cheek pieces on the inside edges to take a share of the plank fastenings. There is usually a vertical member on the centerline, where a wood or metal knee connects the transom to the keel or horn timber. For the sake of appearance, the seams of transom planks should not be caulked. If single planked, the seams of the larger transoms are usually backed with battens. Wide transoms also have a series of vertical stiffeners outboard of the centerline. In a powerboat hull these are frequently spaced to bolt to the ends of long engine stringers.

Most transoms do not have enough radius to prevent the planks from being bent cold. In transoms that do have a lot of radius, the planks can be soaked with hot, wet rags or steamed so they will bend to the transom frame.

KEEL AND DEADWOOD

There are quite a number of keel construction methods, varying with the type of boat, the preference of the designer, and sometimes with the custom of a particular locality. The types most likely to be encountered are illustrated in Figures 8-13 and 8-14. Needless to say, for longevity, only sound timber should go into the backbone members. White oak is the usual material for keel and other backbone members; sapwood should be avoided. Other species of wood can be used as guided by local experience.

The flat-bottomed skiff construction shown in A in Figure 8-13 and at the top of Figure 1-3 (Chapter 1) is very common. It is mostly built upside down with a few forms notched for the keelson and chines, transom and stem set up and securely braced against movement. Sometimes a rabbeted stem is substituted for the two-piece assembly shown, and some builders like twin keelsons instead of one on the centerline. In a two-piece stem, the side planks are cut off flush with the inner stem, and then the outer stem is fastened to the inner, with sealant applied between the two. Before fastening the keel, cut a slot for the skeg.

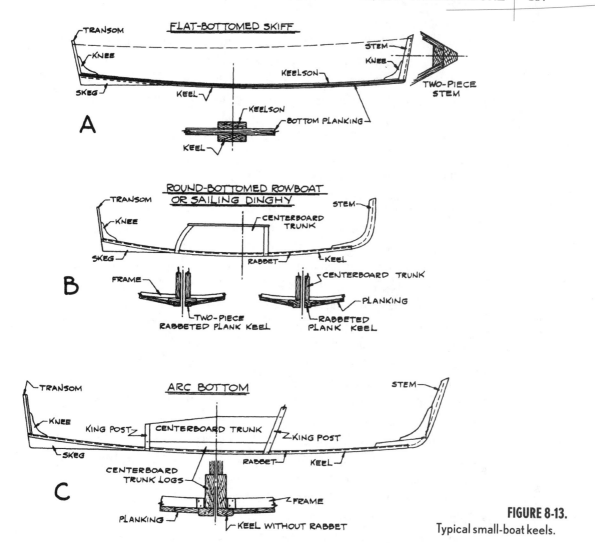

FIGURE 8-13.
Typical small-boat keels.

The rabbeted keel in B in Figure 8-13 is typical construction for a great many boats. As was done for the stem in Figure 8-5, the rabbet should be cut at each station from templates and then cut away between the stations to make a continuous fair rabbet for the planking. The amateur will find it easier to make the two-piece keel if he fastens the pieces together over the molds after first beveling them to form the rabbet.

A generous amount of bedding compound should be applied to all backbone joints, as described earlier in the details of a stem assembly. Regardless of the type of backbone structure, this application is important in order to exclude any water between the joined pieces.

A few of the one-design sailboats use a keel without a rabbet, like that shown in C in Figure 8-13. This is all right, but because the garboard plank (the one next to the keel on each side) is not fastened to the keel, care should be taken to attach the frames strongly to the keel. If the frames butt at the centerline, the floor timbers connecting the frame halves must be well fastened to the frames and keel. In way of the centerboard slot in the keel, the bed logs should be thick to make for good fastening through the keel.

POWERBOAT KEELS

The keel structure shown in A in Figure 8-14 is typical of many modern powerboats. The keel is usually the same thickness throughout and is cut to shape from a template made from the full-size profile. A batten bent into place on top forms a back rabbet for the planking. The rabbet is cut the same as for the little boat in B in Figure 8-13. The horn timber aft is rabbeted. A bronze shaft log with packing gland is installed for watertightness where the shaft leaves the hull. The bottom of the keel may be cut away or continued aft and fitted with a skeg to support the bottom of the rudder. The stern end of the keel would be shaped differently if the boat was designed for twin engines.

Note the two-piece wooden shaft log for a single-engine boat shown in Figure 8-14, B. This is easier to make than a log in a single piece, because the shaft hole in each half can be worked out and grooves for splines can be cut on a table saw or with a plow plane. The purpose of the splines is to swell and prevent leaks in the same manner that stopwaters do, and they are made of softwood such as white pine. It is all right to cut through the splines with bolts so long as the bolt holes are *tight*. The splines swell against the bolts and function just as well as when not cut.

The semicircular grooves that form the shaft hole in a two-piece log can be made on a table saw or even with a portable circular saw by running a series of cuts of varying depths, then cleaning out with a plow plane or "worrying" with gouges. Most professionals prefer two-piece construction to the struggle of boring out a one-piece shaft log. I strongly recommend a two-piece unit.

It is important to seal the tunnel for the shaft to prevent absorption of water, particularly fresh water, unless the wooden shaft log (B in Figure 8-14) is to be submerged all the time; but if the hull is to be stored ashore, say for several months or so, the moisture content might get in the range where decay can occur. There is more about this in the discussion of propeller shafts and bearings in Chapter 20.

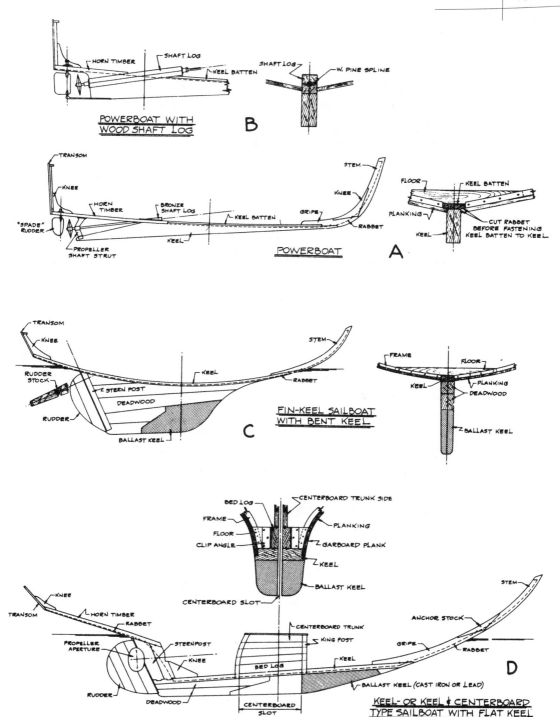

FIGURE 8-14.
A few of the many possible backbone structures for powerboats and sailboats.

FIN-KEEL SAILBOATS

Fin-keel sailboats up to about 30 feet may have bent keels like that shown in C in Figure 8-14. Indeed even larger boats have had this type of construction, with keels thick enough to need steaming to bend the keel to shape. Probably the easiest way to build a boat of this type is upside down, the keel being bent down over the molds and the fin keel added after the hull is turned over.

Attention must be given to the sequence of the bolting in order to properly fasten the fin. The ballast keel bolts usually extend from the casting through the deadwood, keel, and floors, although sometimes they terminate between frames. The deadwood is carefully shaped as called for by the lines. Although it requires hard work if done by hand (another very good reason to acquire a portable electric plane), a lot of effort should be put into the deadwood to make it smooth and fair, not only for the sake of appearance but also to offer a minimum of resistance as the boat moves through the water. The aft edge of the sternpost is gouged out to take the rudder stock and the rounded forward edge of the rudder. While the forward edge of the rudder can be painted by alternately swinging it hard over to each side, it is impossible to paint the concave edge of the sternpost. To prevent accumulation of marine growth, the after side of the sternpost should be sheathed with light copper sheet brought around on the sides just enough for it to be fastened with tacks, or the groove can be heavily coated with epoxy resin. Either method is acceptable.

LARGE SAILBOAT KEELS

The backbone in Figure 8-14, D, is typical of most keel sailboats or combination keel and centerboard sailboats upward of 20 feet on the waterline. The keel in such boats is a thick plank of the same thickness from end to end, but varying in width throughout the length. It is rabbeted for the planking as shown in the section. The vertical position of the keel in the hull structure is drawn in on the full-size profile; then the heights of the keel at the stations it crosses are transferred to the corresponding sections in the body plan to obtain the half-widths of the keel at the stations. A centerline is drawn on the piece of lumber to be used for the keel, the station spacing is picked up and laid off from the full-size profile (the station spacing along the keel is greater than the spacing along the baseline because the keel is at an angle with the base), and the half-breadths of the top of the keel are picked up from the sections and laid off on the keel stock. Draw the outline of the keel with a batten. After the keel is sawn to the shape of the top edge, draw a centerline on the underside of the keel, making sure it aligns with the one on top, and similarly lay off the half-breadths of the keel bottom. The outline of the bottom will give the constantly changing bevel to which to cut the sides of the keel. The rabbet at each section is then templated as a guide for cutting, as mentioned before.

GRIPE AND HORN TIMBER

The gripe is the piece that connects the keel to the stem, and the horn timber connects the keel or sternpost to the transom in some types of power and sailboats. Both the gripe and horn timber are very similar to a stem. The rabbet for the comparatively horizontal horn timber is taken from the sections in the body plan. Knees are used to fasten the various back-bone members to each other. Much of the backbone construction work is made clear by construction sections on the designer's plans.

STERNPOST

The structure between the horn timber and the keel in D in Figure 8-14 and in Figure 10-14, when designed as shown, can be bolted up without fouling the hole for the propeller shaft, but in this arrangement boring a hole for the shaft cannot be avoided. Normally a barefoot auger would be used, with an extension welded to the shank if necessary, and guides devised to keep the hole on course. One source for this auger is W. L. Fuller, Inc. It will on request cut off the standard square end, leaving a round shank that is best powered by nothing less than a ½" electric drill. A heavy-duty "hammer-drill" that hammers while it revolves may reduce the boring time, but I have never tried the tool in this application.

BACKBONE BOLTING

After all the backbone members are shaped, but prior to fastening them together, it is recommended that they be given two coats of a wood preservative. These preparations are inexpensive and well worth the investment for their rot preventive qualities. The liquid should also be poured down the bolt holes before the fastenings are driven. Through-bolts and drift bolts, described at length in Chapter 6, are made and fitted as shown on the construction plan for the boat, and the fastenings must be studied for sequence so the assembly will go together properly. It will be seen as you go along that some of the bolts cannot be driven at this time because they pass through floor timbers (Figure 8-14, A and C) that are not made and fitted in the structure until later. Once again it must be emphasized that all joints have bedding so that no crevices are left for water to seep through or to collect in and possibly start to rot the timbers. Under the washers of through and drift bolts it is advisable to wind a few turns of cotton wicking soaked in paint before the bolts are finally driven home. Very often this treatment will prevent leaks that otherwise would be troublesome or at least annoying. Wicking and a source for it were discussed earlier in this chapter under "Stem and Rabbet." The stopwaters mentioned earlier are fitted after the parts have been bolted.

SCARPHS

It is not always possible to obtain pieces of wood long enough for the keel, deadwood, bilge stringers, clamps, and shelves. Fortunately, sufficient lengths may be found for keels more often than for the other parts, even though an extensive search is required. The backbone requires enough work of the builder without his having to splice the keel, particularly the type shown in D in Figure 8-14. When it cannot be avoided, the long members are pieced out by means of through-bolted joints called *scarphs*. Nowadays these joints in wood are often glued with an adhesive such as resorcinol or a highly water-resistant glue such as thickened epoxy for good measure. If not glued, the joints must be bedded. Bolts are staggered when thickness of lumber permits.

Figure 8-15 illustrates three types of scarphs commonly in use, and it should be noted that all have nibs to prevent one part from slipping by the other when under strain. The joint shown in A is the very common plain scarph that is extensively used for stringers and clamps. The hooked scarph, B, is sometimes employed in backbone members. Just as effective, and easier to make, is the key scarph shown in C. This is simply a plain scarph mortised to take a tightly fitted rectangular key, preferably of durable wood like white oak. In large timbers the key is sometimes made of two wedges driven from both sides at the same time and cut off flush with the sides of the timbers. Such wedges are made with a taper of about one-half inch to the foot.

The scarph with feather edges at the top of Figure 8-15 is marked "incorrect," but if such a joint is properly fitted, adequately clamped, with a couple of nails temporarily driven (to prevent skidding out of alignment when pressure is applied), and glued with a waterproof or highly water-resistant adhesive, then this joint is satisfactory. For an adhesive I would probably use epoxy, thickened to avoid starving the joint. This material is gap-filling and does not require as much pressure as a resorcinol glue. A polyurethane adhesive sealant is a good alternative.

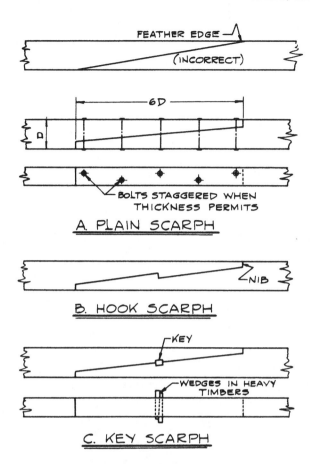

FEATHER EDGE
(INCORRECT)

6D

D

BOLTS STAGGERED WHEN
THICKNESS PERMITS

A. PLAIN SCARPH

NIB

B. HOOK SCARPH

KEY

WEDGES IN HEAVY
TIMBERS

C. KEY SCARPH

FIGURE 8-15.
Common scarphs for joining long members
such as keels, clamps, and stringers.

The scarphed joints and their fastenings may not be shown on the boat plans or specifications. A rough rule for the scarph length is six times the depth of the timber, while the keys and nibs are made up to one-fourth of the depth. If the inexperienced builder should not be able to locate a piece of wood large enough for the keel, the designer or a competent boatbuilder should be consulted for the layout of scarphs most suitable for use with the available material.

TENONS

The mortise-and-tenon joint is sometimes called upon to lock adjoining members having grain perpendicular to each other. The joints between the vertical sternposts and the keel in D in Figure 8-14 are typical. When the wood is not too thin, the tenon is made blind—that is, only partway across the pieces—and therefore it is not visible when the parts are fitted together. Whatever the case, the joint must be made as snug as possible and put together with bedding on the mating parts.

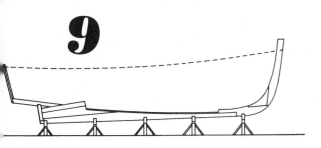

9

SETTING UP

AT THIS POINT IT MUST BE MENTIONED THAT the type of hull planking intended for a given boat will determine the setup needed to build that hull. *If you are not familiar with the various planking possibilities, refer to Chapter 11, "Planking," before returning to the discussion below.*

Just as much care and accuracy should go into the work of setting up as went into the mold loft work and construction of the backbone. Continued attention to detail at this stage will pay dividends in time saved later. The method of setting up depends upon the size, type, and construction of the hull, but in general, most small craft are best built upside down, a method that has much merit. (To contradict this, recently two builders of my 18'7" launch Barbara Anne, which is designed for carvel planking, strip-planked the hull right side up. The builders, of course, considered the height of the hull above the floor.)

Regardless of the size or type of boat you are building, remember to take great care with your setup so that both sides of the hull will be exactly the same.

UPSIDE DOWN OR RIGHT SIDE UP?

There was no question in the minds of the builders of the sailboats shown in Figures 9-7, 9-8, and 9-10 (see pages 200–203) about how to set up; note that the ballast keels and deadwood for these boats are already in place.

On the other hand, the hull in Figure 9-12 is one of hundreds like it built upside down by this company, and for good reason: the hull shown will be planked double-diagonally. A fast and efficient method for overturning these 34- to 80-foot-long hulls was devised early in their development.

With regard to wooden hulls, as well as wooden plugs for molded boats, size alone may not dictate whether to build right side up or upside down. As stated earlier, most small hulls—both sail and power—are best built upside down. This includes flat-, v-, and arc-bottomed hulls, because it is easier to fasten the bottom planks with the hull inverted. It also includes small round-bilged lapstrake hulls that are planked over molds; in this case the fitting of the lapped plank seams is generally simplified with the boat upside down. Cold-molded hulls, too, are better planked upside down.

Strip-planked hulls can be built either right side up or upside down. Hull size, of course, has some bearing on the choice. Remember that it is easier to drive nails downhand. Study the words about strip planking in Chapter 11, then think about the options rather than just plunging ahead. Planking right side up, the hull should be high enough so you can comfortably nail the strips on the bottom. Planking upside down, the hull should be low enough to do the same.

If it has been decided to frame a round-bottomed boat by working on the inside of the ribbands as mentioned in Chapter 8, then the boat should be built right side up to facilitate bending the frames. Any other method would be impractical. In instances where the finished hull will be too heavy or bulky for the lone builder or amateur to turn over, the boat should be built upright.

BUILDING UNDER COVER

Considering that weather can be a drawback if it should be cold and windy, or rainy, or very hot—then your hull should be built under cover if possible. A building also permits work to be done evenings under lights and provides convenient means of overhead bracing of molds and backbone to the roof rafters. A good solid floor is ideal, whether or not it is level and smooth. However, an outdoor construction site can be made to serve well, as many amateur builders have found from experience, although the task of bracing the frame is somewhat more difficult, and weather can bring work to a halt for weeks at a time.

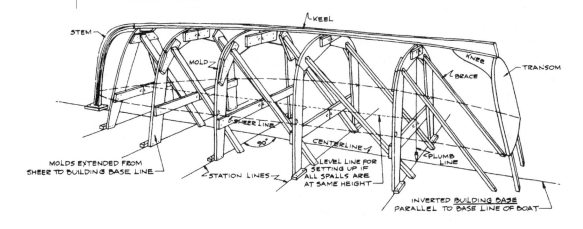

FIGURE 9-1.
The typical setup for building a small hull upside down, shown before the installation of the ribbands.

BUILDING UPSIDE DOWN

When building upside down, a grid must be established and the framework positioned on top of it accordingly. The following is a description of how the 12-foot skiff shown in Figure 9-1 might be set up in such a manner. A centerline is first drawn in on the floor, the station spacing laid off along the centerline, and the station lines squared off from the centerline. As previously described, the molds for upside-down building are extended beyond the sheer to an arbitrary inverted baseline parallel to the baseline of the boat and located above the highest point of the sheer by an amount calculated for convenient working height. The molds forward of amidships are set up on the aft side of the station lines, and those aft of amidships on the forward side of the station lines. The reason for this system will be obvious when the ribbands are applied. If the molds are set on the wrong sides of the station lines, the ribbands will be forced out of their proper position due to the shape of the hull, as shown in the sketch, Figure 9-2.

Use a plumb line to align the centerline of a mold with the boat centerline on the floor, and also use the plumb line or a level to align the upper part of a mold in a fore-and-aft direction. Fasten the molds to the floor with blocks and brace them securely against fore-and-aft movement. You will remember that it was pointed out in Chapter 8 that it would be helpful if the mold cross-spalls were fitted at the same level on all molds; it is now that this fact is realized. If the building floor is not perfectly level, the line of the spalls can be used to determine where shims must be fitted between the floor and the ends of the molds to bring them to the proper height.

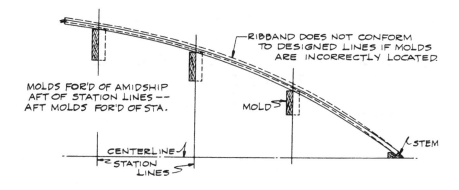

RIBBAND DOES NOT CONFORM TO DESIGNED LINES IF MOLDS ARE INCORRECTLY LOCATED.

MOLDS FOR'D OF AMIDSHIP AFT OF STATION LINES -- AFT MOLDS FOR'D OF STA.

MOLD

STEM

CENTERLINE

STATION LINES

FIGURE 9-2.
Setting the molds on the incorrect side of the stations forces the ribbands out of their proper positions.

It must be emphasized that the utmost care should be taken to align the backbone and molds properly. An extra hour or two spent on this job will be appreciated when ribbands are fitted, frames are bent, and planking is shaped and fastened. The boat will not be the same on both sides if the setting up is not done accurately. The centerline and baseline, waterlines and station lines are all straight lines, and as such, enable the builder to erect the backbone and molds with the use of vertical and horizontal lines just as the designer laid out his lines plan and construction drawings. Shores and braces of sufficient number must be fitted to prevent movement of the structure in any direction. *Take your time here and be accurate.*

Recently I came across a "hands-free" leveling device in a building supply store (see Figure 9-3). Two bubble levels are mounted on a right-angle base, which is strapped to a post, hull mold, etc., to plumb it in two directions. The device is secured with Velcro-type, so-called hook-and-loop straps, or the base could be drilled if necessary to hold it in place with round-head wood screws. The rig should be a boon, especially to a one-man operation, because it frees the hands while offering a visual check in two directions.

Figure 16-4 in Chapter 16 shows how to rig a homemade water level for marking a straight line on a hull using a length of transparent plastic tubing and water tinted with dye to make it easier to read, all at minimum cost. I used a bit of Peters fertilizer,

FIGURE 9-3.
"Hands-free" leveling device.

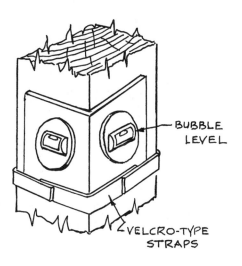

BUBBLE LEVEL

VELCRO-TYPE STRAPS

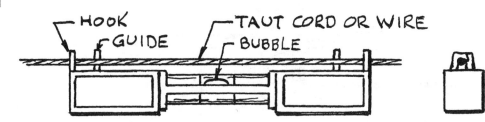

FIGURE 9-4.
Line level.

which was at hand, as a dye. Now builders' supply houses are stocking a more refined water level in several models, starting at about ten dollars.

The same procedure can help you be accurate when setting up if you fix points at the hull ends, say the stem and the transom, then stretch a taut, strong string or wire between the points to ensure molds, etc., are aligned in height. The level line should be checked often using a cheap bubble level called a line level, hooked over the string or cord (Figure 9-4). A new type of water level that has recently appeared in the tool catalogs can make this type of leveling a one-person operation. When the liquid in the adjustable end is level with the fixed end a beep sounds!

To continue setting up: drop the keel—with stem, transom, and knee attached—into position over the molds and screw the assembly to blocks on each mold. Secure the head of the stem to the building floor with blocks to hold it rigidly in position. Brace the transom after making sure it is raked to the correct angle and square across the boat. If everything has been done accurately, the station lines marked on the keel should coincide with the molds. If not, the frame is not properly aligned and must be corrected. One test of fairness is to bend a long batten, with its forward end laid in the stem rabbet, around the molds. The batten should test fair when tried anywhere from keel to the sheer. If not, test and adjust until the batten touches all the molds without forcing. The ribbands should not be installed until the molds have been aligned to your complete satisfaction.

BUILDING OUTDOORS

When building boats outdoors, there are many arrangements that are workable, but probably the most satisfactory for upside-down building is to use as a base a pair of substantial timbers longer than the boat. These should be secured to the ground on both sides of the centerline and made level. The cross-spalls on the molds are fastened to the parallel timbers. Cross-pieces are fastened between the timbers to take the stem head and the transom braces. For building right side up outdoors, timbers are placed on the

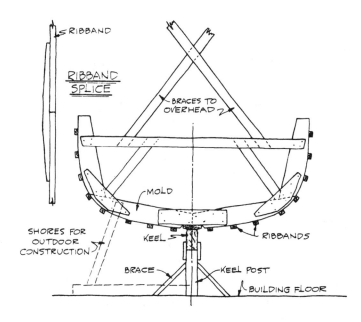

RIBBAND

RIBBAND SPLICE

BRACES TO OVERHEAD

MOLD

SHORES FOR OUTDOOR CONSTRUCTION

KEEL

RIBBANDS

BRACE

KEEL POST

BUILDING FLOOR

FIGURE 9-5.
When building outdoors, construct braces against the keel post (Figure 9-6) and use shores to brace the mold laterally.

ground athwartships at stations and staked solidly against movement. Keel supports are built up with blocks to the proper height, and shores are used to brace the mold laterally (see Figure 9-5). Once again, *take all the time you need to be accurate.*

Another option is to make the keel posts a foot or so longer, depending on the nature of the soil and the terrain, and pound them into the ground after cutting the post ends to a vee shape. Then you must cut the planted posts to the correct height, so once again accuracy is paramount in getting started.

BUILDING RIGHT SIDE UP

In the same manner as described for building upside down, a centerline and station lines are drawn for boats that are to be built right side up. Relatively narrow keels, like those for motorboats, are set on posts erected at each station. The posts must be securely nailed to the floor and braced against movement, as shown in Figures 9-5 and 9-6. The heights of the posts are carefully measured from the full-size profile and checked with the keel template. Quite frequently, keels are held down on such posts by turnbuckles set up between eyebolts in the keel and floor near each end of the keel. Such fastening prevents the hull from being raised off the posts when planking is forced into place with shores and wedges, as this action tends to both lift the hull upward and tilt it to one side.

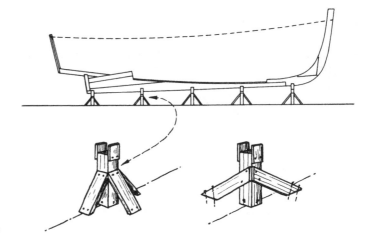

FIGURE 9-6.
Common forms of keel posts.

Posts are also used in sailboat construction, but only to shore the stem. Sailboats are often built on their flat keels, with the ballast keel casting and deadwood added after the hull is planked up. Or the complete backbone may be finished before setting up, as in the auxiliary in Figure 9-7, which shows husky keel blocks being used to prevent shifting of the structure.

FIGURE 9-7.
The backbone of a Rhodes-designed ketch. Note the husky blocks under the deadwood, the shores to prevent side movement of the backbone, and the transom bracing to overhead.

FIGURE 9-8.
The view from the stern quarter of a double-ended auxiliary after frames have been bent inside the ribbands.
Note the excellent bracing of molds and sternpost. The appearance of the ribbands is pleasing as well as
practical. (*Morris Rosenfeld*)

Such keel blocks must be large enough to take substantial fastenings to the
floor and to take the considerable weight of a boat of this type.

One yacht yard builds v-bottomed powerboat hulls upside down, starting with bench-built bulkheads and sawn frames with temporary legs
extended down to cross-spalls at a level clear of the sheerline and located
parallel to the waterlines on the lines plan for the hull; thus the frames can
be plumbed. The floor of the shop is concrete, so wooden sleepers are fastened to the floor as shown in Figure 9-9. The sleepers are of lumber about

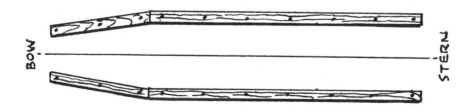

BOW · STERN

FIGURE 9-9.
The layout of wooden sleepers—these are fastened into the shop floor.

4×6 inches laid on the flat. Formerly, these were secured to the concrete the hard way—by boring for lag bolt anchors. These days, however, the sleepers are secured with hardened steel fastening pins driven by a power hammer—bang! and the fastener is driven into the concrete. The sleepers are generously counterbored to minimize pin lengths, and the tool is rented for a few hours each time a hull is set up.

RIBBANDS

After the backbone and all molds have been set up *accurately* and properly braced, the ribbands are applied to hold the parts rigidly in position. Ribbands were mentioned briefly in Chapter 8, where it was pointed out that they are long strips of wood bent around the molds in order to provide a form against which to bend the frames to shape between the molds. The function of molds and ribbands should be made perfectly clear by the photograph, Figure 9-8, which is a rare treat because it is not cluttered up with scaffolding. As considerable pressure is needed to clamp the frames to the ribbands, it is best that they be of moderately hard and strong wood, such as fir or yellow pine. Boats vary to such an extent that there is no general rule for size of the ribbands. They must be stiff to retain the hull shape when the frames are bent against them, but not so heavy that they are hard to bend and hold in place or that they force the molds out of alignment. As a safeguard against distorting the shape of the hull, the ribbands are applied alternately port and starboard. Ribbands are generally bent on the flat from stock such as $1\frac{1}{4}" \times 1\frac{1}{2}"$, and spaced about 10" apart, or $1\frac{1}{2}" \times 2"$ spaced about a foot apart. A sample should definitely be tried around the molds before getting out the stock for all the ribbands.

The differences in ribband sizes between various hull types can be seen in Figures 9-8 and 9-10. Figure 9-8 shows the hull for a moderately heavy cruising auxiliary that has already been framed; Figure 9-10 shows the setup for a racing sloop. A comparison of the ribband sizes for the boats in the two pictures indicates that the racing sloop will have relatively light frames. The ribbands should be in single lengths if possible; otherwise they should be spliced as shown in Figure 9-5. This type of splice tends to eliminate unfair flat spots in the ribbands, but as a further precaution against hard spots, the splices should be located where bends in the ribbands are easiest.

Husky ribbands and close spacing will contribute toward a fair boat. Put them on by fastening the middle first and, working toward the ends, securing the ribbands to each mold with screws having washers under

FIGURE 9-10.

The men at right are fitting ribbands prior to framing a racing sloop. Note mold braces to the rafters of the building and the strongback on top of the mold cross-spalls on the centerline of the boat. (*Morris Rosenfeld*)

FIGURE 9-11.

This mold is being set up and carefully checked for alignment. Other molds are stacked in the background.

FIGURE 9-12.
A v-bottomed hull completely set up with sawn frames and ready for double-diagonal planking. (*Huckins Yacht Corporation*)

their heads. Screws will permit the ribbands to be removed easily as the planking is fitted. The top ribbands should go on first, fitted parallel to the sheer and a few inches above it. The rest of them should be run in fair lines similar to strakes of planking and as illustrated in Figure 9-8. The ribbands are spaced closer where the frames will be bent to the sharpest curves than where the frames will be fairly flat.

Careful mold loft work and setting up will make running ribbands an easy job and will eliminate the task of trimming and shimming molds to get the ribbands to touch all molds and still remain fair. If considerable trouble is encountered fairing the ribbands, it will pay to check the sections by bending a batten into position like a frame on the inside of the ribbands to see if it touches all of them while bent in a fair curve. Running the ribbands is the last job before framing is started, and the hull in this condition usually is the cause of excited anticipation on the part of the builder, for now the shape of the hull may be appreciated.

V-BOTTOMED HULLS

It should be understood without mention that hulls other than the round-bottomed type must be set up, aligned, and made rigid with the same care. There is no point in doing an accurate job of laying down and mold making unless the setup and the work that follows meet the same standard.

10

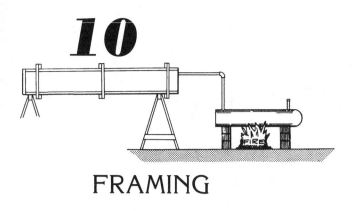

FRAMING

THERE ARE TWO BASIC SYSTEMS for framing a typical wooden hull: transverse and longitudinal. Transverse framing is the most common, and being oriented across the width of the hull, such frames are often called ribs. Transverse frames for round-bottomed wooden hulls are either bent from one piece, as in Figures 1-4 and 1-5 (Chapter 1); laminated from two or more pieces bent on top of each other; sawn from natural crooks of wood; or "double-sawn" from boards and made up of two layers with staggered joints. Small to moderate hulls usually have the bent frames, although in places where material for bent frames is nonexistent, such as islands in the Bahamas, the frames are sawn from crooks or double-sawn according to both the size of the boat and the supply of crooks (see Figure 10-1). Sawn frames for v-bottomed and arc-bottomed hulls are shown in Figures 1-3 and 1-4.

For the longitudinal framing system in general, transverse frames are used to shape the hull, but are spaced farther apart than in the transverse system. Fore-and-aft longitudinals are used to build up the necessary framing strength. This system can become quite complicated for construction in wood, but is well suited for metal boats of welded construction.

In this chapter, discussion is limited to two types of framing suitable for the size of craft likely to be built by the amateur—bent frames and sawn v-bottomed frames. A third, laminated frames, is discussed in

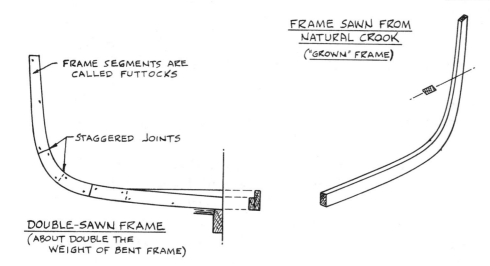

FRAME SAWN FROM
NATURAL CROOK
("GROWN" FRAME)

FRAME SEGMENTS ARE
CALLED FUTTOCKS

STAGGERED JOINTS

DOUBLE-SAWN FRAME
(ABOUT DOUBLE THE
WEIGHT OF BENT FRAME)

FIGURE 10-1.
Sawn and double-sawn frames.

Chapter 4. Before undertaking a craft with other kinds of more complex framing, builders should be certain before starting that they are aware of what is involved.

V-BOTTOMED FRAMES

The lofting and construction of frames for a v-bottomed boat will be better understood by referring to Figures 1-3 and 1-7 and the explanation in Chapter 8. The frames are made from the full-size sections and must be beveled on the edges so the planking will bear against the full thickness of the frame. The process of picking up bevels is explained in preceding chapters.

BENT FRAMES

The bending of frames for a round-bottomed boat seems to disturb the amateur's peace of mind when contemplating the construction of such a hull, but a trial should dispel this fear. For this reason, it is recommended that the novice start with a fairly small boat having light frames in order to gain experience and overcome the mental block that is the principal obstacle to frame bending. We all know that any piece of dry wood may be picked from the lumber pile and sprung to a curve of large radius, but for bending the tight curves found in frames, the wood must be both wet and hot. The

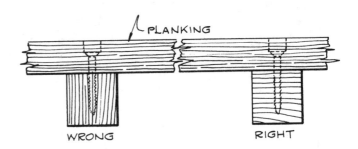

FIGURE 10-2.
Frames should be bent on the flat of the grain—this helps minimize the wood's tendency to split when fastened.

material most commonly used for bent frames in the United States is white oak, because of its durability and strength, while elm is used extensively in Canada, the British Isles, and Europe. Although responsible agencies have proved that oak with a moisture content as low as 12 percent is suitable for bending if handled properly, it is recommended that the builder use unseasoned wood, because it is usually free from surface checks, heats rapidly, and needs only heat to bend rather than the addition of moisture required by dry wood.

The frame stock should be as straight-grained as possible, and this is sometimes achieved by splitting a plank with the grain and then sawing out the frames parallel to the split edges. The stock should be about a foot or so longer than the finished length of the frame. It is best to bend the framing stock on the flat of the grain (Figure 10-2), for not only will it bend more easily this way, but the wood's tendency to split when plank fastenings are driven through it is then minimized. Specifications for some boats call for a flat frame size such as 1" × 1⅜" bent on the flat. However, from the standpoint of theory, a frame is a transverse strength member and thus does its job best when its athwartships dimension is relatively great. If this were carried too far, it would be impossible to bend the frame, so a good compromise is to make the frame square. Then it is just as strong crossways as it is fore and aft, and in practice it may be quickly turned on its other edge if it does not readily bend in the direction first attempted.

SAWN FRAMES FOR ROUND-BOTTOMED HULLS

Rare these days but still in use for large wooden vessels (such as a 90-plus-foot dragger I saw under construction in 1984) are double-sawn frames, Figure 10-1. The frame segments, called futtocks, are customarily riveted or bolted together, depending upon size. The same figure shows a frame sawn from a natural crook. The famous Abaco dinghies are still being built in the Bahamas with this type of frame, made of native hardwood.

STEAMING ARRANGEMENTS

You may have seen the steam box at a local boatyard in action. However, the source of steam does not have to be elaborate when only one boat is to be built. It may be generated in an old hot water boiler from a house, a large kettle, or any similar device rigged so a wood fire may be built under it and the steam piped to the box. The supply of water must be ample for the period of time you plan to work. Watch this point, for the water goes fast.

The steam box is wooden, made as steam-tight as possible by caulking with cotton if necessary, and large enough for a half dozen frames and some room to spare. It is possible that the garboard and one or two other planks will need steaming to bend them in place, so make the box large enough for this job. There must be a door at one end, opposite to the end with the steam supply pipe, and the cracks are packed with rags to prevent steam from leaking out. The box should be located close to the boat, because bending calls for fast work before the frames become too cool. Handle the frames with cotton work gloves. A rough rule for steaming is one hour per inch of frame thickness. A few trials will have to be made to get the hang of it.

Light frames are sometimes made supple in boiling water by placing them in a length of pipe set at an angle with the ground, with a fire built under the pipe's lower end. This scheme works well because, with water in the pipe, there is little danger of unduly drying the frames. Strings should be tied to the frames for pulling them out, and the upper end of the pipe should be stuffed with rags to retain the steam. Typical steaming arrangements are shown in Figure 10-3. Others on the same order may be improvised by the builder.

FIGURE 10-3.
Steaming arrangements.

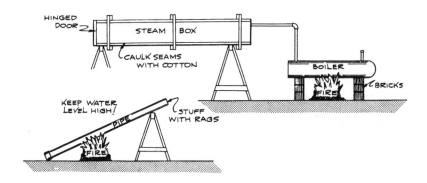

My good friend Pembroke Huckins once built a large hull I designed for him that called for oak frames made of two layers, each 1½" × 3¾", bent one on top of the other. He decided to make the oak supple by boiling it—the first time he had tried this—and was delighted that only a handful of the approximately 280 pieces broke during placement. Figure 10-4 is a mid-ships construction section of Huckins's 73-footer showing the double-bent frames. Note that the clamps, shelves, and stringers have not been shaded in the conventional manner on this drawing, which means these members were made of "nominal" lumber like 2 × 4s, 2 × 6s, et cetera, all readily available in the building area. In addition to the logistical advantage this offered, the lighter material was easier to fit into position. Incidentally,

FIGURE 10-4.
Construction section of yacht *Prudence B.*

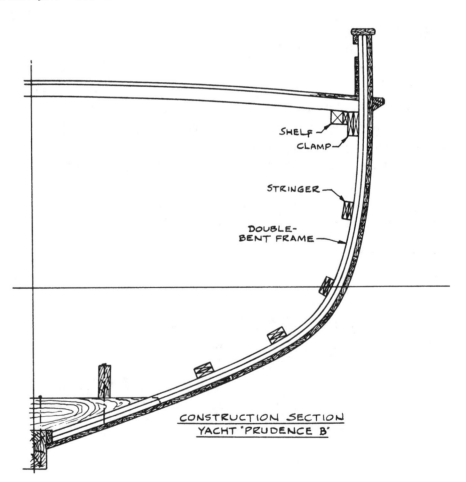

SHELF

CLAMP

STRINGER

DOUBLE-
BENT FRAME

CONSTRUCTION SECTION
YACHT "PRUDENCE B"

years later Pem recalled that he had followed someone's advice and added urea to the water when bending the frames. He thought this might have accounted for the small amount of breakage, and indeed the technique is mentioned in *Wood Handbook* (see Appendix).

BENDING THE FRAMES

Frames may be either bent to shape in the boat against the ribbands or bent on forms and then fitted to the boat cold. The former is by far the easier method, and unless the frames for your boat are relatively heavy or the hull is extremely shapely, this system should be followed. Guided by the frame layout on the construction plan, first mark the frame positions on all the ribbands and at the keel, marking both edges with a thin batten the same width as a frame and making sure the marks are made at right angles to the centerline. Start framing amidships where the bends are less severe. This allows your experience to accumulate as the work progresses toward the ends, where sharp bends are likely to be encountered.

The actual bending procedure goes as follows. Take a frame out of the steam box and as rapidly as possible cut the heel of the frame to fit the keel and nail it in place. Then start the bending by pulling inboard on the head of the frame as you progressively force the frame against the ribbands with hands or feet, all the while twisting the frame to lie flat against the ribbands. By pulling the head inboard, assuming the frames are being bent on the inside of the ribbands, the frame will bend more than enough, and it then can be flattened and forced into position against the ribbands. A gadget like that shown in A in Figure 10-5 may be employed to aid in twisting in the bevel should it be troublesome.

If plenty of hands are available, the frame can be clamped to the ribbands as you bend it; otherwise clamp it at the topmost ribband, give it a downward wallop on the head to make sure that it touches all the ribbands, and then temporarily toenail it to the ribbands so that your clamps will be ready for further duty on the next frame. You will soon learn that the bending must be done quickly once the frame has been removed from the steam box. If possible, two people should work on the bending while a third tends the box. When the boat is designed with frames in one piece from sheer to sheer, there must absolutely be two people bending, one on a side, each working from the keel toward the sheer, in order that the frame can be completely bent before it cools.

In many boats all the frames may be bent as described above. However, the frames in full-bowed hulls and those along the horn timber aft of the waterline in hulls like sketch D of Figure 8-14 (Chapter 8) are often troublesome due to the necessity of twisting in a bevel in a short length. Because of this, it is permissible to depart from bending at right angles to the centerline in the extreme bow and to allow the frames to lie naturally against the planking so they slope forward from keel to sheer. These are called cant frames and are shown in B in Figure 10-5. The same is true of stern frames in a double-ended hull.

FIGURE 10-5.
Bending on frames is easier with two or more people—the goal is to completely bend the frame before it cools. In the extreme ends of a vessel, the frames are not placed at right angles to the centerline, but rather angled to allow them to lie naturally against the planking. These cant frames are shown in B.

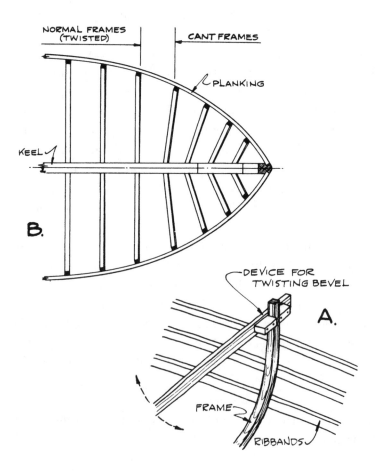

COLD-FITTED FRAMES

Framing the counter stern, as the type of stern in D in Figure 8-14 is called, should be done very carefully if bumps and hollows are to be avoided. In the interest of fair lines, either the frames for such sterns are bent over a mold outside of the boat, as described later, or oversized frame stock is overbent on the ribbands, after which it is removed, straightened to the proper curve, and then beveled to lie against the ribbands. The inner edge is finally beveled to correspond to that on the outside of the frame so that stringers and clamps to be installed later will fit properly. These cold-fitted, beveled frames are similar in cross section to the double-sawn frame illustrated in Figure 10-1. The excess curvature first bent into the frame is accomplished by padding the ribbands with short lengths of wood in way of the frame location. Curvature can be taken out of a frame after it has cooled and set, but none may be added.

If the use of cold-fitted frames cannot be avoided, you must make one or two forms similar to the one illustrated in A in Figure 10-6 over which to bend the frames. To get an idea of the curves required for the forms, bend a piece of soft iron rod or lead-covered electrical wire against the ribbands and use it as a guide to build a form. The frames must always be bent to more curve than necessary, and the form can be padded to vary the shape. When ready to bend, the end of the frame is slipped under the pipe shown in the figure and wedged; then the bending is done with a steady pressure. Leave the frames on the form at least overnight so they will cool and set properly and not lose too much shape when removed. When there is too much curve, the frames can be straightened with a device like that shown in Figure 10-7 on a bench or a corner of the shop building. Reverse curves can be made on the form by bending one curve at a time, allowing the first bend to set well, and then nailing braces across the curve to hold the shape while the reverse is being bent.

Due to tensile stress, the outer fibers of a frame will tend to split when the curve is sharp, but someone found long ago that a metal strap bent along the outside of the frame is a very successful way to combat this breakage. The strap shown in B in Figure 10-6 is typical of the simple scheme involved and is very handy. The tendency to split is also present when bending sharp curves against ribbands. If you find some bad curves, a strap similar to that illustrated may be devised to do the same job. In most cases the strap need only extend somewhat more than the length of the hard bend, such as around the turn of the bilge of a motorboat. After some practice you will be able to judge which bends may give trouble, like those in the S frames forward of the counter of boats like D in Figure 8-14, in which case the frame stock may be split with a fine saw cut as shown in Figure 10-7 to permit the bend to be

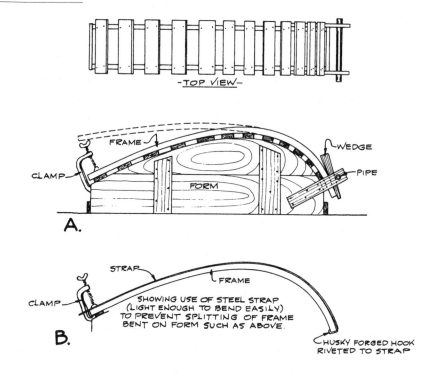

FIGURE 10-6.

Cold–fitting frames are bent around a form. Bending a metal strap along the outside of the frame prevents the splitting of the outer fibers of the frame.

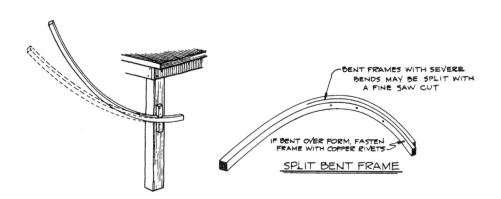

FIGURE 10-7.

If a form is overbent, one solution is to allow the bend to release naturally, as shown on the left, or splitting the form stock with a fine saw, as shown on the right.

made easily. As a matter of fact, this is easier than using a strap when the frames are bent in the hull inside the ribbands. When the frames are bent outside of the ribbands, a strap is not difficult to use. If splitting is resorted to, the frame should be fastened in way of the cut as soon as possible.

LAMINATED FRAMES

Builders and repairers alike, unless they are determined to use the traditional framing methods described earlier, have laminated frames with great success. This involves the same techniques described earlier, but replaces "cold-fitted frames" with thin sections of wood built up in layers using epoxy. You should let each layer fully cure before gluing up the next.

FLOOR TIMBERS

One of the most important members of the hull frame is the so-called floor or floor timber. These pieces of flat-grained material, usually oak, are the strength connection between the frames and backbone. Without floors, severe strains would be imposed on the garboard planks and their fastenings along the rabbet, and the hull would probably not remain tight. Floors are generally placed alongside every frame to ensure that each frame is securely fastened to the backbone, but there are certain exceptions to this rule. You will see plans for some powerboats and light centerboard sailboats with floors located only at every other frame, but in the interest of safety, most boats of the cruiser type, whether sail or power, do not omit any of them.

Floors are set on edge on top of the backbone structure and drift or through-bolted to it, depending upon their location in the boat. Fastenings to frames are either bolts or copper rivets. There are always two bolts through to the keel where the width of the backbone permits, and good practice calls for three or four fastenings to the frame on each side. Floors are shown in Figures 1-3, 1-4, 1-5, 6-2, 8-9, and 8-14 (D) and are clearly visible in Figures 6-4, 9-7, 9-11, and 10-10 (see the corresponding chapters). The latter picture well illustrates the bolting of frames to the floors.

It should be noted in Figure 9-11 that floors have already been fitted to the backbone, although the boat has not yet been framed. This method is common practice for the professional builder, but would be recommended to the amateur with reluctance, because the mold loft work involved for each floor might try his patience to the breaking point. With this system, each floor must be preshaped from a full-size section drawn at each frame, and correct bevels must be cut on three edges before the floor can be bolted in position. In v-bottomed hulls, floors must also be preshaped, being an essential part of each frame. However, the shape is obtained simultaneously with that of each frame being built, and there are not so many of them to make, so the lofting of floors is not as much of a chore as it is with bent-frame hulls.

The thickness of floors should be as specified on the plans and is usually the same as the frames in v-bottomed boats. In bent-frame hulls most of the floors are the same thickness or slightly less than the thickness of the frame. Those under the mast steps and engine beds in both types of boats are made heavier to take the extra strains found in those areas and to accept the fastenings that run through the adjoining parts at these points. Floors in way of ballast keels are bored for bolts through the keel casting and are of a siding (thickness) equal to the ordinary floors plus the diameter of the bolts.

Like all joints in a well-built boat, it is imperative that floors be carefully fitted. They are made to have full contact with the frames, and where the frames twist in the ends of the boat, the floors are beveled off to fit tightly as shown in Section A-A in Figure 10-8. Due to the hull curving in toward the centerline forward and aft of amidships, the twist in the frames will be toward the ends; consequently the floors are placed on the forward side

FIGURE 10-8.
The beveling and fastening of floors is important; good practice calls for using three or four fasteners from the floor to the frame.

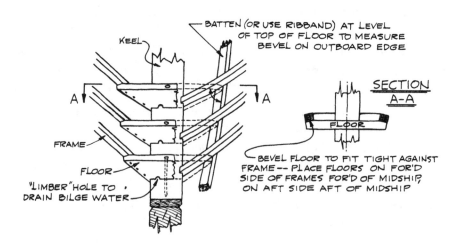

of the frames forward of amidships and on the aft side of the frames from amidships to the stern. An occasional floor may be located otherwise for one reason or another at the option of the designer.

The bottom edge of a floor is beveled to fit the member it rests upon, and many professionals prefer to notch them a half inch or so over the keel to aid in preventing movement of the parts when the hull is stressed. Limber holes are cut on the bottom edges of floors before installation (Figure 10-8) so rain or bilge water will drain to the low point of the bilge for removal by pumping. The outboard edges of the floors are beveled so the planking will bear against them. This bevel may be obtained from a ribband in the vicinity, or a short batten may be sprung around the adjacent frames for the same purpose.

Another builder of my 18'7" Barbara Anne launch design, Maynard W. Lowery of Tilghman Island, Maryland, thoughtfully sent me snapshots taken during construction, and Figure 10-9 shows the neatly fitted floor timbers. Incidentally, Lowery chose to strip-plank this hull with Atlantic white cedar.

Fitting and fastening floors is a chore indeed but very important for the longevity of a wooden hull of normal construction. I know of two sailboats that had additional floors installed after at least 25 years of

FIGURE 10-9.
Floor timbers installed in a professionally built 18'7" utility launch, this one my Barbara Anne design.

service. The work required to install them was almost overwhelming, but both craft were cherished by their owners and were sailed for many years afterward.

LONGITUDINAL STRENGTH MEMBERS

Although fore-and-aft stringers and clamps may not be fastened in place before the hull is all or partially planked, they may be considered part of the hull framing because they are used whether or not the boat is decked. Stringers and clamps are planks on edge fitted on the inside of the frames. They strengthen the hull considerably, and to be most effective they should fit snugly and be carefully fastened. They are made of hard pine or Douglas fir and sometimes oak where weight is not objectionable and maximum strength is the goal. To save weight in the ends of the hull and make installation much easier, the clamps and stringers, in other than the smallest hulls, are tapered in width from a maximum amidships to about one-half the width at the ends of the boat. Stringers and clamps are clearly shown in the photograph of the workboat in Figure 10-10. If material is not available to install these pieces in single lengths, they may be pieced out with scarphs as described in Chapter 8 and as shown in Figure 8-15.

Bilge stringers are used in all round-bottomed boats except the smallest ones, and in powerboats there may be several on each side of the hull. They are not found in v-bottomed boats because of the structural strength of the chines. Stringers give valuable support if a boat should run aground and lay over on her side. There is usually one stringer on each side made up of one or more strakes, and when multiple, the strakes are wedged tightly together. The bilge stringer is fastened to each frame with staggered flathead wood screws, except in heavy construction, where bolts are used. In the highest-quality boats the screws are counterbored and plugged where they will be visible in quarters, and the upper and lower inboard corners of the stringers are sometimes chamfered or beaded with a router for appearance by professional builders. The stringers should be located as closely as possible to the position shown on the drawings, run as far fore and aft as is practical, and depending upon the relative thickness of the piece, sprung or shored in place for fastening.

The sheer clamp is located on the inside of the frames as shown in Figure 10-11. Figure 10-12 has been especially drawn to show that in decked boats the upper edge of the clamp is set down from the sheerline a distance equal to the thickness of decking plus the depth of the deck beams. It is

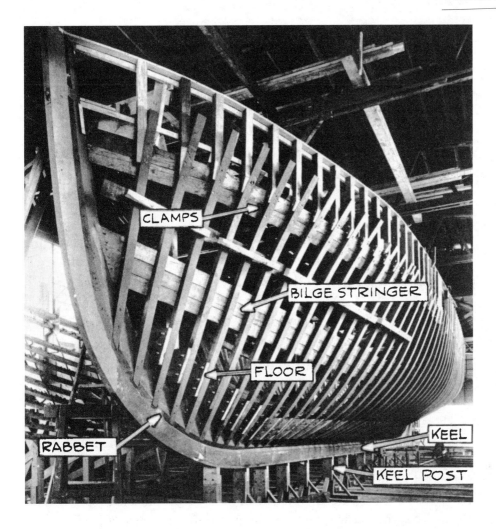

FIGURE 10-10.
Stringers and clamps are fastened inside the frames. This photograph shows why bent frames are often called "ribs." (*Morris Rosenfeld*)

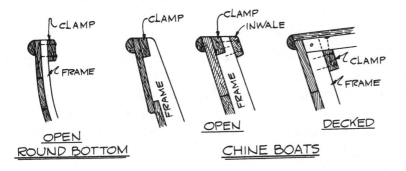

FIGURE 10-11.
Sections showing position of the sheer clamps on various types of vessels.

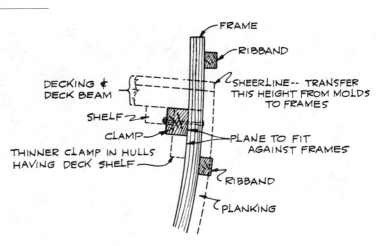

FIGURE 10-12.
In decked hulls, the top edge of the clamp is placed below the sheer.

important to keep this point in mind or else the sheerline will not be at the right height. The clamps are bolted to the frames for maximum strength. This means that if the builder fails to think ahead and completely planks the hull before installing the clamps, the bolts will have to extend through the planking, possibly interfering with the plank fastenings.

There are two ways of getting around this, although I am a little ahead of myself, since planking will be discussed in the next chapter. One way is to fasten the upper two planks in place temporarily until planking is completed. After the molds are taken out of the hull, the two planks are taken off to enable the fitting and bolting of the clamps and then replaced and fastened for good. The other method is to transfer the sheer heights from the molds to adjacent frames, then cut away enough of the molds to install the clamps before planking. The uppermost ribbands hold the frames in position during this work. The molds, of course, cannot be used for another boat without some rebuilding. The clamps are run from the transom to the stem, and the outside faces are planed to fit snugly against the frames. Except in straight-sided boats, this is always necessary if the clamp has much depth (Figure 10-12). Like the bilge stringers, the lower inside corners are sometimes chamfered or beaded for looks.

Clamps in v-bottomed hulls are installed and fastened when the frames are set up, and with the chines, are used to hold the frames in alignment. Because of the depth of v-bottomed frames, the clamps are more often screwed than bolted.

ENGINE STRINGERS

In order to distribute the weight of the engine, and also to aid in elimination of hull vibration, engine stringers are found in all properly designed motorboats. Sometimes of oak, but more often of such woods as fir or yellow pine, the stringers are run as far fore and aft as possible. To accomplish this, they are occasionally pulled toward the centerline forward to permit them to extend farther and still be securely fastened on top of the floors. This applies to both stringers in a single-engine boat and to the inboard stringers in a twin-engine craft. The outboard stringers for twin-engine installations are usually too far out to catch the floors and are set on the frames. They are run straight and cannot be as long as the inner members due to the curving hull shape. It is desirable to have the stringers in single lengths, but if necessary they may be scarphed, the joints being planned to avoid conflicting fastenings.

The stringers are notched ⅜" to ½" over the floors and frames, and through- or drift-bolted to the floors. Outboard stringers not resting on floors are through-bolted to the frames (see Figure 10-13). The centerline of the propeller shaft is laid out from the drawings and the engine stringers spaced equally to each side, the distance being figured from the horizontal center-to-center distance of the engine holding-down bolts, with allowances made for the thickness of the engine bed material.

ENGINE BEDS

In motorboats the engine beds are bolted to the engine stringers, Figure 10-13, and may or may not be notched over the floors. If enough bolts are used to transfer the engine thrust to the stringers, notches are not necessary. The present custom of having the engine in an auxiliary as far aft as possible does not lend itself to the installation of stringers, and in this case the beds are notched over the floors and drift-bolted to them (see Figure 10-14). In all boats the installation diagram for the engine must be consulted to determine the vertical position of the bottom of the bolt lugs in relation to the centerline of the propeller shaft in order to determine the top edge of the beds. Anywhere from ¼" to ½" is allowed between the lugs and the beds for the insertion of hardwood shims when the engine is aligned with the propeller shaft, unless the engine is fitted with mounts with vertical adjustment. These are fairly common these days.

FIGURE 10-13.

Placement of engine stringers and beds for both a single- and a twin-engine powerboat hull.

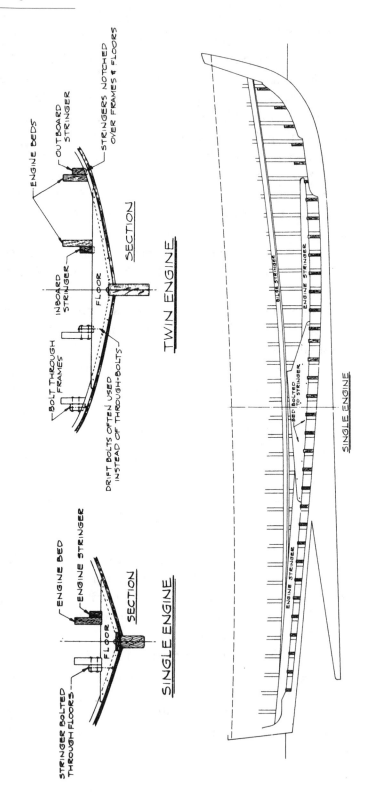

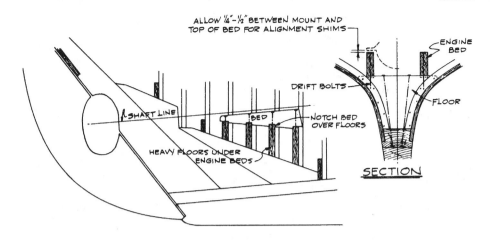

FIGURE 10-14.
Auxiliary sailboat engine bed installation showing the bed notched over the floors.

In some auxiliary sailboats the engine is tucked away so far aft that there is no choice except to make the bed supports of fabricated metal, either steel, hot-dipped galvanized if at all possible, or of bronze in boats of highest quality. It should be expected that the naval architect specified how this should be done. Figure 10-15 is an engine bed support as detailed by the designer of a 35-foot deep-keel sailboat. The metal supports are located in the spaces between the frames.

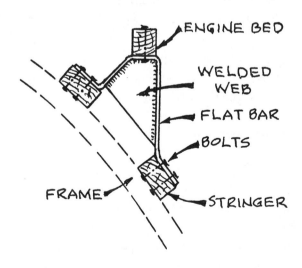

FIGURE 10-15.
A fabricated metal engine bed support is sometimes necessary in sailboat hulls.

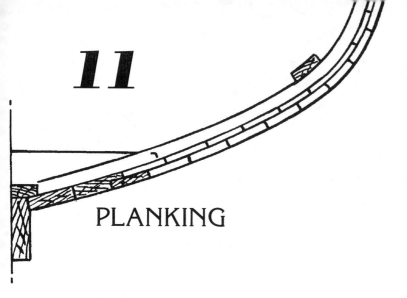

11

PLANKING

PLANKING A WOODEN HULL—with something other than veneers or panels—is often the most difficult part of boatbuilding for the amateur and always one of the simplest tasks for the professional. The beginner has trouble laying out the width of the planks and the run of the planking seams, while the expert does not seem to give it much thought due to accumulated experience and firsthand teaching. The stumbling of an amateur is understandable, because it is not easy to learn planking from a book or even to explain the subject in words. It is strongly suggested that you study the planking on boats in yards, especially of the type you will build. Through the ages a good many methods of planking have been devised, and many of them will be discussed here.

CARVEL PLANKING

It will be well to discuss typical smooth planking first (see Figure 11-1), as over the years this method has been the most common, and much of what is said about carvel planking a round-bottomed boat will apply also to other methods.

The individual planks are called strakes, and for appearance they should be nicely proportioned, shaped so the lines of the seams are pleasing to the eye from every direction. Seams open and shut a little due to shrinking and swelling, and for well-kept appearance, especially on the topsides, the strakes should not be too wide or the seams will become unsightly as well as difficult to keep tight.

Carvel planking is usually made with the seams tight on the inside and open on the outside to receive cotton caulking, which makes the planking watertight. The bevel on the seams is called outgauge (A in Figure 11-1, and Figure 11-2) and should be made so the opening on the outside is about $1/16$" per inch of plank thickness. The planking material should be ordered somewhat thicker than the specified finished dimension to allow for planing and sandpapering and for hollowing the inside face of planks on sharp turns (B in Figure 11-1). Most of the hull planking will not need more than an extra $1/8$" for finishing, but that on the turns may require more. A straight-edge held on a frame will determine the amount (C in Figure 11-1), or you can measure with a profile gauge, which is merely a series of stiff, parallel wires that slide back and forth in a plastic holder but are retained with enough friction to hold them in any desired position. Figure 11-3 shows

FIGURE 11-1.

Terms associated with smooth carvel planking (top). Also shown: beveling of seams (A); the extra thickness needed on planks for finishing (B); and measuring the extra thickness needed by using a straightedge (C).

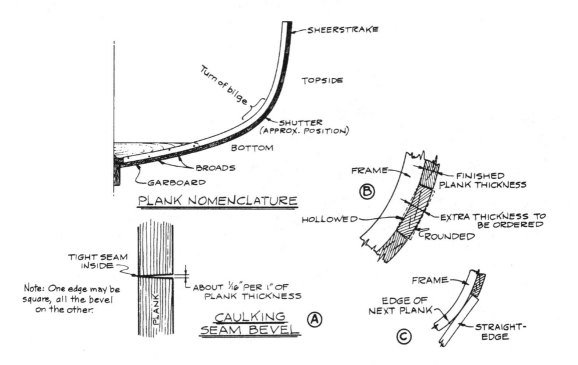

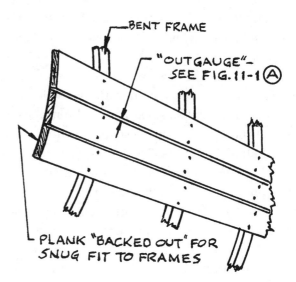

FIGURE 11-2.
Typical carvel hollow-and-rounded planking; also caulking seam (*see Figure 11-1*).

BENT FRAME

"OUTGAUGE"- SEE FIG. 11-1 Ⓐ

PLANK "BACKED OUT" FOR SNUG FIT TO FRAMES

how the gauge works. With this tool the shape can be taken off any piece, such as a molding or, in this case, the curve of the frame. Profile gauges are made in two sizes, one about 6" long and one about twice that length.

Hollowing of planks (B in Figure 11-1, and Figure 11-2) is called "backing out" and is conventionally done using a wooden plane with a convex sole and iron. Some builders grind the iron to work in a regular flat-bottomed plane.

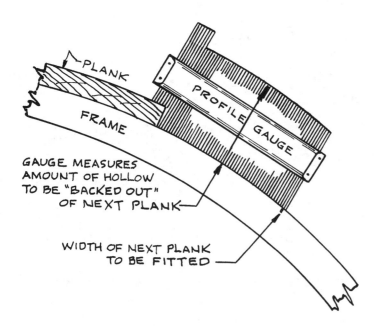

PLANK

FRAME

PROFILE GAUGE

GAUGE MEASURES AMOUNT OF HOLLOW TO BE "BACKED OUT" OF NEXT PLANK

WIDTH OF NEXT PLANK TO BE FITTED

FIGURE 11-3.
Using a profile gauge to measure out the amount of hollow needed on a plank.

Other uses for the gauge will be found during the building of a boat. After a plank is hollowed to fit the curve of the frames, scribe the finished thickness on the edges of the plank and roughly round the outside of the plank before fastening it in place. This will save time later.

It is not recommended that amateurs choose to build, as their first project, a boat having planking that is less than ½" finished thickness. However, if you have the ability as well as the courage to undertake planking less than ½" thick, then go ahead, but remember at that dimension the seams cannot be caulked and therefore must fit perfectly in order to avoid leaks. A hull with thin planking, though, can be covered with fiberglass or other fabric, provided the additional weight does not destroy the reason for thin planking in the first place.

Incidentally, in the language of boatbuilding the strakes of planking are never "installed"; they are *hung*.

BUTTS IN PLANKING

Some small boats can be planked with full-length strakes, but inasmuch as the usual available lengths of planking material are from 12 to 16 feet in intervals of 2 feet, the strakes will ordinarily consist of two or three pieces butted end-to-end. From the standpoint of strength, the location of butts is important, and a plan should be laid out before the work is started, taking into consideration the material at hand. Rather than try to visualize the butts on the frame of the boat, it is much easier to make a rough diagram as a guide.

Figure 11-4 shows a satisfactory way of laying out the butts, and you will note that no two of them should be in the same frame space without three strakes between, and adjacent strakes should not have butts without three frame spaces between them. Butts are made midway between a pair of frames (never on a frame except in massive construction), the joint being backed by an oak or mahogany block as thick as the frame (because the fasteners are the same length as those holding the planks to the frames), and 1" to 1½" wider than the strake of planking. Butt blocks should be sawn to length to fit between the frames, planed on the outside to fit snugly against the planking, and should have their outboard corners generously chamfered to drain water that otherwise might be trapped on top of the block (A in Figure 11-4).

There are those who advocate cutting the length of a butt block short of the space between the frames (see B in Figure 11-4). This is standard procedure when building a v-bottomed boat with widely spaced frames, and it does eliminate any chance of stopping drainage, as shown in A in the figure. Nevertheless, when the ends of the block are properly fitted and

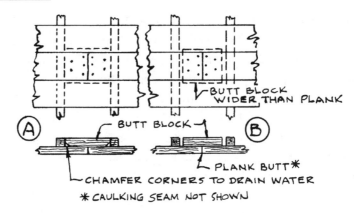

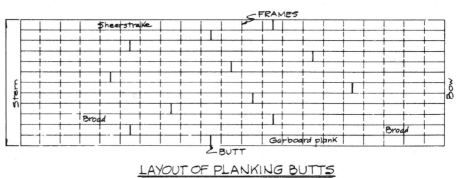

LAYOUT OF PLANKING BUTTS

(No scale necessary for this diagram.)

FIGURE 11-4.

Laying out the planking butts to ensure both strength and good drainage.

bedded, the work goes a bit more easily, especially if the builder is working alone. After soaking the butt block in wood preservative and coating the outside of the block with bedding compound, it can be toenailed to the adjacent frames; then the fasteners are driven through the planks from the outside. Bear in mind that the ends of the planks being butted must also have a caulking seam just as the edges of a plank do, and this must be cut before the plank is hung.

PLANKING PROCEDURE

Let us consider carvel planking a simple round-bottomed boat like the 12-footer used to illustrate loft work in Chapter 7. The normal planking sequence for the amateur is to fashion the sheer strake first, then the garboard, the two adjoining broad strakes, and the bottom planking to the turn of the bilge, and to then alternately plank one strake under the sheer strake and one on the bottom, with the *shutter*, as the last plank is called, coming about midway between the bottom planking and the sheer (see Figure 11-1). Because it is difficult to clamp the shutter, it should be a plank that is fairly straight, without twist, and that does not require steaming.

The first consideration is the total number of strakes to be used, determined by the widths amidships at the longest frame. The garboard will be the widest, and the widths will decrease toward the turn of the bilge, with the topside strakes the narrowest and all about the same width. The sheerstrake can be a little wider than the rest of the topside planks if a rubrail is to be installed.

As to exactly how wide to make the planks on a given boat, this is where your inspection of other boats can help. The following is offered as a general guide to proportion: 6" to 8" for the garboard, diminishing to 4½" for the topsides and 5" to 6" for the sheer strake. These sizes are not hard and fast, but it should be remembered that for good appearance, the topside strakes below the sheerstrake should not be over 4½" wide amidships. Naturally, these widths apply only at amidships, as the frame girths at the ends of the boat are less, and the planks must taper in width toward the ends. Again for appearance, the taper should be uniform.

Bend a thin batten around the midship frame, mark the length from the keel rabbet to the sheer, and lay out the plank widths on the batten. Then lay off the width marked on the batten for the sheerstrake on the midship frame and run a full-length batten around the frames for the purpose of obtaining the bottom edge of the plank. The sheerstrake should be tapered a little at the bow and stern, and the batten must be fair. When the appearance of the line is satisfactory, mark the edge of the plank at the hull's ends and on all the frames, and remove the batten. Of course, it is understood that the top edge of the plank is the sheerline, from which the thickness of the decking, if any, must be deducted.

With the shape of the sheerstrake determined and marked out on the frames, it must be transferred to a plank for cutting. This must be done accurately, so the plank will fit properly without "edgesetting" (springing edgewise into place). The procedure for doing this is known as *spiling*.

SPILING

The shape is obtained with the aid of a spiling batten, which usually is a piece of softwood somewhat longer than any individual strake, about 4" to 6" wide, and ³⁄₁₆" or less in thickness. Several such battens should be on hand, because they will be mutilated with use. The batten is clamped or tacked to the frames; make sure it lies flat against the frames for its entire width and that it is *not* sprung edgewise. Its upper edge should be a little below the top edge of the plank to be made. This does not mean that the edge of the batten will be parallel to the plank edge. If it is, the batten has probably been sprung on edge, and the plank made from the spiling will not fit. The whole idea of the spiling batten is to place it like the plank to be made and so determine the *difference* in shape between the edge of the batten and the edge of the plank. For greater accuracy on hulls with a lot of sheer, a batten with a curved edge must be made if the batten should lie more than a couple of inches from the plank marks.

To use the spiling batten, take your carpenter's pencil compass and set the legs with a gap about ¼" more than the greatest space between the edge of the batten and the plank marks on the frames. With one leg of the compass on the plank mark, make a point on the batten square down from the line of the top edge of the plank (see Figure 11-5). Repeat at every frame and at the ends of the plank, labeling the points with frame numbers and identifying all points for the particular plank with a numbered or lettered circle so they will not become confused with points for other planks later on. Do not change the opening of the compass while spiling the plank. Mark cuts across the batten for the butt, the stern ending, or the stem rabbet, as the case may be. Now take the batten off the boat and lay it on the board that is to be used for the plank (B in Figure 11-5). Still not changing the compass opening, reverse the procedure, and this time, with one leg of the compass on a point on the batten, mark points on the board. Before making any actual marks, test with the compass and shift the batten until the points will be as close to the edge of the plank stock as possible in order not to waste width; then tack the batten against movement.

Mark all the points and the endings of the plank. Remove the spiling batten and run a fairing batten through all the points and draw the edge of the plank with a pencil. Do not worry if the shape of the line is peculiar (such as S-shaped). If the spiling has been done correctly, the plank will fit in place when bent around the frames. Now at each frame on the boat, pick off the width of the sheer strake that was previously laid out with a batten and marked on the frames. At the corresponding frame marks on the board, lay out the plank widths and run a batten through them to draw a line for the lower edge of the plank. If the boat is decked, allow a little extra on the upper edge for the crown of the deck, then saw out the plank.

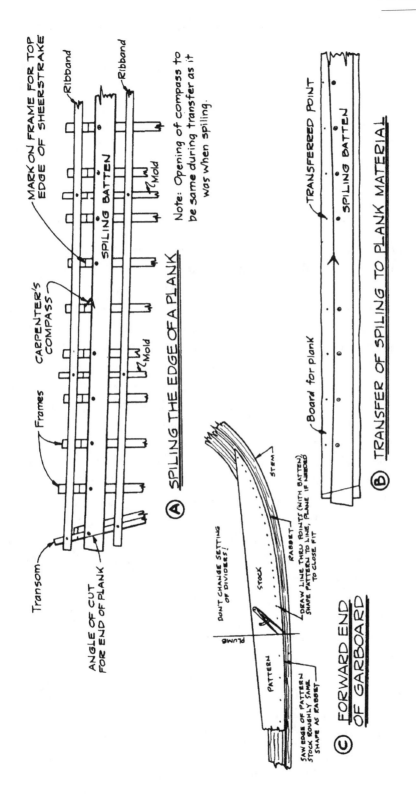

Ribband

Ribband

MARK ON FRAME FOR TOP EDGE OF SHEERSTRAKE

Note: Opening of compass to be same during transfer as it was when spiling.

SPILING BATTEN

Mold

CARPENTER'S COMPASS

Mold

Frames

Transom

ANGLE OF CUT FOR END OF PLANK

Ⓐ SPILING THE EDGE OF A PLANK

STEM

DON'T CHANGE SETTING OF DIVIDERS!

STOCK

RABBET

DRAW LINE THRU POINTS (WITH BATTEN) SHAPE PATTERN TO LINE, PLANE IF NEEDED TO CLOSE FIT

PLUMB

PATTERN

SAW EDGE OF PATTERN STOCK ROUGHLY SAME SHAPE AS RABBET

Ⓒ FORWARD END OF GARBOARD

TRANSFERRED POINT

SPILING BATTEN

Board for plank

Ⓑ TRANSFER OF SPILING TO PLANK MATERIAL

FIGURE 11-5.

Using a spiling batten.

Plane the upper edge for the crown of the deck and the lower edge square and clamp the plank in place. Unless there is something obviously wrong it can be used as a pattern for the same plank on the other side of the boat. (This is why accuracy during setting up is so important.) After that, it can be fastened in place. Bear in mind that the butt end of a plank has to have outgauge for caulking, just as with a plank edge. Incidentally, always use a block of wood between the plank and a clamp so scarring from pressure will not occur.

GARBOARD STRAKE

The garboard plank (the one closest to the rabbet) is likely to be the most troublesome plank of all, but once it is fitted in place the remainder will seem all the easier to fit. What sets this strake apart from the rest is that its shape is determined by the contour of the rabbet and also by its role as a starting point for the rest of the planking. In order to have a nice, fair upper edge from which to start the tapering of the remaining planks, the garboard might be wider at its forward end than at amidships. This is not unusual, because the plank is twisted into place at its forward end, and if it were to be tapered narrower forward than amidships the upper edge might dip down. This is the general rule, although its application depends entirely on the hull form.

To get out the garboard, a spiling is taken for the lower edge by the method described previously, except that the spiling batten should be cut so that the bottom edge comes closer to being an actual pattern for the plank, especially at the stem, where the end of the garboard will be well rounded to fit in the rabbet. The spiling marks must be close together where the curve is pronounced, and they are made plumb vertical from the rabbet line (see C in Figure 11-5).

An extra step at this point, but advisable particularly for the first-time builder, would be to make an accurate pattern of the forward end of the garboard plank, using wood thin enough so it can be twisted to touch the frames without "edge-set" (bending edgewise). The spiling is done the same way as when using a spiling batten, but in this case *make the pattern actually meet the curve of the rabbet.* A good fit will result with no waste of planking material. The garboard should be the only plank requiring special pattern work.

Incidentally, an Australian boatbuilder restoring a 1924 schooner in Florida showed me spiling battens he made from slices of plywood doorskins scarphed to make the needed length. Doorskins about 1/8" thick, used for the faces of hollow-core household doors, are sold by building-material suppliers.

Lay out the width of the garboard at the midship frame and, as you did for the bottom edge of the sheer strake, run a batten on the frames for the top edge of the garboard. The width at the ends of the garboard and the two broad strakes should be such that any excessive curvature is removed, so that the remainder of the strakes will be fairly straight when they are flat before being bent on. This straightening, however, should not be overdone, or there will be too much upward curve at the forward ends of the remaining strakes. As stated before, the garboard will probably be as wide (or a little wider) forward as it is amidships, but the test is to sight the batten you have placed and see that the line it makes is fair and pleasing in appearance from wherever you look at it. In the case of the 12-foot skiff, the width at the transom will be a little less than at amidships. As before, mark the edge on all the frames, remove the batten, and take a spiling of the edge. Saw out the plank, plane the top edge square, and plane the edge against the rabbet so it is open a little on the outside for the seam to receive caulking.

The forward end of the garboard will probably need steaming to get it in place; it is possible that this will be the only plank on the hull that will need such treatment. While the plank is steaming, assemble at hand plenty of clamps, wedges, and material for shores to the floor (if the hull is being built right side up). When ready, fit the forward end of the plank in the rabbet first and clamp it, then as quickly as possible bend the plank in place while it is still limber. Get the plank flat against the frames with shores to the floor. Cut a shore a little short, toenail it to the floor, and drive a wedge between the top of the shore and the plank. If the bottom edge does not lie properly in the rabbet, clamp a piece of oak to the frames above the plank and drive wedges against a block on the plank edge to move it sideways. Never drive a wedge directly against the edge of a plank, or the edge will be crushed. Fasten the plank in place if it fits satisfactorily. If it doesn't, there is nothing to do except to let it cool, when it can be removed and the fit corrected. If you are lucky, it will not need more steaming for replacement. Don't be discouraged, for in a normal boat the garboard is the most difficult plank to fit, and it may even cost you some wasted material before you produce one that is right.

BROAD STRAKES

The next plank to go on is the one above the garboard, called the first broad, and a spiling is taken of the edge that will lie against the garboard. Before running a batten for the upper edge, you have to decide how to taper the width of the plank so the remaining planks will be fairly straight and easy to make. Start by tapering it in proportion to the space between the garboard plank and the sheerstrake. This is done by counting the number of strakes shown on your midship planking layout batten, and at every third or so frame, called the spiling frames, dividing the distance between the top edge of the garboard and the bottom edge of the sheer strake by the planned number of strakes. At this time mark only the width of the first broad on the frames. Now run the batten and look at the line from all directions. It may be that the plank will want to be wider at the forward end in order to straighten it or give it a more pleasing appearance when viewed from forward. If so, make it a little wider, but don't overdo it. When the line satisfies, mark the frames, remove the batten, take a spiling for the top edge, and saw and plane the plank to shape. The next two or three planks are lined out with the same system so that when the turn of the bilge is reached, the remainder of the planks between there and the sheer strake may all be of uniform width and taper.

WIDTH SCALE FOR REMAINING PLANKS

The planks between the last of the bottom planks and the sheerstrake may be lined out by dividing the unplanked girth at each spiling frame into equal spaces. However, the work can be made easier if you use a planking scale made with a batten about $1/8" \times 1"$. Mark on the batten the greatest space still to be planked, which will be near the middle of the boat, and also the shortest space, wherever it may be. Then arithmetically divide the great girth distance by the number of strakes still to go on. Let us say the answer is $4\frac{1}{2}"$; therefore call the corresponding mark on the scale $4\frac{1}{2}"$. Do the same with the shortest girth and, assuming the answer is 3", call the corresponding mark on the scale 3". Now find the number of eighths of an inch there are between the two girth marks on the scale, 12 in this case. Divide the space on the scale between 3" and $4\frac{1}{2}"$ into 12 equal spaces and label them so each one represents $1/8"$. (See Figure 11-6.) You will see that the scale, when applied to the unplanked girth of any frame, will give the width of the strake at that frame.

It takes only a few minutes' time to make a planking scale, and with it you can go along and note the plank widths on as many of the frames as you like for reference when making the remainder of the strakes. From now on, it is unnecessary to run battens, although each plank must be spiled. However, if you find that the seams are not coming out as they should, it is

PLANKING SCALE

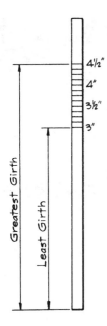

4½"
4"
3½"
3"

Greatest Girth
Least Girth

Example: Assume 8 strakes remaining.
Greatest girth divided by 8= 4½"
Least   "   "   " 8= 3"
4½"– 3"= 1½"= 12 eighths
Divide space between girth marks on
 scale batten into 12 equal parts.
Scale applied to any frame will give
 plank width at that frame.

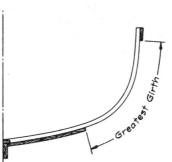

Greatest Girth

Greatest Girth

FIGURE 11-6.
A planking scale makes lining out the last of the planks easier. With it you can mark the plank widths on the remaining frames.

best to run a batten to straighten things out and then divide the remaining space once again.

The ribbands are only removed as they become an interference to making a plank. To keep the hull from becoming distorted, do not put more planks on one side of the boat than on the other. As you fit a plank, make a mate for the opposite side, remembering that the planks are not truly opposite. In other words, due to hollowing, for instance, the planks on opposite sides are not exact duplicates and may be compared to a pair of shoes.

STEALER PLANKS

The typical auxiliary sailboat hull, with the greatest girth to be planked located at a frame well aft of amidships, requires short planks known as stealers. These generally start at the rabbet in the sternpost and end at varying positions forward of the sternpost, depending upon the number of stealers and the shape of the hull. A study of such a hull will show that these short planks are necessary to straighten the remaining planks as the turn of the bilge is reached. The photograph, Figure 11-7, of a hull built over a permanent mold, in the process of being turned over, clearly shows the shape of the stealers along the keel. (Referring to remarks in

FIGURE 11-7.
Stealer planks are used to straighten the remaining strakes as the turn of the bilge is reached.

preceding chapters, the deadwood and ballast keel will be fitted to the hull in Figure 11-7 after it is right side up.) Often, to avoid plank ends that are too pointed to take a fastening, stealers are nibbed into their neighbors, A in Figure 11-8. In this particular type of planking there is no garboard running for the length of the keel rabbet, but it still is possible to have one as illustrated by B of Figure 11-8. There are numerous possible variations, and it is strongly urged that before beginning the job, a study be made of the planking on a boat similar to the one being built for whatever pointers can be picked up.

FIGURE 11-8.
Two methods of using stealer planks.

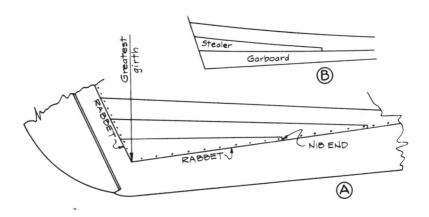

PLANK FASTENINGS

The type of fastening will be as specified on the plans or according to your own choice. Normal planking is secured with three fastenings per plank at each frame where the width of the plank will permit, such as throughout the bottom, and two at each frame in the narrow topside strakes. The fastenings are staggered to the extent allowed by the width of the frames, and planks that cross floors have an additional fastening or two driven into the floor. The butts are fastened with five in each plank end as shown in Figure 11-4. Butts in larger size auxiliaries are frequently bolted. Drilling for fastenings and plugging is discussed in Chapter 6.

After planking, the hull is ready for preliminary smoothing, done by planing with a jack plane and using long strokes to smooth off high areas. With a shorter smooth plane you are liable to plane hollow areas in the planking. Rubbing the hull up and down with palm and fingertips will reveal high spots that are not readily seen with the eye.

As a late teenager during the Great Depression, I was fortunate enough to be taken on as a boatbuilder's helper—probably the only non-Scandinavian working on hulls in that shop. After planing a mahogany-planked hull, the journeyman smoothed off the planking above the waterline with regular rectangular steel scrapers, hand held without holders, and believe me they were artists! Further smoothing was not needed before caulking and paying the seams.

CAULKING CARVEL PLANKING

Before smoothing the hull further, the plank seams are caulked to make them watertight. This is a very critical step in hull building. By caulking too hard it is possible to pull the plank fastenings and force a plank away from the frames; if the caulking is too lightly driven, it will be forced out of the seam by the swelling of the planks when wet. Just the right amount of caulking adds considerable stiffness to the planking.

The entire job of correct caulking is a skilled art, and if the amateur plans to employ professional help with his boat at any stage of construction, here is a good place to do so. Don't let this discourage you from tackling the job, however.

When the plank thickness is $5/8''$ or under, a strand or two of cotton wicking may be rolled into the seams with a caulking wheel or driven with a thin-edged making iron. Thicker planking must have regular caulking cotton in the seams, obtainable at marine supply stores in one-pound packages made up of folds of multiple strands. On a *clean* floor or other surface 25 to 30 feet long, unfold the bundle to the full length of the strands; then separate the strands. They break easily, so handle them with care. Now take two strands of cotton at a time and roll them in a ball. Also make a couple of balls from single strands for use in narrow seams and plank butts or for adding a piece to a double strand for use where the seam is wide. Keep the cotton clean, or else you will have to pick wood chips and pieces of trash off the strands as you use them.

A few caulking tools are shown in Figure 11-9. The caulking wheel is not difficult to make if you are unable to buy or borrow one. Mine is made from a piece of 1⅛" thick × 1⅞" wide × 8" long hardwood; the brass wheel is ⁵⁄₃₂" thick, 1½" in diameter, has a ⁵⁄₁₆" brass axle, and is shaped in section as shown. For regular rather than rolled caulking you can get by with just two making irons: a No. 0 with a ¹⁄₁₆" thick edge and a No. 1 with a ⅛" thick edge. (Just so you know, a No. 00 making iron has a ¹⁄₃₂" thick edge.) A dumb iron is used to open up seams fitted too tight. For certain hulls it is easier to caulk the garboard plank seam at the keel with a making iron having a bent blade; the tool is a "bent iron."

It is said there is something special about using a caulking mallet instead of a hammer—there is a certain ring to it, and resilience. Mine was given to me by a stair builder who worked in a shipyard during World War I. The head is 10" long and 2" in diameter in its middle 3 inches; it necks down to 1½" diameter at the ends. The 14½" long handle is ⅞" diameter at the head end, tapering to 1¼" at the heel. The steel bands are hand forged. Those at the middle of the head are ⅛" thick × ½" wide, while the 1" wide bands at the ends of the head are tapered in thickness from ³⁄₁₆" to a bit more than ¹⁄₁₆".

FIGURE 11-9.
Seam caulking tools.

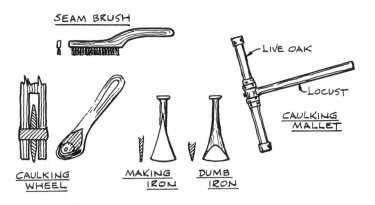

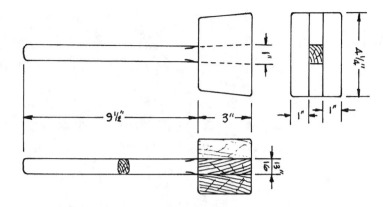

FIGURE 11-10.
A homemade mallet can be used for caulking as well as many other jobs.

A mallet that has worked just as well for me as the traditional caulking tool just described is sketched in Figure 11-10. This was made of hickory scraps culled from a neighbor's kindling supply (which in turn came from scraps culled from an ax-handle manufacturer). More than twenty years ago I assembled it with epoxy resin thickened a bit with a silica epoxy thickener. A mallet such as this is handy for all sorts of jobs, including caulking.

Start at one end of a seam, holding a making iron between the thumb and second finger of your left hand while your first finger is holding the cotton. The iron is across the palm of the hand and held in position by the other fingers. Tuck an end of a cotton strand in the seam with a making iron (normally the No. 0 making iron will do, changing to a No. 1 where the seam widens), leaving a little sticking out to drive into the plank-end seam. The cotton is not fed into the seam in a straight line. Rather, it is gathered in a small loop (see Figure 11-11). The trick is to size the loop just right so the cotton bulks correctly for the width of the seam, and this will necessarily vary if the seams have not been made uniform. After you have driven a few feet of loops, go back to the beginning and drive the cotton in the seam far enough to make room for the seam composition that is put in later. This is being done by the caulker in Figure 11-11. If at any point the seam should not be open enough to take the caulking, drive a dumb iron into the seam to spread it wider. Careful fitting of the planking will reduce the work with a dumb iron to a minimum.

The cotton should not be driven all the way to the bottom of the seam. When finished being driven, it should be in the *middle* of the seam depth,

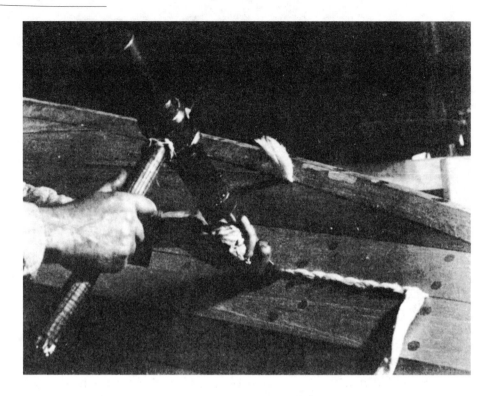

FIGURE 11-11.
Caulking is looped just enough to properly fill the seam. Too much caulking can harm the planking.

formed in a tight rope-shaped strand that should make a slight depression for itself in the plank edges. Heavier blows with the caulking mallet will be needed in hardwood planking like mahogany. Thus, good caulking calls for the right amount of cotton bulk, determined not only by the thickness of the strand but also by the size of the loops, and the right amount of mallet pressure to make the strand force a depression in the plank edges at the right depth. Don't forget to caulk the butts.

Two sources for caulking cotton, wicking, irons, and seam composition are Jamestown Distributors and Hamilton Marine. The WoodenBoat Store carries some caulking tools and supplies as well.

SMOOTHING

After caulking, paint the seams with thickish paint, using a narrow seam brush made for the purpose. If you can find one, this tool is a time-saver. Be certain not to leave any cotton bare of paint. Wipe off any paint that

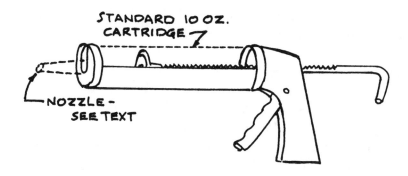

FIGURE 11-12.
Standard finger-operated
caulking gun.

gets on the outside of the planking while doing the seams. When the seams are dry, smooth the hull again with a plane, set for a finer cut this time to get the remainder of the high spots. All the while, rub the palm of your hand diagonally across the planking to find the bumps and hollows. If not smoothed perfectly at this time, the unfair portions will show up when paint is applied, and then the hull must be left as is or else a part of the job must be done over. Sandpaper the hull after planking, gradually using finer grit until it is as smooth as you want it. Garnet paper is better than sandpaper; although more expensive, it cuts faster and lasts longer. Carefully fill the seams with hull seam composition made for this purpose; apply ample pressure with a putty knife to fill the seam to the bottom. New boat planking will swell and push the compound outward, so use a dowel or similar tool to finish the seams a bit hollow.

When the hull size is such that a sore finger might result from a manual run-of-the-mill caulking gun, a device like the one in Figure 11-13 can provide relief. It takes an ordinary 10-ounce cartridge of caulking compound

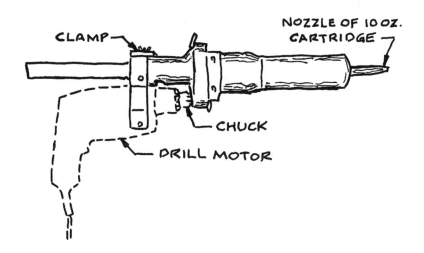

FIGURE 11-13.
Drill-motor-powered
caulking gun.

and is powered by your corded or cordless electric drill. There are also air-powered and cordless electric caulk guns available.

MORE ABOUT CAULKING

The caulking procedure described above is the old standby method and is as good today as it ever was, but modern materials permit the use of a different filling compound for the seams and even permit the cotton caulking to be omitted. So many old hands have sworn that the cotton caulking tightens the whole hull structure, and indeed caulked boats have been so satisfactory for so long that, for that reason and also the matter of expense, I would stay with the method. These new polysulfide and silicone compounds are expensive, and less will be needed if the seam is partly filled with cotton.

Absolutely clean bare wood in the seam is required for proper adhesion of the modern compounds. This is no problem with a new hull, but it certainly would take a lot of work to prepare the seams of an old boat. The cotton and seam sides are not painted in the old-fashioned way, but woods such as teak and Douglas fir, and perhaps yellow pine, have an oil that impairs adhesion and consequently need coating with a special primer made by the manufacturers of the polysulfide compounds. Check the makers' recommendations carefully in regard to seam priming. The polysulfide compounds may be a two-part mix; the silicones are not.

LAPSTRAKE PLANKING

Sometimes called clinker planking, lapstrake planking is very different from carvel planking. In the first place, because of the stiffness of the planking it is possible to plank directly over the molds, the frames being bent in place when the planking is completed. Secondly, inasmuch as one plank laps over the next, the planking must start at the garboard and proceed upward to the sheer strake without any change in order. The nature of the planking prevents efficient smoothing after completion, so each plank is planed before final installation, but a light final sanding may be done after planking and before painting.

If the hull is planked over the molds and the plank overlaps fastened as each plank is fitted, then the frame locations must be marked so lap fasteners will not be in the way when, after the planking is complete, the frames are bent in place and fastened at each lap crossed. The marking could be a problem for an amateur. I suggest the tyro frame before planking, over

FIGURE 11-14.
A 23-foot boat designed by the author and built under his supervision, with plywood lapstrake planking, all strakes scarphed with a dogleg similar to that shown in Figure 11-32.

ribbands bent over the station molds, with the boat upside down. Then each plank can be fastened to the frames as it is hung. I trust the designer is sufficiently knowledgeable about boatbuilding to space the frames so they don't coincide with the mold stations. The frame locations still must be marked on the ribbands so that the frame doesn't wander out of plumb when it is bent; this is easily done by bending a thin strip of wood the same width as the frames, and marking on the ribbands with a pencil at both edges of the strip.

The 23-footer in Figure 11-14 was planked over steamed frames bent over ribbands; thus the molds for making a number of duplicate hulls were made after deducting the thicknesses of planking, frames, and ribbands from the designer's lines plan to outside of planking.

The strakes are lined out and spiled the same as for carvel planking, but the width of the laps must be taken into account when laying out the widths of the planks. Lapstrake planking is used principally for small boats where light weight is preferred. This method of planking is very stiff due to the full-length fastening of the laps along their edges, and thinner material can be used, resulting in a saving of weight.

The section in A of Figure 11-15 shows how the upper edge of each plank is beveled so the next one will fit tight against it for the width of the lap. The bevel varies from one end of the plank to the other due to the shape of the sections. The drawing shows how the bevel may be gauged with a rule at any frame or mold. Your plans should call for a specific width of lap, but the minimum is about $\frac{5}{8}$" on planking as thin as $\frac{1}{4}$" and a little wider as the plank thickness is increased. As a guide when beveling, it is helpful to

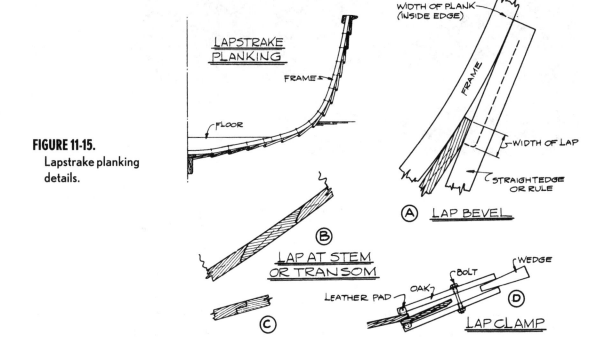

FIGURE 11-15.
Lapstrake planking details.

scratch the lap width on the plank with a marking gauge or mark it with a pencil. At each mold or spiling frame, the correct bevel is cut on the plank for the length of an inch or so. The job then becomes bench work to cut the bevel for the entire length of the plank, using the short cuts as guides.

The planks must be flush where they fit in the stem rabbet or against the transom. This is done by changing the lap bevel to a tapered bevel that looks like B in Figure 11-15 at the ends of the planks. Some builders prefer a tapering half-lap (C in Figure 11-15, and Figure 11-16), but if there is a lot of twist in the plank end a lap like B in 11-15 works better.

FIGURE 11-16.
One type of lap on the ends of clinker planking.

The half-lapped plank ends (Figure 11-16) can be done quickly with a Stanley No. 78 rabbet plane (see Chapter 3) with its gauge set at the width of the plank lap. All beveling of the plank laps must be done accurately or the seam will leak; but the modern marine sealants made from polyurethane or polysulfide have effectively eliminated the need for the perfect fit of the planking laps that was required of the old-timers who built by this method. A bead of one of these products can be easily applied so there is a minimum of squeeze-out when the laps are clamped and riveted.

Something to remember about lapstrake planking: While the shape of any one plank is the same on both sides of the hull, the bevels are opposite. In other words, planks are made right-hand and left-hand.

If the lapstrake boat is being planked over molds, the frame spacing is marked off on the keel and on each plank as it is fitted. The laps are copper riveted (or clench-nailed, as the case may be) between the frame positions as each plank is made and placed in position. (See Figure 6-11 in Chapter 6.) After completion of planking, the frames are bent, using the marks for guides. The planks are then riveted to the frames at each lap. (Rivet fasteners and clench nails for lapstrake planking are discussed in Chapter 6.) The lap rivets should be spaced about 1½" apart in ¼-inch planks, and up to about 3" in ¾-inch planks. At the stem and transom, screws are used to fasten the ends of the planks.

The seam between the stem rabbet and the plank ends is caulked as in a carvel-planked hull. At the transom do not caulk so hard that the planks strain the fasteners.

The shallow throat depth of an ordinary C-clamp does not permit it to clamp the laps, so builders have devised the clamp shown in D in Figure 11-15. A half dozen or so will be needed to hold the planks while the edges are riveted. If the boat is lapstrake-planked over frames in the conventional manner, the planks are clamped to the frames just like smooth planking.

A better type of lap clamp than the one shown in Figure 11-15, D, is the kind made and sold by Walter Simmons. It consists of two pieces of hardwood 1¼" to 1½" thick, a leather hinge, a ⅜" carriage bolt, soft pine clamp pads to prevent marring, and a welded handle (see Figure 11-17). If you are thrifty and have the wood, buy one clamp to see how it is done, then buy the handles from Simmons to make more. Simmons's stock clamp has a 7" throat from the bolt to the opening end, but this can be varied to suit the job. The carriage bolt is driven through a tight hole in one piece

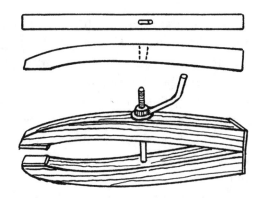

FIGURE 11-17.
Walter Simmons's planking
lap clamp.

of the hardwood, but the other piece has a tapered slot so the clamp can
be adjusted.

GLUED LAPSTRAKE PLANKING

Now that it is possible to find good marine-grade plywood, some designers
and builders are favoring very lightweight hulls using thin plywood lapstrake planking with the laps glued with epoxy. Examples of boat weights
are a 13'10" canoe weighing 44 pounds and a 15'9" sharpie skiff for rowing
and sailing that weighs 68 pounds. These boats and others are to be found
in Tom Hill's *Ultralight Boatbuilding,* a detailed step-by-step explanation
of the glued-seam lapstrake-planking method. (See the Appendix.) Iain
Oughtred's beautiful small-craft designs also are built with glued lapstrake
planking. Some designers, including Brooks Boats Designs (see opposite),
prefer glued lapstrake for strength rather than weight.

CAULKING LAPSTRAKE PLANKING

Walking the docks of a marina I came across a fellow working on a
wooden lapstrake dinghy, which he had upside down. Judging from the
plank edges, which appeared to be about ½", the boat was anything but
flimsy. Curious, I watched him cutting grooves as shown in Figure 11-18.
I noticed he was using a tool the same as one I own: a narrow gouge that
in woodcarver's language is called a veiner. When I asked him what he
was up to, he said the old girl was getting up there in age and a bit weepy
in the seams, so he had let her dry out and was going to fill the grooves

BROOKS BOATS DESIGNS

Brooks Boats Designs (see the Somes Sound 12½ in Chapter 2) uses glued plywood lapstrake planking in many of its designs. Shown here are a few of the steps in building the Somes Sound 12½. (*All photos courtesy Brooks Boats Designs.*)

Planks for glued-lapstrake construction are first spiled, then cut out of high-quality, marine-grade plywood planking stock that has been scarphed to length. On the left, epoxy putty is applied on the lap area in preparation for the next plank. On the right, the plank is on and clamped with a temporary batten. On top of the boat the garboard planks are trimmed to fit the outer keel.

Planks are held on and fair by temporary battens attached with drywall screws to the molds (and for some designs, to small angled blocks between molds), allowing builders to attach more than one pair of planks per day. Battens can be removed and re-used for later planks after the epoxy cures, usually about 24 hours. The set-up of the jig and molds is designed to allow easy access to the hull interior while planking, making it easier to clean up epoxy squeeze-out from the interior after each plank goes on.

After the planks are all attached the battens are removed and the overlapping ends of the planks are trimmed at the stem and transom. Then the laminated outer stem is glued and fastened over the inner stem and ends of the planks. The last residue of epoxy is also scraped off the outside of the hull. Here the centerboard trunk is being fastened to inside the hull with large screws through the keelson in final preparation for attaching the outer keel.

After the hull is planked up several molds can be removed and the centerboard trunk installed with easy access from below (shown here) and above (shown in Photo 3). Clamps made with threaded rod, nuts, and blocks of wood hold the trunk tight to the keelson while screws are drilled for and driven. The trunk is also glued on with epoxy.

(*continued*)

5.

6.

After the hull is taken off the building jig and turned over the sheer clamps are installed along the top edge of the sheer plank and beveled to the camber of the deck. Then the deck framing is installed. Here the coaming knees have been fastened and glued in place a little proud and are being trimmed to the shape of the rest of the deck, using a camber pattern to check progress as wood is planed off. Note the centerboard trunk inside the hull with floors and sole beams being installed around it. Before the deck framing was installed, the bulkhead was attached to a web frame (that took the place of a mold). The web frame provides support for the planks and allows easy access in the hull for cleaning up squeeze out. Installing the bulkhead after the hull was upright was easy and quick.

After the plywood foredeck is installed over the deck framing, temporary forms are fastened to the deck and the laminated coamings are glued up and dry-fit to foredeck and at the transom. The top and bottom edges of the coaming will be marked for trimming before the coamings are permanently installed with screws and epoxy.

with a polysulfide sealer, either 3M-101 or BoatLife LifeCalk. These are both one-part sealants, which means they require no mixing, but they may require a special primer. I would prefer a polyurethane adhesive sealant such as 3M 5200 or Sikaflex 240.

FIGURE 11-18.
Groove cut with hand tool to receive bead of polysulfide sealant.

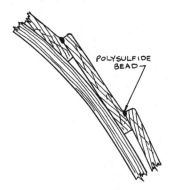

POLYSULFIDE BEAD

FIGURE 11-19.
The Rangeley boat, a classic of fine lapstrake design. (*Dick Durrance*)

DOUBLE PLANKING

The purpose of double planking is twofold: it ensures watertightness without periodic recaulking and a sleek finish that is relatively easy to maintain. Double planking is expensive, because the planking job is really done twice, notwithstanding that each layer of planking is thinner than normal and easier to apply. The total thickness of planking is the same as single planking, but weight can be saved over a single-planked mahogany job by planking the inner layer with a good, lightweight wood such as Alaska, white, or Port Orford cedar. On the other hand, a little of the weight saving is offset by the additional quantity of metal used to fasten the two layers between the frames.

The garboard plank is usually made single so that it can be readily replaced if necessary; also, it is easier to plane a proper caulking seam on a single edge. The sheerstrake and the first broad are also single thickness but are rabbeted for the outer layer as shown in Figure 11-20. The seams of the inner layer are arranged to come at the middle of the outer strakes. The planking is lined out and spiled the same as for a carvel job, for there is actually no difference except that there are two layers. Of course,

FIGURE 11-20.
Double-planking details.

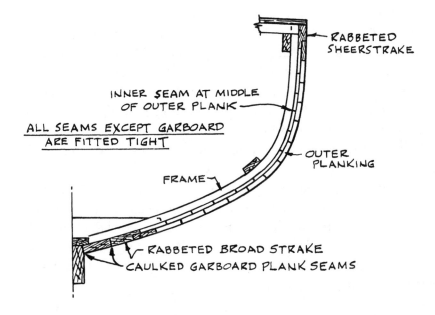

RABBETED SHEERSTRAKE

INNER SEAM AT MIDDLE OF OUTER PLANK

ALL SEAMS EXCEPT GARBOARD ARE FITTED TIGHT

OUTER PLANKING

FRAME

RABBETED BROAD STRAKE

CAULKED GARBOARD PLANK SEAMS

the width of the outer strakes is the primary consideration. The inner strakes are fastened sufficiently with small screws, and when the outer strakes are fitted, the fastenings to the frames are long enough for the total thickness of the double layer. Before each outer strake is fastened, it is first coated on the inside with a double-planking compound. An alternative treatment once used by two of the best practitioners of this planking method—Nevins and Herreshoff—is a thick coating of shellac between the inner and outer layers of planking. All seams are fitted tightly together without outgauge, as no caulking is necessary.

Between frames the layers of planking are fastened together from the inside with screws along the edges of the inner strakes and also along each side of the middle of the inner strakes to fasten the edges of the outer strakes. These fastenings are round-headed screws with washers under the heads. The whole job is very strong because the two layers are so completely tied together. Naturally the outer layer must be thick enough to take the screws from the inside. An example of layer thickness proportion would be a $5/8$" outer layer against $3/8$" inner planking, making a finished thickness of 1".

DOUBLE PLANKING BY THE CUTTS METHOD

Eddie Cutts, who operates the former Ralph Wiley yard in Oxford, Maryland, on the Eastern Shore of Chesapeake Bay, has patented (U.S. Patent No. 4,398,490) a method of building a smooth double-planked hull combining the best qualities of wood, epoxy resin, and Kevlar to produce a frameless leakproof shell without any metal fastenings. Cutts offers a book (available free at his website in PDF format) explaining the Cutts Patent Method in detail (see "Boatbuilding Plans, Patterns, and Hull Kits" in the Appendix). It is necessary to obtain a license to build with the Cutts System.

The enormous strength of Kevlar and epoxy, together with elimination of framing and fastener weight, makes the lightweight hull possible. Further, there is more usable space inside the hull compared to conventional framed hulls, and there is no worry about future disintegration of plank fasteners from galvanic corrosion, electrolysis, or both.

The hull is double-planked over molds—no ribbands are needed as for bent-frame construction. The spacing has to be related to the thickness of the first layer of planking—and I strongly advise consultation with Cutts about planking thickness and cord diameter and spacing. Thickness of the inner plank is greater than the outer by half the diameter of the Kevlar cord.

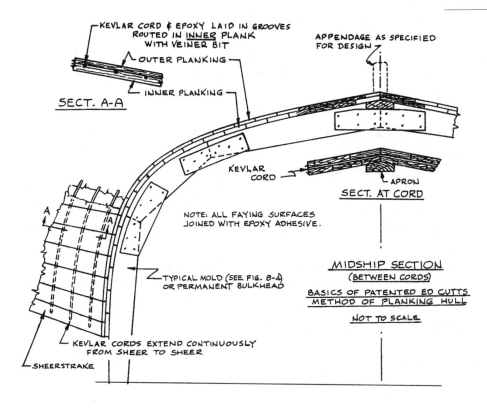

KEVLAR CORD & EPOXY LAID IN GROOVES
ROUTED IN INNER PLANK
WITH VEINER BIT

OUTER PLANKING

INNER PLANKING

SECT. A-A

APPENDAGE AS SPECIFIED
FOR DESIGN

KEVLAR
CORD

APRON

SECT. AT CORD

NOTE: ALL FAYING SURFACES
JOINED WITH EPOXY ADHESIVE.

A

A

TYPICAL MOLD (SEE FIG. 8-4)
OR PERMANENT BULKHEAD

MIDSHIP SECTION
(BETWEEN CORDS)

BASICS OF PATENTED ED CUTTS
METHOD OF PLANKING HULL

NOT TO SCALE

KEVLAR CORDS EXTEND CONTINUOUSLY
FROM SHEER TO SHEER

SHEERSTRAKE

FIGURE 11-21.
The Cutts Patent Method for frameless hull construction.

Before planking, an apron is installed on the centerline and a strake of inner planking is glued to it, as shown in Figure 11-21. Each additional strake is edge-glued (with thickened epoxy, of course, so it won't run out of the seams) and temporarily fastened to the molds until the glue cures. Incidentally, unless the hull is to be varnished bright rather than painted, the appearance (lining off) of the seams is not important.

Fairing and routing for the Kevlar cords is the next step after pulling the temporary fasteners; then the cords are set in the grooves per Cutts's instructions, followed by the outer layer of planking, the seams of which are staggered with those of the inner planks as indicated in the figure.

I don't think a builder lacking high woodworking skill should attempt the Cutts method, but from Eddie's success in using it to build hulls of proper design, it is evident that the method results in extraordinary savings in hull weight.

Sadly, Ed died in November 2009. I hope his son—who has proven he can—will carry on this practice. It's a great process.

BATTEN SEAM PLANKING

This planking system is most closely associated with v-bottomed hulls and owes its name to the fact that its seams are backed on the inside by battens to which the planks are fastened along the edges, as shown in Figure 11-22. One of this country's largest producers of v-bottomed stock cruisers used seam batten construction for many years, and it is a method being used again for building replicas of the beautiful varnished mahogany runabouts of pre–World War II. Batten seam construction has been popular with amateurs, because lining out the plank edges is fairly simple. The frames may be spaced relatively wider because the planking is stiffened by the battens. Figure 11-23 shows a well-built frame ready for planking.

A marine sealant such as a polyurethane adhesive sealant is applied to the batten in way of plank being fitted; this eliminates having to caulk the seam. However, the seam between the garboard plank and the keel is caulked in the usual manner.

FIGURE 11-22.
A typical section through batten seam construction. Note the two-piece chine, which is not always used. Be guided by the plans for the hull.

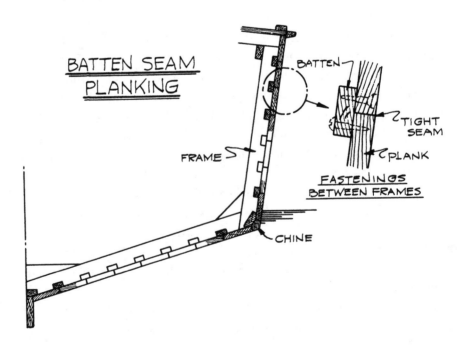

To build a boat by this method, the v-bottomed hull is set up with chines and clamps fitted and fastened in place. The seam battens are then clamped to the frames, having been located by dividing each frame into a number of equal parts, the spacing depending on the width of the available planking material. The plank widths may be greater than with carvel planking, say an average of 6" amidships. The battens are sighted for appearance, and when they have been adjusted, if necessary, so that they look fair, the top and bottom edges are marked where they cross the frames, stem, and transom frame. With the battens removed, the framework is notched so the battens will be flush with the inside of the planking when fitted. The battens are fastened in each notch with one or two flathead screws.

A plank is clamped so it overlaps a batten, and pencil lines are drawn along the edges of the batten from the inside. Thus the shape is obtained, but remember the net width of the plank is to the middle of the batten, so half the batten width must be deducted from (or added to) each edge of the plank. If the frame spacing is very wide and there is no clamp against the planking at the sheer, as in the boat in Figure 11-22, the sheerline may be preserved by spiling the top edge of the sheerstrake from a fairing batten sprung around the frames. Screw-fasten the planking to the frames and to the battens along the edges.

STRIP PLANKING

Strip planking—planking a hull with narrow edge-fastened strips of solid lumber—has enjoyed popularity in certain areas for many years. Currently the edge-fastening system consists of an adhesive plus nails to hold the strips together during the curing cycle of the adhesive. Strip planking was also practiced before the era of waterproof adhesives, but the fits between the strakes of planking had to be as near perfect as possible. The skin resulting from modern edge fastening produces a dimensionally stable structure that lends itself to sheathing with fiberglass or other such synthetic materials. This planking method can be used to build either round- or v-bottomed hulls, and I have even seen strip-planked trunk cabin sides.

Strip planking is reasonably easy for the amateur, *the shape of the hull dictating just how many complications will be encountered.* Unless girths of the hull from keel to sheer are the same throughout the length of the hull (and normally they will not be by any means), there is usually more to strip planking a hull than just nailing one parallel-sided strip to another just like it. It is easy to understand that when the girths vary, something must be done to compensate for this, just as with carvel planking.

The dimensions of the strips are a matter of design, but they are usually at least ½" thick, and anywhere from the same dimension in width up to a width of one and one-half times the thickness. There is an advantage to using square strips: it gives the builder the opportunity to select the best grain. Due to the natural expansion and contraction of wood, the strips are best laid with the grain running in the direction shown in C in Figure 11-24. Thickness is governed by the shape of the hull—the strips must bend on the hull without coming close to breaking. At the other end of the scale, the strips must be stiff enough to remain fair when sprung to the shape of the hull.

Sections through strip planking are drawn in Figure 11-24. The amount of curvature regulates the amount of beveling required, as can be seen in A in the figure. Note the open seams around the turn of the bilge on the unbeveled strips. The smaller the boat, the greater the relative curvature to be reckoned with. Some builders hollow one edge and round the other

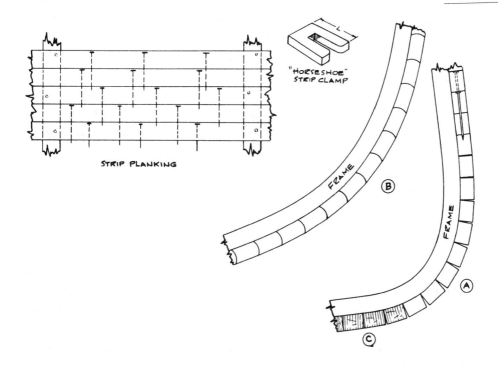

FIGURE 11-24.
Strip-planking details.

to eliminate beveling (B in the figure). If the gaps between strips are not too great, they can be filled with an epoxy putty or a polyurethane adhesive sealant such as 3M 5200, but don't apply the adhesive sealant strake by strake; rather, wait until the contents of a 10-ounce cartridge can be used up to save cost.

If the strips are not long enough, they must be scarphed. (See "Sawing Strips of Wood for Scarphing" later in this chapter.) You can make a miter box of sorts for doing this by hand, or the cutting can be done on a bench saw or with a radial saw. The length of the scarph should be about five times the strip thickness. Scarphs should be glued on the workbench, not on the boat.

The length of the nails when no adhesive is used to bond the strips together, or when the glue is resorcinol, ideally is about 2 to 2¼ times the width of the strips, but due to curvature in the sections this is not always possible, so be guided accordingly. With epoxy glue, nails 1½ times the strip thickness are ample because of the gap-filling ability of the epoxy, thickened of course as mentioned previously.

The choice of metal for the nails is largely a matter of economics. If cost does not matter, either Anchorfast Monel or silicon bronze nails are the first choice. When getting down to pennies, it is all right to use hot-dipped galvanized common wire nails, because they are buried in the wood (or should be!), not exposed to water. The spacing and number of nails should be just sufficient to clamp the strips tightly in place while the adhesive cures. Nailheads are set just barely below the surface of the wood with a nail set. Some like to drive the nails at an angle to the strip for a locking action. If the hull mold contains bulkheads or other permanent framing, every other strip or so should be fastened to such a member with a nail or screw.

Before epoxy resins became available, resorcinol glue was used between the edges of strip planking. Resorcinol is a very good adhesive; however, it needs pressure during curing time and is not noted for its ability to fill gaps. In strip planking there is sufficient pressure possible from the nail fastenings, but the fits between the adjacent strakes of planking must be pretty close or the resorcinol will run out of the seam. Now there are epoxies, which do not need much pressure, and to which a filler can be added, thickening the adhesive so it won't run out of the joint if the fit is less than perfect.

There are options when it comes to setting up a mold over which to build a hull with strip planking. The edge-fastened skin is so stiff that the number of frames that would be needed normally for the same thickness carvel planking is drastically reduced. Or the frames might be omitted altogether, with the hull planked over temporary transverse molds of suitable number to shape the hull—but do not remove the temporary molds without a number of braces across the hull at the sheer to retain hull shape. Bulkheads and a few frames, if needed, can be added to the structure later, or bulkheads can be part of the setup and left in the hull. The hull is best built right side up (unless it is to be quite large) and is best set up in a building with plenty of overhead clearance so that the keel can be high enough off the floor that there is a minimum of working time in a stooped position. To contradict this, Fred Bates, a designer-builder in Damariscotta, Maine, chose to build one of his popular Pogo designs, a 23-foot powerboat, upside down. Figure 11-25 most likely proves his point in this instance.

The builder should be advised that strip planking is often a two-person job, because the wide interval of molds or bulkheads minimizes the number of places where strips can be clamped into position. However, the reduced number of molds needed for this planking method means a saving of time and material in the setup.

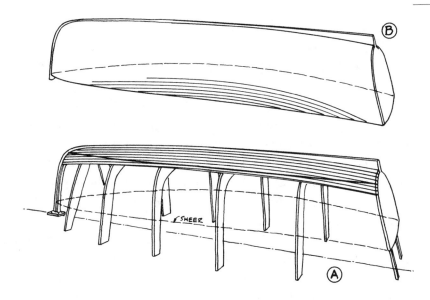

FIGURE 11-25.
Fred Bates built his 23-foot powerboat upside down—this eliminated the need for the tapering of the seams. In (A) planking strips are put in place temporarily.

Some of the best strip-planking workmanship ever turned out was done by Ralph Wiley in his yard on the Eastern Shore of Maryland. A few of his strip-planked deep-keel sailboats that I saw were planked with mahogany strips about 1¼" square. The parallel-sided strips extended from the sheer and ran to well below the waterline, where Wiley then tapered the strakes suitably and worked the edges to bevels for perfect glue fits. The planking was, of course, started at the keel and was planned in advance to determine where the tapering would stop and the parallel-sided strips would take over. In my opinion, beveled strip planking thicker than ⅞" is just too much of a job for the first attempt by the amateur. Wiley's hulls, between 30 and 40 feet long, were built right side up.

Before tapering frightens us unduly, let us look at a layout, used by Fred Bates for strip planking hulls of simple form, that eliminates tapering. Referring to A in Figure 11-25, planking strips are laid starting at the keel and are temporarily held in place, not permanently fastened. Then a distance equal to a number of strip widths is laid off from the sheer at each frame or mold, and a line is drawn on the strips by springing a batten through the points. The strips are carefully marked for exact location, then removed and cut to the line, and are permanently replaced with glue and fastenings. The remainder of the hull is planked with parallel-sided strips to the sheer.

Fred has a good scheme for keeping the strips of planking aligned while nailing. He makes a dozen or so of the horseshoe clamps sketched in Figure 11-24. These are cut from scrap ¾" plywood, varying the depth L, with a slot width of slightly more than the strip thickness.

When Fred told me he was about to build another strip-planked hull and mentioned the cost of the lumber, I suggested (and he heeded my advice) that he rip the planking strips from the wide stock with a thin-kerf carbide-tooth circular saw blade, because the thinner kerf would lower the cost of the wasted sawdust by about half. The 7½" diameter blades, which are available from Woodcraft, Inc., have a 1.8-mm-wide kerf, while the 10" ripping blades have a kerf of less than ³⁄₃₂".

We must reckon with the ingenuity of boatbuilders, both amateur and professional. Attention has been called to a variation of Fred Bates's strip-planking system devised to avoid tapering strips in width. In this case the planking strips were too thin for edge fastenings, structural strength of the hull skin depending entirely upon edge-to-edge epoxy adhesive. Starting at the sheer line, full-length strips were applied to about half of the girth at the midship mold (no *permanent frames* were employed in this instance); then, starting at the keel, full-length strips were applied until the strips intersected with the topside planking, leaving an area still to be planked that tapered from approximately amidships, depending on the shape of the hull, to zero at the ends of the area. Therefore the remaining strips were beveled (mitered might be a better description) in width at each end to butt against the already planked topsides. Each strip is then shorter in length as the planking is completed.

The description given me was not complete. It must be assumed, however, that the thin planking had to be supported by closely spaced molds to which the strips were temporarily fastened until the epoxy cured. The numerous molds are the price paid for a very light hull, but this could be amortized if a number of hulls were made from the same mold setup.

A number of Rhodes-designed sailboats were built using parallel strips with rounded and hollowed edges. There was no tapering of the strips; they started at the keel and ran out at the sheer, as indicated in B in Figure 11-25.

Ray Kargard of Marinette, Wisconsin, produced a Rhodes one-design sloop whose shape was particularly well-suited to strip planking. Ray planked with round- and hollow-edged strips machined on all four sides in a single pass. For production purposes, molds were erected upside down; the frames were bent over permanent ribbands. The sheerstrake was spiled and the lower edge made convex to mate with the hollow edge of the first strip. The garboard plank was also spiled. Finished widths for the sheerstrake and the garboard compensated for differences in the section girths.

Still another version of strip planking that I have seen was a method where hull strips were laid on diagonally. This unusual strake arrangement resulted in a herringbone appearance as one looked down into the hull, a 30-odd-foot Charles Wittholz design that was built right side up.

STRIP PLANKING FOR CANOE CONSTRUCTION

Since the third edition of this book I clipped a sketch of strip planking for canoes from one of the informative news bulletins published by Gougeon Brothers, one of the major suppliers of epoxy resins for boatbuilding. The cedar strips were as shown in A in Figure 11-26, but a Gougeon Brothers technical advisor said that the strip manufacturer had gone out of business. In lieu of this source, he suggested that builders acquire suitable router bits and make their own strips. (Note that the "cove and bead" bits shown in Figure 11-26B will not yield a a v-shaped joint as in the sketch of the canoe planking.) Be sure to check the cutter dimensions carefully before purchasing.

SAWING STRIPS OF WOOD FOR SCARPHING

This is as good a time as any to show how easy it is to prepare wood strips for scarphing to a length-to-thickness ratio of 10:1 or thereabouts. Experienced bench sawyers know there are several ways to do this, so only one will be demonstrated. (See the plan view sketch of a bench saw table,

FIGURE 11-26.
Strip planking possibilities for canoes.

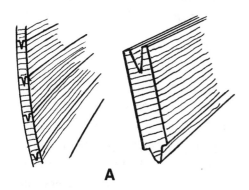

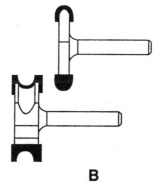

A   B

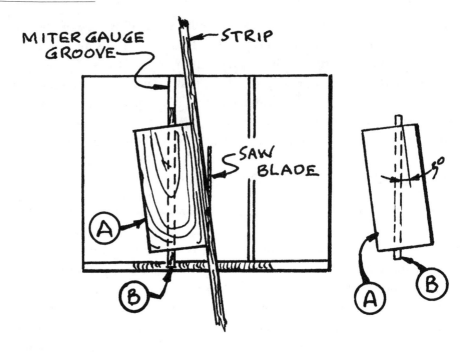

FIGURE 11-27.
An overhead view of a table saw, showing how to cut strips to be glued and scarphed into longer lengths.

Figure 11-27.) A in the figure is a block of wood worked to fit the miter gauge groove of your saw table, fastened to the block at about 5 degrees to the edge, then waxed to make it slide easily. The procedure is then obvious.

In addition to planking strips, the same routine can be used when necessary to lengthen small-craft parts such as inwales, chines, and the like.

The subject of strip planking cannot be concluded without mention of the famous Casco Bay Hampton launches with yacht finishes built by Richard S. Pulsifer of Brunswick, Maine. Pulsifer works alone except when bending frames, and he produces four boats each year. Each side of the hull is planked with over fifty strips, and the deck is also stripped.

DURAKORE

The Baltek Corporation markets an innovative strip-planking material called DuraKore. It is made of flat panels consisting of end-grain balsa bonded on both sides with 3/16" (1.5 mm)-thick faces of luan veneer with the grain of the faces in the same direction, like standard plywood panels. The adhesive is waterproof resorcinol glue. The resulting panels are then slit by Baltek into strips parallel with the grain of the face veneers and

FIGURE 11-28.
A 22-foot strip-planked Hampton utility launch. (*Peter Ralston photo courtesy Richard Pulsifer*)

perfectly finger-jointed at the ends for simple splicing to any length. The strips can be curved in both directions, and due to the end-grain core can be twisted when necessary at the ends of a hull, depending upon the shape of course, somewhat easier than solid lumber strips. One builder twisted it 90 degrees in 36 feet.

Layup of DuraKore strips is usually done inside female molds, with thickened epoxy adhesive applied to the edges of the strips as planking progresses. The strips, of course, must be temporarily fastened to the molds until the epoxy has cured. But this is not the end—synthetic fabric and resin must be applied to both sides of the DuraKore laminate for additional structural strength. The available sizes of the 8-foot-long DuraKore strips range in thickness from ½" to 1" and in width from ⅞" to 1¾".

The hull can be round, vee, or a combination of both like the one in Figure 11-30, in which the vee bottom (also known as v-bottom) is laid up with DuraKore strips inside female station molds. The photo may be deceiving, however, because at the stern end (foreground) the first layer of fiberglass reinforcement is hanging down, concealing the thickness of the DuraKore. The hull bottom at the stern actually looks like Figure 11-31. Further forward in the hull bottom the second layer of inner reinforcement skin is being applied.

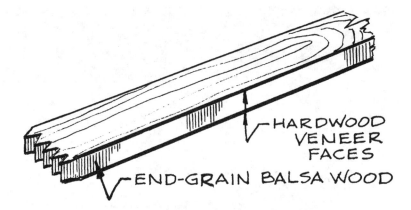

FIGURE 11-29.
DuraKore planking strip.

HARDWOOD
VENEER
FACES

END-GRAIN BALSA WOOD

FIGURE 11-30.
V-bottom laid up with DuraKore strips, which were also used for the curved topsides.
Note that the outboard edges of the bottom are horizontal to form a "spray-knocker" chine.

FIGURE 11-31.
The hull bottom at the stern of a DuraKore-built boat.

I like the DuraKore scheme of hull construction, but the first-timer should be aware of what is involved—starting with complete lofting and construction of a substantial setup of the female molds. Gluing the Dura-Kore strips end to end is only the beginning of the hull, and certainly the planking procedure requires helpers. Then when the layup of the Dura-Kore strips is complete, both sides of the hull must be sheathed with fabric and resin. When complete, though, the hull is very strong and comparatively lightweight. The whole process is one that a professional shop could accomplish quickly once the hull mold is set up.

Construction of hulls cored with DuraKore has caught on worldwide. Baltek has a well-done brochure on the method, available upon request.

Although I have not seen illustrations for it, I cannot see any reason for not assembling a DuraKore hull upside down over male station molds, particularly small craft within the realm of the do-it-yourselfer. This should in fact be easier, because the molds for a small craft will be spaced closer, leaving no room for a person to stand between molds as is necessary when laying up inside upright female molds (unless of course the hull is being "split-molded" in two separate halves, as is sometimes done for convenience).

I have not seen how DuraKore strips are terminated at the forward end of the hull, but can think of several arrangements. This, however, is a designer's decision.

PLYWOOD PLANKING

The fact that a hull is v-bottomed does not automatically mean that it can be planked with plywood: plywood can be bent without distortion in only one axis at a time and thus should be used only to plank hulls designed with its limitations in mind. The sections of vessels designed for plywood construction generally consist of developable curves—curves that consist of portions of cylinders and cones. It should not go unnoted that experienced builders have succeeded where theory dictates the impossible. However, the methods used just about defy written description. Suffice it to say then, that you should review the plans of your boat carefully before deciding to plank it with plywood panels.

Plywood is stiff material; therefore, planking thickness can be less than it would be with conventional wooden planking. Also an advantage is its ability to cover large areas quickly. Often, standard plywood panels will be too short for you to plank in one panel from bow to stern. If so, either special panels must be ordered or else the regular panels must be butted end to end. These joints, which should be detailed on the plans, are generally made with good-size butt blocks. The joints should be waterproof-glued and well fastened with screws or rivets.

Note that plywood panels butted end to end do not want to bend in a fair curve due to increased stiffness in way of the butt block. It is much better to join the panels by scarphing, and as indicated in Chapter 4, you can scarph plywood yourself or suppliers will do it for you.

While being fitted, the plywood should be fastened with just enough screws to hold it in place. When the fit is satisfactory, remove the panel and apply marine or waterproof glue to chines, rabbet, frames, etc., and bend the plywood on again, again with just a few screws to hold it. Working as fast as possible because of the glue, drive the remaining screws, of which there are a great many. Work from the middle of the panel toward the ends, drilling for screws and countersinking the heads slightly below the surface of the panel so they can be made invisible with marine surfacing putty or similar material.

I have tried the WEST System 410 Microlite Fairing Compound, which is mixed with epoxy resin, and found it easy to apply in shallow depressions in wooden surfaces or over cured polyester or vinylester surfaces. It sands and feather-edges beautifully.

Some builders use plywood instead of solid lumber for the inner layer or even both layers of a double-planked hull, even when there is considerable curvature. They apply the plywood in pieces as large as will bend on the hull and in this way save labor over the usual double-planking method. Several years ago I saw a number of commercial boat hulls 55 to about 75 feet long planked in this manner, and have learned since that the builder also made a 90-odd footer.

Many builders, too, of lapstrake boats switched from solid lumber to marine plywood. A shop that has tooled for a production run will typically plank a hull over a rugged jig consisting of inverted section molds and permanent ribbands. When boats are built one-off, the setup is more conventional, and the planks are cut and hung like solid stock. However, in both cases—custom and production—the plywood is generally scarphed to glue a "dog leg" as required by the shape of each plank (see Figure 11-32). At the sheer a three-piece dog leg may be required, but this procedure minimizes the amount of sheet material needed for an S-shaped plank.

GLUED SCARPH

FIGURE 11-32.
Scarphed stock with dogleg to suit curve of plank, a savings (in this example) of 40% in width.

In the foregoing I mentioned framed plywood-planked hulls, all of which have a beveled chine piece at the intersection of the topside and bottom planking even in boats only 6 feet long. Unless the boat is a pram (one of the easiest to plank with plywood), and depending upon the hull shape, the chines sometimes must be soaked with hot rags or steamed to bend them into place. In a pram with flat or moderate vee sections, the sides are planked first and the bottom simply overlaps the sides for the entire length of the chines. A in Figure 11-33 shows a section through the chine of a pram and is also representative of the greater part of the length of a conventional v-bottomed dinghy. In the latter, however, the forward end of the bottom planking must be twisted into the stem rabbet (D).

A in the figure shows the outside of the planking as lofted from the plans (see Chapter 7); "t" is the deduction for the planking thickness allowed when making a frame; the black shading is the material to be cut off the chine and the edge of the side planking. Again, all of the above is typical of a pram-type hull or the greater length of the chine corner of other hulls. It is in the length approaching the bow that things can be puzzling at first glance, because of the angle between the side and the bottom, but it quickly becomes obvious that the joint at the chine can no longer be a simple overlap. When one tries a dry run of fitting one of the bottom panels, it becomes apparent the forward end must be secured first, and it is time for another pair of hands.

The sections show what happens. As we proceed forward from the simple bevel in A, the angle toward the bow becomes too steep to properly fasten the side planking (B), so a change must be made from a lap (A) to a miter joint (C). Here is where you must think. Cut the length as short as possible with a sharp chisel, yet not short enough to increase the difficulty of twisting the panels to make them meet as in D at the stem rabbet.

A template of the bottom panel is recommended, especially forward, so wasted material can be avoided. One material for templates is hollow household doorskins. These are plywood, about 1/8" thick by 38" wide by

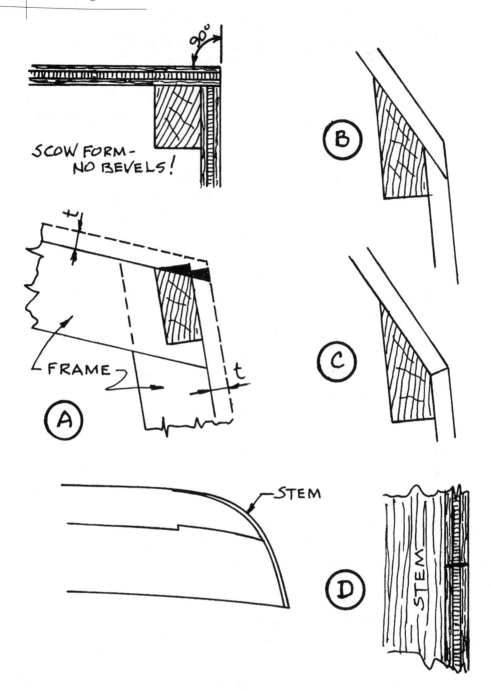

90°

SCOW FORM—
NO BEVELS!

t

FRAME

t

Ⓐ

Ⓑ

Ⓒ

STEM

STEM

Ⓓ

FIGURE 11-33.
Plywood planking: sections at chine.

70" long, relatively inexpensive, and sold by building supply stores. In any event, use material thinner than the planking plywood to make a pattern of the shape.

After the plywood for half of the bottom has been shaped and is ready to be fastened in place, you must be extremely ingenious to do this job without help—for two reasons. First, the stern end of the plywood must be held up while adhesive is spread where the bow end is to go. Second, when you plan to begin fastening you will discover that there is nowhere to use clamps. The bow area of the bottom—the area marked X in Figure 11-34—is the most troublesome when planking with plywood unless the hull is a pram or similar design with but little twist at the bow. A well-known rule for bending plywood: Always clamp into place and secure first the area where the greatest curvature occurs.

FIGURE 11-34.
The bow area on the bottom is the most troublesome spot when planking in plywood.

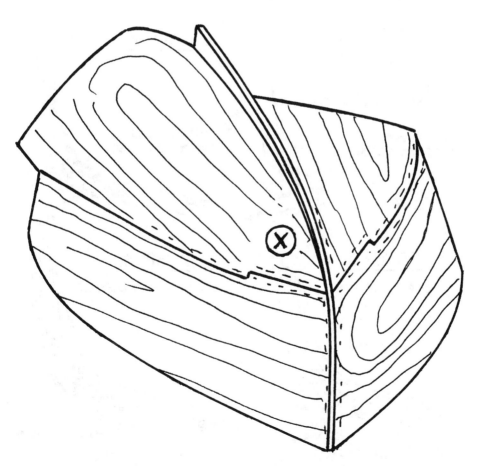

STITCH-AND-TAPE PLYWOOD HULL CONSTRUCTION

V-bottomed hulls without conventional framing only appeared on the scene during the last three decades. These are called "stitch-and-tape" (or stitch-and-glue, tack-and-tape, or glued-seam) designs, and a generous number of plans for these boats are on the market.

Typically, the drawings for stitch-and-tape hulls show the shapes of the plywood panels with enough dimensions so a batten can be run through the points and tacked in place. The lines are marked with a sharp pencil, cut wide of the line, and then planed carefully to the line.

On the other hand, there are plans available from firms that furnish full-size patterns for cutting all the plywood parts for the hull. This saves a good bit, if not all, of the layout work.

The sections through the corner in Figure 11-35 make it obvious why this method of joining the panel edges at the chine corners has been

FIGURE 11-35.
Stitch-and-glue joint at chine corner.

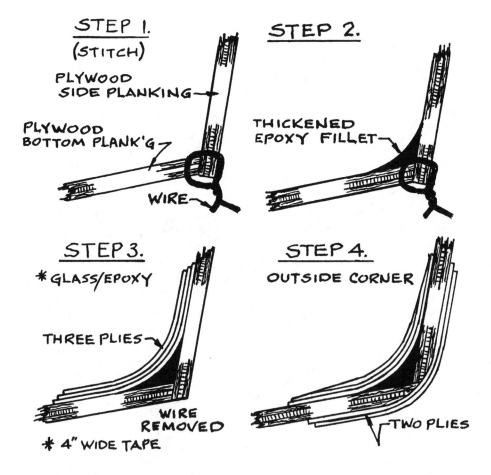

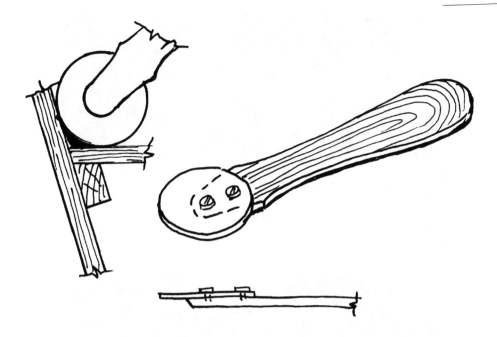

FIGURE 11-36.
Typical homemade tool for filleting thickened epoxy or similar material.

dubbed "stitch and glue." At this time the favorite adhesive seems to be epoxy, thickened so it will not sag when the inside filleted corner is formed with something like the plastic top from a coffee can (tea drinkers can use a short piece of PVC pipe). This ensures that the joint will be at least as strong as the wooden parts, and probably more so. (See Figure 11-36.)

The wire "thread" can be had in bubble-packed rolls sold in building supply stores; 18-gauge is about right. The spacing of the twisted wire ties may vary with the amount of curvature of the panel. Of even easier use are plastic ties, also available from your local hardware store.

The edges of the fiberglass tape should be feathered for a neat appearance. Be very careful not to cut into the plywood.

For a hull like a small dinghy I would not cover the plywood skin with fiberglass—rather I would use the best grade of waterproof plywood in the first place and then finish with one of the super-slick marine coatings on the market today. This will save the cost of fabric and resin, eliminate all that messy sanding to produce a smooth surface, and reduce weight, but the choice is yours.

FIGURE 11-37.
Gypsy, a 15-foot plywood Phil Bolger tack-and-tape design built by H. H. "Dynamite" Payson, from whom plans are available. (*Dynamite Payson*)

FIGURE 11-38.
Another Bolger/Payson tack-and-tape plywood hull, the 12' 3" Bobcat, built from eight panels of $\frac{1}{4}$" × 4' × 8' plywood. Plans are available from Payson. (*Dynamite Payson*)

COLD-MOLDING

A cold-molded hull consists of multiple layers of thin veneers (as thin as $1/16"$ for small boats) or strips bonded to each other with a waterproof adhesive to form a stiff, strong skin. Generally, the first layer of strips is laid up diagonally at about 45 degrees to the centerline of the mold or frame, the second layer at 90 degrees to the first, the third at 90 degrees to the second, etc. Depending upon the designer's specifications, sometimes as many as five layers of thin strakes are used to build up the desired thickness. While the glue is curing, the strakes are secured with staples, nails, or screws, which are usually removed after the glue sets up. As noted in the section on adhesives, the modern waterproof glues—resorcinols and epoxies—set up at room temperatures, thus the reason for the term cold-molding.

For the past 25 years or so, the most popular method for fastening cold-molded construction is by *vacuum bagging*. This may lie beyond the scope and capabilities of some amateurs, but you can read about it in the Appendix.

Although all cold-molded hulls are built upside down, they can be built by various methods. The method used by most amateurs is to laminate a skin over a skeletal framework, which usually consists of some sort of backbone, transverse forms (some of which are bulkheads and frames), and longitudinal stringers. Another method is to build up a hull on a male mold, which may be either a strip-planked plug or a form with closely spaced ribbands. In this case, the supporting structure does not become a part of the hull; the finished shell is lifted off the form, and structural members, such as bulkheads and transverse frames, are installed as necessary. Still another method combines these two: the first layer of planking is strip-planked over a skeletal framework and then successive layers of planking are laid on diagonally.

Each method has definite advantages for particular applications, and there are variations within each method as to skin thickness, number of planking layers, and the number and weight of internal strengthening members. The designer draws up his construction specifications with the intended vessel's size, its shape, and its purpose in mind. In the last 35 years, the cold-molding process has been the subject of much scientific research and development. The end result has been that designers have been able to specify hull construction scantlings with strength-to-weight ratios approaching that of aluminum.

Whatever the method chosen, cold-molding has several attractions. A hull built with a cold-molded skin can be built very light because of the stiffness of the laminated planking, or if desired, a very stiff hull can be built by laminating the hull up to a desired thickness. Either way, the hull construction entails lighter work than that needed to construct a wooden hull by the traditional method. The interest has been heightened for many because high quality is easier to achieve when working with light materials. Tied closely to this is the availability of the superb adhesives, particularly the epoxies. To cap it all off, the dimensional stability of laminated planking means that the outside of cold-molded hulls can be sheathed with fiberglass or other fabric. Thus, it is possible for the amateur to build a tough, strong, long-lived hull that might otherwise have been beyond his ability with other methods.

However, although it might seem to the amateur that laminating up a hull of thin strips is child's play compared to bending frames and spiling and cutting out planks, there is no substitute for skill and care in any facet of boatbuilding. The lines must still be accurately lofted, and a true and sturdy mold must be constructed. There is still a great amount of spiling to be done to get the joints between the planks to butt tightly against one another. Indeed, some professionals have opined that, to build a cold-molded boat, a builder must go through a complete planking routine for each layer, meaning that the hull is planked not just once, but at least three and perhaps as many as five times, depending upon the numbers of layers. In addition, some hull shapes can prove tricky to build; hulls with reverse curves seem to give a great amount of trouble, and one professional builder has stated that such hulls should not be attempted by anyone less than a really skilled, patient craftsman.

There are four excellent books that deal with cold-molding at considerable length. These are *Modern Wooden Yacht Construction* by John Guzzwell (out of print but available through online booksellers), *The Gougeon Brothers on Boat Construction, Cold-Moulded and Strip-Planked Wood Boatbuilding* by Ian Nicolson, and *The New Cold-Molded Boatbuilding* by Reuel Parker (originally published by International Marine but now published by WoodenBoat Books). Parker has built a number of fine, large vessels with this method, including a couple of 50-foot sharpie-style schooners that he has lived aboard for long periods prior to selling. As I was preparing the fourth edition of this book in 1993, he built a 60-foot cold-molded sailboat and sheathed it with Xynole polyester fabric. (See discussion in Chapter 5.) Much can be learned about the details of cold-molding from these books, which have been written by those with a great deal of experience with this type of construction.

FIGURE 11-39.
The first skin being applied to a framework of molds, bulkheads, and stringers. (*John Guzzwell*)

I recently read a description of cold-molded planking by a boatbuilder who called the final smoothing backbreaking, something for the amateur to note. (The hull, of course, was not dinghy-sized.) And it bears repeating that epoxies are highly toxic, and to use them without thorough skin and respiratory protection is to court trouble. More than one professional boatbuilder has become so sensitized to epoxy as to break out in rashes when merely in the proximity of cured epoxy resin! Many others, however, have avoided problems by using the proper precautions.

HOT-MOLDED HULLS

A cold-molded hull could be called a laminated hull, but "cold-molded" distinguishes the method from "hot-molded." After World War II the availability of a truly waterproof adhesive made possible the fast production of hulls laminated of three or more layers of thin strips of wood laid up over a male plug. The adhesive was laid in sheets between each layer of veneer. The plug was then moved into an autoclave and subjected to heat and pressure that made short work of curing. Made this way were dinghy, daysailer, outboard-motor-powered runabout, and even deep-keel sailboat hulls. I crewed aboard a 30-odd-foot hot-molded sloop, so I know that hulls at least that long were produced. Hot-molding as a production method was not practical for small-volume boatbuilding, and with the introduction of fiberglass the hot-molding process suffered a natural death.

DIAGONAL PLANKING

Although it predates cold-molding by quite some time, diagonal planking is very similar to cold-molding. In fact, as it is practiced now, using waterproof glue between the planking layers instead of fabric soaked in a waterproofing agent as was formerly done, it can be considered a form of cold-molding. What makes it a bit different is that it employs strakes that are thicker than veneers, and it often consists of only two layers of planking. Because of the greater strake thickness, this method is used mostly on v-bottomed powerboats, where the change in shape that each strake encounters is much less severe than on round-bottomed hulls. The planking is generally fastened to a framework consisting of keel, chines, clamps, and transverse frames (or in some cases, a fewer number of transverse frames or bulkheads together with longitudinals). A frame hull awaiting double-diagonal planking is shown in Figure 9-12, Chapter 9. I watched hulls of up to 58 feet being built with two layers of $3/8$"-thick mahogany; this increased to $5/8$" thick for hulls 60 to almost 90 feet long.

The scheme of diagonal planking is shown in Figure 11-40 and can be seen to be similar to that of cold-molding. The planking material is made of uniform width, 2" to 4" wide, depending upon the size of the hull. The first layer is laid up at a 45-degree angle to the keel and is secured with glue and screws or annularly threaded nails to frames, chine, and keel or sheer clamp, with the edges of the strakes also being glued to one another.

Toward the bow, the planks must be tapered, as the convergence of the bottom and the topsides tends to change the angle of the planks too much out of parallel with those amidships. Tapering brings the planks back approximately into line; the angle is not critical, as long as the planks cross several frames.

The second layer is glued to the first and is also edge-glued, then fastened in place with screws to the keel, chines, clamps, and frames. To

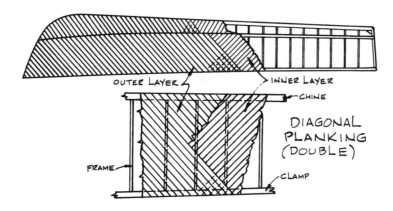

FIGURE 11-40.
Diagonal planking.

provide clamping pressure between frames, the intersections of the inner and outer strakes are clout-nailed. The copper clout nailheads are countersunk while the nails are backed up by a helper inside the hull. When planking strakes are ⅝" thick or more, the fastenings between the framing can be wood screws driven from the inside to eliminate puttying over the heads on the outside of the hull. After the adhesive has cured, the planking is smoothed by sanding, then sheathed with synthetic cloth and epoxy resin.

One custom builder of double-diagonal-planked hulls uses a laminated keel (Figure 11-41). After being glued, the keel is machined to a

FIGURE 11-41.
Detail of planking and keel shoe at centerline of keel—all laminated with waterproof glue.

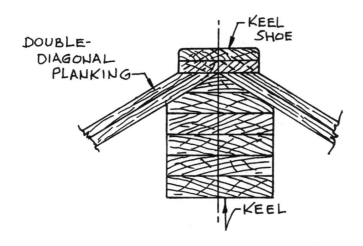

continually changing bevel, and when set up the ends of the two layers of planking are beveled at the centerline, then planed off flat to the width of a keel shoe laminated in place. (The frames, gussets, and keelson are not illustrated in the figure.) All told, this makes an enormously strong structure. I observed about eighty-five of these boats, of lengths from 34 to 86 feet, under construction, and I have nothing but admiration for these staunch hulls.

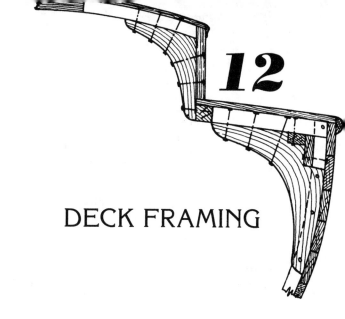

DECK FRAMING

12

THE DECKING OF A BOAT normally is laid on transverse beams, which not only provide support for the deck but also help to hold the sides of the hull together. The latter aspect is important in all boats designed to be decked, especially in sailboats. These days, however, innovative construction methods for lightweight racing sailboats sometimes combine both transverse and longitudinal deck framing.

CLAMPS AND SHELVES

The deck beams must be of good size and strongly connected to the hull if they are to contribute the strength required of them. In small boats they are fastened to the clamp and the frame heads (Figure 12-1, A and B). As hulls increase in size, an additional stiffening member called a shelf, or deck shelf, is fitted on each side of the boat. The shelf is generally of the same material as the clamp, and its position on the flat against the clamp provides a greater landing area for the beam ends, which are fastened through it instead of the clamp.

In small craft, screws are used as fastenings, but in larger vessels through-bolts are always used. Bolts have the extra advantage of being able to be tightened if necessary, whereas screws through beams are not accessible once the boat is decked. To lessen the concentration of fastenings in

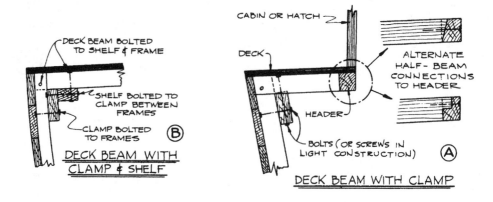

FIGURE 12-1.
Deck beams on small boats are fastened to clamps and frame heads.

the vicinity of the deck beams, shelves are fastened to the clamps *between* frames (see Figure 12-1). They are sprung in place on edge in single lengths when possible, or in several pieces joined by scarphs, with the joints located toward the ends of the boat, or they can be laminated. The inner edges may be left square, but the outer edges should be planed to fit snugly against the clamps. The shelves must be fitted with a pitch corresponding to the camber of the deck beams so that the beams will bear on the shelves' entire width. The best way to get the bevel is to temporarily set a few deck beams in place so the bevels may be measured every few feet, or at least at every station. The edges of the shelves can then be planed to the proper angle (see A in Figure 12-2).

FIGURE 12-2.
Fitting the clamps and headers to agree with camber of the deck.

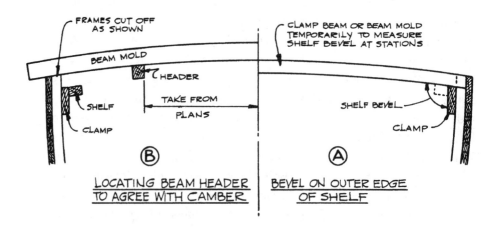

When the clamp and shelf are bolted together, they function as a single member, shaped like an angle iron, that contributes strength and stiffness in two directions; for maximum benefit, *they should be connected at the ends of the hull.* At the bow this is done with a breasthook, which is a knee of sorts fitted between the shelves and bolted to them. The hook was often sawn out of a natural wood crook, either of oak or hackmatack. Just as good a connection is a piece of oak or a laminated plywood sandwich laid on top of the shelves and through-bolted (A in Figure 12-3).

The shelf/clamp assemblies join one another at the stern via the transom. For a flat transom, this connection takes the form of quarter knees, which are sawn from crooks and bolted in place on top of the shelves and against the transom cross framing at the underside of the deck. With a curved transom, the connection is more difficult. In this case the knees must have the proper deck camber and fit the transom curve as well. Unless you are a skilled loftsman who can work out the intersection of the deck and transom on the floor, it is best to make these pieces by the cut-and-try method.

The plan view shape is easy to obtain, as it is shown on the deck framing plan for the boat. The shape of the top edge of the knees is best obtained on the boat. Install the deck beams for the 5 or 6 feet ahead of the transom and at intervals of 3 or 4 inches on each side of the centerline, clamp a batten on top of the beams, its aft end just touching the inside of the transom. Mark the transom at the underside of the batten each time the batten is clamped; a line through the marks will represent the underside of the decking as well as the top curve of the quarter knees. The battens can also be used to measure the bevel needed for the aft edges of the knees. Shaped as they are in every dimension, these pieces are really quite a job for the amateur, and thus a job to be proud of when completed for the first time.

DECK BEAMS

The deck beams should be made of oak or ash where maximum strength and durability are desired, and of spruce where lightness is a consideration. There should be a beam at each frame, and they should be cambered, both for strength and so the deck will quickly shed any water that comes aboard. Where the camber is normal, the beams can be sawn to shape. Where there is high camber, such as is often found in cabin tops, it is best to laminate the beams of three or more pieces over a form, using waterproof glue. Beam construction is shown in A in Figure 12-4. Most of the beams will have the same siding, but at hatches, mast partners, and the ends of

FIGURE 12-3.

Alternate methods of fastening deck beams.

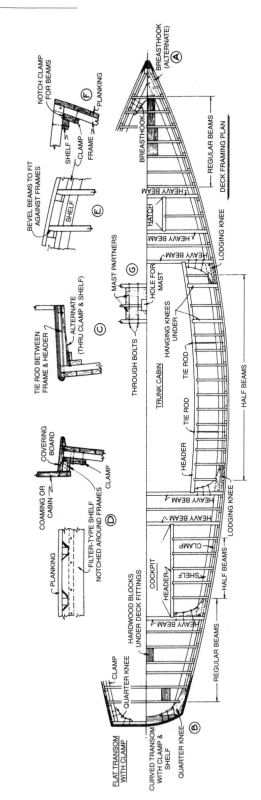

cabin trunks, the beams should be heavier by about 75 percent than the regular beams (see Figure 12-3).

Although it is customary to represent the beams and frames on the plans in the manner shown in Figure 12-3, E in the figure shows that the beams must be beveled to fit against the frame heads. This is because the frames are twisted to lie flat against the planking, which curves toward the centerline toward the ends of the boat. Due to a combination of deck camber and flaring hull sections, the inboard corner of the clamp must sometimes be cut away so the beams will land on a flat surface instead of a point. This is sketched in F. Remember that what counts is the close and careful fitting of all structural parts of the hull.

DECK BEAM CAMBER

The amount of camber is given on the plans or in the specifications and is stated as a depth of curve of so many inches for a given length, using the length of the longest beam. To make a beam pattern, or a beam mold as it is called, the procedure in B in Figure 12-4 is followed, or the camber may be laid out easily with the mechanical method shown in C. The method shown in B is self-explanatory and is suitable when only one camber curve is needed, but C is faster and very useful should you run into a cabin top where each beam has a different camber. In this method, three nails are driven in the pattern board, one at each end of the beam length and one at the center of the beam length at the top of the arc. Then two straight-edged battens, each longer than the longest beam by at least 2 feet, are placed snugly against the nails as shown and tacked together rigidly enough to hold the angle between the battens. The camber curve can then be drawn by sliding the batten assembly from the centerline to one end of the beam and then to the other, always holding the battens in contact with the nails at the ends.

Still another way of laying out the camber for a deck beam pattern is easy if you have a handheld calculator—and who doesn't? Perpendiculars are erected on a baseline at the centerline and at points one-quarter of the needed pattern length each side of the centerline, on which the specified camber or crown is laid off as C. Then the total camber, C, is multiplied by decimals as shown in Figure 12-5 and laid off above the baseline on the perpendiculars. (Note: for clarity only one-half of the camber curve has been shown as W.) With the points down, a batten is used to draw the curve through the nine points, that is, the centerline and four points each side of it.

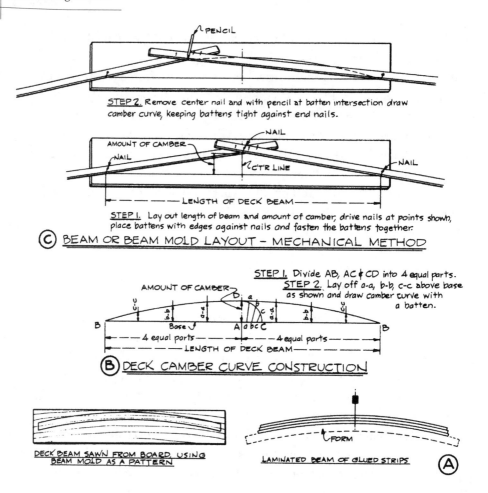

STEP 2. Remove center nail and with pencil at batten intersection draw
camber curve, keeping battens tight against end nails.

STEP 1. Lay out length of beam and amount of camber; drive nails at points shown,
place battens with edges against nails and fasten the battens together.

Ⓒ BEAM OR BEAM MOLD LAYOUT – MECHANICAL METHOD

STEP 1. Divide AB, AC & CD into 4 equal parts.
STEP 2. Lay off a-a, b-b, c-c above base
as shown and draw camber curve with
a batten.

Ⓑ DECK CAMBER CURVE CONSTRUCTION

DECK BEAM SAWN FROM BOARD, USING
BEAM MOLD AS A PATTERN

LAMINATED BEAM OF GLUED STRIPS   Ⓐ

FIGURE 12-4.
Beam construction showing ways to measure camber.

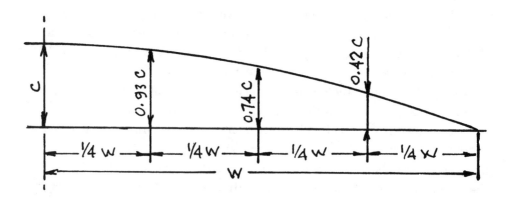

FIGURE 12-5.
Mathematical layout of deck beam camber curve.

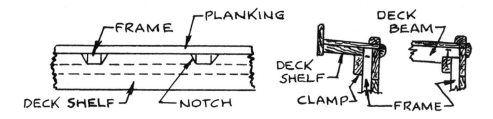

FIGURE 12-6.
On small boats, wide deck shelves can be fitted instead of using a header.

HALF BEAMS AND HEADERS

At the sides of deck openings the beams are short (Figure 12-3) and are termed half beams. The opening is bounded by the strong beams mentioned previously and the fore-and-aft headers into which the half beams are notched and fastened as shown in A in Figure 12-1. The old-timers always dovetailed the half beams, but the connection is more often made by the easier method shown in the sketches. The headers must be elevated to coincide with the camber of the beams, and the procedure is to make a couple of beam molds, clamp them in the space between the strong beams, then pull the header up to the mold, all the while springing the header to its planned dimensions from the centerline of the boat (see B in Figure 12-2).

In powerboats and small sailboats with narrow side decks, a wide shelf is sometimes fitted to save making and fastening a header and a dozen or so short half beams. To clarify this Figure 12-6 has been drawn, partly to show that the clamp in this case is set below the underside of the deck by the thickness of the shelf. The deck will rest on the shelf, which is notched for the heads of the frames and extends for the length of the deck opening, that is, cockpit or cabin. Where the deck is the full width of the hull, the deck beams are notched for the clamp as shown.

DECK TIE RODS AND LODGING KNEES

When the decking consists of planks rather than large pieces of plywood, the deck framing is stiffened with tie rods running between frame heads or clamps and the headers (C in Figure 12-3). These fastenings also take some of the load off the connections between header and half beams. For additional stiffening there may be "lodging" knees in the deck frame to provide strength at ends of large openings in the deck or at masts. These knees are sawn from hackmatack or oak crooks and are planed on top to conform with the deck camber. They are bolted or riveted to the beams and shelf or clamp (see Figure 12-3). Alternatively, the knees may be made from marine plywood, and further laminated to a specified thickness if necessary. For further discussion see "Modern Construction" later in this chapter.

DECK BLOCKING

Wherever there are fittings on deck such as cleats and tackle blocks, there should be blocks fitted between the beams to take through-fastenings. The blocks provide more wood for the fastenings to bear against, and they distribute the load to the beams in the case of shearing forces, and over a greater area of decking when upward strains are encountered. The blocks can be of oak, mahogany, or plywood and should be planed on top to conform to the deck camber and sawn to a tight fit between beams. Blocks are shown in the deck framing, Figure 12-3.

MAST PARTNERS

The deck framing plan in Figure 12-3 is for a sloop having its mast stepped through the cabin trunk, the top of which has large blocks called mast partners fitted between beams. These blocks are always as thick as the depth of the deck beams between which they are fitted, and they are made of hardwood or laminated plywood and through-bolted. The supplementary sketch, G in Figure 12-3, shows a set of typical mast partners, whether located in the trunk top or the main deck.

All comparatively large deck frame surfaces, such as blocking or lodging knees, should be coated with thick bedding as the decking is laid. This serves to keep out water should there be a leak in the vicinity. Take special care to treat the raw edges of any plywood used.

HANGING KNEES

The forces exerted on a boat by seas and by masts in sailboats work to collapse a hull in a manner similar to the way that a packing box from which the ends have been removed collapses when a man stands on it. These forces try to hinge the hull structure at the deck corner—this is only one of the reasons why properly sized and located fastenings are important if long hull life is to be expected. Brackets called hanging knees are fitted for

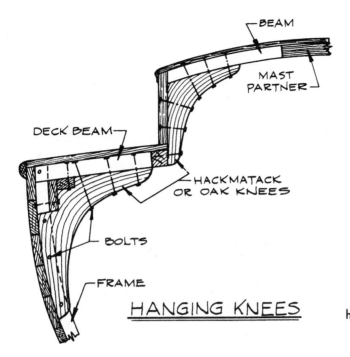

BEAM

MAST
PARTNER

DECK BEAM

HACKMATACK
OR OAK KNEES

BOLTS

FRAME

HANGING KNEES

FIGURE 12-7.
Hanging knees of oak or
hackmatack (larch) at a mast
partner.

resisting such sideways strains. Like lodging knees, they have been traditionally made of natural crook oak or hackmatack and always through-fastened insofar as possible. Metal, in the form of flanged plates, plates and angles, or castings, is often used for knees and has the advantage of not splitting with age as wood is liable to do. Hanging knees are generally used in pairs at the masts and singly at the ends and midlength of long deck openings. Figure 12-7 shows typical wooden hanging knees at the mast partners of a sloop having its mast stepped through the cabin trunk.

Figure 12-8 shows an alternate method to natural crook or metal knees, using marine plywood instead. Thickness will depend upon the size of the boat, ranging from a single thickness ½" or ¾" to heavier if needed (built up by laminating with ½" or ¾" thick pieces); once again, through-bolts in snug holes are used insofar as possible.

MODERN CONSTRUCTION

The quarter knees, lodging knees, and hanging knees described earlier as oak or hackmatack natural crooks are used in traditional construction. The problem with such knees is to find them and then to pay a reasonable price for them. It should be realized that there are modern materials and techniques available for small craft that can eliminate the need for traditional

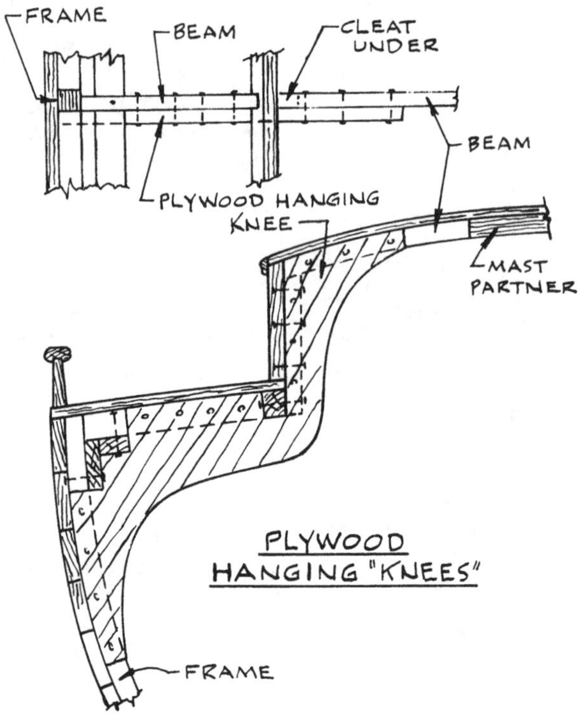

FIGURE 12-8.
Hanging knees made of plywood.

FIGURE 12-9.
Yacht designer Philip L. Rhodes took this snapshot in the winter of 1935–36, during construction by F. F. Pendleton in Wiscasset, Maine, of a 67-foot-overall yawl. Visible are the bent frames, bilge stringer, clamp and shelf, deck beams, and, in the foreground, a few of the floor timbers atop the horn timber.

crook knees of oak and hackmatack. As pointed out before, knees can be laminated of wood or plywood or be made of flanged metal plates. Or, knees need not be used at all due to the enormous stiffening provided by modern materials: a well-fitted and secure plywood deck can do the work of lodging knees, and properly secured plywood interior joiner bulkheads in effective locations often take the place of hanging knees.

To sum up, tie rods and lodging knees are not needed when the decking is plywood, and strategically located joiner bulkheads, when effectively designed, can make hanging knees unnecessary.

In any case, be guided by the plans for your boat. The designer should provide details of the structure in way of masts when panel material is used for weight and labor savings.

If there are a number of bulkheads and full-height joiner partitions in a hull, as is common in many power cruisers packed full of cabins, head enclosures, etc., a deck consisting of two layers of plywood glued together can be supported by these bulkheads and partitions with a minimum of other deck framing—just a few transverse beams or longitudinals where it is necessary to reduce the span of unsupported areas.

13

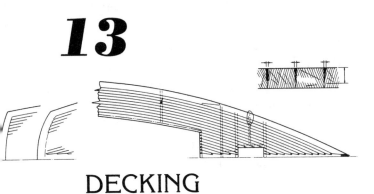

DECKING

DUE TO THE AVAILABILITY of waterproof plywood and synthetic fabrics, various decking methods described when this book was first printed in 1950 (then under the title of *Small Boat Construction*) are now virtually obsolete. They are of interest still to restorers and to traditionalists, but discussion here will be brief.

TONGUE-AND-GROOVE DECK

Tongue-and-groove nail-fastened boards make an inexpensive deck because the width of the material, anywhere from 4" to 6", permits the deck to be quickly built, with the boards parallel to the centerline of the boat as in A in Figure 13-1. Very often these decks are made of nondurable material, unseasoned in the first place, and quick to rot if the deck covering leaks. The straight-run deck is not as strong as other types, and the tongue-and-groove construction has the disadvantage that the thin upper edge of the groove tends to warp between the fastenings (B in Figure 13-1). The only covering for a tongue-and-groove deck of wide boards that will come and go easily with the moisture in the air is old-fashioned canvas duck. The groove warping shows through the canvas as ridges and the canvas life is shortened by wearing along these ridges.

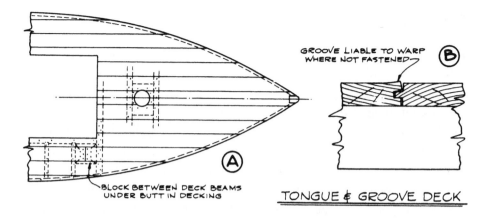

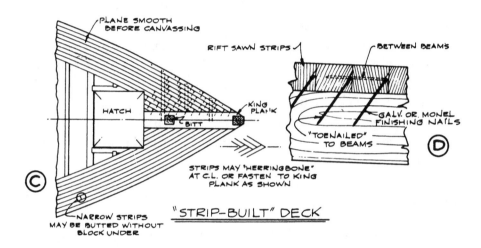

FIGURE 13-1.
Decking options include tongue-and-groove and strip-built.

Unless the boards are laid in single lengths, there must be joints in the decking, and these should be scattered as much as possible. For strength and to prevent curling, the butt ends must be well fastened, and it is not practical to make such a butt on a deck beam. Instead, the ends are fastened between the deck beams to blocks similar to planking butt blocks.

These decks are generally fastened with common galvanized nails; with age the fasteners have a way of working upward and poking holes in the canvas, causing it to leak. Galvanized wood screws would be better, and annularly threaded bronze nails better still; but on the whole, a tongue-and-groove deck really does not have much to recommend it except low cost, and in time even this is doubtful.

STRIP-BUILT DECK

The strip-built type of decking shown in C in Figure 13-1 is strong, rather quickly laid, and suitable when the deck is ½" thick or better. The strakes are usually square, or perhaps just a little wider than their thickness, and for maximum rigidity they are sprung to the curve of the deck edge. It is best to cut any laid decking from rift-sawn boards and lay it with the edge-grain up, for this way there will be a minimum of shrinking and swelling across the width of the deck (see Figure 4-3). Galvanized finishing nails are used for fastening and are satisfactory because they are hidden and not exposed to seawater. The fastidious, of course, can substitute nonferrous Monel or bronze nails at many times the cost and eliminate all misgivings. The strakes are fastened to each other between the deck beams and toenailed to the beams as shown in D of Figure 13-1. At the deck edge, the outermost strip is fastened to the sheerstrake of planking.

If a strip-built deck is built with waterproof-glued seams like a strip-planked hull (Chapter 11), it will be enormously strong if the seams are fitted reasonably tight. After being planed smooth and sanded, such a deck can be finished bright, painted, or covered with canvas (refer to "Canvas-Covered Decks" below) or light synthetic cloth and then sanded and painted.

PLYWOOD DECK

A main deck or cabin top of marine plywood is strong, light, and quickly laid. The arrangement of the pieces of plywood must be planned with care to provide maximum strength for the deck and for minimum waste of material, taking into consideration openings in the deck for hatches, cockpit, and cabin, together with the size of the panels available. In the previous chapter, the function in construction of lodging knees under the deck at openings and at masts to minimize horizontal racking was mentioned. Following the same reasoning, the plywood should be cut so seams do not come exactly at the ends of large openings in the deck as shown in A in Figure 13-2. The butts should overlap as shown in the sketch, and joints should be located between the beams where the panel ends can be securely screw-fastened to a butt block underneath. Joint locations are not as important if the plywood is waterproof-glued to the deck beams, because this adds considerably to the horizontal strength.

The deck panels should be fastened around the edges and along the deck beams with closely spaced flathead screws or annularly threaded

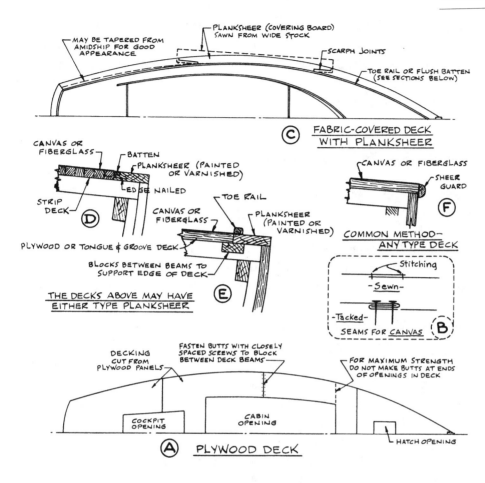

FIGURE 13-2.
Details on fitting a plywood deck and covering a deck with canvas or fiberglass.

nails. Countersink the fastening heads slightly below the surface and cover them over with a surfacing putty, non-oil-based if the deck is to be covered with fiberglass (or other synthetic) cloth and resin.

A well-fitted plywood deck properly glued to the deck framing can be fastened with nonferrous staples. Plywood up to ½" thick can be fastened with coated Monel or plastic staples driven by compressed-air-powered staplers. The coating increases the staples' holding power so it is just about impossible to withdraw these staples from white oak deck beams. (See Chapter 6.)

When a plywood deck is specified to be ¾" in thickness or more, the curvature due to camber and sheer might make laying the deck in a single thickness very difficult or even impossible due to the stiffness of the thicker panels. As soon as it is obvious that the flat panels will not conform to the surface, the job must be done by using a double thickness, such as two layers of ¼", ⅜", or ½" plywood, which should be waterproof-glued together to provide the most strength.

CANVAS-COVERED DECKS

Because boat decks—both laid and plywood—are still being covered with cotton canvas in certain areas by some builders, the method merits a brief description.

Canvas for covering should be bought wide enough to go over the entire deck in one piece if possible, allowing enough width to turn down over the edge of the deck. If a suitable width cannot be had, get a canvas worker to sew two strips together so that there will be a seam down the centerline of the boat. When unable to use sewn canvas, tack it on the centerline with a double fold. Seams are sketched in B in Figure 13-2.

The weight of the canvas varies from 8-ounce for small boats to 10- and even 12-ounce for decks that are liable to get considerable wear. Although there are canvas cements on the market, it is recommended instead that the canvas be laid in *wet* marine paint (not house paint). This of course will be applied to the deck just before laying the canvas.

First stretch the canvas fore and aft along the centerline. The canvas should be stretched as tight as possible, and this is at least a two-man job. It is better accomplished by rolling the ends of the canvas around sticks so that more area can be worked on than can be handled by just your two hands. Pull the canvas down over the edges of the boat and secure it with tacks, which will be hidden by moldings. Tacks should be copper or Monel, never steel or even galvanized, and should be very closely spaced in order for them to hold the pressure.

After the ends are fastened, start working amidships, pulling from opposite sides of the boat and tacking as you go along until the canvas is completely fastened around the edges. Where the canvas covers openings for cabin and hatches, cut it about 4" inside of the openings, stretch it tightly, and temporarily tack it to headers and beams; it will be turned up inside deck structures later as they are added to the boat.

When the canvas has been completely fastened, it is a good idea to apply the deck paint undercoater. Believe it or not, one of the best methods is to wet the canvas to further shrink and stretch it just before painting. Do this with a scrubbing brush and paint the surface before the canvas is dry. At any time later, one or two more coats of flat paint can be added, then a final coat of deck paint.

COVERING SURFACES WITH FIBER-REINFORCED PLASTIC (FRP)

I am only going to touch on covering the most dimensionally stable wooden structures—plywood panels, diagonally planked cold-molded hulls, or glued-seam strip-planked hulls (Chapter 11)—with synthetic fabrics such as fiberglass cloth, Dynel, and Vectran. There is often disagreement about covering these surfaces: should the cloth be laid on bare wood and then saturated with resin, or should the bare wood be coated with resin, and the cloth laid in the tacky resin, smoothed, and immediately saturated with another coat of resin? I don't think it makes much difference, but I have found that the "wet first" method makes an already messy job even worse.

There are several books about covering wood with fiberglass or other synthetic fabric written by people used to dealing with the inexperienced. One of these is *How to Fiberglass Boats*, by Ken Hankinson, which provides a straightforward account of fiberglassing procedures and should be read prior to a first attempt at fiberglassing.

Polyester resin is the most widely used of the resins and should be of the "laminating" type until the last buildup coat; this coat, which will be sanded smooth, should be "finish" resin. The book mentioned above describes how to make an additive that changes the laminating resin to a finish resin, the latter giving the hard and sandable surface necessary for painting. Finish resin can also be purchased.

Stable surfaces like plywood can be covered with a single layer of cloth, while corners, such as the chines of a v-bottomed boat, are reinforced with doubling strips. The adhesion of the wood surface is improved if rough sanded.

Do not use an oil-based putty or filler in dents or over the heads of fastenings. Instead, make a putty by mixing a powder such as Cab-O-Sil, microballoons, or microspheres (sold by resin suppliers) into the resin to thicken it.

Epoxy resin has a greater adhesion to wood than polyester but is significantly more expensive. However, epoxy does minimize the risk of the overlay delaminating from the wood. In addition I prefer epoxy to any other resin when covering a surface that has been previously painted. When using epoxy resin with fiberglass, care must be taken to choose a compatible cloth whose binder will not be dissolved by the epoxy.

FRP-covered decks are painted after being sanded smooth, a so-called fiberglass primer being used as the first coat.

If the cabin sides and such items as hatch coamings are to be finished bright, the decks should be covered before the installation of the deck joinerwork. When everything is to be painted, the watertight method is to build the cabin, etc., and turn the fabric up against it for an inch or two, "feathering" the edge of the covering by tapering it with the sander so it is not visible in the finished job.

Some fabrics, notably fiberglass, are also available in tape form. These narrow strips are good for strengthening and making watertight exterior woodwork joints that will be painted.

Warning: Heed all safety precautions when working with synthetic fabrics, resins, and their catalysts and/or hardeners.

DECKS WITH PLANKSHEER

The completely canvas-covered deck needs a molding on the sheerstrake (F in Figure 13-2) in order to hide the edge of the canvas. An attractive alternative is a deck with a varnished or contrasting colored covering board at the edge of the deck (Figure 13-2, C). This piece is called the *planksheer* and is sawn from wide boards. The joints between segments are scarphed rather than merely butted, and are generally screw-fastened from the top to butt blocks under the deck.

The canvas is stopped at the edge of the planksheer in either of two ways. The inner edge of the planksheer can be rabbeted (Figure 13-2, D), the canvas run down into the groove and tacked, and the groove filled with a tightly fitted batten of wood to match the planksheer. Another way is to employ a toe rail set at the inner edge of the planksheer as shown in Figure 13-2, E. The fabric is tacked along the edge, and the toe rail is fastened over the canvas with plugged screws. This is also a suitable termination for decks where the covering is synthetic fabric rather than canvas.

The outermost strake of a strip-built deck is edge-fastened to the planksheer for support, but the outer edge of a tongue-and-groove deck would be sprung downward if stepped on between beams where unsupported, perhaps to the extent of tearing the canvas—fiberglass covering a tongue-and-groove deck is not recommended—and splitting the edge of the decking. To prevent this, and also to support the ends of the deck planks where they run out at the edges, there must be blocks fitted between the deck beams.

CAULKED DECKS

There are two types of caulked decks. In larger yachts, where weight does not make too much difference, deck planking 1" thick and upward is laid. In smaller boats, where weight is important, thinner decking is laid over a sub-deck of marine plywood.

There is no denying that the old-time caulked decks were prone to leak, usually over someone's berth, but waterproof plywood has come to the rescue. Covered with FRP to prevent rot, plywood becomes an ideal underlayment even for the thicker caulked decking.

A typical laid and caulked deck is drawn in Figure 13-3 for a sailboat, and the construction also applies to powerboats. The planksheer is fitted first as described before; then the narrow strakes are sprung parallel to the edge of the planksheer. The reasons for the narrow strakes are twofold: they may be sprung without too much trouble, and the narrow material will not shrink and swell much or check. The wood for a laid deck must be clear and should be in long lengths. Any joints are located so they are quite far apart in adjacent strakes. The wood must be rift-sawn so the grain can be laid on edge, because flat grain will eventually lift and splinter—a condition that is both unsightly and hard on bare feet. Suitable woods are good white pine, Douglas fir, Port Orford cedar, and teak. The last named is the best and, like most good things, by far the most expensive. It has a natural oil that seems to make the deck everlasting (if given reasonable care), and it does not have to be varnished or painted. Scrubbing with salt water in the sun will bleach it out to a whitish color so that, together with its long life, there is no deck quite equal to teak.

Teak decks do get dirty and do not look well if neglected, but since so much teak trim is being used on fiberglass boats to offset their otherwise antiseptic appearance, there has been a flood of teak cleaners and treatment systems put on the market. Most of them do a good job and are easy to use, but be certain to follow directions because adjacent painted parts can be damaged by some teak cleaners.

Until the chemists got busy making up new seam sealers, standard practice was to bevel the edges of the deck strakes for caulking to make them watertight, as shown by the enlarged sections in Figure 13-3. The seams were caulked with cotton, then filled with a heated seam glue, which, in time, left much to be desired. Caulking with cotton can be eliminated by filling the seams in the decking with polysulfide adhesive sealants (such as 3M #101, BoatLife Caulk, and Thiokol) that can be run in simple, square seams like the one shown in the figure. After the decking is laid

FIGURE 13-3.
Details of a laid deck, including caulking.

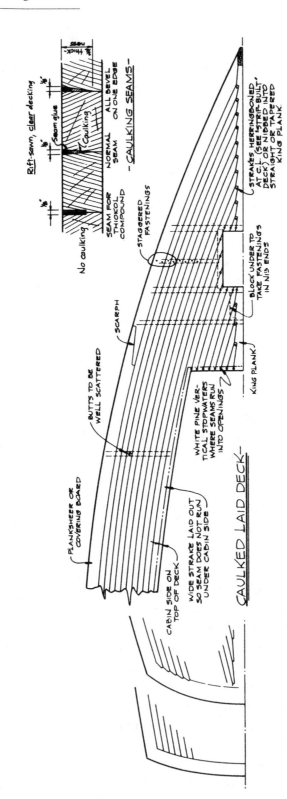

and secured, the open seams are masked with tape. The cartridge-packed seam filler is then applied with a regular household-type caulking gun or a drill-motor-powered gun (see Chapter 11). Care must be taken to avoid air bubbles by keeping the tip of the cartridge at the root of the seam so it is filled from the bottom up. The seams are overfilled, and the excess filler is cut off with a *very* sharp chisel after the polysulfide has completely cured a few days after *paying* (as seam filling is called). Be sure to check whether the caulking compound should be applied *only* to pre-primed seams, and if so, don't fail to use the primer recommended. This is very important, because if the sealant does not adhere to the wood you'll have an expensive rework on your hands. Best make a trial using scrap before paying the entire area.

A 1⅛" or 1¼" thick deck will have strakes about 1¾" wide, and this proportion is about right as the thickness of the decking becomes greater in larger boats. Your plans will specify what the designer wants. It is suggested that you use flathead screws as listed in the table in Chapter 6, Figure 6-6. The screws will be countersunk and plugged with bungs of the same wood as the decking, and due to the size of the plug, there will be room for just one fastening at each deck beam. Note in Figure 6-6 that the screw gauge may be reduced for decking, resulting in a smaller bung at times.

It is noted in Figure 13-3 that the strakes may be herringboned at the centerline like the strip-built deck or nibbed into a king plank as drawn. Either way there must be blocks under the deck at the centerline to take fastenings. It is not desirable to let deck seams run under cabin sides, and to avoid this, the strake next to the cabin opening is made wider, as drawn in Figure 13-3. Sometimes the decking strakes are run parallel to the cabin sides, requiring the ends to be nibbed into the planksheer as well as the king plank. Quite a lot of fitting is needed, as the taper on some of the nib ends will be very long. Still another way of decking is to run the planks straight fore and aft, nibbing both into the planksheer and a margin plank around the cabin (unless the cabin sides, too, are straight) and fastening the plank ends to blocks under the deck where the lengths run out at the sides. You will find that the method used in Figure 13-3 is not only common but also pleasing to the eye. When planking is completed, the seams are caulked and payed; then the entire surface of the deck is planed and sanded smooth.

Planking a laid deck over a sub-deck of marine plywood is similar to constructing a conventional laid deck, with the exception that the strakes are not being fastened directly to deck beams. The decking

should be thicker than the plywood sub-deck; as an example of proportions, a ⅜" fir plywood sub-deck would be covered with a ⅝"-thick
teak overlay. Plugging fastening holes can be avoided if desired by
back-screwing the teak to the plywood from underneath. This is labor-
intensive, but some deem it worthwhile. Pains must be taken to prevent rotting of the sub-decking should there be a leak in the seams of
the teak strakes. In fact, the best builders cover the plywood with light
FRP cloth before laying the teak deck. As an alternative, the teak can
be laid on plywood covered with polysulfide or even polyurethane
adhesive sealant (without allowing it to cure, of course)—a messy but
effective job.

Vertical-grain pre-milled teak decking made for installation over a plywood sub-deck is available from suppliers. The ½" thick strakes are 1¾"
wide and have a ⅛" wide by 3/16" deep groove for caulking cut on one edge.
(When two strakes are butted edgewise, the total groove for caulking compound is ¼" wide by 3/16" deep.)

Figure 13-4, part of a detail I drew for a Rhodes-designed sailboat during
the late 1940s, illustrates this kind of construction, as well as three examples of boatbuilding nomenclature: *strake, planksheer,* and *sheerstrake.*

If the teak strakes are not back-screwed, the ⅝" thickness mentioned
earlier is sufficient for counterboring and plugging screw holes in the conventional manner.

FIGURE 13-4.
Planking a laid deck over plywood.

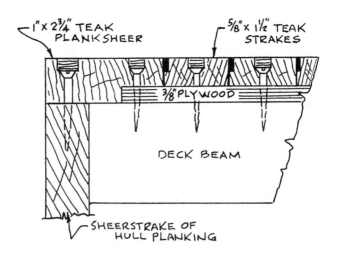

PREFABRICATED TEAK DECKING, ETC.

While inspecting a steel restaurant boat under construction on the east coast of Florida a few years ago, I noticed a crew on the forward deck smoothing the humps and hollows in the welded steel plating with a troweling compound I was later told was an epoxy-based mixture. Near the stern, where the deck surface had already been cured and faired, large sections of teak decking with strakes *already caulked* were being laid. The prefabricated sections had been made on the opposite coast of the state.

I contacted the decking contractor, Teakdecking Systems, and was given a booklet containing an explanation of services available and a very impressive list of yacht builders and individual boats—ranging from a popular 31-foot powerboat through the large so-called megayachts—that had purchased either complete weather decks or lesser areas such as cockpit soles, flying bridge decking, etc. Installation of decking is *not* limited to metal decks.

If teak is in the offing, this firm is worth investigating. There is obviously an economic advantage to dealing with a specialist: Teakdecking Systems can fabricate decking faster than its boatbuilder customers can, and it has an enormous stock of teak, all of it old-growth wood from Southeast Asia.

FIGURE 13-5.
Installation of prefabricated teak decking on a large yacht. (*Teakdecking Systems*)

14

DECK JOINERWORK

THE AMOUNT AND CHARACTER OF DECK JOINERWORK will vary with the type of boat. Open boats like daysailers will have simple cockpit coamings, while larger yachts might have a deckhouse, cabin trunk, hatches, watertight cockpit, and bulwark rail. This work should be done carefully and neatly because, regardless of how well you have built your hull, the occasional visitor will make a snap appraisal of your boat based on the appearance of the deck structures. Proper maintenance, too, is necessary, for nothing looks worse than bare and stained woodwork, peeling varnish, or scarred and dirty paint. Even though it is said that a book cannot be judged by its cover, my advice is to take a great deal of care when finishing parts that meet the eye and to keep them shipshape. A discussion about finishing with various protective coatings is found in Chapter 16.

CABIN TRUNK AND COCKPIT COAMING

The plans of your boat will show you the kind of cabin and coamings (along with heights and half-breadths), type of toe or bulwark rail, size and location of hatches, and other related information; the best I can do is discuss joinerwork details in general. The largest structure you will tackle is the cabin trunk, or deckhouse, depending upon the design. If the curve of the cockpit coaming on deck is a continuation of the cabin side, it will be best

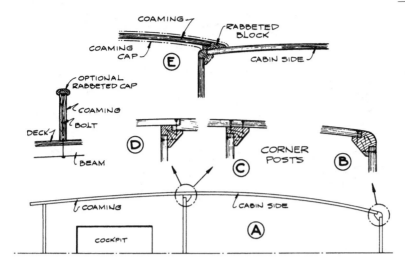

FIGURE 14-1.
Deck joinerwork options, including alternate methods of attaching corner posts.

and easiest to make both coaming and cabin side out of one long piece as in A in Figure 14-1. Long, wide mahogany boards are usually available for this, but if not, the width can be made up by edge joining the board with glued splines. If the cabin side is to be of plywood longer than standard panels, these can be made up in the same way.

The shape of the bottom edge of the cabin side, whether it is to rest on the deck or overlap it, is best obtained with a template of thin wood carefully held in place at the deck opening and scribed to the shape. The top edge is taken from the mold loft floor, where it was laid down from the plans. *Remember to leave a little extra on the top edge so it can be planed to the camber of the trunk top.*

The old-timers dovetailed the corners of the trunk—beautiful but almost unbelievably exacting and time-consuming work—while general practice nowadays is to fit the ends into suitably rabbeted corner posts and to fasten them with glue and plugged screws (see Figure 14-1, C). When making corner posts, make the rabbet deeper by ¹⁄₁₆" or so than the thickness of the cabin sides, and after assembly, work off the radius corner to a perfect fit.

The sides of the cabin, rather than being vertical, should be sloped *inboard toward the centerline* slightly to keep them from appearing to lean outboard. Sometimes for aesthetic reasons the cabin sides are sloped inboard considerably. This can be a chore for the amateur builder, but the results are often more than pleasing. It is easy to fit the cabin sides inside the deck beam headers as shown in B in Figure 14-2, but such a joint is

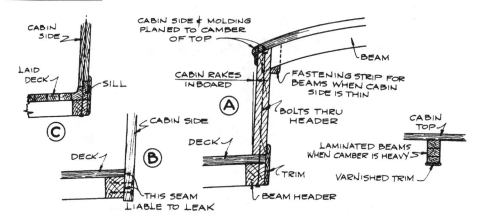

FIGURE 14-2.
Alternate methods of fitting the cabin sides to the deck.

difficult to keep watertight unless the deck is fiberglassed and the fabric turned up against the cabin side for a couple of inches. If the cabin sides are to be finished bright, making turned-up fabric impractical, great care must be taken to fit and bed the cabin sides against the deck edge to ensure watertightness. Thus, it is best to set the cabin sides as shown only when the deck is canvas covered or fiberglassed. With a laid and caulked deck, the best way is to make a rabbeted sill piece as sketched in C in Figure 14-2. This job is a real challenge, but it is absolutely first class.

Permit me to digress for a moment. I have noticed that a number of shippy-looking traditional-type sailboats are being designed with cabin trunk sides that, in plan view, are straight. And yet, when a mast is stepped through the trunk, there is a structural advantage in *not* having straight sides. To prove this, cut a strip of cardboard and hold it straight on a table; note how easily it hinges along the bottom edge (A in Figure 14-3). Now spring the strip to a curve and note the resistance to bending when loaded sideways (B of the same figure).

When trunk sides of solid lumber are specified to be as thick as 1¼", they should be fastened with bolts through the deck and beam header, with the bolts countersunk into the top edge. Drilling must be very carefully done so as not to ruin the lumber. When the cockpit coaming is thinner than the cabin

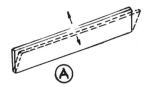 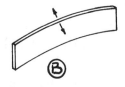

FIGURE 14-3.
Use a strip of cardboard against a table edge to demonstrate the benefits of a curved cabin trunk side—when curved there is more resistance to bending.

side, make it out of a separate piece and let it into the trunk at the after end as shown in D in Figure 14-1. When the cabin and the coaming are not in a continuous curve, the coaming is usually fastened to the cabin sides through a rabbeted block (E in Figure 14-1).

Strangely enough, I have seen only one cabin trunk for a sailboat that had strip-built sides, nailed and glued the same as planking of this type. With the mast stepped through the trunk top, the cabin has to be strong, and this is one way to do it easily, discounting amateur labor. In the one case that I saw, female forms were set up, against which the strips were clamped athwartships; the work went quickly and the trunk was very strong.

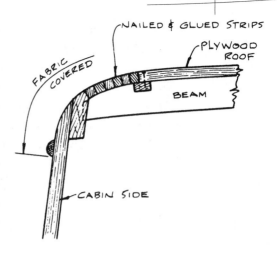

FIGURE 14-4.
Strip-planking the edge is one method of joining a curved cabin roof and side.

Sometimes the intersection of the cabin roof and sides is designed with considerable curve at the edges, like that shown in Figure 14-4, or even more so. Depending upon whether the roof is single- or double-planked, it might be impossible to give a quick bend to the plywood edges, especially in view of the curve in plan view. In this case a solution is to strip-plank the edge as shown.

TOE RAIL

Small sailboats are fitted with toe rails on deck (A in Figure 14-5) that are used as a foothold when the boat is heeled, and from long use, have come

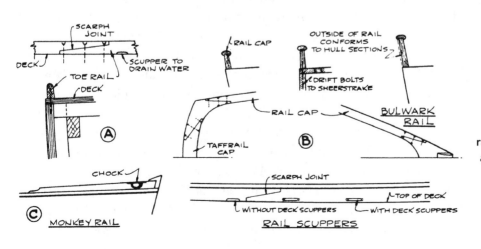

FIGURE 14-5.
Toe rails, bulwark rails, and monkey rails. Scuppers at the rails are also shown.

to be looked on as being decorative as well as practical. The rails are either set slightly inboard of the deck edge or at the inboard edge of the covering board, as mentioned in Chapter 13, and are fastened with plugged screws. Where joints are necessary, the butting pieces are scarphed. The under edge of the rails has scuppers cut at and near the low point of the sheer so that rainwater and spray will drain overboard. The rails may be of the same thickness throughout, but more often they are tapered on the inside face. Small toe rails may be of constant height from end to end, but they look better when tapered; the heights are frequently shown on the lines plan.

BULWARK RAIL

Larger boats have what is called a bulwark rail. In most large yacht designs these rails are tapered in height from bow to stern and usually tapered in thickness. Details are shown in B in Figure 14-5. Bulwark rails are secured by drift bolts run about every 18" through the deck into the sheerstrake, and are topped with a neatly shaped cap, screw-fastened and plugged. The cap is sometimes omitted for economy. Joints in both rail and cap are always scarphed, and the bottom of the rail is scuppered to drain water that otherwise would be trapped on deck. If no deck scuppers (pipes that drain water from the deck overboard through the hull near the waterline) are fitted, then the bottom of the rail scuppers must be at the deck level to drain rainwater. When there are deck scuppers, the bottom of the cuts in the rail are placed about ½" above the deck so that ordinary rainwater will not run through the scuppers to streak the topsides with dirt. The forward end of the rail is fitted into the stem rabbet, and the cap is shaped at the stem and across the transom as shown in B in Figure 14-5.

Installation of the bulwark rail will call for some ingenuity on the part of the builder. Templates should be of thin wood, sprung in place, and the bottom edge shaped to fit the deck. Then the rail heights at the stations are laid out, and a batten is run to fair the top of the rail. It will be a problem to hold the template in place, and the magnitude of the problem will vary with the type of boat. Bear in mind that the outside face of the rail conforms to the hull sections; that is, the rail is not installed vertically on a normal boat; thus the bottom edge bevel constantly changes. Jigs from the cabin sides and coamings and across the fore and after decks must be devised to hold the template in place, and then the rail while fastening. It is very likely that at least the forward section of the rail will need steaming to get it in place unless the rail is laminated. Much care must be taken to fair the rail sections into each other at the joints so they will be smooth.

Laminating can eliminate some of the heavy work in larger boats, but it requires a jig.

Sailboat bulwark rails often have a track to carry an adjustable fore-and-aft pad eye for a headsail sheet lead block; thus the rails must be structurally strong.

MONKEY RAIL

Boats without a true bulwark rail sometimes are dressed up with a short monkey or buffalo rail (take your choice) forward (see C in Figure 14-5). This is handy as a foothold when handling an anchor in a heavy sea and can be fitted with chocks for anchor and dock lines.

SLIDING HATCH

A sliding hatch is necessary to give headroom over companion ladders and elsewhere. The hatch must be rugged enough to take the weight of a man sitting or standing on it. The cover may be flat across, but looks much better when cambered like the deck. It can be of plywood, either one or two layers glued together, but the classier covers are constructed of solid lumber, as shown in Figure 14-6. The cover is made on a pair of beams sawn to the camber, using material $7/8$" thick and about 3" wide, with the butting edges grooved for soft white pine splines, which stiffen the hatch as well as prevent leaks. The joints are waterproof-glued, and the top pieces are fastened to the beams with plugged screws.

The logs may be constructed in a variety of styles as shown in Figure 14-6, some of which are easier to make than others. A common slide is shown in sketch A with brass tongues on the beam ends to slide in grooves in the logs. The edge of the cover is protected with a piece of split brass tubing, while the tops of the logs are sheathed with brass strips that interlock with the split tubing to keep spray out of the hatch opening. The arrangement in sketch B is similar in operation, having a rabbeted beam header that slides in the log groove. The top of the log may be sheathed if desired, and the molding on the edge of the cover makes it adaptable to canvas covering. The logs shown in sketches C and D do not have grooves, for the covers slide directly on the logs, making it necessary to sheathe them to prevent wear of the surface. In C the sliding friction is minimized by having an angle between the brass strips, so contact is at one edge only. In D there is a piece of brass let into the cover at the ends only, and it should project slightly, so the wooden cover will not touch the log. The arrangements

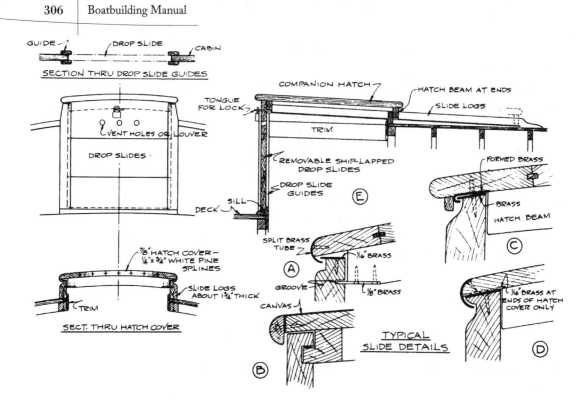

FIGURE 14-6.
Details of companionway slides and covers.

shown in the sketches are typical and others can be devised. The metal parts can be stainless steel, but brass is quite easy to work.

An elevation at the centerline of a sliding hatch is illustrated by sketch E, Figure 14-6. The length of the logs as they extend beyond the companionway is determined by the distance from the aftermost hatch cover beam to the forward end of the hatch opening. Beyond the required length, the logs are finished with an ogee curve. Fasten the logs to the deck beams and headers with plugged screws. The bottom edges of the logs just forward of the apron must have scuppers cut in them to drain trapped water.

Strive to make the cover slide freely—nothing is more aggravating than one that sticks.

COMPANIONWAY CLOSURE

The simplest way of closing the opening in the aft end of the trunk is to fit drop boards that slide between guides, as shown in Figure 14-6. A slot can be cut in the top slide to take a brass padlock tongue screwed to the bottom of the hatch cover beam, or a cabinet lock may be fitted. The top slide should also have ventilation holes or louvers to circulate air through the boat when it is locked up. A shaped sill is fitted on the deck to keep water from running off the slides or main deck into the cabin. Double doors, usually paneled, are sometimes substituted for the drop boards.

HATCHES

Openings in the deck are covered with hatches made to be watertight or reasonably so. At sea, particularly, hatches that leak are an unspeakable nuisance, making for discomfort during the watch below, so every effort should be exerted to construct them so they fit well and function satisfactorily. The pieces forming the cover (unless the cover is plywood) are preferably splined as described for the sliding companion hatch. The frame around the cover is half-lapped at the corners (here, again, the old professionals used dovetails, which I consider to be too difficult for the amateur), and it is very important that the detail in sketch A of Figure 14-7 be followed. If the half lap is reversed from that shown so that the end screws in the top pieces are in the side frame that is parallel to the top pieces, the swelling of the top in width will force the corner joint apart. In other words, all screws across the width of the top must be in the same piece of frame.

The hatch coamings vary in detail according to preference or practice, but all are either through-bolted or fastened from the bottom with long, husky screws. The corners of the hatch coamings are dovetailed together or rabbeted and screw-fastened as shown in G in Figure 14-7, and set in marine bedding compound on the deck. In fact, bedding compound is used to keep out water under *everything* fitted on deck, whether it is woodwork or such fittings as cleats, fill plates, etc. Use a polyurethane adhesive sealant such as 3M 5200 or a polysulfide-based compound such as BoatLife's Life Calk.

Sketch B illustrates a crude workboat-type hatch not very suitable for a yacht, and although frames like C are used, they are too light to be any good and should be modified into something like D, which will stay together and is fairly watertight when dogged down. The type shown in sketch E has the coaming grooved for a rubber gasket. A refinement of this is the hatch construction shown in Figure 14-8, which is the best of the lot and not too difficult to build. It is a mistake to make the parts of hatches too light. Flimsy hatches and hatch hardware just do not stand up to the abuse they must take.

The hinges shown are made by a couple of the marine hardware firms and are quite satisfactory. Through-bolt the hinges wherever possible.

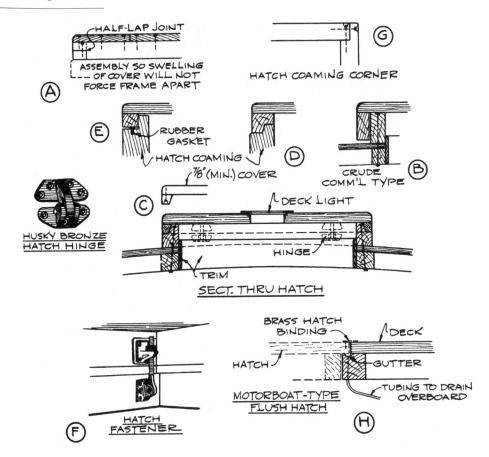

FIGURE 14-7.
Details of hatch coaming corners and closures.

Note that the hatch in Figure 14-8 is shown with a plastic top. This is optional, but it admits a lot of light to spaces like the galley. Unless a strong material such as Lexan is used, it is a bit risky to use a hatch with a plastic top on the main deck of a sailboat where a crewmember is liable to jump on the hatch with considerable force. If a light is wanted in a wooden main deck hatch, it is safer to use a round one with a bronze frame, like the one shown in the hatch section in Figure 14-7.

When the deck joinerwork is to be all painted, a hatch cover of marine plywood—fiberglassed if fir—is satisfactory. Some like to hinge the hatches at both forward and after sides, which is effected by fitting two sets of hinges and replacing the individual pins with a removable rod to engage both hinges on the desired side. The covers are locked from below with cast brass hooks and eyes, or dogged down tight with a bronze fastener of the type shown in sketch F of Figure 14-7 (available from marine hardware

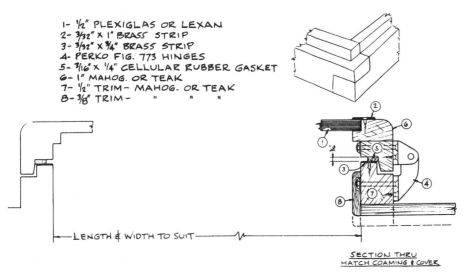

1- ½" PLEXIGLAS OR LEXAN
2- 3/32" X 1" BRASS STRIP
3- 3/32" X ¾" BRASS STRIP
4- PERKO FIG. 773 HINGES
5- 7/16" X ¼" CELLULAR RUBBER GASKET
6- 1" MAHOG. OR TEAK
7- ½" TRIM- MAHOG. OR TEAK
8- 3/8" TRIM-   "   "   "

LENGTH & WIDTH TO SUIT

SECTION THRU
HATCH COAMING & COVER

FIGURE 14-8.
Details of a homemade hatch.

suppliers), located at the corners opposite the hinges. Such fasteners are especially good where a gasket must be pulled down.

The builder now has the option of buying excellent hatches instead of making them. Hatches of cast aluminum alloy frames with strong lights of polycarbonate sheet (Lexan) are also available; they're made by Bomar, Lewmar, and others and come in a large selection of sizes (see Figure 14-9). Some of these hatches are designed with sailboats in mind and have a minimum number of protrusions so that sails can be hurriedly passed through the hatch without catching on anything.

FIGURE 14-9.
A cast aluminum hatch by Bomar.

Some complain that the plastic-topped hatches sweat, and this is also true of metal hatches. Sweating of the metal hatches can be considerably reduced or stopped entirely by applying granulated cork to the underside. Of course, it is possible to make a minimum-sweating hatch out of another material—wood!

FLUSH HATCHES

Cockpits usually have flush hatches over engines, tanks, and storage spaces; these often are constructed as shown in sketch H, Figure 14-7, in an effort to keep rain, spray, and washdown water from running into the bilges and dripping on equipment on the way. This usual method is pretty poor because it does not take much water to overflow the shallow gutters or much dirt to clog the drain. A better method is to use a system of channel-shaped sheet stainless steel or aluminum alloy gutters attached to the hatch opening framing, wide enough to project under the opening, and having a good-size overboard line, say ¾" at least.

NONWOOD WINDOW FRAMES, RUBRAILS, ETC.

Cruising boats with deckhouses often use windows rather than portlights, and it is usually simpler to purchase these instead of making them. They are leakfree, easy to install, and there is a selection of stock sizes or they can be made to patterns furnished by the boatbuilder. Materials used are aluminum alloy anodized to resist corrosion (fasteners to secure these should always be stainless steel) or rigid vinyl.

Figure 14-10 is a section through a heavy-duty fixed rigid vinyl window frame. Window frames are also made sliding or hinged. Stock and custom

FIGURE 14-10.
Section through rigid vinyl fixed window frame for wooden cabin side.

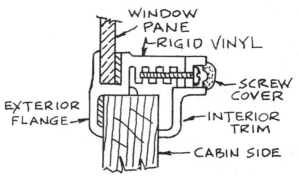

windows of this type in a multitude of styles can be obtained from Freeman Marine, Waterway Systems, and B & J Aluminum Windows.

Taco Metal makes aluminum alloy windshields for utility-type craft or runabouts or will sell the extruded parts and assembly hardware for the do-it-yourselfer. The Taco line also includes nylon deck cleats and many styles of extruded vinyl and aluminum alloy rubrails, continuous hinges, and other kinds of hardware including stainless steel.

WATERTIGHT SELF-BAILING COCKPIT

A watertight cockpit as fitted in sailboats is simply a well sunk below main deck level with scuppers to drain water, whether it be from rain or heavy spray and seas. The sole of the cockpit can be fiberglass-covered plywood, preferably made of nonskid, or bare teak.

The boat plans should provide details for the cockpit scuppers and whether or not they should be crossed in sailboats to take care of heeling—that is, whether the port scupper discharges through the hull on the starboard side and vice versa. There are various ways to fit scuppers flush with the cockpit sole; probably the easiest is to buy flush-fitting scuppers from one of the marine hardware outfits. Above all, the scuppers *must* be generously sized so that the cockpit well can drain rapidly should a sea break aboard.

The cockpit sole is laid on beams that may extend to the hull sides, or it may be supported by beam headers, which in turn are suspended from the main deck headers by long rods with threaded ends for nuts (see A in Figure 14-11). A rabbeted water table is fitted at the intersection of the cockpit ceiling and the sole (C in Figure 14-11). The cockpit ceiling may be permanently installed or fitted with hinged doors for access to storage spaces not occupied by fuel and water tanks, exhaust piping, etc.

Many prefer cockpit seats lowered below the main deck level (B in Figure 14-11) for the feeling of security it gives. If the boat has a raised doghouse, the designer must plan the lowered seats with care in order not to restrict the visibility of the person at the helm. The seats are most comfortable if sloped and fitted with a slanted lazyback. They require beams and headers for support, the latter of which are secured to blocks under the main deck beams at the ends of the cockpit. (See dotted lines in B, Figure 14-11.) Sloped seats must be scuppered with copper or other noncorrosive tubing at least ½" in diameter (if possible) to drain water; also, the seats may be arranged with hinged sections over storage spaces.

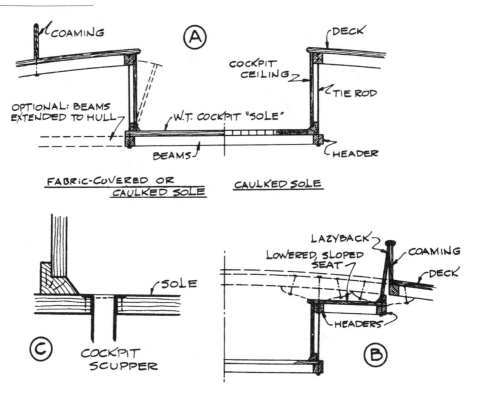

FIGURE 14-11.
Cockpit details.

SEATS AND LOCKER LIDS

Hinged seats and locker lids on deck are prone to warp due to changes in moisture. This occurs in both solid lumber and plywood. One way to minimize this is to make a series of cuts parallel to the long direction and on the underside of the piece. This is done on a table saw or with a portable circular saw. Cleats are fitted as shown in Figure 14-12 and securely fastened while the seat is *flat,* clamped if necessary.

SHEER GUARDS

The hull guard at the sheer, if the boat is designed for one, can vary from a simple half round or rectangle for smaller boats to a fairly heavy, builtup guard for larger hulls. The latter type can be difficult to make and install, considering the shape of the deck in plan and the changing bevel of the sections of the boat from bow to stern. The most difficult job is to install a

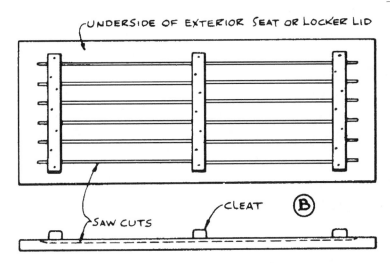

UNDERSIDE OF EXTERIOR SEAT OR LOCKER LID

SAW CUTS

CLEAT (B)

FIGURE 14-12.
Details of a seat or locker lid.

guard at the bow of a powerboat having a full deck line forward and a lot of flare. For the larger hulls a guard must be laminated to the shape of the deck line and sawn to the bevel of the sections. The fastening of guards is very important, for they are there for the purpose of protecting the hull and must not come loose when subjected to a blow either from the side or vertically, or a combination of both.

Sometimes a rubber-like guard, often in conjunction with an aluminum alloy extrusion, is used in place of wood shod with metal half oval, provided a suitable shape can be found, and there are quite a number of these sold by marine supply houses. Taco Metals has an extensive variety of extruded guards.

Lower guards to protect hulls at the stern where there is tumblehome (hull wider below the sheer than at the sheer) take some hard knocks at times and also must be securely fastened. Depending upon the construction of the hull and deck at the sheer, the sheer guard sometimes needs blocking between the frames to take the fastenings, which, for heavy-duty guards, are preferably through-bolts.

15

INTERIOR
JOINERWORK

FROM THE BEGINNING OF THIS MANUAL it has been assumed
that the builder is familiar and reasonably skilled with woodworking tools,
having undertaken basic household projects. With this experience, the
cabin joinerwork should prove to be the easiest task in the construction of
the boat. Be advised though that this work may not proceed as rapidly as
one might wish, because parts must be made to fit the shape of the hull in a
work space that is comparatively cramped. The joints and finish can be as
plain or as fancy as desired, commensurate with the ability of the builder.

Note: If we assume for the moment that the sheerline of the boat being
built is an average of 4 feet or more above the shop floor, and that the boat is
a cruiser about 30 feet long with a fair amount of interior joinerwork, then
the builder should consider having power saws on deck if the arrangement
of the boat permits, or a platform with power saws at approximate sheer
height if the building site permits. Either setup saves hours of time spent
climbing out of the boat and back in again, often to make just a cut or two.
Currently on the market there is a good selection of moderately priced,
downsized bench and band saws—very handy tools for onboard joinerwork, and often seen now in the boatshops.

The boat designer's drawings of sections through the interior or his
specifications should but often do not show details of joinerwork construction methods; in case these are lacking or sparse, I will show some typical

structural methods. In a small craft there are not too many different details to be planned, although there might seem to be a multitude of them the first time around. Even in a hull large enough to sleep four or more persons there are only a few bulkheads and doors, the rest of the interior joinerwork consisting of berth tops and fronts, lockers, drawers, the galley work top, and the all-important icebox. Any finished carpentry in the nature of cabinetwork is enhanced by neatly fitting joints and a smooth finish, so the time spent in fitting parts and pushing sandpaper really pays off with the satisfaction of a job well done.

PLYWOOD INTERIOR JOINERWORK

Waterproof plywood makes interior work much easier than in years past because this material saves labor by permitting parts to be quickly cut from large sheets rather than fabricated from boards. Bulkheads and large partitions are a good example, as these can be made of plywood in a fraction of the time formerly needed to make them either of paneling or of tongue-and-groove material.

FINISHING PLYWOOD INTERIOR SURFACES

Assuming that plywood will be used, the finish can be of any of several basic types. The most attractive of these is a real wood finish. This can be achieved by using a plywood faced with mahogany, teak, or other such veneers available in waterproof panels, stained or natural, and finished with multiple coats of varnish, each rubbed down with fine sandpaper or bronze wool between coats. Natural wood can also be finished with wax-based material, tung oil, or tung oil varnish. The tung oil liquids can be applied by hand with a soaked rag or a brush, the excess being wiped off soon afterward. The surface should be allowed to dry for a day, then buffed with bronze wool and recoated until the luster is pleasing. Moldings for trim around locker openings, etc., must be made of solid lumber. Flats such as tabletops, exposed shelves, and the like are best covered with a phenolic finishing material like Formica to match the natural wood finish. In such cases, the plywood can be of less expensive fir. The natural wood decor is for the perfectionist who has the time, skill, and patience to make perfect-fitting joints throughout.

Another choice is to go with a completely painted finish or a combination of paint with natural wood trim, such as mahogany. For a painted finish, the use of faced plywood like MDO (Chapter 4) is best because it will save one or more coats of paint. Even though most of the surfaces will be painted, it is practical to cover the galley counter and other flats that receive hard wear with Formica or a Formica-type overlay. (Formica is but one type of "high-pressure laminate.")

A third choice is to cover most of the vertical surfaces with one of the tough, washable vinyl wall coverings and to paint the parts that are not practical to cover with a harmonizing color. Again, the horizontal surfaces that take wear and tear should be covered with overlay or painted. The trim can be painted to match or contrast, or it can be natural wood finish.

Still another finish is to use an overlay as much as practical on both horizontal and vertical surfaces, either in colors or wood grains. It is a little tricky to work with until you get used to it, but an attractive and unusually durable finish results. The panels are adhered to clean plywood with so-called contact cement, which is applied to both surfaces and allowed to set up dry to the touch before the surfaces are joined. Once the two cement-coated surfaces contact each other, they are stuck for good, so they must be carefully positioned. One method of preventing premature contact is to use what is known as a slip sheet, made of a piece of brown paper the same size as the Formica part to be cemented. The cement-coated surfaces are allowed to set up dry to finger touch, the slip sheet is laid on the wood while the Formica is lined up perfectly, and then while holding the parts aligned, the slip sheet is pulled out from between the surfaces so the parts can be joined.

Plywood helps reduce the weight of joinerwork; there is no sense in installing weight in the form of furniture that is overly strong. The plans for the boat should specify the thickness of the plywood, but if they don't, a general guide for bulkheads is ½", ¾" in the larger hulls; dresser tops, counters, and minor partitions need not be over ½" in any boat where weight saving is desired. Shelves in lockers and elsewhere can be ⅜" or ½" depending upon the area. Be guided by common sense, because with glued and screwed parts, high strength can be achieved with plywood structures, and the lighter panels reduce cost.

Sometimes in sailboats the mast is stepped on deck, and somehow the thrust must be carried to the hull. In some cases the bulkheads in the immediate vicinity of the mast are used for this purpose; thus they may be heavier than normal.

JOINING PLYWOOD INTERIOR PANELS

When bulkheads or partitions are larger than can be cut from one plywood panel, the pieces must be joined. The simplest way is to use a butt strip of plywood glued and screwed to the bulkhead pieces, but this does not look good unless it is located inside a locker or otherwise concealed from view. The neatest butt is made with a spline as shown in section A of Figure 15-1, using a glued plywood spline, but you must have the woodworking machinery to cut the grooves accurately or have a mill do it for you. Still another way to join two plywood panels is to scarph them together, cutting the scarph with an attachment for a portable circular saw called a "Scarffer." This is shown in Chapter 4, Figure 4-9.

INTERIOR JOINERWORK DETAILS

Sections B through E in Figure 15-1 show different ways of building corners for bulkheads, while F shows a vertical section through a galley or bathroom counter. The toe space shown at the base of the counter is well worth the trouble it takes to construct. It is a minor but important feature that facilitates making up berths or standing closer to counters. Dimensions for a toe space should be 3" × 3" (unless greater height is needed above the sole for extra thick coverings); glue and screw all faying surfaces.

Another good detail to incorporate is shown in sketch G of Figure 15-1. This shows sea rails that have been brought down to counter level at their ends to enable dirt to be cleaned out of corners. Sea rails are used to keep things from falling off counters and should be about 1" high, or even higher when you want to retain something like a portable radio.

FIGURE 15-1.
Details of interior joinerwork, including a method of joining plywood (A).

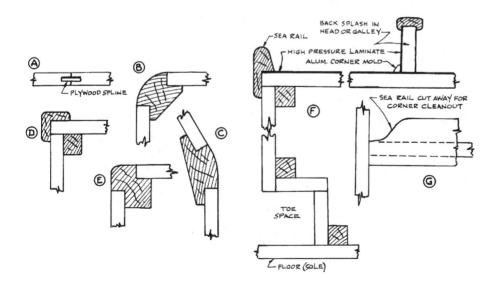

The interiors of early small production cruising sailboats were antiseptic in appearance, all parts stark white or nearly so, the exception being remnants of carpeting cemented to the inside of the hulls in the way of berths, etc., to hide the ugly raw fiberglass. Later—and this was still true of powerboat interiors I inspected at the manufacturing plants in 1991—teak trim was added to relieve the monotonous expanse of white.

Better grades of boats, both stock and custom, have gone in heavily for teak interiors, either oiled or varnished, the latter usually with satin rather than glossy finish. Nowadays the do-it-yourselfers, as well as the professionals, have stock teak trim parts available to them to make things easier. Figure 15-2 illustrates just a sampling of the Seateak line of moldings sold by many of the marine supply stores. In the figure, A is called berth molding; B is for door frames; C is an opening cap; D a bulkhead or partition corner; E a simple quarter-round trim; and F is an ell-shaped "corner killer." A super work saver made for sea rails is illustrated in G: (a) is an inside corner piece, and (b) is an outside corner. The moldings are made to mate with both ½" and ¾" thick panels.

Also available are a kit of parts to make a louvered door, either left- or right-handed, and parts from which to assemble a tambour closure.

In addition, the Seateak line has premachined and preassembled teak items such as a soapdish, a liquid-soap holder, tissue and paper towel dispensers, glass and toothbrush holders, towel bars and racks, several sizes of pinrail-type utility shelves, and electrical switch and outlet covers.

FIGURE 15-2.
Seateak line of moldings: berth molding (A), door frames (B), hatch opening cap (C), bulkhead corner (D), quarter-round trim (E), ell-shaped for corners (F), and sea rail alternatives (G).

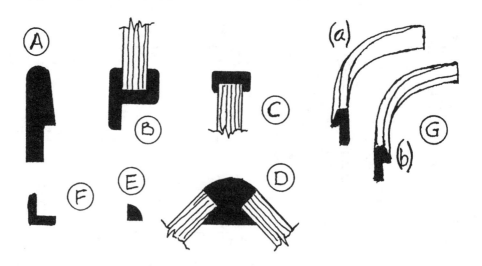

BALSA-CORED PANELS

Before further discussion of interior joinerwork detail, an alternative panel should be described. Baltek Corporation has long been importing balsa wood from Ecuador. Many people have used balsa during their youth to make model aircraft or boats. The wood has also been used extensively as a lightweight core between fiberglass skins to build boat hulls, as mentioned in Chapter 5.

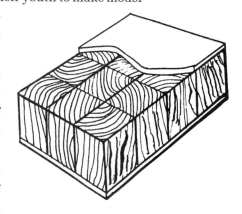

One such product, called DecoLite, is a sandwich consisting of end-grain balsa between faces (see Figure 15-3). The panels have a place in any type of boat where a saving of weight is desired and can be afforded. Uses include bulkheads, partitions, and cabin soles. The panels are flat and stiff, and five choices of facings, or skins, are offered: a variety of hardwood veneers; clear fiberglass; high-pressure laminates (the uptown term for Formica-type materials); ash; and teak. Baltek produces these panels

FIGURE 15-3.
Construction of DecoLite panels.

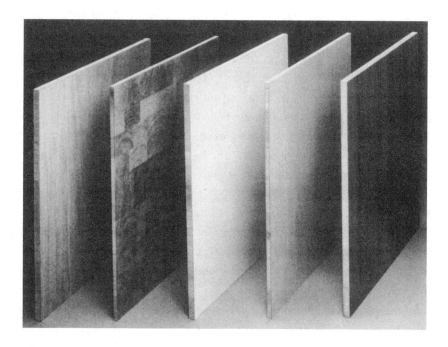

FIGURE 15-4.
Baltek DecoLite panels with various facings. *Left to right*: Hardwood veneer; clear fiberglass; high-pressure laminate; ash; and teak.

in 48" × 96" size, ½" and ¾" thick. Clear fiberglass is also made 1" thick. Bonding is done with polyester resin.

Average weight in pounds per square foot of the samples sent to me is about 0.96 for ½" and 1.15 for ¾". In round numbers these are 65 percent and 50 percent, respectively, of the weight of Douglas fir plywood—an appreciable savings.

For more information about Baltek products for boatbuilding, write to the company or have a look at its website. (See Appendix.) It has prepared a series of sketches showing ways of butting DecoLite panels.

Defender carries Baltek products, as well as other composite products, and is happy to sell them by the sheet instead of the truckload.

A unique combination of balsa strips with hardwood veneer, called DuraKore, is an interesting alternative for strip-planking hulls, as discussed in Chapter 11.

OTHER ALTERNATIVE MATERIALS

Polymer sheets. First, what is a polymer? Give up? It is a chemical compound or mixture of compounds, especially with high molecular weight, formed by polymerization (which is the process whereby small molecules combine into larger ones with repeating structural units). If you handled a piece you would say it is a hard plastic. One maker of marine polymer sheet, King Plastic Corporation, has an ad in a trade paper that reads, "You've come to rely on polymers to take the place of teak and other woods." Well, that may be overstating things a little, but marine polymer sheet does have its uses. A King brochure explains that its photographs show ladder treads, a transom platform, cockpit lockers, grabrails, and both deck and interior joinerwork, perfectly flat or bent to curves. The polymer sheet is made in seven different colors or can be matched to a sample. Panel sizes are ¼", ½", ¾", and 1" thick; 54" × 96", 48" × 96", and 48" × 120". At 60 pounds per cubic foot, the panels are fairly hefty. There are several plastics suppliers on the Web advertising the availability of StarBoard in smaller amounts, cut to specification. Gluing StarBoard (and other polymer sheets) is a bit of an issue. The glue that StarBoard recommends as the only suitable one is quite expensive and is still not always successful; generally it is best to fasten StarBoard with stainless steel bolts or screws.

Honeycomb panels. These lightweight structures generally have a wood or synthetic exterior, with an interior core of foam, kraft paper, aluminum, or composite materials—Nomex, for example. Nida Core, which has a polypropylene core, is gathering adherents as a relatively inexpensive, lightweight, durable, and easily worked alternative to plywood and balsa-cored panels for interior furniture. Noah's Marine Supply stocks Nida Core and many other cored panel materials used in boatbuilding. Jamestown Distribiutors is another good source.

SCRIBING FOR SHAPES

Where berth platforms, shelves, and the edges of bulkheads and partitions lie against the hull, their edges are curved and must be fitted by a process similar to spiling planking. This requires the use of heavy cardboard or light wood for making templates. In the case of a horizontal part, the template board must be held level athwartships for the most accurate results, while the template board for a bulkhead must be held normal (90 degrees) to the centerline of the hull. Similarly, the points of dividers or a carpenter's compass must be held normal to the centerline when scribing points for a horizontal part, and level when scribing the shape for a bulkhead. If these procedures are not followed, the parts will not be correctly shaped, and further fitting will be required. The bevels for the parts can be taken off at intervals and marked on the template board. The template board is cut to the scribed line and used as a pattern (see Figure 15-5).

Bulkheads are often located on one side or another of a frame. Fastening a bulkhead to a frame is simple, unless the frame is not plumb vertical, which is often the case when the frames are bent rather than sawn. In such cases, the frame must be shimmed to true up the bulkhead. Thus, when framing a boat, it pays to be particularly careful to have the bulkhead frames be as true as possible. For bulkheads located between frames, a strip similar to a frame must be installed so that the bulkhead can be fastened to the hull. In v-bottomed hulls and in some round-bottomed ones, a strip can be bent cold to the inside of the planking, but where there is too much shape for this, you must either steam bend the wood, saw a frame to shape, or bend in a strip made pliable by numerous saw cuts on its inside edge. (See A in Figure 15-6.) The spacing of the cuts is determined by trial and error, and a strip like this is best placed where it won't be visible in the cabin.

DRAWERS

Drawers are best made of solid lumber, using ¾" for the fronts, ½" sides, and backs rabbeted for a bottom of ½" plywood or hardboard such as tempered Masonite. They must have a device to prevent them from opening at sea. (See B in Figure 15-6.)

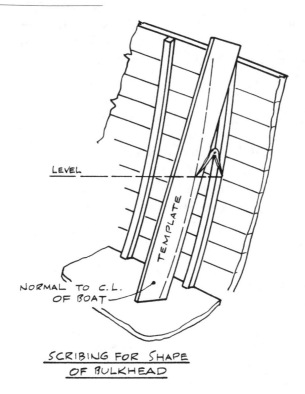

LEVEL

TEMPLATE

NORMAL TO C.L.
OF BOAT

SCRIBING FOR SHAPE
OF BULKHEAD

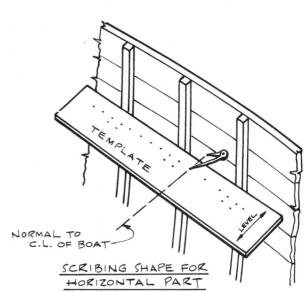

TEMPLATE

NORMAL TO
C.L. OF BOAT

LEVEL

SCRIBING SHAPE FOR
HORIZONTAL PART

FIGURE 15-5.
Two methods of scribing for shape.

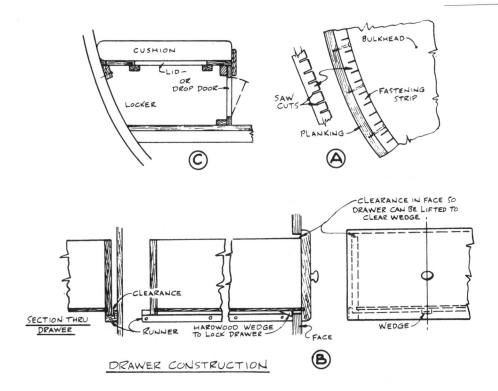

FIGURE 15-6.
Fastening a bulkhead to a frame (A) and details of drawer (B) and locker (C) construction.

Occasionally a product developed for residential use is made of non-corrosive material enabling it to be used as well in boats at sea. A case in point: injection-molded plastic parts manufactured for custom cabinet drawers. These parts utilize a three-point support system that may be simpler to build or install than the old method of hanging a drawer on side runners as shown in Figure 15-6.

The alternative system described here (there are others on the market) employs a mass-produced tee-shaped wooden track on the centerline of the bottom of a drawer opening, where it is secured to a short cleat. Support at the outer end of the track depends upon where it is located—for example, at a bulkhead or partition, or against the hull, etc.

A molded track holder—secured to the back side of the drawer at the bottom—engages the track, while the bottom edges of the drawer sides slide along an angle-type molded part located on each side of the drawer opening in the cabinet or berth front. (See Figures 15-7 and 15-8.) The molded parts are made of a slippery, low-friction material. In making a selection

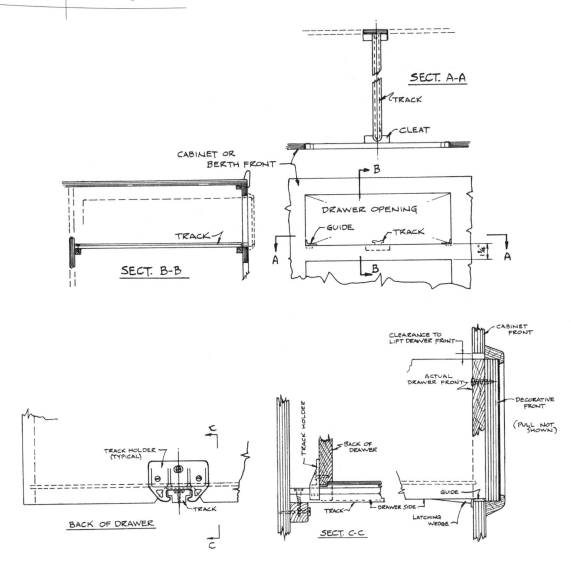

FIGURES 15-7 AND 15-8.
Drawer construction details.

it is advisable that a careful detail of drawer construction be worked out and tested to satisfaction before plunging ahead with a quantity of drawers.

INTERIOR FASTENERS

Fastenings in interior woodwork are screws for the most part. Do not use steel nails unless they are hot-dipped galvanized. In plywood joinerwork many of the fastenings can be hidden by the trim. In varnished trim, the fastening holes are counterbored and plugged or concealed by matching putty if the fastenings are nails set below the surface of the wood. Plugs in varnished work are set in either Weldwood Plastic Resin Glue or an aliphatic liquid glue such as Titebond or Titebond II or III. Epoxy would work well, too, especially if you are setting a number of plugs at one time.

Do not expect plated-steel hardware, such as hinges, drawer pulls, or lock sets, to survive forever in a boat. Although expensive, the hardware should be brass or bronze, either plain or chrome-plated, or stainless steel.

NONCORROSIVE MARINE LOCKS

Many have been frustrated trying to find hardware that does not rust. These days many marine suppliers carry noncorrosive locks for hinged and sliding doors and cabinet locks.

LOCKER DOOR CATCH

The catch shown in Figure 15-9 was used by Nevins and other sailboat builders about forty years ago; brass elbow catches are still made in the United States and England. The reasoning behind this type of catch is to eliminate protrusions that are a danger and a nuisance down below when at sea in heavy weather. Nevins lined the finger hole with a brass ferrule. Nowadays there is so much teak in boat interiors that several manufacturers make hole liners of that material.

EXTENSION SETTEE BERTHS

In Figure 15-6, C shows a typical detail section through a fixed berth, assuming plywood construction. The larger cruising sailboats often have a berth

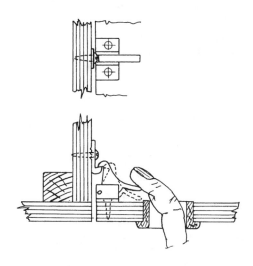

FIGURE 15-9.
Typical installation of elbow catch for locker door.

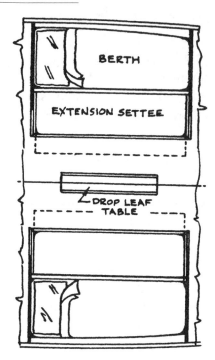

FIGURE 15-10.
Main cabin settees slide to berth width in cruising sailboats with sufficient beam.

against the hull each side and settees at a lower level inboard of the berths, and when the beam of the hull is sufficient the settees can be extended farther inboard to make them usable as additional berths (see Figure 15-10). This is done by making them slide to expose cushion width that is normally concealed under the hullside berths, which are higher above the cabin sole. Making such a sliding settee without prior experience can be a real head-scratching exercise; therefore Figure 15-11 has been prepared to illustrate a method that was furnished to a good number of builders of boats designed by the late Philip L. Rhodes.

FIGURE 15-11.
Philip Rhodes's details of an extension settee.

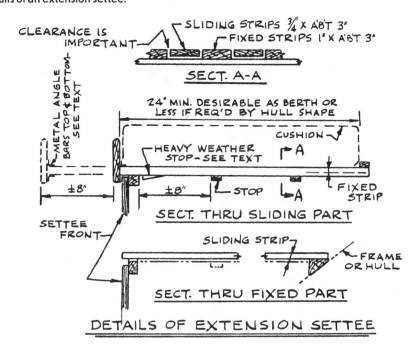

The usual increase in settee width is about 8". The scheme shown in the figure uses solid lumber strips about 3" wide. About half of them are ¾" thick; the other half, the pieces that slide, are 1" thick. It will soon be realized that the construction has to be tailored to the shape of the hull at the level of the settee. The fixed strips are fastened inboard to a cleat secured to the top edge of the settee front, while outboard they are fastened to another cleat, which in turn is attached to the frame or the hull skin, as the case may be. The ends of the seat front and headers terminate at partitions or partial bulkheads at the ends of the settee.

The sliding section consists of a cushion retainer inboard with small brass or aluminum angle bars to which the sliding strips are fastened. Outboard, the sliding strips are fastened to a cleat and also another cleat that limits the travel. A single small wedge about mid-length of the sliding assembly prevents movement inboard during heavy weather.

VENTILATION

Proper ventilation of the hull is one of the most important items that will contribute to the long life of a wooden boat. Passage of air must be provided for at all times, all the while keeping fresh water from entering the boat and becoming trapped. (It must be remembered that the boat may be kept for most of its life at a mooring or a slip, unprotected by a roof.) Other than patented devices made of molded plastic, etc., the most practical ventilator developed is the cowl ventilator mounted on a box having a baffle against water, as illustrated in Figure 21-5, Chapter 21. This will bring in air from the outside, but air must be able to flow *through* the boat after it gets inside. There must be openings in ceilings (the hull lining) and lockers; where bulkheads are watertight, each compartment must be provided with a source of air for ventilation.

Doors to lockers and cupboards should have vents for passage of air at top and bottom, not only for the preservation of the hull, but also so clothes and other stowed gear will have a chance to dry out before they mildew. A few suggestions for locker door ventilation and typical door frame and stop details are shown in Figure 15-12.

Not shown in the figure but suitable for ventilation areas of locker doors are attractive panels of woven caning. Natural cane is available in a number of weaves, but in one yard where I worked the first installation of natural cane could have been a complete disaster if the yacht owner had not insisted on this material. In our Florida climate the cane shrunk when humidity was low, without any visible effect, but on days with high

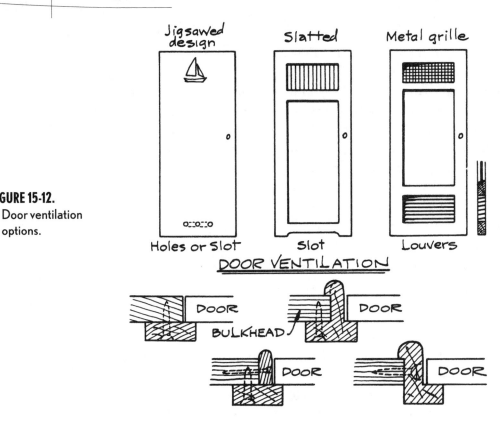

FIGURE 15-12.
Door ventilation
options.

humidity it swelled and looked terribly amateurish. Perhaps we did not
know how to use natural cane; but we subsequently used artificial cane
with good results. For caning supplies, try the Woodworkers' Store or
Albert Constantine. Both of these firms carry many items of interest.

Ventilation is also of importance in boats built of materials other than
wood to minimize the chance of mildew and musty odors, which are sometimes extremely difficult to remove.

CEILING

Ceiling is a lining on the inside of a wooden or metal hull that is used to con-
ceal structural members, to protect stowed gear from sloshing bilge water,
or to strengthen the hull. For the latter purpose, in larger yachts the ceiling
is usually 40 percent of the thickness of the planking. It is spiled to shape
when the hull form requires it, and the strakes are wedged tightly together
before fastening. For appearance, the inner edges of the ceiling are lightly

beveled so that the seams form a vee on the inside, and before fastening, the outside of each strake is painted or treated with a wood preservative. In the finest yachts the fastenings are counterbored and plugged where they would be visible in the quarters. This type of ceiling extends upward from at least the cabin sole, to an inch or two below the sheer clamp, the space at the top being left for the circulation of air.

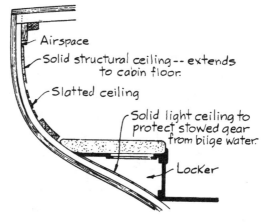

FIGURE 15-13.
Ceiling options.

In small boats, light ceiling ¼" to ⅜" thick is sometimes used for the sake of appearance rather than strength and may be slatted if desired. At the outboard side of a bunk, the ceiling prevents the discomfort of frames pressing against your body, but one of the best reasons for ceiling in small boats is to protect gear stowed under berths and in the bottom of lockers from being wetted by sloshing bilge water when the boat is heeled down in a lump of a sea. For this purpose the ceiling seams must be tight, and thin tongue-and-groove can be used. Small-boat ceiling should be kept light; excessive thickness is useless. White cedar or pine is suitable and may be fastened with nails or screws. Ceiling is shown in Figure 15-13.

In boats where the shape of the topsides will permit it, a sheet-type ceiling is bent into place. This can be of light plywood or hardboard, the latter being either plain or perforated with many small holes such as pegboard.

In boats where the ceiling is decorative rather than structural—particularly in motorboats—light plywood lining used to hide structures can be painted or covered with vinyl fabric or Formica-type material. The inside of fiberglass hulls, particularly forward where hull curvature is greatest, can be covered with carpeting stuck to the hull with an adhesive, or there are "hull liners" now made for this purpose. These materials are vinyl with a foam backing.

CABIN SOLE

Cabin sole is the proper name for the flooring inside the hull. It must have hatches to enable ready access to the bilge, tanks, piping, valves, etc. In small boats a removable panel on the centerline is usually sufficient to serve all purposes, but make sure of this, for there is nothing more frustrating than not being able to get at, say, a seacock; lack of access can be downright dangerous in an emergency. Plywood is an excellent material for the sole because it saves much labor and can be fitted in large pieces. The plywood can be painted for the simplest finish, or covered with vinyl flooring either in one piece or laid in squares. There are aluminum and stainless steel hatch bindings for use with the vinyl coverings. Do not make the hatches too tight, for the plywood often swells just enough to make a hatch bind.

In a seagoing sailboat it is practical to make a sole nonskid by adding a compound to the final coat of paint. It is not pretty, but it is practical. A bare teak sole is nonskid; however, it is expensive and it will hold grease stains. High-quality yachts often have soles of ¾" teak laid in strakes about 2" wide with a ³⁄₁₆" thick strip of wood, light in color like holly, between each strake. The strakes are preassembled in the shop by gluing and edge-nailing the holly to each strake of teak. Plywood panels are now available faced with teak and holly to resemble the solid wood sole.

In cabins where a carpet will be used, the sole needs only one coat of paint. A carpet is warm on the feet on a chilly morning, but it requires cleaning with a vacuum to be properly shipshape, and should not be used near open hatchways. Indoor-outdoor carpet, made of synthetic fibers that will not absorb moisture, has become very popular with boatmen. It is light enough to be taken up and cleaned on the dock.

The sole is the first of the interior joinerwork to be installed in the hull, and it must be carefully planned ahead to establish the hatch locations. In addition, it must be adequately supported by beams and headers.

HEADLINERS

Headlining—unheard of until people started making the insides of boats look more like homes than boats—is a covering for the underside of deck beams and cabin tops. The most popular headlining material is a vinyl fabric made just for that purpose, the best ones having an anti-mildew treatment. Other headliner materials are hardboards having decorative finishes, acoustical tileboard, and light plywood with vinyl or Formica-type covering.

THERMAL INSULATION

Inexpensive, lightweight fiberglass insulation on the underside of decks and cabin tops adds to comfort both summer and winter whether or not air-conditioning is installed in the boat. The easiest kind to use is a type having a thin face of white plastic material on what is meant to be the down side, away from the deck above. It can be cut to fit between deck beams and stapled in place. The only way to make it look decent, though, is to cover it over with headlining.

ICEBOX

The icebox, which looks so simple when used, is very time-consuming and difficult to construct. For this reason, if any of the ready-made boxes suit your boat, you will be much better off buying one. There are several makes on the market with a capacity of about 4.5 cubic feet, which amounts to about 50 pounds of ice. They are all plastic and have polyurethane insulation. They are built for under-counter installation, and if space permits, two of them can be placed side-by-side or stacked. These boxes are also made as electric refrigerators, but I am not going to get into the batteries, chargers, generators, and shore lines that are needed for even the smallest of refrigerators, because the service conditions can vary so widely.

When building an icebox into a wooden boat, there are some important points to remember. Space should be left between the hull and the box structure for the circulation of air, and that part of a wooden hull that will be hidden should be treated with a wood preservative or paint. Space is always limited in a boat, and to make the most of the area allotted to the icebox, the outboard side should be shaped somewhat to the hull form. The section in Figure 15-14 is typical of the situation in many boats, and here again plywood simplifies the job. Basically the box consists of an inner and outer shell, with insulation in between and a watertight liner inside.

Make the outside box first, leaving the top off, and brace it to the hull, making sure not to obstruct passage of air, as noted above. Add posts in the corners and intermediate stiffeners on bottom and sides to support the inner shell and to take its fastenings. Then coat the inside of the outer box with bitumastic paint and, while it is still wet, line the box with felt paper laid with overlapping joints. This is a vapor barrier. The insulation—I suggest polyurethane foam available in planks—is then cut to fit between the corner posts and the stiffeners. Next make the inner plywood box. As for the drain, it must lead either overboard or, if the bottom of the box is below the waterline, to a sump tank. It is an invitation to rot to drain fresh water into the bilges of a wooden hull. The sump tank can be removable for dumping overboard or piped with a two-way valve to the bilge pump. Of course the drain should be at the low point of the bottom of the box.

Before making the box top, the liner must be fitted. A liner of stainless steel sheet with soldered, watertight joints is ideal, but the inner plywood

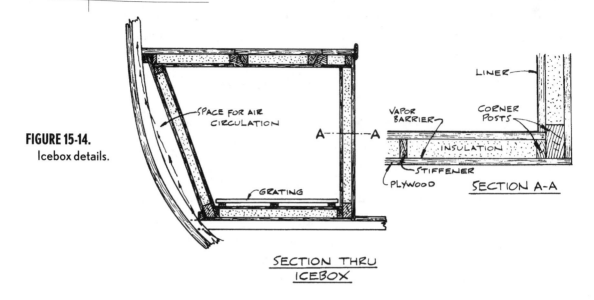

FIGURE 15-14.
Icebox details.

SPACE FOR AIR CIRCULATION

LINER

VAPOR BARRIER

CORNER POSTS

A----A

INSULATION

GRATING

STIFFENER

PLYWOOD

SECTION A-A

SECTION THRU ICEBOX

can be fiberglassed instead, even though smoothing the corners is tedious. The final finish should be smooth to make cleaning easy.

Whenever possible, a top opening is best for the icebox, because less cold air is lost when the box is opened. Sometimes a front door is unavoidable, but the cold air will pour out quickly, and so will the contents when rolling at sea.

The finished weight of a built-in box is significant. Limit the outside of the box to ½" thickness, the inside to ⅜". In fact, you might omit the inside wooden box and fiberglass right on the insulation—but first make certain that the resin is not a solvent for that insulation!

Finish the box with light wooden gratings in the bottom, and fit adjustable slatted partitions to separate food from ice.

READY-MADE WOODWORK

If you want to save time as your boatbuilding project nears completion, you can use ready-made parts made up by a mail-order supply house. One such outfit, H & L Marine Woodwork, Inc., makes, among other things, a complete line of dish, magazine, and book racks; grabrails and binocular boxes; paneled and louvered doors; and gratings and tillers. Most items are made of teak, mahogany, or oak. Atlantis Outdoor Kitchens makes a wide range of cabinetry products designed and built for outdoor use, some of which may be appropriate for marine use.

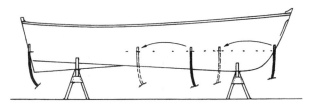

16

FINISHING

WHEN A HULL HAS BEEN PLANKED, it is advisable to protect it because, depending on the size of the boat, much time could pass before completion. This is especially important should construction be outdoors and not well covered to avoid moisture or hot sun.

Wood preservatives were mentioned earlier in this book, but it is not amiss to state again that all wood that will become inaccessible should be treated before it is hidden. I recall touring a plant of what was then the largest manufacturer of wooden boats and observing a number of overhead signs that read NO BARE WOOD in letters at least a foot high. In this chapter, however, we discuss the finishing of surfaces that are exposed and accessible.

In Chapter 15, "Interior Joinerwork," there is a discussion about finishing vertical and horizontal surfaces with Formica-type materials or with washable vinyl wall-covering material, and also finishing natural wood and plywood faced with mahogany, teak, and the like. The following will take it from there.

SANDING AND SMOOTHING

These are necessary evils, and the more time you devote to these tasks the better your boat will look. Needless to say there are health hazards involved, so get yourself a mask and *wear* it to guard against inhaling dust and fumes. An ordinary dust mask will suffice if the material you're sanding is nontoxic, but if you're going to be sanding toxic materials, ensure that you use a sanding respirator. More about this in Chapter 22, "Safety."

When you sand planking, you may luck out and not find many dings, scratches, and hollows, but if not, the blemishes must be filled and sanded so they are flush with the adjacent surfaces. Since preparation is generally acknowledged to be 90 percent of the job, give it the time it deserves. For shallow fillings above the waterline, I like to use a marine trowel cement, like Interlux Surfacing putty, after the first application of undercoater. Another option for shallow blemishes and hairline cracks is a glazing or spot putty, which is fast-drying and is sold in squeeze tubes at automotive paint supply houses. There are many fairing compounds on the market, some made by the marine paint people, some not, some single-part, some two-part. During my last job I must have seen a ton of polyester autobody filler used; it is quick-drying when properly mixed to instructions. Look for a compound that shrinks a little, but even so, don't try to fill deep blemishes all at once when using polyester putty. For deeper repairs I have used WEST System 410 Microlite filler mixed into epoxy resin. I find it easy to sand and feather. I doubt that any of the two-part preformulated fairing compounds would do a better job, and they are a lot more expensive.

COATED ABRASIVES

There is much more to coated abrasives than meets the eye. (Though to many of us these materials will always be known collectively as sandpaper, a strict interpretation would have to point out that they contain no sand, and sometimes—when fiber backing is used—no paper.) First, there is the grading of the grit that is going to do the cutting for you. One system is by number: from 40 for coarse to as high as 600 for really fine. Other makers grade by the slants, such as 5/0 for coarse, which you will probably never use, to 10/0, which you also will probably never use. Going by the numbers, think of 60 as coarse and 220 as fine enough to smooth your varnish and paintwork.

Then there is the density of the grit. On closed-coat sheets, belts, and discs, the grit solidly covers the area; the grit on open coat covers only

50 percent to 70 percent of the backing surface. Closed coat is used the most; open coat is useful for sanding gummy materials, because the open area between the particles of grit permits the removed material to drop off more easily.

Not all sandpaper has the same kind of grit material. Garnet is a natural mineral with a reddish color and very sharp edges; it is best used for softwoods. Aluminum oxide grit, which is whitish to gray-brown in color, is tough and durable and considered the best for hardwoods. For an extremely fine finish and for metals, synthetic silicon carbide is often used with water (sheets marked "wet or dry") or oil as a lubricant.

Next to consider is the backing material. Backing may be paper or cloth; the latter is more expensive and is generally used when sanding by machine. Paper backing is graded A to F, A being the lightest in weight. You will find 220A easy to find, as are C and D, called "cabinet papers," for grits coarser than 220. Be careful not to wrinkle the A-weight papers when hand sanding; it is easy to do.

Abrasive life can be extended considerably by cleaning the handheld abrasives with a brush and the papers on the machine sanders with a $1\frac{1}{2}" \times 1\frac{1}{2}" \times 6"$ stick of latex rubber sold as an abrasive cleaner. The amount of dust removed when the stick is held against the abrasive surface while the machine is running is proof that it is a money-saver. Abrasives are not low-cost items.

When sanding wood, the smoothest scratch-free finish will result from hand-sanding after machine sanding. Always sand wood *with* the grain, and remember that no amount of coatings will hide a rough finish—for a first-class varnish job, the wood has to be as smooth as glass. Never use a coarser grit than necessary or time and material are wasted, and always work from coarse to fine, never the reverse, which is another waste. When switching from coarser grits to the finer, clean the wood with a painters' "tack" cloth so you can see how the work is progressing.

I have two palm-type finishing sanders that use sandpaper sized $4" \times 5\frac{1}{2}"$, made by quartering standard $9" \times 11"$ sheets. To minimize the chore of cutting a number of these at one time, I place a slotted pattern on a full sheet, run a pencil through the slots to mark the quarters, then cut as many as possible, depending on the grit, with sheet metal shears (see Figure 16-1). A similar pattern can be made for marking sandpaper into thirds, sized for orbital/straight-line sanders. To ease the often frustrating procedure of inserting the ends of the sheet into the clamps of the sander, a "kinker"— made by adding wooden jaws to a spring clamp—will turn the edges of the paper into the required curve (see Figure 16-1).

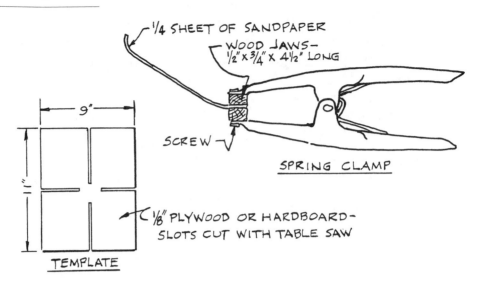

FIGURE 16-1.
I use a template to mark and cut multiple pieces of sandpaper with a table saw. I also use a spring clamp to bend the edges of sandpaper to make the sheets easier to fit into the clamps of the sander.

Figure 16-2 shows a variety of hand-sanding blocks—flat, convex, and concave—which have worked well for me. As dimensioned, these are operated with quarters of standard 9" × 11" abrasive sheets. I use white pine for the blocks and contact cement for the $\frac{1}{4}$"-thick cellular rubber facings.

In the early 1970s an adhesive was introduced for sticking abrasive sheets on sanding discs, either portable or bench-mounted. This entailed coating the disc and pressing the abrasive sheet in place; then, when the useful life of the abrasive was over, it was removed and the disc cleaned (I put the disc in a bucket of water to make peeling the sheet easier) and recoated to take another sheet. The first improvement came with the introduction of abrasive sheets coated with a pressure-sensitive adhesive (PSA); the disc itself did not have a coating. This method of sticking abrasives to uncoated discs is still widely used, but a further step forward has been made with the introduction of Velcro or Velcro-type (hook-and-loop) fasteners to adhere the abrasive to a disc or

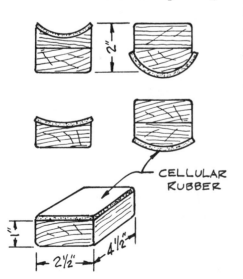

FIGURE 16-2.
A variety of hand-sanding blocks.

a rectangular sanding pad. This is a fast way to attach abrasive sheets, but they might cost twice as much as plain, uncoated sheets. Both PSA and Velcro sheets save time over the original system of cleaning and recoating the pad each time a sheet is changed.

Please have a look at the discussion of power sanders, particularly random-orbit sanders and detail sanders, in Chapter 3.

REPAIRING ABRASIVE BELTS

Sanding belts are expensive, so it is maddening when an almost-new belt breaks at the splice. An acquaintance of mine has made a repair or two by rejoining the ends of the belt with ordinary contact cement after preparing the splice by scraping away the failed adhesive.

MASKING TAPES

The only way for an ordinary person to neatly apply coatings—paint or varnish—is to mask off areas adjacent to the one being coated to ensure clean-cut divisions. (An exception to masking occurs when a steady-handed person is cutting in bottom paint below a topside paint or a boot-top stripe.) Masking tape should be applied with care, making sure the tape edges are pressed down firmly, but lesson one is not to buy the cheapest tape in the store, even if it is to be removed after a few hours. At the risk of being branded a stockholder, I have learned to stick (no pun intended) with 3M tapes, including the 3M Scotch brand. And I'm not alone; on the table before me, I have the catalogs of three marine supply houses that do not list any other brand.

The details of the product line changes from year to year, but 3M makes a multitude of tape products with specific purposes and recommendations in a wide price range. Generally the more expensive tapes can stay on the boat for longer periods, and they give you a finer line. Some of the tapes use a vinyl backing (as opposed to the familiar paper); these tapes can be applied in conformance with a fairly sharp curve, which the paper ones cannot. Here are the currently available 3M masking tapes most useful in boatbuilding:

- ScotchPaint Masking Tape #233. Conformable, hugs curves and contours, goes on quickly and stays put. Not for extended outdoor use; in fact, plan ahead so this type of tape can be removed at the end of a workday. Widths ¼" to 3".

- Scotch Fine Line Tape #218. An extruded matte-finish green polypropylene tape. Good color line separation due to the minimal thickness, which allows stretching on curved surfaces; also has good solvent and moisture resistance. But it's not for extended outdoor use. Widths ⅛" to ¾". (This was my favorite for masking half-hull models until I discovered #471.)

- Scotch Long Mask Masking Tape #2090. Crepe-paper backing makes tape conformable and smooth, provides UV stability and adhesive transfer up to seven days. Widths ¾" to 2".

- Scotch Silver Weather Resistant Masking Tape #225. Silver-colored backing reflects UV light to provide weather resistance for up to a month. Widths ¾" to 2".

After unpacking and using tape for the first time, do not leave the roll banging around in the shop, because in time the edges of the tape will collect enough crud to spoil a clean, crisp, masked edge. Although tape descriptions mention easy tearability, if you are brushing coatings you should refrain from tearing it; rather, cut it clean across with a sharp knife to avoid pointy ends that can protrude and interfere with brushing.

BRUSHES

Brushes are available in a variety of materials and a wide range of prices. What you need is a brush that holds a generous amount of paint or varnish. Some of the brands with synthetic bristles are thin and just don't have the capacity. If you are inexperienced, you will have to learn what kind of brushes you like best, and how to take care of them.

In my estimation there are two good all-purpose types of brushes: those with pure China bristles (pigs' bristle) and those with a mixture of 40 percent ox hair and 60 percent China bristle. In either case, they should be thick. Epifanes is currently marketing a line of high-end China bristle brushes available from Jamestown Distributors and the Wooden-Boat Store.

High-priced brushes made with badger hair are considered by some to be the ultimate for finish work. Recently I saw badger brushes 1" to 3" wide in a Florida chandlery, so these quality brushes are around if you are hell-bent to spend the money. Jamestown Distributors sells them for less than the Epifanes brushes, as well as a complete selection of China bristle brushes and utility grades as well. But I would be inclined to save the badger hair brushes for the most exacting varnish work, otherwise using plain bristle brushes (but never nylon).

Years ago in a yard on the St. Lawrence River, I watched three painters varnish the topsides of one mahogany runabout after another, getting them ready for the summer folk. They were using oval brushes that held a lot of varnish, and they finished each boat in a matter of minutes. The boats had been sanded beforehand and needed but a quick rub with a tack cloth in that clean environment. Some professionals use inexpensive polyfoam throwaway brushes for applying varnish—no cleaning, and that is a great idea! Cleaning bristle brushes is a must unless you are a millionaire.

Here is what International Paint Company recommends before using a new brush: Remove loose bristles by tapping the brush vigorously against the palm of your hand or twirling it between your palms. (Use a brush spinner, as described below, if you have one.) Then soak the brush in the solvent or thinner of the paint system you are using to remove dust particles, shake well to remove excess liquid, and shampoo the brush with a warm soap (not a detergent) and water. Rinse well in water, then comb (yes, there are paintbrush-bristle combs) the brush carefully to remove twists and curls—be sure the bristles are straight.

After each use, clean the brush with a solvent or thinner compatible with the paint system being used to remove all traces of the paint *before* it sets up. Finally, wash the brush in soapy water, rinse well, comb, wrap in kraft paper (I have never seen a boatyard painter use anything except newsprint, but paper towels work fine too), and let dry before storing either flat or hanging on a nail. Never store a brush up on its bristles.

Some brush-wielders prefer (and of course they argue that their way is the only way) to saturate brushes in oil after cleaning and before storing. A sign painter once told me he used motor oil for the purpose. He stored his brushes flat on their sides and remarked that the oil kept the bristles "well fed."

PAINTING

For countless years I used what might be called the "standard" oil-based alkyd enamel topside and deck paints, and frankly I probably still would if I had a boat to paint. (In the meantime, I use those paints when finishing half-hull models.) The various marine paint makers still offer conventional enamels as well as undercoaters, and fir plywood especially should have a coat or two of a sealer such as Interlux 1026. The alkyds are gradually being replaced by the one- and two-part polyurethane paints such as Interlux Perfection and Brightside. Yachts tend to be finished to the highest gloss achievable, but owners of commercial boats often prefer a flat or semigloss finish. A flat finish masks blemishes that in gloss stand out like a sore thumb. Interlux sells flattening agents to bring the gloss down for this purpose in its one- and two-part topside paints. Depending on climatic conditions and service, marine alkyd enamels will stand up anywhere from one to three years, and then it is time for a good sanding to minimize paint buildup, followed by a fresh coat of the finish paint, unless there are dings to repair. The polyurethanes ought to last a good deal longer.

If the area being painted is dirty from particles of dust and the like—perhaps a tack-rag wipedown was not done immediately before starting—then stop, unless you don't care. The dirt showing up could also be from an unclean brush or dirt in the paint. Clean the brush thoroughly, then strain the paint into a clean container. Throwaway paint strainers are sold by paint stores. These cone-shaped strainers are made of paper, with a fine mesh cloth near the apex of the cone.

A concern over health hazards came to the fore when the two-part polyurethanes used for painting aircraft broke into the marine market several years ago, offering long life and high gloss. The first was U.S. Paint's Awlgrip, followed by Sterling and DuPont's Imron. When these are sprayed, there are many precautions to be taken, including lung protection in the form of respirators, and skin protection from gloves and paper or Tyvek coveralls. Given the hazards, attempts to apply these high-tech materials by brush and roller were inevitable. I met one boatyard painter and one do-it-yourselfer who claimed brushing was easy if careful attention was paid to *both* temperature and humidity. Once again, heed the instructions furnished by the makers. There is a video available, produced by U.S. Paint, called *Your Step by Step Guide to Brushing Awlgrip,* on Amazon for about $25, which ought to apply to all the two-part polyurethane paints. Certainly an amateur can learn to spray paint, but it is a high art, in my opinion, and might not be worth mastering for finishing one boat. Often it is possible to do all the prep work and have a pro come to your site to do the actual spraying, which could be a cost-effective way to get a nearly perfect finish.

The major paint makers have protective coatings for aluminum alloy and steel structures (or ballast keels of nonmetallic sailboats) and will help you set up proven procedures. They also have a line of paints for interiors, where there is no reason not to use high-quality latex paints. Water cleanup is a welcome change from solvents.

Interlux recently introduced a polyurethane hull paint called Interspray 800, which it claims to be gloss-rated at 98 out of a possible 100. Unlike other polyurethanes, it can be used to cover dings without recoating the entire area.

The two-part epoxy coatings include Interprotect 1000, a basecoat for repairing and sealing damaged gelcoat of fiberglass hulls; Interlux 2000, a rapid-cure epoxy for new or undamaged fiberglass hulls; Interlux 404/414 Epoxy Primekote for fiberglass, wood, and prepared aluminum alloy; and Interlux Primocon for bare steel. These epoxies should always be overcoated when used above the waterline, because they have very little UV resistance.

BOTTOM PAINTS

I am purposely not commenting on antifouling bottom paints because there are so many questions about the ingredients now that the environmentalists have gotten into the act, which is all for the best. There are too many people out there who do not care what they ruin or kill. Not too many years ago the very effective bottom coatings containing mercury were banned, and a number of proposed substitutes were also found to be harmful. Not all formulations are effective in all areas. Seek local knowledge; it could save you money.

Old-fashioned bottom paints used to die after a few days ashore, but now there are antifoulants that retain their effectiveness after a long period hauled out. Do your homework, and when you have made a choice, carefully follow the manufacturer's instructions. Always!

In almost every area there is a yard catering to do-it-yourselfers. If you scrape the bottom yourself instead of having the yard do the dirty work, ask about the disposal of scrapings. If the yard handles this for you there is no problem, but if you are responsible, don't shovel the muck overboard. The same concern holds for disposal of used abrasive papers—the yard should have containers adjacent to the work areas for trash you created and a separate one for used thinners, solvents, paint cans, and other hazardous materials.

If your boat is waterborne infrequently and otherwise remains on a trailer or stacked-stored, antifouling bottom coatings are not needed. In this case the savings will help pay for the dry-storage charges.

WATER-BASED COATINGS

In response to queries about water-based or water-reducible coatings, I have to say I don't know anything except what I read in the catalogs, where I have noticed them in increasing numbers. One catalog describes such a coating as a lacquer, another as a varnish.

VARNISHING

Traditionally, the finest yachts had vast areas of varnished deck joinerwork of teak or mahogany; indeed, the antique or classic boats and yachts that have been cared for are an unforgettable sight to behold. In current construction, for various reasons, any large areas of varnished fine woods are most likely to be faces of plywood rather than solid lumber, and if fortunate the faces are of veneers thick enough to survive a few refinishings to bare wood. Nowadays, varnished wood ("brightwork") is limited to trim moldings used to accent fore-and-aft lines such as the sheer of the hull.

Teak and mahogany are moderately hard and resistant to scarring, but both of them can be dented by abuse and suffer from neglect. Their natural appearance, though, has appeal to many, and such a finish takes work to produce initially and to maintain. These woods have an open grain that must be filled for a smooth finish. Clear, natural filler is used for teak, while paste filler stains of desired color are applied to the mahoganies. The wood must be sanded to a perfectly smooth finish before filling; then the filler, thinned to brushing consistency, is spread on and allowed to dry to a dull appearance, at which time the excess is wiped off across the grain with clear cotton waste or rags. This is easy after a little practice. After a day of drying, the first coat of varnish can be applied. When this is dry, it should be sanded with a fine-grade abrasive. Repeat for six coats or more and you will have a finish that you will be proud to show off. The work and work area must be clean and free of dust while varnishing.

Varnishing brightwork is a labor of love. All the large manufacturers make varnishes with and without protection against ultraviolet rays. I have been around yacht captains most of my life and have always been amused by their loyalty to certain brands. For these chaps, picking a varnish is like picking a liquor or an anchor. One captain whose brightwork always appeared in tiptop shape mixed two different brands of varnish together and smugly refused to reveal the proportions.

A Dutch varnish called Epifanes has invaded the U.S. market, and I have heard it praised. It has a UV inhibitor and has been used in the Caribbean, an excellent testing ground, for many years. But regardless of the kind of varnish used, the essentials of varnishing remain the same: cleanliness, absence of moisture, and *light* sanding between coats, just enough to kill the gloss.

Those inexperienced with varnishing techniques are advised to read Rebecca Wittman's *Brightwork: The Art of Finishing Wood* and *Brightwork Companion*. (See the Appendix for more information.) One thinks of the high-priced oval brushes touted for varnishing as the ultimate, but Wittman advocates the use of foam brushes, which do not require time-consuming cleaning because they are simply thrown away. Even if, as some argue, foam brushes don't last as long on a big job, or load as well, they would certainly be handy for small to medium jobs.

I can recall when UV inhibitors in varnishes were unheard of, but anything that retards the effects of sunlight should be welcomed. I have never cruised aboard a crewed yacht that did not have the dew wiped off the brightwork with a chamois before breakfast.

Practical Sailor magazine periodically runs more or less rigorous tests of products like varnish, and it can't hurt to keep current with these results. Most recently, it has been regarding Epifanes Wood Finish Gloss, Pettit Hi-build, and West Marine's Skipper's Varnish as the best choices overall. As with many materials choices discussed in this book, this is *not* a sensible place to prioritize cost.

"OIL" FINISHES

Small open boats in the New England area are often coated inside when new with an oil mixture, frequently made by the boatbuilder, rather than with paint or varnish. Simple to apply, an annual coat freshens appearance and helps preserve the hull. However, a first-class job requires surface preparation similar to that for a good varnish finish—that is, all blemishes, pencil marks, and the like must be removed prior to finish treatment.

OLD DOWN EAST DECK COATING FORMULA

For many years of my early life, I lived a few hundred yards from a fleet of "head" boats that took passengers fishing in coastal waters. After unloading after a trip, the crew always flushed off the wooden decks with salt water. The crewmembers were always noncommittal when I asked the makings of whatever they treated the laid wooden decks with that made them shed water like a duck. The most I ever got was "oil." So we are indebted to Hamilton Marine for a formula for a deck oil that has been handed down for many years. The following quantity of deck oil is said to treat 100 square feet:

1 quart turpentine
1 quart boiled linseed oil
½ pint pine tar
½ pint Japan driers

This makes a deck oil with a dark amber finish. Add less pine tar for a lighter color, more for a darker color.

MARKING THE BOOTTOP

Nothing looks worse to yachtsmen than a ragged division between the topside and bottom paints. Assuming that the builder has had the foresight to mark the designed waterline at the stem and stern for reference during construction, just about the easiest way to mark the boottop is to first plot the straight waterline at frequent intervals along the hull and then lay off heights to the boottop as scaled from the plan of the outboard profile. Level straightedges are set up at the ends of the boat as shown in Figure 16-3, and then a length of thin, strong cord or wire is stretched tightly between the edges and moved inboard until it barely touches the hull, where a point is marked. By moving the cord in and out on the straightedges alternately at opposite ends, points on the waterline may be marked as often as desired. Be sure to keep the cord tight, for if it is allowed to sag, the waterline will not come out straight. If the boat is level fore and aft and there is room to work, a builder's level or transit may be used to run in the line. The boottop or stripe is often curved (sheered) for appearance, and offsets above the waterline can be taken from the plans and plotted as shown in the figure. A batten is tacked on the hull to fair the points and mark the line, which is done by scribing with the broken

FIGURE 16-3.
Marking the boottop.

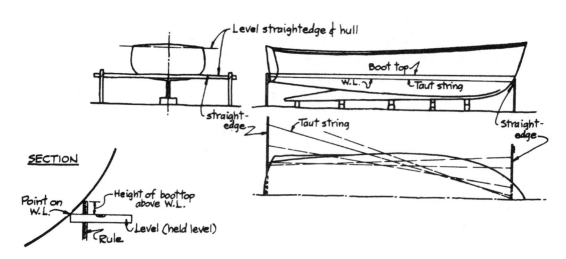

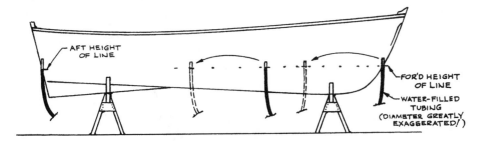

FIGURE 16-4.
Using water-filled tubing to mark the boottop.

end of a hacksaw blade or similar device or with a so-called race knife made for scribing wood.

Another method I have used to mark a straight line in profile on a hull is based on the fact that water seeks its own level. This is best done with a helper; also, the hull must be level both athwartships and fore and aft. A piece of transparent tubing with an inside diameter of about ¼" is needed. For a small craft the tubing should be longer than the line to be marked—well, not really, but the cost of tubing is small compared to hiring a land surveyor to mark the level line.

Figure 16-4 shows the method for marking points after the tubing has been filled with water that has been dyed. The helper holds one end of the tubing vertically with the water level even with the desired height at one end of the hull. The other end of the tubing is also held vertically, and points are marked as closely as needed to tack a batten through the points prior to scribing the line. For a nonwooden hull the points are marked closely enough to apply masking tape in a fair line. Once started, the marking is rapid.

The figure also shows how a piece of tubing shorter than the length of the boat is used. After the length of the tubing makes it impractical to mark further, move the helper's end of the tubing to the last point marked and proceed as before. This can be done provided another method has been used to level the hull before marking has been started.

PAINTBRUSH AND ROLLER SPINNER

In all the years I had been around boatyards, I had never heard of a paintbrush spinner until I came across it in one of Walter Simmons's writings. The scheme is to put the brush handle in the chuck, or a paint roller outside

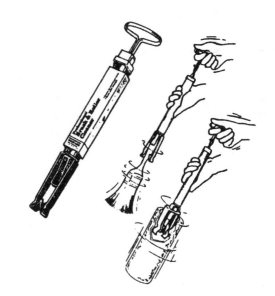

FIGURE 16-5.
Spinner for cleaning paintbrushes and rollers.

the chuck, dip it in solvent, and spin the brush or roller clean. It works. I do the spinning in a trash can or a large brown grocery bag. The brush bristles appear frightened after the spinning ordeal—wrap in paper to reshape.

HAND CLEANER

A chap building an epoxy-glued strip-planked hull from one of my designs wrote to tell me how much happier he has been since he discovered 3M Paint Buster Hand Cleaner #05975, which he found removed even partly cured epoxy. (Of course, he should have worn gloves.) GOJO is another widely available citrus-based hand cleaner that seems to work on most of the messy stuff that gets on your skin when you work around boats.

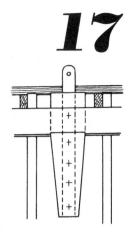

17

SAILBOAT MISCELLANY

SAILBOAT PEOPLE AND POWERBOAT FANS don't always approve of each other, so in this edition I decided to save powerboaters the trouble of stumbling through the following sailboat items by gathering the topics in their own chapter.

BALLAST KEEL

The ballast keel casting for sailboats will be of cast iron or lead and will be bolted either through the keel or through both the keel and floors, as preferred by the designer. Bolts will be shown on the plans and are the largest-diameter fastenings used in the construction of the boat. They are made of rods threaded on both ends for nuts, and on the inside of the boat are set up on heavy washers under which are grommets consisting of a few turns of cotton wicking soaked with a marine sealant. Tobin bronze or Everdur bolts are used to hold lead keels, while good galvanized wrought iron or Monel bolts are used when the keel is cast iron.

Because of the weight of the metals—450 pounds per cubic foot for cast iron and 710 for lead—the size and location of the ballast must be carefully figured by the designer and just as carefully reproduced by the builder. Templates for the keel are made from the mold loft lines and, as noted in Chapter 20, the keel pattern is made with a shrinkage rule. Shrinkage of lead and iron castings is 1/8" per foot.

The boatbuilder can make the pattern for a cast iron ballast keel, but the casting must be done by an iron foundry because of the high temperatures required. On the other hand, for a lead keel, the amateur or professional boatbuilder can make the mold *and* pour the casting.

Recently I studied the plans for the noted L. Francis Herreshoff's H-28 ketch and saw an item of interest. The lead keel is bolted through the 2½"-thick wooden keel only at the ends. Between the ends, 5/8"-diameter hanger bolts that penetrate the lead 3 inches or more are specified, one per frame bay and staggered each side of the centerline. This is labor-saving; I have no idea whether this was standard practice at the famous Herreshoff Manufacturing Company.

CAST IRON KEEL

When the keel is iron, the pattern is made of soft pine, and for a rectangular keel (A in Figure 17-1) the job is quite simple. For a more shapely keel the pattern entails more work; in either case the sections should be constantly checked for accuracy as the pattern nears the finished shape. The pattern for a shaped keel is made of layers of pine anywhere from 1" to 2" thick that are screw-fastened and glued together. Those familiar with model building can see that the lift (sometimes called "bread and butter") method of construction may be used here by drawing waterlines through the keel, spaced the same as the thickness of wood used, and sawing each layer roughly to shape before fastening them together.

The holes for bolts through an iron keel are cored, and care must be taken to locate the cores in relation to the bolt spacing, always taking shrinkage into account. The core in the bottom of the keel is enlarged in diameter to take the nut, allowing enough depth to cement over the nut to close the hole in the casting. A core box is made only for the longest core needed, as the molder can break cores off to proper length for the shorter ones. When a centerboard is located in way of the ballast keel, the board's slot must be cored.

The iron casting should, if possible, be given a coat or two of anticorrosive paint such as Interlux Primocon before it starts to rust. First bring the casting to bright metal by sandblasting, or by grinding with 36-grit discs. If fairing is required to achieve a smooth keel, make up a paste of epoxy with

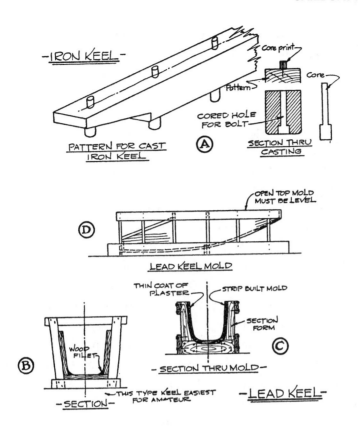

FIGURE 17-1.

An iron keel must be sand-cast in a foundry, while a lead keel can be cast in a mold at the building site.

a fairing-type additive, trowel it on the low spots, and sand smooth. Deeper pits may require multiple applications to get a really fair surface.

LEAD KEEL

When a willing foundry is within a reasonable distance, boatbuilders sometimes make a male pattern for a sand-cast lead keel and let the foundry make the mold and pour the casting. Making the pattern is a relatively easy job as compared to making a sand mold at the boatshop. The big keel manufacturer is Mars Metal, which claims it can cast lead keels from 500 to 100,000 pounds. (See the Appendix.) Of course, if you have a local foundry that will do the job, you are in luck.

Accuracy is particularly important when making patterns for lead castings. Each *cubic inch* of lead weighs about 0.41 pound. As a comparison, cast iron weighs about 0.26 pound per cubic inch.

A rectangular lead keel mold is quite simple to make (B in Figure 17-1), as it can be made with planks, with either wood or plaster fillets used to shape the corners when necessary. It must be remembered that the keel will be heavy, and this requires that the mold be strong so that it will not break apart when the lead is poured and that the mold be supported by husky braces and shores. The inside of the mold is given a thin coat of plaster to prevent it from burning. The plaster and the mold must be *perfectly dry* before starting, as the lead will spatter if poured into a wet mold and workmen may be burned.

Making the mold for a shaped lead keel (C in Figure 17-1) is quite a task and is a good reason to have the keel sand-cast in a foundry. As shown in the section, forms are made to the outside of the keel, plus the thickness of the mold, at stations and half stations. They are then set up rigidly (D in Figure 17-1), and the mold is strip-built inside of the forms. As the strips are fitted, they are edge-nailed to each other and to the forms. The inside is finished to a set of templates representing the finished keel plus an allowance for shrinkage. Gouges and round-bottomed planes are used for this work. The casting will reflect the degree of smoothness of your mold.

Lead, fortunately, has a low melting point, but at the least, you will need a large iron melting pot, supported by bricks so a roaring wood or charcoal fire can be built under it, and several iron ladles. Better still is a melting pot with a pouring spigot or pipe leading over the mold and a metal trough to distribute the molten metal over the length of the keel. The top of the open mold must be level. A centerboard slot can be taken care of by a plank of proper thickness to act as a core. More than enough lead must be on hand to allow for discrepancies, and some of the pigs may be placed in the mold before pouring. Several hands will be needed, because the pouring must be carried on to completion before the top of the lead already in the mold starts to solidify.

Start to pour when the lead in the pot is hot, distribute it in the mold, skim the slag from the top, and puddle the molten lead to prevent the formation of air pockets. Add pigs to the pot as you pour, and they will quickly melt in the hot lead if the fire is kept blazing. Allow at least a day for the casting to cool before removing the mold. The top surface of the lead casting can be smoothed with a woodworking hand or electric plane. The holes for the keel bolts are drilled with a barefoot wood auger or with a twist drill lengthened by welding a rod to the end, used in an electric drill of ample capacity. Either drill must be frequently withdrawn to clear the lead shavings, and kerosene is used as a lubricant. Where necessary, the outside of the keel is smoothed with coats of trowel cement, and the cement is then sanded. The keel casting is liberally coated with thick white or red lead where it fits against keel and deadwood.

Adding 1 percent antimony to the lead makes it easier to drill or to plane smooth.

WOODEN SPARS

Traditional wooden sailboats most often had solid wooden spars; the more modern ones have hollow wooden masts and booms to save weight. Otherwise, aluminum alloy spars have captured the field. As a result, there are dozens of extruded sizes and shapes from which to select a spar of proper strength.

Wooden spars are preferably made of spar- or aircraft-grade clear Sitka spruce because it is a light, strong wood. (See Chapter 4 for sources of Sitka spruce.) Clear fir and pine run rather far behind as second choice. Inasmuch as a mast is a column, the maximum sectional area is required at midlength of the longest unsupported panel, so to further save weight aloft, the mast is tapered from the point of greatest cross-sectional area to the head and sometimes to the heel as well. The edges on which sails are set, the top of the boom and the aft side of the mast, are made straight so the sails will set as they should.

When using modern waterproof glue, fastenings in spars are not required or even desirable, as they add weight up high where it is detrimental to the stability of the boat. As a matter of fact, hollow glued spars were in use years before truly waterproof glue was known, water-resistant casein glue being relied upon together with coats of varnish to protect the joints from moisture. This type of glue was mixed with water until creamy.

A number of adhesives are discussed in Chapter 6. Today, if cost does not matter, epoxy glue is very strong, and "slow" hardeners are offered by some suppliers for more "open" time. Stepping down in cost, the aliphatic glues such as the Titebond line ares strong, but I think they would set up too fast unless the spar is small. A cabinetmaker in Florida, where summers are long and hot, told me he slows down aliphatic glue with water, but this could affect the strength of the glue. So it appears that a glue made from powder mixed with water, such as Dap's Weldwood Plastic Resin Glue used by sparmakers for many years, will give the maximum working time. Resorcinol-resin glue is also a fine adhesive, but traditionalists who varnish wooden spars object to the purple glue line.

Sitka spruce, fortunately, is available in long lengths, and the majority of amateur-built boats will have spars that fall within the range of available lengths. When joining is required, the individual pieces are scarphed on the flat, the length of the joint being made about 10 times the thickness of the piece. Considerable patience as well as sharp tools are needed to make a perfectly fitting feather-edged joint of this type. Theoretically a glued joint is as strong or stronger than the wood, so that splices could be adjacent to each other, but inasmuch as a glued joint will be locally stiffer than the adjoining unjointed pieces, it is best to stagger the scarphs as much as possible. Figure 17-2 shows a scarph and typical hollow spar sections in use today.

The simplest mast to make is a hollow, rectangular box spar. This section, with the fore-and-aft pieces rabbeted, is preferred by some builders because it is easier to control skidding of the glued surfaces. The section next in simplicity is the round spar made of hollowed-out halves. The larger spars, both the oval section and the round section made of staves, are the most difficult to make and would be quite a job for the amateur. Of the two, the oval is the easier in the smaller sizes, as it consists of two round halves and two tapered side pieces. The wall thickness of oval and round spars is always tapered in the interest of weight saving.

Some of the smaller sailboat classes use a solid mast with a groove routed out for the boltrope on the luff of the mainsail. This groove can be made by first making a saw cut with a circular saw and then routing out the groove in the saw cut, using a very-high-speed cutter with a shank narrower than the saw cut (see Figure 17-2). To make a boltrope groove in a hollow spar made up of two rounded halves, the groove is hand gouged or machine routed on each half before the sections are glued together.

FIGURE 17-2.
Typical wooden spar sections. Most small craft have rectangular hollow masts and booms.

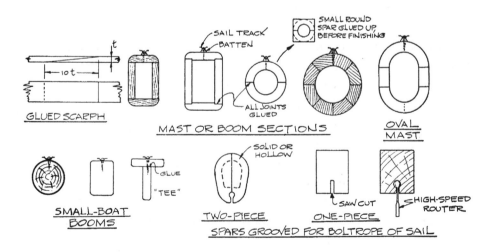

The T-boom is used on smaller sailboats, which also sometimes have solid rectangular booms.

HOLLOW RECTANGULAR SPARS

Probably the easiest way to make a box spar, unless the builder has extensive machine tools, is to order the spar material dressed four sides to the dimensions at the maximum section of the spar. It is desirable to add a slight thickness, say 1/32", for dressing up and finishing after the spar has been glued. With such material at hand there is nothing to do but taper the pieces in accordance with the designer's detail plans. This is done by laying off the width at the spacing shown on the plan for the spar, fairing the shape with a long batten, and then sawing and planing the edges to the lines. The width layout for the forward and aft pieces is done from a centerline because both edges are shaped. Duplicate sides may be temporarily nailed together and made at the same time. Be sure to keep the edges square, or else a perfect glue joint with 100 percent surface contact cannot be made. Here again, epoxy adhesives are a boon to the amateur because of their gap-filling ability and minimum clamping pressure.

When only one or two spars are to be made, a makeshift spar bench may be devised by nailing a series of short boards horizontally to a wall or fence, with legs down to the ground to support the outer ends (see A in Figure 17-3). All supports should be level and at the same height, or the top edges shimmed to be so, as upon them will be placed the side of the spar that is to be straight, that is, the aft side of the mast or the top side of the boom.

Shellac, which dries fast, has long been the sparmaker's choice for coating the interior surfaces of a hollow spar (though varnish will do the job too). Be careful not to coat the surfaces to be glued. Use a marking gauge to scribe the width of the side pieces on the forward and aft pieces and shellac between the lines. The filler pieces at the ends of the spar and elsewhere as called for by the plans are fitted, and shellac is also omitted in way of these. Because solid filler blocks have been known to swell and either split the spar or cause poorly glued joints to open up, some prefer the pad-type fillers glued to the inside before assembly as shown in B in Figure 17-3. A long solid filler fitted at the heel of the mast is bound to locally stiffen the mast due to the sudden increase in sectional area. The late Phil Rhodes, one of the great yacht designers, insisted upon a block cut as shown in C in Figure 17-3 to avoid this situation and also advised running saw cuts longitudinally on the block to allow for expansion. Provide drain holes in all solid fillers except the one at the masthead, so moisture will not collect and start rot.

FIGURE 17-3.
Sparmaking details.

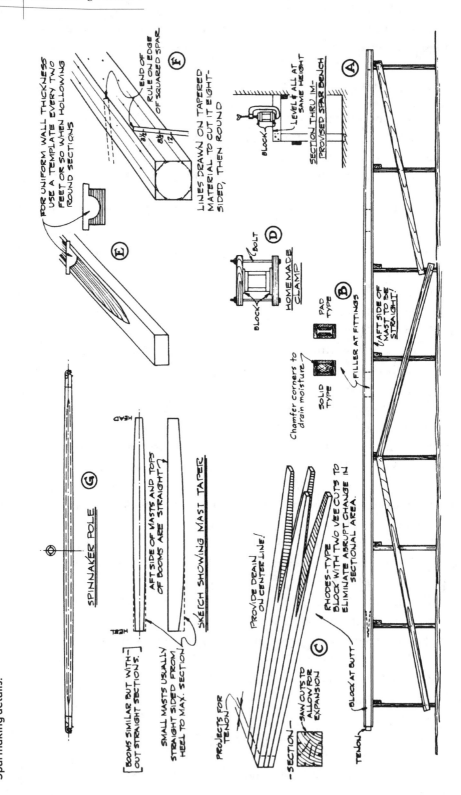

When everything is ready, mix the glue strictly in accordance with the instructions, paying particular attention to those regarding temperature and working life after mixing. Once the glue is mixed, spread it quickly and thoroughly. Before gluing make sure there are enough clamps at hand; it is surprising how many are needed, as there should be one every few inches or so to apply the pressure required for the glue, particularly resorcinol. Although Figure 17-4 shows a boom that is larger than any that the average amateur would attempt, it is a good illustration of the number of clamps used by a builder to ensure a perfect job. All kinds of clamps may be utilized if their openings are sufficiently wide to clamp the spar plus pieces of scrap used under the clamp pads to distribute pressure and prevent scars. If the number of your clamps is insufficient, you can make satisfactory spar clamps of two husky pieces of oak or ash joined together at the ends with bolts of at least ½" diameter (see D in Figure 17-3).

The clamps should not be removed for at least 24 hours to allow glue to develop full strength. Finish the spar by scraping the excess glue from the seams, round the corners, and then sand all sides smooth, gradually working down to fine abrasive paper. If a varnish finish is wanted—Sitka spruce has a beautiful appearance when finished clear—apply at least five coats, carefully sanding off or dulling the gloss between coats.

FIGURE 17-4.
Many clamps help ensure that the glue bonds well in spar construction.

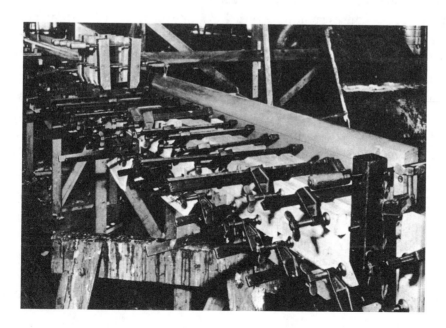

ROUND HOLLOW SPARS

Even though a boat may have a rectangular mast and boom, the spinnaker pole (G in Figure 17-3) will be round, made in symmetrical halves around a centerline. First, get out two pieces of stock that will be square when clamped together and equal to the diameter of the pole in the middle. Mark centerlines on the mating surfaces of the material; then lay out the inside of the pole, that is, the part to be hollowed. Make hollowing templates (E in Figure 17-3) for points every two feet or so apart and constantly use them to check as the wood is cut away. The templates control the wall thickness of the finished spar and guard against ending up with walls that are too thin or not uniform in thickness. The hollow portion is ended in a quick taper, as shown on the sketch, so that pole end fittings will be attached to solid wood.

When the halves have been glued together, the spar must be laid out on the outside, and then the square assembly is tapered. The walls will then be of equal thickness all along the spar's centerline. The next step is to cut the corners off the square and make it eight-sided. This is done by drawing guide lines as done in F in Figure 17-3. The following description is an example of how the guide lines might be laid out. At any point along the length of the tapered assembly, the end of a rule is placed even with one corner, and the rule is pivoted until the 12" mark lines up with the opposite corner. Points are made on the wood at the $3\frac{1}{2}$" and $8\frac{1}{2}$" marks on the rule. This is repeated at every foot, and a batten is run through the points to draw a line. These figures should be varied to suit differences in the diameter of the spar, because for ease of layout, the rule should be almost square across the spar. The ratio of $12:8\frac{1}{2}:3\frac{1}{2}$ can be reduced or enlarged to suit any size of spar. For smaller spars of, say, 5" diameter, the figures can be halved. Therefore, the end of the rule is held on one corner of the spar, and the 6" mark on the other, with points made at the $1\frac{3}{4}$" and $4\frac{1}{4}$" marks. When guide lines have been drawn on all four sides, it is a simple matter to make the spar eight-sided with a drawknife and plane and then to round it off to be finished by sanding. A round mast for a marconi sail will be straight on the aft side, but the method of making it is the same.

RIGGING ATTACHMENTS FOR WOODEN SPARS

Not too many years ago almost all masts were round and the upper ends of the standing rigging were spliced in a loop, dropped down over the masthead to the desired location and held in position by shoulder cleats on the mast. With the introduction of the marconi rig and the systems of stays for supporting it came taller masts, and the manufacturers of wire rope started to make what is called strand, a rope consisting of a single wire core with eighteen wires twisted around it. This is known as 1×19 construction. It has more strength than any other rope of the same diameter and is logical rigging to use to reduce windage. It is very stiff and difficult to splice and is therefore not suitable for looping around a mast, particularly one with an elongated oval or rectangular section. Consequently, spliced rigging has practically disappeared and the ends of the wire rope are fitted with swaged stainless steel terminals, which are attached to the mast by means of tangs. Most tangs are made of strong sheet metal, like Everdur (silicon bronze) or stainless steel, and are held to the mast by one bolt and a number of wood screws calculated to take the outward and downward stress components of the stay. It is the job of the naval architect to design tangs that are both light and strong, and each tang is usually carefully detailed for the job to be done.

The tangs can be made by a machine shop or a rigging specialist, or the enterprising amateur can tackle the sheet metal work by fitting his band saw with a metal cutting blade. Besides making the tangs exactly according to plan, the builder must drill the holes for the tang fastenings with care. Loose holes will permit the tangs to slip, possibly overloading a few of the fastenings instead of letting all of the fastenings do their share of the job. Figure 17-5 shows tangs for double lower shrouds on the mainmast and mizzenmast of a ketch. These particular tangs,

FIGURE 17-5.
Tangs for the shrouds on a mainmast and mizzenmast.

designed by the staff of Phil Rhodes, are an example of a simple, strong fitting. They are well made by the builder. The material is Everdur 1010 half hard; the bolts are tubular to save weight aloft. Straps encircling the mast with clips for the heels of the spreaders are found a few inches above the tang bolts.

Fore-and-aft bolts for tangs have nuts on the aft side of the mast that would interfere with the sail track if it were laid directly on the mast's aft face. To get around this, the sail track can be laid on a batten that has been glued on the mast and cut away for the nuts. Battens are also sometimes desirable on booms to prevent sail slides from binding due to contact with the boom at their edges. The screws for the sail track go through the batten and into the wall of the spar. At certain points of extra strain, such as at the extreme ends of a track and at reefed positions of the mainsail headboard, through-fastenings rather than screws should be used.

MAST STEP

The compressive load from the mast is taken by the mast step, which is of some hardwood like oak. The step is given a length of several frame spaces to distribute the load over the hull via the floor timbers, and in boats of any size it is placed in notches in the floors after first having been notched itself. When carefully done, the resulting joint at each floor will prevent movement of the step in any direction, and in addition, it is drift-bolted to the floors (see C in Figure 17-6). The mortise in the step to take the mast tenon should have a drain hole drilled at the low point so that water will not collect and rot the step. A typical step is shown in B in Figure 17-6, but like many other boat details, there are other types of steps, particularly in small craft, and details will be found on the plans.

Masts are sometimes stepped on deck or on the cabin roof. The thrust load is then carried down to the hull by a stanchion or by strategically located joiner bulkheads of ample strength.

VERTICAL TIE ROD

The forces from the thrust of the mast and the upward pull of the rigging tend to collapse the hull, so that in moderate-size boats it is well to fit a tie rod between the mast step and mast partner as shown in B in Figure 17-6. The rod is threaded on both ends for nuts that are set up over washers. Just take up the nuts snugly when installing them, as there is no need to try to pull the deck and step together!

With the advent of plywood bulkheads and well-fitted adjacent parts, the tie rod is no longer as important as it once was.

STANDING RIGGING CHAINPLATES

Unless masts are designed to be free-standing, they are kept straight and prevented from breaking by wire rope standing rigging. The mast loads are transmitted to the hull by straps called chainplates. The chainplates must be designed equal to the task, and the designer should show on the construction plan locations and details of the chainplates with the size and number of fastenings.

It is a simple matter to calculate the strength of the metal parts, but their fastenings to the hull can be insufficient. The area of the wood in the hull against which the bolts bear must be equal to the strength of the shroud. Sometimes the chainplates are bolted through the planking and a frame and are located either on the outside of the planking or between the planking and a frame. However, it is better to bolt them to backing blocks between frames that are cut to bear against the clamp. (See A in Figure 17-6.) Blocks of this type eliminate the necessity of cutting frames with fastenings, which weakens the hull somewhat at that point.

Inside chainplates are to be preferred, as on the outside they

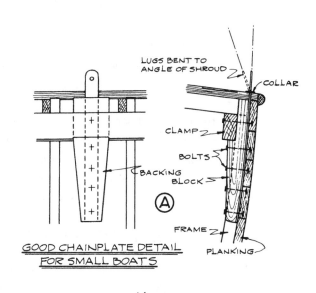

GOOD CHAINPLATE DETAIL FOR SMALL BOATS

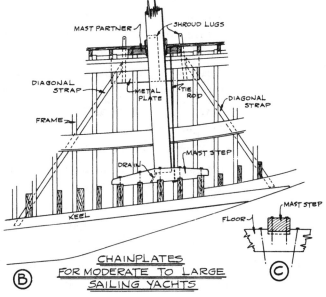

CHAINPLATES FOR MODERATE TO LARGE SAILING YACHTS

FIGURE 17-6.
Chainplate details for various size craft.

will show unless neatly let flush into the planking, and the metal may bleed and discolor the topside paint. It is best to use corrosion-resistant metals such as bronze, Monel, or Type 316 stainless steel for both plates and bolts, because due to corrosion, there have been many cases of chainplates torn out under stress. This may result in a broken mast. There are several types of small-boat chainplates peculiar to various classes, and these are shown in detail on the plans for the boats. Referring to chainplates in general, the end of the lug extending above deck should have only slightly rounded edges so as not to reduce strength unnecessarily. To stop leaks, the hole through the deck should be filled with a sealant or fitted with a metal collar set in sealant.

Sailing yachts of the more expensive type with a waterline length upward of 28 feet are fitted with a rectangular bronze plate between the frames and the planking to which lugs for the shroud turnbuckles are bolted or riveted. Diagonal metal straps extending to the keel are riveted to the plate and screwed to each frame crossed and the keel. This arrangement, shown in B in Figure 17-6, distributes the rigging loads over a large area and prevents the distortion of the hull, called hogging, often noticed in the sheerline of old wooden boats. The planking rather than the frames is carefully notched for the straps as each strake is fitted.

ALUMINUM ALLOY AND CARBON SPARS

The plans for the boat you are building will probably call out the specifications for the parts if the spars are to be made of aluminum alloy. There is now a large choice of sizes of extruded sections for masts, booms, spinnaker poles, and the like, and also a large choice of fittings to complete the rig and make it work. Sailboat rigging is a business of its own and is best left to the experts if you do not have the details of what you need. There are ads in the sailing magazines for many spar suppliers and sailmakers ready to help with your problems if you have decided to use aluminum spars. See the Appendix.

In Figure 17-7, the first two extruded mast sections on the left of the upper row are for the larger boats, while the other sections simply have a groove for the luff boltrope.

Carbon and other composite spars are becoming the dominant technology in certain (high-end) parts of the boatbuilding world. Composite spars are made, generally speaking, in a similar fashion to fiberglass and other molded hulls: layers of the composite material, usually carbon fiber, are laid up in a female mold with resin pre-impregnated or applied between

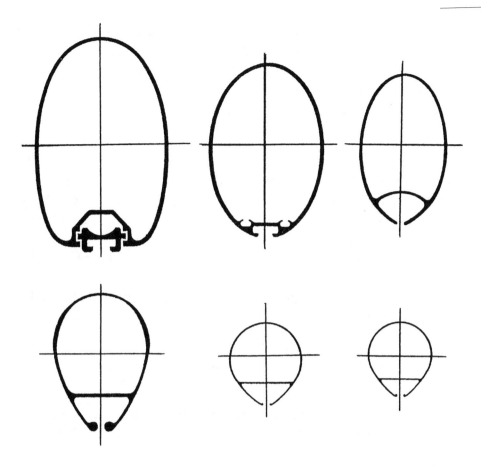

FIGURE 17-7.
Just a few of the many aluminum alloy extrusions for sailboat masts. (*Dwyer Aluminum Mast Company*)

layers, then the molded unit is baked. Usually the spar sections are molded in halves (lengthwise) and bonded together into one unit after removal from the molds. This allows a fair amount of hardware installation and other detail work from inside the spar, before bonding.

Other spars are made in a similar fashion, but the fiber is wound on a male mold (or mandrel) before baking.

Southern Spar, which has a U.S. facility in Rhode Island, states on its website that there are several advantages to the composite process other than the obvious weight advantage: much stiffer spars can be produced; thinner spars with less windage are possible; and, in general, there is much greater flexibility in design than with aluminum, because each mast is largely handmade. Another advantage that occurs to me is that they don't corrode in salt air. Don't be too sure that the wooden mast you are admiring on that brand-new gold-plater is varnished spruce. Nowadays it's as likely to be carbon fiber with an eerily effective faux-wood finish. Maybe it will come someday, but for the time being there is no do-it-yourself method for composite spar-building, I'm sorry to report.

WOOD SHELL YACHT BLOCKS

There is enough interest in fitting out sailboats, especially the traditional types, to create a limited market for wood shell blocks similar to the thousands produced by the late Merriman Brothers of Boston, which offered wooden block shells of both ash and lignum vitae, and bronze sheaves with plain or roller bearings. Pert Lowell Company (U.S), A. Dauphinee & Sons, Ltd. (Canada), and Conrad Blocks (Australia) all have their own lines of these beautiful fittings. There are also magazine articles to guide you in the fabrication of your own shell blocks, said to be a fascinating pursuit in itself.

FIGURE 17-8.
Ash shell yacht block with bronze and stainless steel parts. Although Bainbridge Blocks, the manufacturer of this block, is no longer in business, others have stepped in to fill the void. See the Appendix for sources.

18

STEERING

BESIDES BASIC SEAWORTHINESS AND METHOD of propulsion, whether by engine or sails, the most important feature of a boat is its steering control. There are a number of choices, depending on the type and size of the craft.

RUDDERS

A rudder consists of a wood or metal blade and a stock through which force is transmitted to the blade and around which it pivots. Except for common types of powerboat rudders, it is attached to the hull by hangers called gudgeons and pintles. The location of the rudder is either inboard, meaning forward of the after end of the waterline, or outboard on the transom or sternpost (on a double-ender). Further, the rudder is either unbalanced, with all the blade area abaft the stock or pivot point, or it is partly balanced, with a percentage of the area forward of the stock. In the latter case, the force required to turn the rudder is reduced.

Powerboat Rudders

Modern powerboat rudders are now almost invariably made of metal, although formerly they were often of wood. The most common type has a blade of cast manganese bronze bossed for a rolled bronze or stainless steel stock that is inserted in the head of the rudder. In Figure 18-1, A shows this type of rudder supported at the top by the rudder port, a stuffing box to prevent leaks where the stock enters the hull, and at the bottom by a pintle riding in a hole in a metal skeg. A spade-type rudder is sketched in B in Figure 18-1 and is made in the same manner, but is not supported at the bottom and is more liable to catch lobsterpot buoys and the like. It is a clean design and results from an effort to reduce underwater resistance by cutting away the deadwood, so there is no way of supporting the bottom of the rudder. On twin-screw boats a spade-type rudder is used behind each of the propellers and gives excellent steering qualities. The two types of rudders sketched may be purchased in a number of sizes. Spade rudders are now frequently fabricated of welded stainless steel; they are either a single plate blade or a hollow double blade having an airfoil section.

Cast bronze rudders of the shapes shown in Figure 18-1, as well as variations, are made by Marine Associates, Buck Algonquin, and Edson

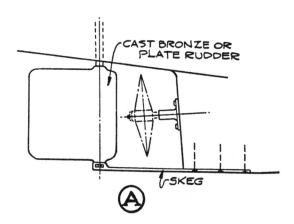

FIGURE 18-1.
Cast bronze rudder shapes.

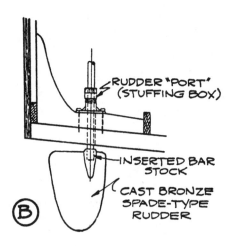

International. (Addresses of these and other sources are listed in the Appendix.)

Small-Sailboat Rudders

Small centerboard sailboats have an outboard rudder as shown in A in Figure 18-2. The blade may be of one or more pieces, depending upon available material, but in any case it should be doweled with bronze rod to prevent warping, and the grain direction of the wood should be alternated from piece to piece for the same reason. The blade area below the surface of the water is streamlined in shape, as indicated on the sections in the sketch, with the maximum thickness being about 25 percent of the blade width aft of the leading edge of the rudder. When gudgeons and pintles of the common variety seen in any marine hardware catalog are used, the rudder may float up and become disengaged from the boat, leaving the skipper with a tiller in hand but no control over the boat. To prevent this, the rudder may be weighted with an insert of lead heavy enough to offset the buoyancy of the blade, or the upper pintle can be drilled for a cotter pin just below the gudgeon. The tiller is fixed, or preferably made to hinge so it can be raised when tacking.

In shoal water localities the small-boat outboard rudder is often made with a pivoting blade so that it may be raised to clear obstructions (see B in

FIGURE 18-2.
Small-sailboat rudders and fittings.

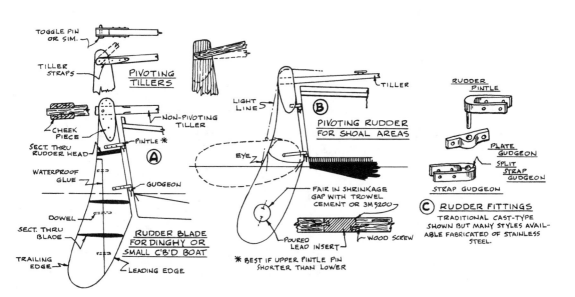

Figure 18-2). This is done by pivoting the blade between long cheek pieces riveted securely to a filler of the same thickness as the blade. A lead insert is needed to prevent it from rising due to buoyancy or the forward motion of the boat. A light line is used to raise the rudder while sailing over shoal areas.

Some of the standard fittings available from marine stores are sketched in C in Figure 18-2. Besides these, several of the marine hardware manufacturers make sets of fittings for small outboard rudders that prevent the rudder from coming off, yet leave the rudder readily removable from the transom. Rudder fittings should be through-bolted or riveted.

Large-Sailboat Rudders

Figure 18-3, A, shows the rudder for a keel sailboat in which the stock is run down far enough to take a few bolts through the piece of blade next to it. A strap is fitted as shown at the end of the stock to prevent it from bending from pressure of water against the blade when the rudder is turned. At the bottom of the rudder, a pintle and gudgeon are fitted for support. Unfortunately, the variety of rudder shapes and thicknesses is so great that stock fittings are not available and patterns must be made for castings. These fittings are usually detailed by the designer with enough dimensions so that, together with templates made on the hull and rudder, the necessary patterns can be

FIGURE 18-3.

Various rudder arrangements.

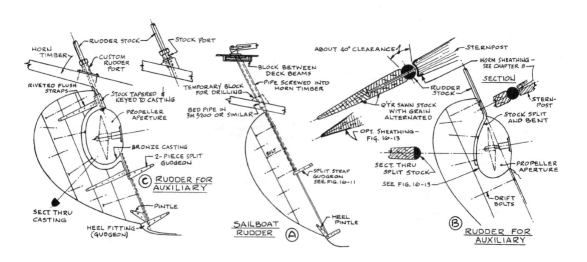

turned out for the use of the foundry. It is inadvisable to use anything but nonferrous metals for rudder fittings. The best materials for rudder stocks are tough, strong Tobin or silicon bronze rod or stainless steel. A rudder is a vital, very important part—*do not skimp on the quality of fittings.*

Larger rudders must be made of pieces that are doweled or drift-bolted together as indicated by the plans. The size of dowels and bolts should be shown by the designer and may be decreased in diameter near the trailing edge, where the blade is thinner, so the wood will not be weakened by the fastenings. Dowel holes must be parallel to one another or the pieces cannot be joined together, and all fastenings must be kept in the middle of the blade to prevent their coming through when the blade is tapered. Drift bolts used in heavier rudders do not have to be parallel to each other, and when driven at varying angles, they lock the pieces together. Drifts driven from the trailing edge have a slot cut far enough in from the edge so the head will be hidden, and then a piece of wood is inserted to fill the slot. The enlarged section in A in Figure 18-3 shows how the blade is tapered. It may be seen that the amount of work required to make a rudder should not be underestimated.

If the builder is fortunate enough to have a thickness planer, some hand labor can be saved by planing each piece to its thickness at the forward edge. Otherwise all tapering is done with plane and spokeshave. The sketch also shows how the grain is alternated in adjacent pieces to prevent or minimize warping, and how the after edge of the sternpost is hollowed out so water will flow past the deadwood onto the rudder with a minimum of disturbance. As mentioned in Chapter 8, the edge of the sternpost is sheathed with copper about $1/32$" thick for protection from worms and to eliminate painting, which is practically impossible without unshipping the rudder. The sheathing is carried around the sides by an inch or so and secured with copper tacks. The forward edge of the rudder blade begins aft of the center of the stock so that the rudder can be turned hard over without fouling the sternpost. With the rudder arranged as shown in A in Figure 18-3, water is kept out of the hull by screwing a threaded brass or bronze pipe into a hole drilled in the horn timber. The hole must be just the right amount smaller than the pipe so the threads will take hold, and it must be drilled at the correct angle. The best way to start the hole is to cut through a block (shown dotted in the figure) having its face at right angles to the center of the stock. This can be laid out from your mold loft drawings, and a drilling guide can be devised to ensure that the hole is drilled at the proper angle.

Rudders for Auxiliary Sailboats

When a sailboat is fitted with an engine and the shaft is on the centerline, there must be a hole or an aperture cut in the deadwood and rudder in which the propeller can turn (B in Figure 18-3). The aperture should not be larger than necessary, but its size must be such that the propeller blades will not strike the rudder when revolving. The edge of the aperture can be checked on the mold loft floor by setting up a semicircular disc of the same diameter as the propeller on the propeller centerline, and then hinging a piece of thin plywood or heavy cardboard on the centerline of the rudder. The aperture is cut away by trial until the "rudder" can be swung 40 degrees off center and still clear the propeller blades (see Figure 18-4).

It is not sufficient to end the rudderstock at the top of the aperture: it must either partly surround the opening as shown in B in Figure 18-3 or completely encircle it as shown in C. Sometimes the latter method is carried out by casting the complete stock in one piece from its upper end to the

FIGURE 18-4.

Determining the size of the aperture for a propeller and details of sheathing the rudder's trailing edge.

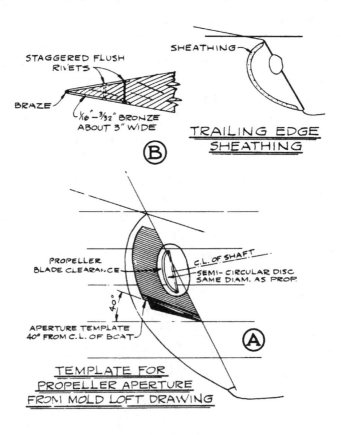

pintle below the aperture, but a long pattern is needed, the casting is not the easiest to make, and quite a lot of machining is required to finish the job. A shorter casting around the aperture, as shown, is hard to beat for strength, and except for grinding rough spots from the casting, the only machining needed is to taper, bore, and keyway the upper end for the stock, drill holes in the blade straps, and turn a pintle or bore for an inserted pintle on the lower end. The blade straps shown are cut from flat bronze and secured with countersunk rivets. The stock, of course, is made from bronze shafting, tapered and keyed to match the aperture casting, and is secured with a pinned nut on the lower end. A rudder made like this may be removed from the hull without digging a deep hole by taking off the two-piece split gudgeon and the stock and lifting the rudder enough to disengage the bottom pintle from the heel gudgeon. A stuffing box is shown on the horn timber. This will very likely be a special job, as seldom can standard fittings be adapted, due to the angle between stock and horn timber. The upper end of the stock of any rudder has a keyway for a standard tiller fitting, or in larger boats for a wheel steerer. There are several varieties of each of these items made by the marine hardware manufacturers.

An expensive and by no means necessary refinement to a rudder is to bronze-sheath the trailing edge, as illustrated in B in Figure 18-4 and in the photograph, Figure 18-5. This is made by templating the shape of the

FIGURE 18-5.
Fastening the bronze sheathing on a rudder with rivets.

trailing edge and band-sawing the sheathing from a sheet of bronze about $1/16$" to $3/32$" thick, and there is much waste. The edges of the curved strips are filed smooth and laid on the rudder to mark a rabbet that is cut so the sheathing will be flush with the surface of the blade. Fastening is by means of countersunk head rivets, as shown, and the trailing edges are brazed together, then ground reasonably sharp. Sometimes the rudder on a new boat will vibrate so that it chatters considerably, a condition remedied by sharpening the trailing edge somewhat, but the sheathed rudder is perfect from the start and is usually fitted on cruisers and racers of the finest quality.

STEERING CONTROLS

There are various means of transmitting directional forces to the rudder, starting with the simple tiller for an outboard rudder shown in A in Figure 18-2. When the rudder is inboard, more complicated methods must be used. Some sailboats have an Edson-type steerer with the wheel and gearing attached to the upper end of the rudderstock. These gears must be carefully aligned and securely fastened to the structure. Other sailboats have the wheel farther away from the rudder and use a pedestal steerer connected to a quadrant on the rudderstock with a length of sprocket and chain and wire rope running over sheaves. Edson International, one of the world's largest producers of sailboat steerers, issues a catalog that is practically a design handbook. A recent Edson innovation utilizes husky push-pull cable steering from a pedestal in lieu of cable-over-pulley connections to the rudder tiller. This greatly simplifies the installation.

There are several types of steerers for powerboats. One method uses a reduction gear steerer at the wheel and chain and wire rope similar to the sailboat pedestal steerer. Others use a gearbox at the wheel or elsewhere in the system and connect to the rudder arm with shafts, solid or pipe. A more modern type of steerer, suitable for small to medium sizes of boats, uses a rack and pinion at the wheel and a heavy push-pull cable from the rack to an arm at the rudder. This is by far the simplest type of steerer and is seen in many boats because it is the least expensive to install.

The fortunate builder has good detail of the steering system on his plans; otherwise he has been left on his own to work it out. The steering should be installed before too much of the interior joinerwork has been built. It is most important that all steerer and gear parts be securely fastened to prevent movement of units such as the steerer and wire rope sheaves. The latter should be through-bolted and should be carefully aligned to reduce friction and eliminate wear on the wire rope. All parts should also be non-ferrous whenever possible.

Due to the high cost of labor, manual hydraulic steering has almost become standard with the stock powerboat manufacturers. This type of steering consists essentially of a pump that is turned by the steering wheel, a hydraulic cylinder, and a reservoir, all connected by three tubes or hoses of small diameter. There can be two or more steering stations—it makes little difference as long as there are no leaks in the piping—so the more the number of stations, the more advantageous the system. One drawback, and this is a matter of design, is the great number of steering wheel turns from hard over to hard over of the rudder. In larger boats, the number of turns can be reduced by introducing a power-driven pump instead of a manually operated one. Some well-known suppliers of hydraulic steering components are Hynautic, Inc., Wagner Marine (USA), Inc., and Teleflex, Inc.

19

TANKS, PLUMBING, ETC.

SMALL CRUISING BOATS HAVE AT LEAST a freshwater tank, a sink with supply and drain, a toilet and possibly a sewage holding tank, and, depending on method of propulsion, a fuel tank and engine cooling. As the size of a boat increases, additional piping systems become necessary. To avoid minor annoyances or major problems, tanks must be installed properly and care taken to ensure safety by using approved materials put together to be leakproof. In this chapter we discuss the basics.

FUEL TANKS

Due to the danger of explosion and fire, the construction and installation of fuel tanks, particularly gasoline tanks, should not be taken lightly. Both installation and construction are well covered by standards set by the American Boat and Yacht Council, written by people with long experience, and by the U.S. Coast Guard. The standards are only as good as your compliance with them, so heed them well. (See Chapter 22, "Safety.")

The standards specify the all-important matter of tank materials. Monel Alloy 400 remains probably the finest metal from which to make tanks, either for gasoline or diesel fuel, but it is extremely high in cost. Steel remains the most inexpensive material for diesel tanks but must not have a coating of any sort on the inside. A recent development is the approval of certain alloys of aluminum for the construction of fuel tanks. Now tanks can be welded of alloys 5052, 5083, or 5086. The latter is the most resistant to corrosion from seawater and is used for hulls, many of which are not painted above the waterline.

When buying a fuel tank, be sure it bears the label of the manufacturer as called for by the standards and that it shows it was tested. Also, be sure that it has a tab for connection to the bonding system of the boat.

One caution about aluminum tanks concerns the connection of metal fittings, such as metal tubing and metal ends of fuel hoses, to the tank, because the metal may not be galvanically compatible with the aluminum alloy. One way to avoid trouble is to weld half of an aluminum pipe coupling to the tank and then screw a stainless steel pipe bushing into the female threads of the coupling half. The bushing reduces the size of the opening; therefore you must start out with a coupling that is a size or two larger than usual. Fill and vent connections to the tank are normally of hose, and these can be slipped over and clamped to aluminum alloy tubular fittings, either straight pieces or 90-degree elbows, beaded for hose and welded to the tank.

In 1986 fuel line hoses were introduced that are not affected by the alcohol-type additives replacing leaded gasoline fuels.

There has been some discussion in boating periodicals about corrosion of stainless steel fuel tanks in stock small craft where the tanks are installed so low they contact bilge water, and the proponents of polyethylene for fuel tanks have had much to say about the benefits of this material. It is certainly true that such location of stainless steel tanks can be dangerous and should be avoided; neither would I install aluminum alloy fuel tanks low in the bilges. Stock nonmetallic tanks are made by Tempo Products Company and Vetus. (Addresses of these and other sources are listed in the Appendix.)

All valves in the fuel piping, including those at the tank for the fuel suction to the engine (and fuel return line in diesel systems), must be of the approved packless type, which do not leak at the stems.

One final word: openings in the tank for any purpose are not permitted anywhere except on the *top* surface of the tank.

A tank manufacturer that has made hundreds of aluminum alloy fuel tanks for stock and custom boatbuilders as well as for the one-off people is Florida Marine Tanks, Inc. You may be able to find a custom tank fabricator in your area. In the Northeast, Luther's Welding in Bristol, Rhode Island, is a good bet.

DO-IT-YOURSELF PRESSURE TEST

I was but fifteen years old when I saw a gasoline-powered commercial fishing boat explode and two bodies blown upward. Thus early on I learned respect for fuel with the flash point of gasoline. Many years later while building a utility launch for myself I heard that all the gear on a steel lifeboat converted to an auxiliary cruiser was for sale because the hull was no longer repairable. I bought the engine and the fuel tank, with the condition that the tank pass my test for leakage. It met standards in that there were no openings except on the top surface, but otherwise there was no history attached to the tank. I plugged all openings on the top except a flange for a 1½" fill pipe, then screwed 7 feet of 1½" pipe into the flange and filled the tank and fill pipe with fresh water. This exerted a pressure of $7 \times 0.433 = 3.03$ pounds per square inch (psi) on the surface of the tank.

(Obviously, 0.433 is the pressure head in pounds per square inch exerted on a surface by a liquid, in this case fresh water, which weighs 62.4 pounds per cubic foot. Not so obvious is that the inside diameter of the length of pipe used to build up the pressure head does not make any difference.)

After half a day without any signs of a leak I knew it would be safe to install that tank. In due course a label was attached to the tank showing capacity, test pressure, and date of test.

DECK PLATES FOR FUEL TANK FILLS

The location of a fuel fill should be such that any spill or overflow will not drain into the hull or the middle of a self-draining cockpit. Why not the cockpit? Because gasoline fuel could collect here before draining—enough fuel to cause a disaster with the smallest spark. Fuel fills are generally sited on side decks, outside coamings.

There is a large fine in the United States for spilling fuel overboard, and when a boatbuilder becomes a boatowner he must remember that a fuel fill located to protect the boat from spillage does not give him a license for sloppiness.

Use fill plates that are stamped to show the contents of the tanks they serve. This will help prevent, but not guarantee, fuel from being pumped into a freshwater tank or vice versa. As you can imagine, either mistake presents a serious problem!

FUEL TANK VENTS

The location of the fuel tank vent is important, particularly in sailboats, in order to prevent seawater from contaminating the tank and thereby causing engine failure or expensive residual damage. Referring to Figure 19-1, we can see that in a common rail-down sailing situation, the vent route shown as drawn is not safe. A horizontal loop (indicated by dashed lines) in the same boat is still only safe to 45 degrees. When the loop is vertical, extending to the underside of the cabin roof, things are better, but can be improved by extending the vent to the centerline of the boat. Heavily ballasted craft may still have positive stability when heeled beyond 90 degrees, so the vent locations warrant close study.

The examples in the figure assume that the tank is located along the centerline of the hull; otherwise, each case must be examined separately.

Through-hull fittings for fuel tank vents are readily available. Most come with a flame arrester screen and are made to connect with a ⅝" I.D. vent hose.

FIGURE 19-1.

The vent route for a fuel tank on a sailboat needs to accommodate heeled waterline levels.

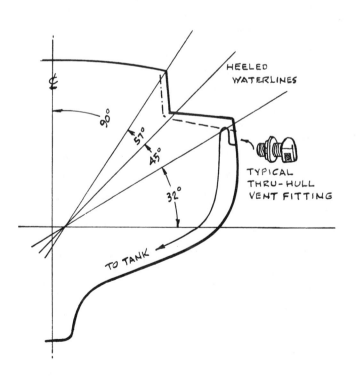

FRESHWATER TANKS

Freshwater tanks should be just as carefully built, tested, and installed as fuel tanks. One difference is that there *should* be an opening in the bottom of the tank—the outlet. This is used to drain the tank when a boat is unused or stored in freezing weather. Suitable water tank materials include Monel Alloy 400, superior in quality and cost, stainless steel (Type 316 is the best in salt atmosphere), aluminum alloy, polyethylene, and fiberglass, provided the interior is treated to remove taste and odor.

TANK CAPACITY CALCULATION

Figure 19-2 shows tank shapes commonly used in boats and how to calculate their capacities by figuring the volume in cubic inches and dividing by 231 to find contents in U.S. gallons. Boatbuilders, when faced with the installation of an unplanned tank, seem always to work the capacities from inch dimensions. If dimensions are taken in feet and fractions, the cubic capacity is multiplied by 7.48 for the answer in gallons.

The cylindrical and rectangular tanks A and B are straightforward to figure. Shape C is typical of a tank installed under the cockpit of a sailboat. The sides are parallel, but the top and bottom are not, due to hull shape. The cross-sectional area W times H is the average of the area of the ends, or the same as the area at midlength of the tank. Shape D is often used for tanks located under the sole of a cabin, and again the volume is the length times the average of the area of the ends. The W measurements are taken at midheight of the ends.

Sounding Tanks

Sounding a fuel or water tank that has a straight, vertical fill pipe makes it easy to determine the amount of liquid in the tank and, conversely, the amount needed to fill the tank to full capacity. Marking a wooden dipstick to sound a rectangular tank is easy. Simply work the formula given in B in Figure 19-2, using one inch as the height (H). This will give the number of gallons per inch of height. Mark the stick with fine saw cuts every inch or two inches from the bottom end, depending on the proportions of the tank. If you have a set of steel numbers, stamp the number of gallons above the saw cuts. If not, write them on a card or in a notebook. When there are a number of tanks, the sticks must be identified as well.

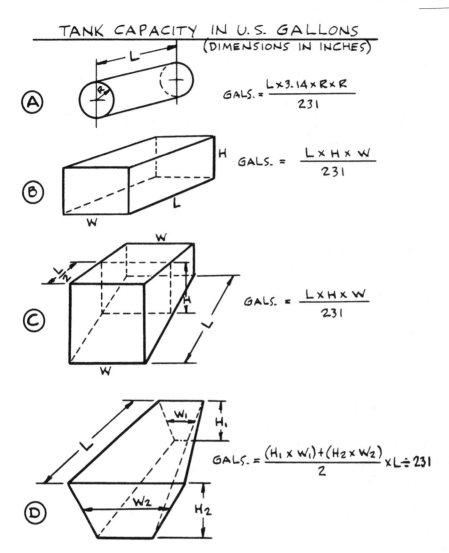

TANK CAPACITY IN U.S. GALLONS
(DIMENSIONS IN INCHES)

(A) $\text{GALS.} = \dfrac{L \times 3.14 \times R \times R}{231}$

(B) $\text{GALS.} = \dfrac{L \times H \times W}{231}$

(C) $\text{GALS.} = \dfrac{L \times H \times W}{231}$

(D) $\text{GALS.} = \dfrac{(H_1 \times W_1) + (H_2 \times W_2)}{2} \times L \div 231$

FIGURE 19-2.
Various methods of determining tank capacity.

A dipstick painted flat black is best; the wetted length is instantly apparent.

Calibrating a dipstick to sound a cylindrical tank is another matter. Such a tank is usually installed horizontally. A in Figure 19-2 shows how to figure the amount of liquid on a cylindrical tank in percentage of total capacity of the tank, assuming the dipstick will have 10 divisions in a length equal to the *inside* diameter of the tank (A in Figure 19-3). It's simple with a handheld calculator.

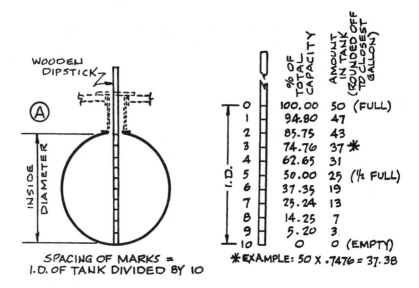

FIGURE 19-3.
Calibrating a dipstick for sounding a cylindrical tank installed horizontally; a 50-gallon-capacity tank is used as an example.

It is assumed that, for the safety of lives, when a tank is used for a highly volatile fuel, an accidental overflow of fuel or fumes will not be trapped anywhere on board the boat.

PLUMBING

Copper used to be an accepted material for piping for salt water or hot and cold fresh water, but it has its drawbacks, such as an annoying tendency to develop pinholes. Now not only is the tubing costly, but so are the fittings to hook it up. The marine supply stores have other piping materials, such as nylon-reinforced vinyl hose, which is nontoxic, tasteless, and odorless, for both hot and cold water systems; clear polyvinyl tubing for sink and other drain lines and *cold* freshwater lines; and PVC (cold water) and CPVC (hot and cold water) piping, fittings, joint cleaner, and joint cement. These polyvinyl chloride items are available in Schedule 40 standard wall thickness and Schedule 80 thick wall. (The "schedule" dimensions are the same as brass or steel pipe.)

Hose ends should be secured only with 100 percent stainless steel hose clamps (both the strap *and* the tightening mechanism).

SEACOCKS

Seacock is another name for a valve made to close an opening in the hull—an opening for a water intake, or toilet discharge, or the like. A real seacock—unlike an inexpensive, ordinary, residential valve—is made of a corrosion-resistant material other than common brass. The best of them will have a base drilled for bolts through the hull and a backing block or plate; the base is tapped for a threaded through-hull fitting. It is good practice to use seacocks for pipe openings below a line about 12" above the maximum draft of the boat. Your marine store probably stocks seacocks made by Perko, Groco, or Wilcox-Crittenden. All three makes have marine UL-approved seacocks, meaning the product has had proper testing.

MARINE TOILETS

The piping for a marine toilet requires special attention. Installation instructions normally advise the use of a so-called vented loop in the discharge line, and suggest that the loop be at least 6" above the deepest waterline of the boat. Indeed, the vented loop is a safe installation that guards against siphoning water back into the boat, but I would modify this to locate the loop *as high as practical* in sailboats, and in the case of rail-down sailing make it a strict rule on board that the seacock be closed except when the head is in use. Installation of marine toilets has gotten a tad more complicated with the passage of laws compelling the use of holding tanks within protected waters. Y-valves can be used to provide the option of using the onboard tank or discharging waste overboard.

The last point brings up another: *all* seacocks *must* be located where accessible. If the seacock has a detachable handle, then a hook or other suitable stowage should be provided adjacent to the valve itself.

Use full-flow seacocks rather than those which, when open, have a flow area less than that of the pipe size.

The toilet piping in Figure 19-4 is only schematic. For example, it may be more practical to mount the loop more nearly 90 degrees to what is shown, that is, mounted along the hull. Also, the intake seacock should be located forward of the discharge seacock.

Intakes for engine cooling, etc., must have scoop strainers over the opening on the outside of the hull and also good-quality intake strainers on the inside of the hull between the seacock and the device pumping the water.

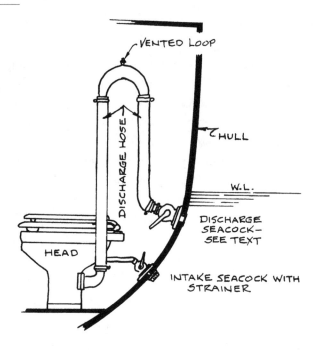

FIGURE 19-4.
Section of hull showing a marine toilet installed below the waterline. Note, for boats in protected waters an internal holding tank would be required (not shown here).

HOLDING TANKS

U.S. federal laws now require that marine heads (toilets) not be discharged close to shore. Rather, contents are now flushed into holding tanks in the boat, which are then emptied at properly equipped marinas or other facilities. Alternatively, composting heads may be installed. You can find the necessary pumps, tanks, hoses, valves, deck fittings, and bits and pieces at West Marine, Defender, and the other marine supply stores. The West Marine catalog has an excellent "Advisor" on the legal and technical aspects of these installations. On a smaller boat and when only short stays aboard are contemplated, it's hard to improve on the simplicity of the humble covered bucket or the Porta-Potti.

20

MECHANICAL AND ELECTRICAL

ONBOARD MECHANICAL AND ELECTRICAL SYSTEMS are becoming increasingly complex as the years roll by. This chapter discusses some of the basics. Information on new and updated methods and equipment can be found in yachting and commercial craft publications and online sites. Advancements in LED lighting, hybride power systems, and "fly-by-wire" control systems are occurring at lightning pace—read all you can and use this chapter as a foundation for how you adapt the new systems to your project.

Zogo, a hybrid diesel-electric launch designed and built in Maine, is just one recent example of a unique approach to solving the propulsion puzzle for a powerboat. (*Molly Mulhern*)

PROPELLER SHAFTS AND BEARINGS

Propeller shafts must be made from strong, noncorrosive material. At this writing two of the best metals, Monel Alloy 400 and the higher-strength Monel Alloy K-500, have just about priced themselves out of the pleasure-boat market. These are high in nickel content, and this is probably the reason why little people, unlike governments, cannot afford them. A somewhat weaker metal, although "standard" for many years, is Tobin bronze, but this seems to have disappeared (but don't overlook the possibility of finding a used Tobin shaft) and been replaced by various stainless steel shafting materials, notably Armco's Aquamet 17, 18, and 22. If the shaft is going to be turning most of the time, as in commercial boat use, then Aquamet 17 is a strong, suitable metal, but in typical intermittent yacht service Aquamet 22 is a better choice. During the 1980s Aquamet 22HS was developed, and its strength is impressive. In the 2"- to 3"-diameter range, for example, yield strengths have increased enormously; Aquamet 22HS has a yield strength in tension of 105,000 pounds per square inch (psi) versus 75,000 psi for Aquamet 22, and a yield strength in torsion of 70,000 psi, compared to 50,000 psi. Horsepower of engines used in pleasure craft has been increasing, so the higher-rating Aquamet 22HS is beneficial in holding down the diameter and thus the weight of shafting. Shafts of this alloy may not exhibit as much corrosion resistance as those of Aquamet 22, however.

If your boat plans do not specify the shaft diameter, American Boat and Yacht Council standard P-6 has charts for selecting the sizes of shafts for the materials mentioned above and also for bearing spacing.

Typical shafts have a keyway machined on one end for the propeller shaft coupling to the engine, while the outboard end has a taper with keyway to match the propeller hub bore and threads for the propeller locking nuts. The tapering must be carefully done so the propeller will fit properly and is best left to a shaft supplier who is set up for this work. For instance, standard taper for the propeller is ¹⁄₁₆ inch per inch, which is an angle of 3°34'47" (total included angle). Dimensions for machining the shaft end and propeller hub have long been standardized, at least in the United States, and the relevant SAE data is usually tabulated and illustrated in the catalogs of the propeller makers. When setting up the length of your shaft, allow one shaft diameter's clearance between the propeller hub and the strut.

Figure 20-1 shows a longitudinal section at the shaft centerline of a twin-screw motorboat. The same section applies to a common single-screw

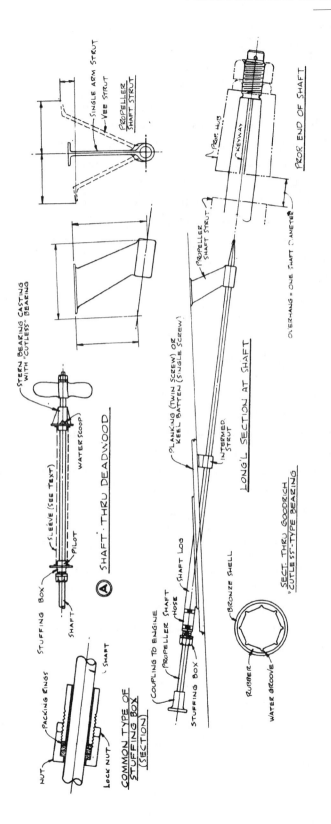

FIGURE 20-1.
Various shaft details of shaft including propeller strut details, as well as stuffing box details.

motorboat with a keel batten and cutaway skeg. It shows the usual modern arrangement of a rubber-necked shaft log with a stuffing box inboard to prevent water from leaking into the boat around the shaft, and a strut to support the shaft at the propeller. Intermediate struts are used when the shaft is sufficiently long to require additional support.

The stuffing box and the shaft log are both of bronze and are connected by a short length of rubber hose secured by clamps. The hose helps to reduce vibration due to minor misalignment of the shaft. Shaft logs are made in the several angles that have proved the most useful for the majority of boats, but they may have to be shimmed with a wedge of wood in your boat to get the correct alignment. The base flange of the shaft log must be made water-tight by bedding the flange with a generous amount of bedding compound or adhesive sealant. Wherever possible, the base should be through-fastened with silicon bronze bolts; otherwise wood screws of the same metal should be used.

The shaft hole through the wood should be treated with epoxy resin, because the hole is difficult to clean and paint later with the shaft in place and is therefore susceptible to worm damage. This precaution is very important indeed.

Some shaft logs are designed with a tube integral with the base. The tube is a lining for the shaft hole and is cut off flush with the outside of the hull. This type of shaft log is rather special and is not used as frequently as the kind that terminates at the base.

Another type of special shaft log is sometimes used in moderate- to large-size boats where the shaft is quite long in proportion to the diameter and it is desirable to have a bearing between the first intermediate shaft strut and the engine. In this case shaft logs are made that have a short length of bearing. The bearing is housed so the forward end is not exposed to a flow of water; water lubrication is provided by engine cooling water tapped into the log forward of the bearing. The water used is part of that usually piped into the exhaust line for cooling, but the diversion is not detrimental, because only a small amount is sent to the shaft log bearing. This type of shaft log is specially made up and not found in marine supply catalogs.

Some perfectionists object to a stuffing box that drips water, even only a normal amount, and for years I knew of only one shaft seal with zero drip, but such seals are now available. One of these is the Lasdrop, made by the Lemania Company and said to have American Bureau of Shipping approval. (Addresses of this and other sources are listed in the Appendix.) The descriptive brochure lays out the entire device in color, much better

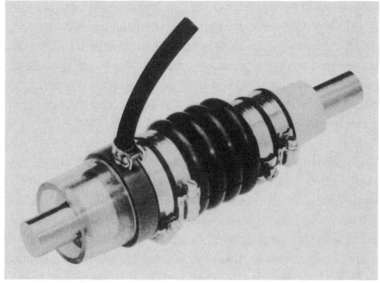

FIGURE 20-2.
Lasdrop propeller shaft seal. (*Lemania Company*)

than the photograph, Figure 20-2, and explains the function of the hose going into the top of the seal assembly. That hose is either to supply water as a lubricant to the seal faces in high-speed boats, which may have dry stern tubes when at planing speeds, or used as a vent line in low-speed displacement hulls to make the unit self-priming.

A part of the propulsion setup that is almost always a special item is the propeller shaft strut. As specified by the plans, it is either the single arm or the vee type, and due to the angle of the shaft and the shape of the hull it is nearly impossible to find a stock strut that will fit. There are, however, some adjustable struts on the market that might just do the job. Otherwise, enough dimensions on a sketch (as shown in A in Figure 20-1) or a mock-up must be sent to a strut manufacturer so he can make up one or a pair to fit the boat. Most struts are made of cast bronze.

Struts are fastened through the planking and the inside blocking with silicon bronze or manganese bronze bolts. The heads of the bolts should be oval and countersunk and should have a screwdriver slot to keep the bolt from turning while it is tightened. These bolts are best ordered from the strut manufacturer; specify the length needed.

You might as well have the strut maker install the bearing in the strut. It is hard to beat the Goodrich "Cutless"-type bearing, which is made of rubber bonded to an outer shell of bronze or, if the hull is aluminum alloy or steel, to an optional plastic-type shell. This type of bearing has grooves that channel in water for lubrication and for washing out silt and sand, thus minimizing shaft wear. The shell of the bearing is lightly pressed into the strut and secured with one or two set screws. The bearings are four times the shaft diameter in length when used as the aftermost bearing, and they are often reduced to half length in intermediate struts, so that one standard bearing can be cut to make two intermediate ones.

In Figure 20-1, A also shows a typical arrangement when the shaft of a single-engine boat goes through the deadwood. The stuffing box is inside the hull, the stern bearing outside. The latter has a Cutless-type bearing and a water scoop on each side of the casting for bearing lubrication. The stuffing box can be had "rubber necked," with a piece of hose between the stuffing box and the casting. Both the stuffing box assembly and the stern bearing are stock marine hardware items and are readily available.

Water will fill the hole for the shaft and must be prevented from leaking into the hull through joints in the deadwood structure. This is done by fitting a tube between the stuffing box and stern bearing castings, either a lead sleeve as shown in A in Figure 20-1 (the lead is easily flanged by hammering) or a bronze tube special-ordered from a marine machine shop. The pilots of the castings can be tapped for the ends of a threaded pipe. The castings should be fastened to the wood with hanger bolts. Today fiberglass tubes are also used; they are available from Spartan Marine (see the Appendix).

The stuffing box packing is square, either waxed braided flax or Teflon-impregnated asbestos braid, and is installed as individual rings, with the joints staggered so they are not all in line, thus preventing leakage.

When you have secured a propeller on the shaft with the thin nut against the hub, followed by the thick nut, don't let anyone tell you it is wrong! Not long ago the Society of Automotive Engineers, which provides the marine propeller bore and shaft taper standards, revised their propeller shaft-end drawing to show the nuts properly arranged (see Figure 20-3).

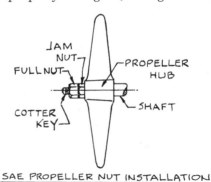

FIGURE 20-3.
The proper arrangement of the nuts on the shaft end.

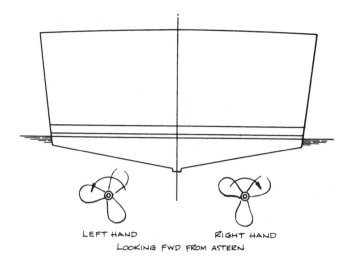

LEFT HAND   RIGHT HAND

LOOKING FWD FROM ASTERN

FIGURE 20-4.
Shaft turning direction defines whether to install a left-hand or a right-hand propeller.

DIRECTION OF PROPELLER ROTATION

Screw propellers are made either right-hand or left-hand. Looking forward from astern, a shaft that turns clockwise requires a right-hand propeller and a shaft that turns counterclockwise takes a left-hand propeller. It is customary for the propellers in twin-screw boats to be of opposite rotation and to turn outboard as shown in Figure 20-4.

ALIGNING PROPELLER SHAFT COUPLINGS

If there is misalignment between the engine and propeller shaft couplings, there will not only be unnecessary vibration when the engine is running but also possible damage to the rear bearing and seal of the reverse gear. The shaft should be installed first and the engine mated to it. If there are only two support bearings for the shaft—the stern bearing or strut bearing and a rubber-necked shaft log—block up the shaft inboard of the shaft log to prevent the shaft from sagging at the rubber neck. Lacking a feeler gauge, test for alignment between the coupling halves by inserting four strips of paper as shown in Figure 20-5. You can tell by gently pulling on the strips whether the pressure, and thus the gap, is the same for all pieces. Hardwood and thin brass shims are used under the engine mounts until

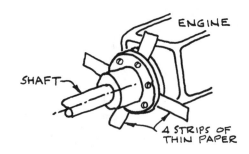

FIGURE 20-5.
One method of testing shaft alignment.

the alignment is as perfect as possible. The final test is to tighten down the engine and still have good alignment of the couplings.

Many engines are equipped with adjustable mounts that need but a wrench to lift or lower them a few thousandths of an inch, and some of the larger engines have jacking screws built into the mounts for the same purpose. Regardless, the fit of the coupling flanges is the important point.

If aligning of the engine is done with the boat out of water, it must be tested again when the vessel is launched because some hulls change shape when waterborne, throwing out the alignment that was done while hauled out.

PULLEY DRIVES

The boatbuilder is often faced with figuring out a v-belt pulley ratio when a bilge pump or extra generator is to be driven from a power takeoff pulley on an engine. The formulae below are handy for finding pulley diameter or speed in RPM.

Driven pulley:

$$RPM = \frac{diameter \times RPM\ of\ driver}{diameter\ or\ driven}$$

$$Diameter = \frac{diameter \times RPM\ of\ driver}{RPM\ or\ driven}$$

Driving pulley:

$$Diameter = \frac{diameter \times RPM\ of\ driven}{RPM\ of\ driver}$$

$$RPM = \frac{diameter \times RPM\ of\ driven}{diameter\ of\ of\ driver}$$

ENGINE CONTROLS

The engine is almost always located some distance away from the steering station of the boat, so remote controls must be installed for operating the throttle, the reverse gear, and an emergency shutdown in the case of some two-cycle diesel engines. This used to be done with complicated linkages of rods, pipes, and bell cranks and was a job of major proportions. One of the greater boons was the advent of the hydraulic reverse gear, requiring but fingertip effort on a small lever on the gear instead of the many foot-pounds of effort needed to operate the old manual clutch. This led to the push-pull cable controls now seen in most boats, a method that drastically reduced the time and cost of installation. The engine control system now consists of an attractive set of levers at the steering station and two push-pull cables running from the levers to the engine, one each for gear and throttle. The control maker usually has kits for each brand of engine for connecting the engine end of the cables to the gear and throttle. These save hours of making brackets for each job.

The length of cables between control levers and the engine can be almost unlimited, but they should be installed with a minimum number of bends, and the minimum bend radius for the size of cable being used must not be exceeded. Contrary to the opinions of some, it is a mistake to restrict the movement of push-pull cables. They should only be secured sufficiently to keep them from interfering with other equipment. A little time spent planning the cable runs will show which way has the least number of bends. The control manufacturers furnish excellent instructions for making the installation.

A variation of a control head with two levers per engine is the single lever control favored by many operators. Two cables per engine are still required, so the installation is planned the same as when there are two levers.

When two or more control stations are planned and would require long runs of cables with many bends, consideration should be given to hydraulic controls for the throttle and gears. Hynautic, Inc., has a system that may do the job for you.

ENGINE EXHAUST SYSTEMS

The purpose of an engine exhaust system is to get rid of the gaseous products of combustion safely (without setting the boat on fire). The exhaust system also reduces the noise level and prevents water from backing up into and damaging the engine under all conditions of heel and trim. Such an arrangement is depicted in Figure 20-6, but this schematic does not show the effect of heel.

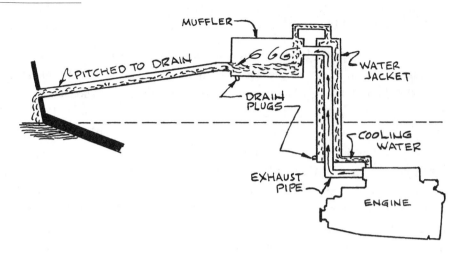

FIGURE 20-6.
The basics of engine exhaust disposal.

Sailboats pose the worst problems because they often sail rail down. Figure 20-7 shows how to avoid a problem caused by heel. The water-jacketed tube for years was made of copper, a material relatively easy to work (NFPA 302 forbids the use of copper in contact with *dry diesel* exhaust gases), but copper is subject to pinhole leaks. Nowadays stainless steel is more commonly used. In sections where it is safe (see Figure 20-7) the exhaust can be hose that is *approved for marine use.*

In any event, metal water-jacketed sections are on the heavy side and expensive to make. Whenever possible the systems shown in the sketches thus far can be replaced by the so-called waterlift system. One type of waterlift system is illustrated in Figure 20-8, which shows typical installation with the exhaust outlet of the engine both below and above the waterline. Any restrictive dimensions should be heeded.

There are also vertical waterlifts that may better suit your hull. The makers should provide installation instructions.

ENGINE CONNECTIONS

Water, fuel, and electrical connections to an engine should always have slack so vibration cannot cause premature failure of the lines. Cooling water lines to the engine should be hose, double clamped at each end with stainless steel hose clamps whenever possible. On the other hand, fuel lines should be hose of approved type with threaded end and *never* clamped. The reader should heed the regulations described in the safety chapter.

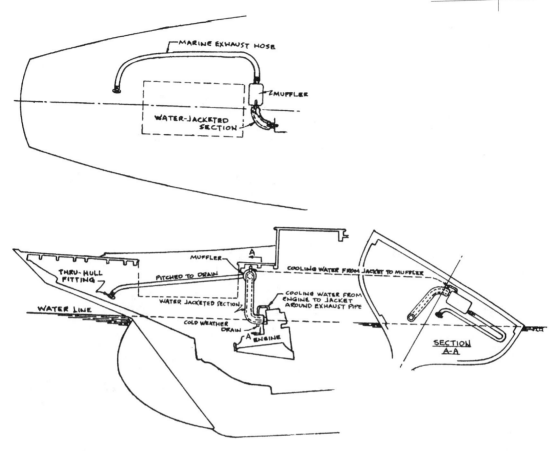

FIGURE 20-7.
Details of water jacket installation on a sailboat.

A good number of boats have sunk because exhaust hoses have been inadequately clamped to the adjoining rigid pipes or tubes. Figure 20-9 shows the minimum clamp widths and hose overlap permitted by the American Boat and Yacht Council standard on this subject.

ELECTRICAL SYSTEM

Here is a part of modern boatbuilding that can get a builder into a lot of trouble. If he is lucky, there will be only one voltage on board, such as 12 volts direct current. However, more often these days there will also be 115 volts of alternating current from a shoreline connection. This would be used to operate a charger to keep the batteries topped off, and also perhaps to operate the AC side of a dual-voltage refrigerator when the engines are not running and to operate air-conditioning while dockside. Progressing further, an AC independent generator on board can be used to provide conveniences

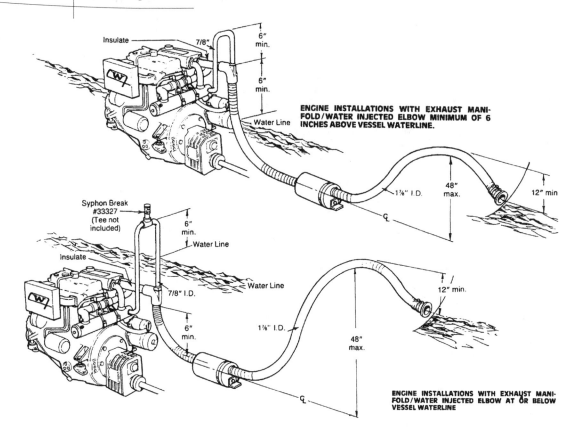

FIGURE 20-8.
Waterlift-type muffler installations. *(J. H. Westerbeke Corporation)*

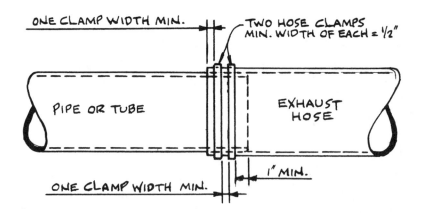

FIGURE 20-9.
Double-clamping hose connections is critical for safety.

such as an AC-powered cooking range, heating or air-conditioning, television, etc. And further along the line there can be *two* AC voltages in use aboard, and also *two* DC voltages, such as 12 and 24 or 12 and 32. The complications are endless; in some of the larger yachts there seems to be no end at all. But this has been recognized, and there are ABYC standards that *attempt* to keep things manageable.

In terms of material, the standards are a guide to the all-important matter of overload protection to avoid fire and to the type of insulated conductors necessary to cope with the various environments aboard a boat. The conductor size is governed by the length of the wire and the ampere load to be carried, and the wires of the conductors should be stranded rather than solid to minimize failure from vibration. Connections must be by approved crimped terminals and should be soldered as well. Advice from an old friend: Solder electrical wire crimped connections with 60-40 rosin-core solder, *not* acid-core solder.

If you have access to ABYC standards, you'd best read and heed them well, remembering that the recommendations contained therein are a result of concern by the boatbuilding industry to help boatbuilders and owners avoid trouble. When a boat is large enough to have electrics, be sure to also heed the ABYC advice on bonding the equipment on board. A list of ABYC-recommended practices appears in "Safety," Chapter 22.

The U.S. Coast Guard also has something to say about electrical installations, due to tragic experiences in the past, particularly in boats with gasoline engines. The Coast Guard's guideline for safe electrical system installation is listed in the safety chapter.

Life is being made easier for the boatbuilder by the appearance on the market of switchboards meeting recognized standards. For years, the only hardware store–type switchboard available to boatmen was a small 12-volt DC panel having six to a dozen toggle switches and automotive-type fuses for circuit protection. Now, there are DC panels and combination DC and AC panels of various sizes, all having approved circuit breakers and meters to show loads and the condition of batteries. There is a sufficient selection of panels and load capacities to take care of the circuits used in many boats, and this often eliminates the necessity of having to utilize custom-designed, custom-built switchboards. Newmar, Blue Sea, and Paneltronics all have products in this area (see the Appendix). The panel in Figure 20-10 is for boats with only direct current. Available on a stock basis are panels designed as alarms, such as the engine, bilge water, and engineroom alarm panel in Figure 20-11. Also available is one that

FIGURE 20-10.
Typical neat, compact DC electrical
panel for small craft. (*Blue Sea*)

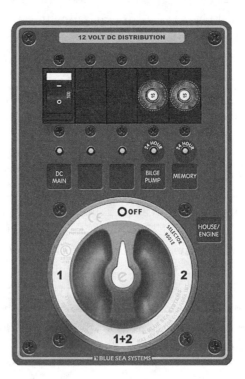

FIGURE 20-11.
A specialized DC distribution panel that
includes a battery switch. (*Blue Sea*)

detects extremely dangerous cooking-gas fumes that escape due to a leak in the piping.

Another maker of AC/DC circuit breakers is Paneltronics, which will provide a design manual upon request.

My boat-designer friend Fred Bates has over the years sold several hundred sets of plans for his 23-foot powerboat Pogo, a craft with just basic living accommodations. The schematic wiring diagram, which I have simplified somewhat by omitting wire sizes, is shown in Figure 20-12 and is typical of the direct-current systems in many small craft.

FIGURE 20-12.

Schematic wiring diagram for 23-foot cruiser.

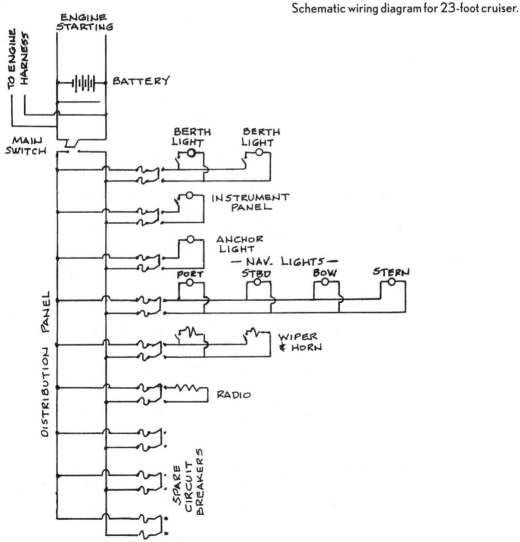

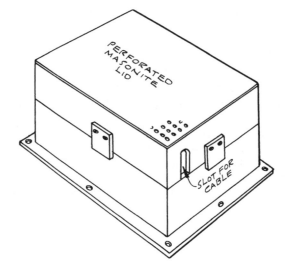

FIGURE 20-13.
A suggested battery box design.

BATTERY STORAGE BOXES

The electrolyte in a lead-acid storage battery is very destructive to wood and certain metals, so it is important to prevent spillage. The worst thing that can happen is for an unsecured lead-acid battery to overturn; therefore the battery, whether it consists of a single or multiple units, must be secured. New batteries, including gel-cell and AGM, are closed and do not poise the same potential for damaging leakage; however, all batteries are extremely heavy, so securing them well to the vessel is mandatory. For small craft, covered molded plastic cases with straps and hold-down fittings are available. In larger boats there might be a bank of two engine-starting batteries and a bank of two to eight ship's-service batteries, for which custom boxes must be built.

One of the simplest containers is made of plywood, with its interior made acid-resistant by carefully and completely lining the box with fiberglass. The inside dimensions of the box should be about ¾" larger all around than the battery to provide space for spilled water, which can be removed by suction with an oven baster. A couple of expendable wooden blocks can be used to keep the battery from shifting despite the clearance. The top should be of a material such as Masonite, ventilated so that explosive hydrogen generated when the battery is being charged will not be trapped. A top also guards against the possibly dangerous sparking that would take place should a tool be accidentally dropped across the battery terminals.

Figure 20-13 is a suggested battery box for the do-it-yourselfer.

21

POTPOURRI

AS I STATED IN THE BEGINNING, you won't learn everything there is to know about boatbuilding from one book unless the boat is the very simplest type. Indeed, larger craft seem to be becoming more complex due to the vast assortment of equipment available, but fortunately most manufacturers are very cooperative and will assist the boatbuilder or owner. Following are a few miscellaneous items that did not seem to have a place in the foregoing, but that I did not want to omit because some readers might find them of interest.

OARS AND OARLOCKS

The sketch in Figure 21-1 answers questions most often asked about the relationship between the location of oarlocks and the rower's seat in a standard rowboat, based on "rules" handed down over the years. The gunwale construction of the boat may or may not require a rowlock pad as is indicated in the sketch. The 7½" dimension is to the top of the socket of conventional oarlocks.

The rower's thwart is best made 8" to 9" wide to give the part of your body that sits a good grip when rowing vigorously; a wider seat is not as good.

A few years ago I visited, on a bank of the historic Penobscot River, a shop called Shaw & Tenney, where oars and paddles have been made

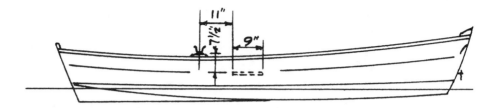

FIGURE 21-1.
Measurements between rowing seat and oarlock placement.

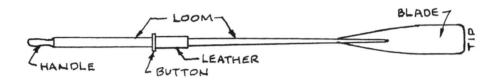

FIGURE 21-2.
Oar nomenclature.

since 1858. The shop recommends an oar length based on the athwartship distance between the centers of the oarlocks. One-half this distance + 2" = X, then X ÷ 7 × 25 = overall length of the oar in inches.

LETTERING AND CARVING

Try painting the boat name and hailing port ("name and hail") on the stern or elsewhere instead of hiring someone else to do it. Paint containing lead, still the favorite of sign artists, is available in well-stocked paint or art supply stores.

Another challenge is carving nameboards, hailing ports, and the like. If you are inexperienced, I advise you not to start hacking away without consulting Jay Hanna's *The Shipcarver's Handbook.*

FIGURE 21-3.
The author's first attempt (years ago) at carving and gold-leafing a name board, for the stern of a catboat with an outboard rudder (thus the space between B and C).

FIGURE 21-4.
A carved trailboard.

WATER TRAP VENT

There should be a circulation of fresh air through a boat even when it is otherwise closed up. The vent shown in Figure 21-5 was developed for sailboats at sea some years ago and remains popular and practical for any type of boat, as it permits ventilation while excluding rain and flying spray. The cowl can be turned as desired for best results. The removable screen should not be used unless there are insects, because screens reduce the effective opening by about 25 percent. The cowl can be one of the pliable rubbery plastic kind that bend when a rope crosses it. The tube into the boat can be plastic, aluminum, or copper. The box can be installed either fore and aft or athwartships.

The top of the box can be made of wood as shown or of Plexiglas or Lexan at least ½" thick, either of which will admit a bit of light into the space below. (Lexan is preferable to Plexiglas because it is less liable to scratch.) Fasten the plastic with oval-head wood screws in oversize holes, because the expansion of wood and plastic is not the same. Use a sealer like silicone caulk or silicone rubber between the edge of the wooden box and around the screws in the plastic. Bed the box itself with a good caulk or adhesive sealant.

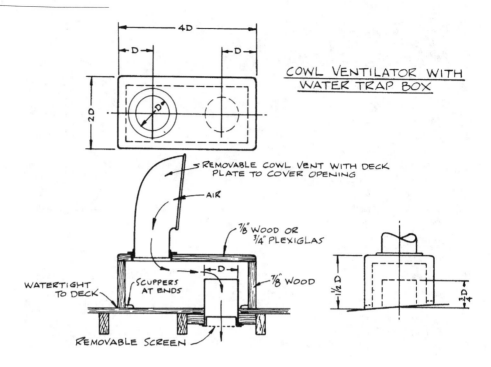

FIGURE 21-5.
Construction details of a cowl vent.

If a wooden box is not appropriate, consider a soft PVC cowl vent with built-in water trap.

DAVITS

Davits are used for handling anchors and dinghies aboard yachts and for other purposes on commercial boats. Aluminum alloy pipe, anodized if possible for protection against corrosion, has become a popular material for davits because of its light weight. This is good when, for one reason or another, a davit must be removed from its socket and stowed and thus needs manhandling. Davits can also be made of stainless steel pipe or tube or of ordinary steel pipe, the latter preferably hot galvanized after shaping and welding whatever fittings are needed on the davit. I worked up the accompanying chart, Figure 21-6, some years ago when scores of small craft going to war were clamoring for davits for all sorts of uses. If you know the load and the reach (dimension A), the chart will give a pretty good idea of the pipe size needed. The chart has a built-in safety factor of four using ordinary steel pipe. A davit is basically a cantilevered beam, so if a load swung outboard will heel the boat much, or if rolling seas are

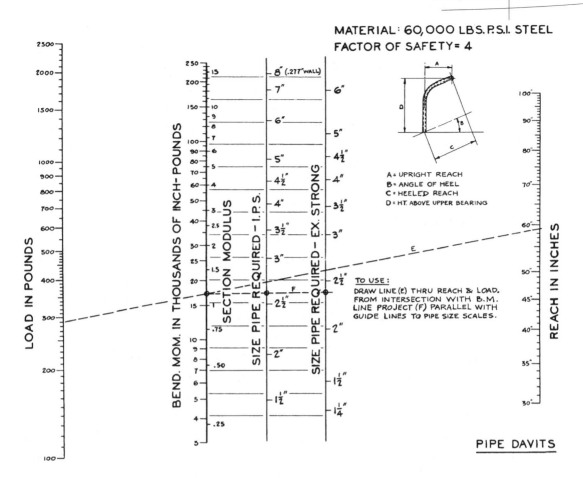

MATERIAL: 60,000 LBS. P.S.I. STEEL
FACTOR OF SAFETY = 4

A = UPRIGHT REACH
B = ANGLE OF HEEL
C = HEELED REACH
D = HT. ABOVE UPPER BEARING

TO USE:
DRAW LINE (E) THRU REACH & LOAD.
FROM INTERSECTION WITH B.M.
LINE PROJECT (F) PARALLEL WITH
GUIDE LINES TO PIPE SIZE SCALES.

PIPE DAVITS

FIGURE 21-6.

Use this chart to calculate the appropriate diameter for davits based on the load they are to carry.

expected, the reach should be increased as noted on the chart. A larger
pipe size will then probably be indicated.

Anodized aluminum alloy davits of various capacities, ranging from
150 pounds for anchors and up to 1,500 pounds for small boats, are made
as stock items and can be had with a tackle arrangement, with a hand-
operated winch, or with an electric winch in various voltages. The reach,
dimension A in Figure 21-6, is usually limited to 6 feet.

PATTERNS FOR CASTINGS

While a great many fittings for boats may be purchased from the stocks
of marine hardware manufacturers, there are always a few items that
are special. Here the amateur can save money by making patterns and

having a foundry pour the castings. To name a few of the fittings that are usually special for the sailboat, there is the jibstay fitting, permanent backstay fitting, propeller aperture casting, rudder gudgeons and pintles, and sometimes light cast-bronze floors when tanks are located under the cabin floor. Parts usually made of cast material for powerboats include propeller shaft bearing struts—it is seldom that the off-the-shelf struts fit properly—rudders, and transom platform brackets. Some of the standard fittings can be homemade, too, but this does not always pay unless you have time to burn.

Cast parts, especially for use underwater, are usually made of manganese bronze, and there are several different alloys, ranging in tensile strength from about 40,000 psi to upward of 100,000 psi. Above water, aluminum alloy castings are sometimes used where saving weight is important. Some of these alloys are not very resistant to salt water, and protective finishes for aluminum put out by some of the marine paint makers should be used. Anodizing also offers good protection if applicable to the alloy of your fittings.

The patternmaking and casting processes will be but briefly outlined, as people with wood and metalworking experience probably know all about them already. Any kind of wood may be used for patterns provided it is given a smooth finish, but soft pine is preferred because it is easy to work. The fitting is drawn on the wood, using fine lines for accuracy (patternmakers use a knife rather than a pencil). Because the molten metal will shrink during cooling, the pattern is made oversize by the amount of shrinkage expected. The shrinkage of bronze is $3/16$" per foot, and if any amount of work is to be done, a two-foot shrinkage rule should be purchased to make the layout work easier. Such rules can be obtained at good hardware stores and are made in shrinkages of $1/8$", $3/16$", etc., per foot of length. A two-foot rule made for $3/16$" shrinkage will actually measure $24\frac{3}{8}$".

Inside corners on patterns have fillets to provide strength in the castings and for ease of molding. Large, thin sections at an angle to each other have proportionately larger fillets than thicker-walled sections (see A in Figure 21-7). Fillets may be purchased from a patternmaker's supply house in wax strips, which are stuck in place with a heated fillet tool as shown, or they may be made of leather and secured in place with glue. For a small job you can get along with paraffin wax. Knead the soft wax and work it into the corners, making it uniform and smooth with a fillet tool, which is simply a steel ball on a handle, or with a dowel or a metal rod. The pattern must have a smooth finish for release from the molding sand. Patternmakers finish with several applications of shellac rubbed down between coats.

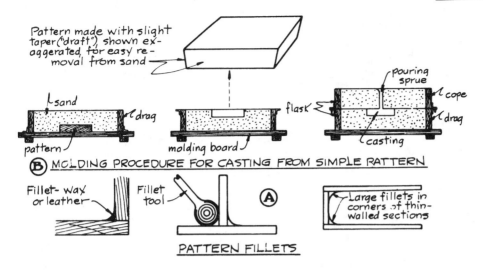

Pattern made with slight taper ("draft"), shown exaggerated, for easy removal from sand

sand

drag

pattern

molding board

flask

pouring sprue

cope

drag

casting

(B) MOLDING PROCEDURE FOR CASTING FROM SIMPLE PATTERN

Fillet- wax or leather

Fillet tool

(A)

Large fillets in corners of thin-walled sections

PATTERN FILLETS

FIGURE 21-7.
Details of making a mold for casting a metal fitting.

A maker of wooden duck decoys introduced me to a semigloss clear wood finish, which is lacquer-based and can be applied every two hours. Rub between coats and after the final one with No. 0000 steel wool; this will produce the desired slick finish on wood that has been well sanded previously. Also, when the pattern is made, you must give the sides of the pattern a slight taper, called draft, so it may be easily removed from the mold by the molder. This is better understood by referring to B in Figure 21-7.

This discussion is not to be regarded as a short course in molding, but the procedure is interesting to know. For small work, such as boat fittings, a small platform called a molding board will be used, and on it will be placed a box without ends to retain the sand used for the mold. The finished mold consists of two boxes, one upon the other, called the cope and the drag, and together the assembly is called a flask. Dowel pins on the cope fit into sockets on the drag and keep the two in alignment. The pattern is placed in the drag and covered with sand of such a nature that when packed hard it will stick together; the drag is then turned over. With the pattern still in the mold, the surface of the sand is coated with a powder so that when more sand is added, the two surfaces will part. Then the cope is added, filled with sand, and rammed solid. The cope is lifted off and turned over, and the sprue (a passage for pouring the molten metal) and some small vent holes to carry off gases are cut with molder's tools. The pattern is removed from the drag, leaving a space to be filled with metal.

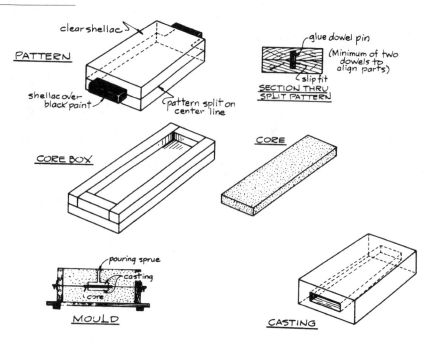

FIGURE 21-8.

The pattern, core, and mold for a simple hollow casting.

A flat pattern, as shown in Figure 21-7, is easy to remove, but a deeper one, or one with a complicated shape, is more difficult to take out without breaking the sand unless the pattern sides have proper draft. The casting is ready to be poured when the cope is replaced on the drag. The sprue is cut off the finished casting by the foundry.

The molding procedure for the simple block pattern in B in Figure 21-7 is easy, but a study of the mold shown in Figure 21-8 will indicate that to produce a casting shaped like the pattern, the pattern would have to be split along the centerline. Further, if the casting is to have a hollow portion, the hollow area must be kept free of molten metal; this is done with a core of sand shaped like the desired hollow. A simple core, as shown, is made by ramming sand into an open-top box until full and then baking the sand to make it hard and strong enough to withstand the pouring of the molten metal. Cores of irregular shape are molded in a split box with dowel pins. In the pattern, the core is extended beyond the length of the casting so the imprint of the core extension in the mold will support the core. This is shown in the figure. The core print, as it is called, is painted black so the molder will understand the core. When the casting has cooled and been taken from the mold, the core is easily broken out.

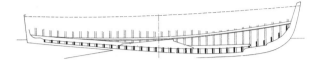

22

SAFETY

A SOUND HULL IS ONLY THE BEGINNING of a safe boat, unless it is the simplest of craft like one made to be paddled or rowed. As soon as holes are made in the hull underbody for through-hull fittings or machinery and electrical installations are made, precautions must be taken to prevent leaking, sinking, fire, or explosion. Newcomers to boatbuilding are fortunate in having information available to keep them out of trouble. Not too many years ago this knowledge was not so easy to come by. Many lessons were learned the hard way—sinking caused by a rotted hose attached to a valveless underwater through-hull fitting, loss of fire control from the wrong kind or an inadequate number of fire extinguishers, fire and/or explosion because a fuel line to an engine was installed without slack and broke from vibration, loss of life because passengers aboard a sinking boat could not find the life preservers. Such occurrences are preventable.

The very nature of boats calls for deck levels of varying heights to be accessible by steps and ladders. Risk of injury can be reduced by having an adequate number of handrails and grabs that are securely fastened in place with through-fastenings whenever possible. Similarly important are the adequate height and fastening of safety rails and lifelines around the edges of all decks accessible to those aboard.

AMERICAN BOAT AND YACHT COUNCIL

This nonprofit council was formed in 1954 by members of the boating industry who were concerned with safety. Over the years dozens of members have served countless hours in the preparation of standards for safe practices in the general areas of hull, equipment, machinery, electrical systems, and engineering. Ample time has been given for comment and criticism of each of the standards before they have been approved; therefore the standards do not represent one-sided opinions.

Membership in the American Boat and Yacht Council (ABYC) is open to all and includes a complete set of standards, copies of new standards as they are developed, and revisions to existing standards.

There are numerous and detailed standards in each of the council's general divisions mentioned above. If membership is not desired, the ABYC standards are for sale on an individual basis. It may well prove less expensive, though, to join up and receive them all. Following is a list of ABYC standards that should be of interest to boatbuilders:

Standards and Technical Information Reports for Small Craft from ABYC

Table of Contents—July 2010

Project	Title	Date
A-1 (ANS)	Marine Liquefied Petroleum Gas (LPG) Systems	July 2006
A-3	Galley Stoves—Corrected July 2010	July 2007
A-4	Fire Fighting Equipment	July 2008
A-6	Refrigeration and Air Conditioning Equipment	July 1999
A-7	Liquid and Solid Fueled Boat Heating Systems	July 2006
A-14	Gasoline and Propane Gas Detection Systems	July 2007
A-16	Electric Navigation Lights	July 2005
A-22	Marine Compressed Natural Gas (CNG) Systems	July 2006
A-23	Sound Signal Appliances (Corrected 07/05)	July 2004
A-24	Carbon Monoxide Detection Systems	July 2007
A-26 (ANS)	LPG and CNG Fueled Appliances	July 2006
A-27	Alternating Current (AC) Generator Sets	July 2004
A-28	Galvanic Isolators	July 2008
A-30	Cooking Appliances with Integral LPG Cylinders	July 2006

Project	Title	Date
A-31 (previously A-20/A-25)	Battery Chargers and Inverters	July 2010
A-33 (ANS)	Emergency Engine/Propulsion Cut-Off Device	July 2009
E-2	Cathodic Protection	July 2008
E-10	Storage Batteries	July 2006
E-11 (previously E-8/E-9)	AC & DC Electrical Systems on Boats	July 2008 (2009 technical amendment)
H-1	Field of Vision from the Helm Position	July 2010
H-2	Ventilation of Boats Using Gasoline	July 2008
H-3 (ANS)	Exterior Windows, Windshields, Hatches, Doors, Port Lights, and Glazing Materials	July 2008
H-4	Cockpit Drainage Systems	July 2008
H-5	Boat Load Capacity	July 2004
H-8	Buoyancy in the Event of Swamping	July 2004
H-22	Electric Bilge Pump Systems	July 2005
H-23	Installation of Potable Water Systems for Use on Boats	July 2008
H-24 (ANS)	Gasoline Fuel Systems	July 2010
H-25	Portable Gasoline Fuel Systems	July 2010
H-26	Powering of Boats	July 2007
H-27	Seacocks, Thru-Hull Fittings, and Drain Plugs	July 2008
H-28	Inflatable Boats	July 2010
H-29	Canoes and Kayaks	July 2007
H-30	Hydraulic Systems	July 2001
H-31	Seat Structures—Corrected July 2010	July 2007
H-32 (ANS)	Ventilation of Boats Using Diesel Fuel	July 2008
H-33 (ANS)	Diesel Fuel Systems	July 2009
H-35	Powering and Load Capacity of Pontoon Boats	July 2005
H-37	Jet Boats–Light Weight	July 2006
H-40 (ANS)	Anchoring, Mooring, and Strong Points	July 2008
H-41 (ANS)	Reboarding Means, Ladders, Handholds, Rails, and Lifelines	July 2009

Project	Title	Date
P-1 (ANS)	Installation of Exhaust Systems for Propulsion and Auxiliary Engines—Corrected July 2010	July 2009
P-4	Marine Inboard Engines and Transmissions	July 2004
P-6 (ANS)	Propeller Shafting Systems	July 2010
P-14	Mechanical Propulsion Control Systems	July 2010
P-17	Mechanical Steering Systems	July 2008
P-18 (ANS)	Cable Over Pulley Steering Systems for Outboard Engines	July 2008
P-21	Manual Hydraulic Steering Systems	July 2003
P-22	Steering Wheels	July 2008
P-23	Steering and Propulsion Controls for Jet Boats	July 2001
P-24	Electric/Electronic Propulsion Control Systems—Corrected July 2010	July 2007
P-27	Electric/Electronic Steering Control Systems	July 2007

Industry Conformity Standards

Project	Title	Date
S-7 (ANS)	Boat Capacity Labels	July 2010
S-8 (ANS)	Boat Measurement and Weight	July 2010
S-12	Outboard Motor Transom and Motor Well Dimensions	July 2002
S-30	Outboard Engine and Related Equipment Weights (Corrected 2006)	July 2005

Technical Information Reports

Project	Title	Date
T-1 (ANS)	Aluminum Applications for Boats and Yachts	July 2010
T-5	Safety Signs and Labels	July 2002
T-10	Hull Identification Number (HIN)	July 2005
T-17	Compass Installation	July 2000
T-19	Fabrication Equipment, Procedures, and Materials Quality Control	June 11, 1990
T-24	Owner/Operator's Manuals	July 2002
TA-27	Batteries and Battery Chargers	July 2001

Project	Title	Date
TE-4 (previously E-4)	Lightning Protection	July 2006
TE-30	Electrical Propulsion Systems	July 2009
TH-22	Educational Information about Carbon Monoxide	July 2008
TH-23	Design, Construction, and Testing of Boats in Consideration of Carbon Monoxide	July 2004
TY-28	Boat Lifting and Storage	July 1998

NATIONAL FIRE PROTECTION ASSOCIATION

While going through the files in the office of a naval architect—it had to have been 1935—I came across a small booklet called NFPA 302, which offered safety advice for pleasure craft. Today the booklet has grown in size and scope; basically about fire prevention, it is called *Fire Protection Standards for Pleasure and Commercial Craft up to 300 Gross Tons.* Information includes lightning protection, engine and exhaust systems, electrical, cooking, and auxiliary appliances including CNG and LPG fuels, and fire protection equipment. The standards parallel those of the ABYC. For more information, contact the National Fire Protection Association.

FEDERAL SAFE BOATING REGULATIONS

Poor design, construction, and equipment installations that resulted in explosions, fire, and loss of life have inevitably led to the enactment of laws in the United States governing gasoline fuel systems, electrical systems in boats with gasoline-fueled engines, safe loading and safe powering, and level flotation in case of swamping. The American Boat and Yacht Council, under contract to the U.S. Coast Guard, prepared "compliance guidelines" to ease the burden of boatbuilders—either manufacturers or backyard builders—to determine whether their product will meet the regulations. In my opinion, the standards required by law are the same as the practices recommended by the ABYC.

Copies of the *Boatbuilder's Handbook* may be obtained from the U.S. Coast Guard Office of Boating Safety (http://www.uscgboating.org/regulations/boatbuilder_s_handbook/downloads.aspx).

Part 1—Regulations and Other Information
Part 2—Safety Circulars #64 and an excerpt from #83
Part 3—Consumer Fact Sheets

Compliance Guidelines

Subpart I—Electrical Systems Applies to all inboard or inboard/outboard gasoline-powered boats and boats that have gasoline auxiliary engines such as generators.

Subpart J—Fuel Systems Applies to all boats powered with gasoline engines (except outboard engines); all boats with gasoline auxiliary engines, such as generators; and gasoline fuel tanks that are permanently installed in inboard and inboard/outboard boats.

Subpart K—Ventilation

Subpart C—Safe Loading and Subpart B—Display of Capacity Information

Subpart F, Subpart G, and Subpart H—Flotation Requirements Applies to monohull boats less than 20 feet in length. It does not apply to sailboats, canoes, kayaks, or inflatable boats.

Safety Standards for Backyard Boat Builders (also available online) is a boon to the home builder and includes directions on how to work up the safe loading calculations for boats under 20 feet long to which the law applies. In addition, it tells how to go about attaching a "capacity label" and a "certification label" to the hull, and how to obtain a hull identification number (HIN) for your boat. The regulation for the HIN spells out how you can establish the number yourself (each letter and number in the HIN means something), and the height of the figures and exactly where to cut them into the hull. The HIN must not be removable, and it identifies builder and date, all of which is helpful in case of theft of the boat. At the last building yard I was employed by, I took it upon myself to engrave the HIN with a Dremel tool; a Coast Guard representative visited several times a year to check our compliance.

It is hoped that all these things will not discourage a would-be backyard builder; a careful study of the safety regulations will show that their intent is good.

Many government regulations seem to consist of endless pages of solid text, making them difficult to read. Not so the guidelines put out by the Coast Guard. These clearly illustrate with simple line drawings what is acceptable and what is prohibited. The Coast Guard's booklet *Federal Requirements for Recreational Boats* (www.uscgboating.org/regulations/federal_regulations.aspx) is worth acquiring. Should you have further questions, you can contact the nearest Coast Guard station or a local Coast Guard auxiliary. The latter usually will give you a courtesy inspection by appointment for compliance with the regulations.

It goes without saying that a boatowner in the United States must have life-saving and other equipment aboard, as specified in the *Federal Requirements* booklet. (Vessels built to carry passengers for hire are subject to another set of regulations.) Besides fire extinguishers of approved type and number, there must be personal flotation devices (PFDs), usually called life jackets or cushions, for each adult and child on board (even aboard canoes and kayaks). With certain exceptions, craft over 16 feet in length must also carry flares.

Sailors on seagoing sailboats most often, and especially at night when the seas are up, wear a harness that can be snapped on a side deck lifeline or onto a specially rigged lifeline near the centerline of the deck so it can be reached from either side.

I was working in a West Coast yard just before the Los Angeles-to-Honolulu race, the Transpac, one year. When entrants checked the race circular they found a new requirement to carry a man-overboard pole— a pole of a certain length with ballast at the bottom, flotation to more or less keep the pole upright, and a flag at the top. No store in the area stocked these, so for a few weeks we had a windfall.

SHOWER STALL DOORS AND ESCAPE LADDERS

It occurred to me one day years ago that we were building expensive yachts for well-to-do people, and that, while becoming well-to-do, most of these people had also become elderly. While considering what special safety precautions we could take to help them continue to enjoy their boats, I thought about our shower/bath facilities. When simple curtains gave way to doors, the shop always hinged the doors to swing inward, because that made it easier to keep the water in the stall. However, shower spaces in yachts tend to be minimal in size, so if an occupant should faint, the inward-swinging door would make it very difficult to reach him to provide aid. So I made a rule: no more inward-swinging doors. I mentioned this to Lysle Gray of the ABYC, and he pointed out that about a third of the entrance doors to the toilet rooms he had checked also swung inward, presenting the same problem if the space is small. He also noted that most builders provide escape hatches (emergency exits from below deck) that many people are unable to negotiate without a ladder. Escape ladders should be kept handy for such hatches.

PRODUCT TESTING

A step for safety beyond mere words has also been taken. Manufacturers of stock boats can now have their products tested for compliance with American Boat and Yacht Council standards and so labeled when the product meets the requirements.

SHOP SAFETY

If you are as old as I am and worked in wooden boatbuilding in what is justly called the good old days, you probably did not give much thought to safety, except perhaps fire protection. Circular saw blade guards were probably thrown away because they are a nuisance. (Nowadays they are kept handy for shop safety inspections.) The identifying mark of an old hand was the number of missing fingers. Otherwise I can't recall anything that was particularly dangerous, but I remember when, as a helper, I was assigned to the yard mill, which was in a separate building. There was no dust-collection system, so when I was on the receiving end of the thickness planer the shavings shot up in the air and came down all over me. When I undressed the night of my first day in the mill, my mother informed me that, henceforth, I was to shed my clothes in the bathroom, where it was easier to sweep up the mahogany and oak shavings. When a hull was finished in that shop, the jointers took over, along with the painters. Back then the coatings were oil-based paints, varnish, and "copper" bottom paints, all very simple compared with today's fancy coatings, which are applied by workers dressed as for a trip into space. Once I worked a half day helping bend steamed frames, and wore the cotton gloves loaned to me by the framing leader for the duration of the operation. Otherwise gloves were not worn.

Now, eighty years later, there are enough health hazards in boatbuilding to drive one into office work. Modern construction materials appear to be hazardous to skin, lungs, vision, and what have you. Even wood dust (particularly Western red cedar, and to a lesser degree mahogany and teak) from sawing and sanding has been declared harmful if inhaled. It is difficult to avoid the dust, so you must protect your lungs with an appropriate mask or respirator. (See "Personal Protection," below.) Dust-collecting vacuums are standard equipment in safety-conscious boatbuilding shops.

The strong odor from polyester resin used when laminating or sheathing with synthetic fabrics is caused by the presence of styrene. The proportion of styrene in the resin is now limited by the Occupational Safety and Health Administration (OSHA), because styrene has been found to cause cancer in animals. Acetone, extensively used for cleaning in shops doing fiberglass laminating or repairs, has also been found hazardous to health, yet some workers (and I have seen this) use acetone to clean their skin—a practice that is bad indeed.

Dust-collecting vacuums assist in keeping noxious fumes out of the shop airspace.

The list of harmful liquids is a long one and includes solvents of all kinds, resins (especially epoxy resins), wood preservatives, paint and paint strippers, and on and on. One type of dust that may not appear harmful to you, but is, is dust from pressure-treated wood. I keep all suspect liquids outside my garage workshop, principally because of fire hazard, and I do no mixing indoors. One boatbuilder I know who usually has two or more fiberglass sailboats under way in a shop that reeks of styrene built an unattached cement block outbuilding for all his polyester layup of hulls, decks, and parts, and to store dangerous materials. The odor of the main shop improved at once. Plenty of ventilation is a must, and a dust-collection system is just as necessary. I have noted an increasing number of dust-collection-system tubes and fittings in the catalogs of woodworking tool suppliers, making it a bit simpler to cope with the problem.

An item related more to shop health than personal health is the care of electrical cords. A good practice followed in one shop where I worked was to disconnect at the end of each day the many electrical extension cords to the tools in the boats under construction and to any tools in the shop that were not hard-wired.

Worthwhile safety articles have been published over the years in *WoodenBoat* magazine, which has back issues available online. These include "Boatyard Hazards" by Peter Spectre and "Gearing Up for Safety" by Mary Lou Dietrich, both in *WB*#79, November/December 1987; and "Boatbuilders, Beware" by Paul Lazarus, in *WB* #93, March/April 1990. The articles discuss in depth the chemicals everyone should guard against (I never knew there were so many different kinds of gloves for protection of the hands). Other recent articles concerning safety precautions include boatyard chemicals (#200), fire safety (#178), hearing protection (#117), and router use (#207).

PERSONAL PROTECTION

A first-aid kit is basic equipment in the shop to take care of the usual minor injuries such as wood or metal splinters and cut fingers. (Recently, for the first time, I noticed one of these kits prominently displayed by one of the larger building supply/home improvements stores.) Most injuries, though, can be prevented by taking the proper precautions. When grinding or using machines that spray wood particles, protect your eyes by wearing shatter-proof goggles or a full face shield, both of which can be worn over prescription glasses. Hand protection is needed mostly to guard against splinters when handling rough lumber and to prevent contact with solvents, epoxies, and other chemicals, and you can assume most chemicals are hazardous. Marine supply houses carry coverall suits made of paper or of Tyvek, a lightweight, tough fabric that resists tearing and is especially suited to protecting spray-gun operators. Some also carry Tyvek sleeves or gauntlets. These should be considered when working with epoxy resins, as there should be no contact between resin and skin.

Protection against inhaling fumes or dust is made possible by wearing appropriate masks, filters, or respirators—and the distinctions are important.

There are more choices. If your marine supply store does not have what you need, try a store specializing in automotive finishes.

There has also been an ever-increasing amount of discussion in the boating trade papers about hearing protection in the shop. Those working in the vicinity of noisy machines should be equipped with hearing protectors.

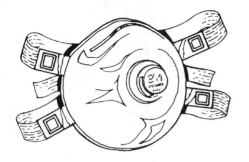

FIGURE 22-01

Two 3M-brand respirators. *Left*: #8540 Easi-Air Spray Paint Respirator.
Right: #9913 Dust/Mist Respirator.

Inasmuch as I have been living for a good number of years with what I'll call for want of a better description a background of escaping steam, I finally acquired a set of earphone-type protectors. Now I don them every time my circular saws and thickness planer are in operation, and I don't miss the screams of those machines one bit.

VACUUM BAGGING

USING THE ATMOSPHERE TO CLAMP WOOD

by J. R. Watson, illustrations by Robert LaPointe

I HAVE A FRIEND WHO HAS BEEN BOATING ALL HIS LIFE, and he says that the three greatest recent innovations of our field are solar panels, epoxy resin, and vacuum bagging. All three harness a readily available force: solar captures electromagnetic energy generated by the sun; epoxy utilizes the electrical attraction of molecules; and vacuum bagging uses gravity—and the atmospheric pressure it causes—to our advantage.

For holding things in place, gravity is often our friend. Flat surfaces can be held together with weights: A 27-lb. concrete block placed on its end exerts 1.3 lbs. per square inch (psi)—sufficient to press mating parts together while a contact or low-pressure adhesive cures. Such an arrangement is viable as long as the clamped parts are thick enough to distribute the force. But if a greater area is to be thus clamped, you have to haul a lot of blocks, and your work surface had better be strong enough to support all the weight.

Gravity is also often our foe. When a surface is inclined, vertical, or overhead, it is not as useful. Other forces, supplied by clamps, fastenings, and plops of various configurations, must be used. Material thickness controls the number of clamps needed. For example, suppose you are fastening ¼"-thick stock with a C-clamp with a small footprint (typically ½" diameter) and exerting a maximum force of about 350 lbs. Only those areas directly under the pad or a short distance from it will have sufficient pressure to make contact between the gluing surfaces; farther away, the surfaces might not have any pressure at all, or may even be forced apart. So, larger pads must be inserted to distribute the clamping force.

With thin stock, we often use staples—lots of them. They take a long time to remove, and they leave holes. Other methods of exerting pressure include the screw, bolt, or spring clamps, tie wraps, wire, and nails. All exert only localized pressure and not much of it. Often, thin wood veneers bonded to low-density cores are impossible to hold in place with mechanical clamps or fastenings, and placement of weights on such surfaces may be impossible due to surface curvature or overhead orientations. At some point in time, someone must have said, "If only there were a way to apply even, firm pressure . . . ." And, as a result, somewhere, at some time someone conceived the use of vacuum to do that.

416

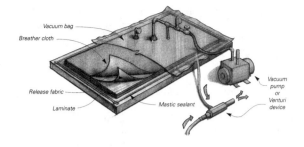

1. Vacuum pumps and materials

Vacuum can be generated by mechanical pumps or venturi devices. Release fabric rests directly on the wooden laminate and prevents the breather cloth from bonding to the wood. Breather cloth covers the release fabric and allows air to be drawn from all parts of the envelope. The vacuum bag rests atop the breather cloth and forms half the airtight envelopes. Mastic sealant provides an airtight seal at the perimeter of the mold. The plumbing system provides passage and control of the vacuum from either a pump or a venturi device to the envelope.

WHAT IS VACUUM BAGGING?

The air we breathe is a fluid, just as water is. The biggest difference is its density. A cubic foot of fresh water weighs 62.2 lbs. per cu. ft., while air weighs .004 lb. per cub ft. Imagine a diver descending just 30′ beneath the surface, and one can observe the effect of pressure. A foam wetsuit will compress; its thickness will be decreased in all directions about his body. At 30′, one experiences almost 15 psi of pressure. Air exerts pressure in the same manner, but less of it. We're located pretty deep in the atmosphere—about 55 miles. At the Earth's surface, the weight of the air is equivalent to that of water 34′ deep. As a result we experience about 15 psi of pressure.

We capture this force with a vacuum bag, and use it as a tool to exert pressure on components so they can be held in place until an adhesive takes over. What is especially beneficial is that pressure is exerted in all directions—even overhead. The vacuum bagging system is simple; its basic parts are an airtight clamping envelope and a method for removing air from that envelope until the adhesive cures.

VACUUM PUMPS

The heart of a vacuum system is the vacuum pump. Powered vacuum pumps are mechanically similar to air compressors, but work in reverse so that air is drawn from the closed system and exhausted to the atmosphere. Vacuum pumps are designated by their vacuum pressure potential or "Hg maximum" (Hg is the chemical symbol for mercury), their capacity in cubic feet per minute (CFM), and the horsepower required to drive the pump.

The Hg maximum level is the maximum vacuum (measured in inches of mercury) recommended for the pump. This translates to the maximum amount of clamping pressure that can be generated. Two inches of mercury (2" Hg) equals about 1 lb. per square inch (1 psi) of air pressure. (Remember that one atmosphere equals 29.92" Hg, which equals 14.7 psi.) If you are vacuum bagging a 1 sq. ft. laminate, a 20" Hg vacuum will yield 10 psi clamping pressure or a total of 1,440 lbs. of clamping force over the entire laminate. If you are laminating a 4′ × 8′ panel, the same 20" Hg (10 psi) will yield over 46,000 lbs. of clamping force spread evenly over the entire panel.

The capacity, or rate at which a pump can remove air (rated in cubic feet per minute or cfm), is also an important consideration in the selection of a pump. If the vacuum bagging system (the mold, bag, plumbing, and all scams and joints) were absolutely airtight, any size pump should be able to eventually pull its rated Hg maximum vacuum regardless of the size of the system. However, creating a perfectly airtight vacuum bagging system is nearly impossible, especially as the system gets larger or more complex. The greater the cfm rating, the closer the pump can come to reaching its Hg maximum and maintaining an adequate clamping force against the cumulative leaks in the system. A vacuum pump with a high cfm rating will also achieve an effective clamping force more quickly. This is an important consideration if the working life of the adhesive is limited.

The horsepower rating of the pump motor is an indication of how efficient the pump is and is not in itself an indication of how well a pump is suited to vacuum bagging. When selecting a pump, use the "Hg maximum" and cfm ratings as guides, rather than horsepower. Smaller pumps designed for specific applications may trade off either vacuum rating or air capacity to suit a particular job. Generally, to get higher "Hg maximum" and cfm ratings, more horsepower is necessary. Pump motors that are useful for moderate boatyard vacuum bagging may range from ½ hp to 2 hp; pump motors for larger production operations may be as big as 5 hp or 10 hp.

The size and shape of the mold and type and quantity of the material being laminated will determine the minimum pump requirements. If you are laminating flat panels consisting of a few layers of glass or flat veneers, 5" or 6" Hg (2.5–3 psi) will provide enough clamping pressure for a good bond between all of the layers. If the area of the panel is limited to a few square feet, a 1 or 2 cfm pump will be adequate to overcome the system leakage and maintain that clamping pressure. As the panel area increases, the cfm requirements increase proportionately. A displacement of 3.5 cfm may be adequate for up to a 14' square panel; for larger jobs, a pump with a capacity of 10 cfm may be required. Poor seals in the plumbing system or envelope, or material that allows air leakage, will require a larger-capacity pump to maintain a satisfactory vacuum. The more airtight the system, the smaller the pump you'll need.

A higher "Hg maximum"-rated pump will be required if you need more clamping pressure to force laminations to conform to a complex mold shape. Curved or compound mold shapes and/or laminations of many layers of stiff veneers or core materials may require at least a 20–28" Hg vacuum to provide adequate clamping force. Again, if the panel size is limited to a few square feet, a 1 or 2 cfm pump with a high "Hg rating" will work if the envelope is airtight. However, a large panel or hull may take a minimum of a 10 cfm pump to reach and maintain enough clamping force to press all of the laminate layers into the mold shape and produce glue lines of consistent thickness throughout the laminate. Generally, the best pump for a specific vacuum bagging operation will have the largest air-moving capacity for the vacuum/clamping pressure required while operating at a reasonable horsepower.

I learned about vacuum pump types the hard way. In one of my first attempts I borrowed my wife's new upright sweeper. It performed admirably until it seized up in a cloud of smoke and ozone. A vacuum sweeper's motor relies on air passing over it for cooling. With a great seal on my airtight mold, the cooling system quickly failed. So, a word to the wise; use a bonafide vacuum pump.

Vacuum pump types include piston, rotary-vane, turbine, diaphragm, and venturi. They may be either a positive or a nondisplacement type. Positive-displacement vacuum pumps may be oil-lubricated or oil-less. Oil-lubricated pumps can pull a higher vacuum and are more efficient and longer-lasting than oil-less pumps. Oil-less pumps, however, are cleaner, require less monitoring and maintenance, and easily generate vacuums in a range useful for vacuum bagging. Of the several types, the reciprocating piston and rotary-vane pumps are most common. Piston pumps are able to generate higher vacuums than rotary-vane pumps, but they vibrate and generate higher noise levels. Rotary-vane pumps may pull less vacuum than piston pumps, but they offer several advantages: They are able to move more air for a given vacuum rating. In other words, they can remove air from the system more quickly and can tolerate more leaks in the system while maintaining a useful vacuum level. In addition, rotary-vane pumps are generally more compact, run more smoothly, require less power, and cost less to buy.

Non-positive-displacement vacuum pumps have high cfm ratings, but generally operate at vacuums that are insufficient for most vacuum bagging. A vacuum cleaner, like the new one I had to purchase for my wife, is an example of a non-positive-displacement or turbine-type pump.

Air-operated vacuum generators are simple, low-cost venturi devices that generate a vacuum by using airflow supplied by standard air compressors. Their portability and relatively low cost, along with the availability of compressors in many shops and homes, make them ideal for small vacuum bagging projects. Single-stage generators have a high vacuum rating but move a low volume of air, limiting the size of the vacuum bagging operation. Larger two-stage units are comparable to mechanical pumps for most vacuum bagging operations, but require a proportionately large compressor to run them.

A dry run is a good idea the first time a new pump is employed. Keep in mind that the pump should be able to hold a vacuum continuously until the adhesive reaches an effective cure, which may take as long as 12 hours.

VACUUM BAGGING MATERIALS

A variety of other materials is needed to complete the vacuum system and facilitate the laminating process.

Release fabric is a smooth woven fabric that will not bond to epoxy. It is used to separate the breather (see below) and the laminate. Excess epoxy can wick through the release fabric and be peeled off the laminate after the laminate cures. It will leave an even, textured surface that, in most cases, can be bonded to without additional preparation. You want a release fabric that you can blow air through; too tight a weave can result in air-entrapment problems. Others can transfer a contaminate to the substrate and jeopardize subsequent adhesion. When removing release fabric, pull as close to 180 degrees as possible. Apply steady, firm pressure. Don't jerk, but pull evenly.

Breather (bleeder) cloth allows air from all parts of the envelope to be drawn to a port or manifold by providing a slight air space between the bag and the laminate. Polyester blanket (baby blanket) works well; so does bubble-type swimming pool cover material, or even burlap.

The vacuum bag, in most cases, forms half of the air-tight envelope around the laminate. If you plan to use a vacuum of less than 5 psi (10 Hg) at room temperatures, 6-mil polyethylene plastic can be used for the bag. Clear plastic is preferable to an opaque material to allow easy inspection of the laminate as it cures. For high-pressure applications, specially manufactured vacuum bag material should be used. A wrinkled-type film may eliminate the need for breather cloth. Vacuum bag material may be of heat-stabilized nylon film that can stretch; it is available at 60" wide. For wider projects it can be joined together with mastic sealant.

Mastic sealant is used to provide a continuous airtight seal between the bag and the perimeter of the mold. The mastic may also be used to seal the point where the manifold enters the bag; to create pleats; and to repair leaks in the bag or plumbing. Typical mastic sealant is tan or yellow in color and feels like used bubblegum. It comes in tape form measuring ⅛"–½"on a roll with a paper separator. The unique thing about this material is that it adheres only to smooth surfaces such as glass or plastic and to itself—and it adheres tenaciously.

Other methods of sealing the bag exist. Mosquito screen molding, for example, is generally used with permanent molds. Another approach is to use a soft material (like surgical tubing or door gasket) attached to a wooden frame that can be spring clamped down to create a seal (the bag itself can be attached to this frame as well).

THE PLUMBING SYSTEM

The plumbing system provides an airtight passage from the vacuum envelope to the vacuum pump, allowing the pump to pull a vacuum as it removes air from the envelope. A basic system consists of flexible hose or rigid pipe, a trap, and a port that connects the pipe to the envelope. A more versatile system includes a control valve and a vacuum throttle valve that allow you to control the vacuum at the envelope. A system is often split to provide several ports on large laminations or may include some type of manifold within the envelope to help channel air to a single port. A variety of pipe or tubing can be used for plumbing so long as it is airtight and resists collapsing under vacuum.

Vacuum hose is designed specifically for vacuum bagging and autoclave laminating. It is available, along with fittings, pumps, and other vacuum bagging materials, from manufacturers specializing in vacuum bagging equipment. Because of its high cost, this type of plumbing system is most appropriate for large-scale or production laminating operations. Other types of wire-reinforced hose may work, but they should be rated for crush resistance or tested under vacuum for the appropriate length of (cure) time. Semirigid plastic tubing, with adequate wall thickness, can be used for a plumbing system, but it is often awkward to handle.

Rigid ¾" PVC or CPVC pipe, elbows, T's, and valves work well. They are low-cost and available at most local hardware or plumbing supply stores. The pieces do not need to be cemented (the vacuum holds them together) and can be arranged to suit any configuration. This type of plumbing system, because of its low cost and versatility, is ideal for small-scale or occasional laminating operations.

A **vacuum port** connects the exhaust tubing to the vacuum bag. It can be designed specifically for the purpose or built from commonly available materials. One of the simplest ports is a hollow suction cup that sits over a small slit in the vacuum bag. Cups designed for use with car-top carriers can be easily adapted by drilling a hole through the center of the cup to accept the plumbing. If the port is placed directly over the laminate, place several layers of breather material over this area to prevent the port from making a permanent impression in the laminate.

A **control valve** should be incorporated into the vacuum line to allow you to control airflow at the vacuum bag. The control valve affects the rate of air removal, but not the ultimate vacuum. A second valve, the **vacuum throttle valve,** can be placed between the control valve and the vacuum bag. This valve, incorporated with a T fitting, acts as an adjustable leak in the system to control the vacuum bag pressure. For convenience, valves should be placed close to the bag.

A **trap** should be incorporated in the line as close as possible to the vacuum bag. The trap collects any excess adhesive that gets sucked into the line before it reaches the valves or pump, and it prevents a buildup of adhesive in the line. A trap can easily be built with a small section of pipe, a T, and an end cap.

A **vacuum gauge** is necessary to monitor the vacuum level during the cure time. Most gauges read in inches of mercury from zero (one atmosphere) to 30 (inches Hg below one atmosphere). The reading of negative pressure inside the bag equals the net pressure of the atmosphere pressing on the outside of the bag. To approximate this reading in pounds per square inch, simply divide the reading by two. A vacuum gauge, available at most automotive stores, can be modified by threading a hollow suction cup (similar to the port) to the base. A 1½" PVC pipe cap, with a hole drilled and tapped to match the gauge, will also work. The open end of the cap is sealed to the vacuum bag with mastic over a small slit as with the vacuum port.

A **manifold** can be used in some situations to assist in air removal from the vacuum bag. It can be a thicker section of breather material or other material that provides a channel for air movement under the vacuum bag to a port. I used a 1" PVC pipe with holes drilled along its length to vacuum bag a 39' wing mast (Figure 6, page 422).

HOW IS VACUUM BAGGING UTILIZED?

Imagine that you have to make a whole bunch of laminated bulkheads, bunk tops, and shelves. After cutting all the pieces to shape, they could be placed onto an airtight table and in one bonding application be assembled in a single operation. A flat, rigid mold is a useful tool (Figure 2).

Flat and rigid molds

If you are laminating into wet resin, you will replicate the degree of finish of your mold surface. In most cases, a smooth finished surface is the goal. So, when a local junk store had a deal on flawed 40" × 40" card table tops of safety glass with radiuses on the corners and edges—I found them to be perfect for an airtight, perfectly smooth rigid mold. Other materials that work well are plastic laminates such as Formica (select a gloss surface over textured or frosted), a smooth metal surface like sheet aluminum, or Mylar film like the back side of that used for drafting. With the exception of the Mylar, most mold surfaces have to be waxed with a release such as Megular's Mirror glaze No. 8 mold-release wax, TR-104 Hi Temp mold-release wax, or sprayed with Stoner #F.497.

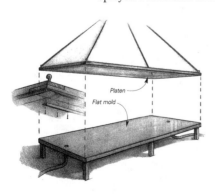

Platen
Flat mold

Curved and shaped surfaces

More complex molds can be built to establish about any desired shape, then sealed to become airtight. The laminations produced from these shapes can then be used-as-built, or further deflected to produce boat parts. This approach is best suited for long, narrow shapes such as those found on multihulls—although some monohull designs were developed for it.

2. Flat and rigid molds

Flat, rigid molds with flat, matched platens allow efficient lamination of bulkheads, berth flats, and shelves.

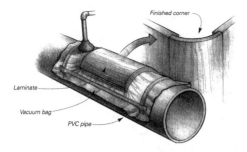

Finished corner

Laminate

Vacuum bag

PVC pipe

3. Curved and shaped molds

Molds made from PVC pipe can form corner laminations.

PVC pipe can be used as a mold to make round parts and corners (Figure 3). Of course, the mold could also be an actual hull. After a layer of planking (say strip planking) is laid and is made airtight, subsequent layers of thinner stock can be vacuum bagged to that surface until the desired hull thickness is achieved. Typically, one or two coats of epoxy are required to make a wooden surface sufficiently airtight. The impetus for such an approach would be optimum surface contact with the elimination of fastening holes, and overall labor savings. Several builders have used this technique to produce small cold-molded hulls (Figure 4), and Hodgdon Yachts employed it for planking the impressive 124' sloop *Antonisa* and 155' kerch *Scheherazade*. On large craft such as the Hodgdon boats, the hulls usually are divided into sections of reasonable size so the crew can apply the adhesive, the prefitted planking, and the vacuum bag before the epoxy kicks off.

Prefitting involves the spiling of individual veneers so their edges meet properly over the hull's curved surface. On smaller craft, such as a Tornado catamaran, both sides and two layers of veneer are laid up in one operation.

Flexible molds

A plastic laminate bonded to thin plywood or aluminum sheet will create a surface that is airtight and smooth (Figure 5). A seal can be made between this surface and the vacuum bag. The wet laminate is placed flat on the mold and a slight vacuum applied that is sufficient to hold the layers lightly together but still allow them to slide past one another. Then the mold may be bent into a curve (but not a compound one!) and held this way until the laminate cures and a curved panel is produced.

Free-form

This technique was used to produce a 39' wing mast of plywood and resin-impregnated honeycomb with stringer reinforcement (Figure 6).

The plywood skins and stringers were cut to length. Honeycomb panels were fitted to fill between the stringers. Adhesive was applied to all components. A ¾" PVC pipe with ¼"-diameter holes every 4" served to distribute the suction, and it was place the length of the mast laminate. A vacuum bag was placed to surround the wet laminate, and a light vacuum (2 or 3 lbs) was exerted to hold the components together but still allow the pieces to slide on one another, allowing further shaping. The unit was then placed into guides that aided in forming the mast section to the desired shape. Once the shape was established, greater vacuum was exerted until the adhesive cured.

Begging with a Shop-Vac

A low-pressure mold can be used, for example, to clamp a canoe deck or to bond decorative veneer onto a small item (Figure 7).

4 Hulls as molds

After a layer of planking is laid and made airtight, subsequent layers of thinner stock are vacuum bagged on that surface. (For some boats, the strip planking becomes part of the hull. For other projects, the strips remains on the molds.)

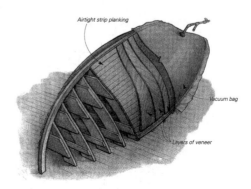

Airtight strip planking

Vacuum bag

Layers of veneer

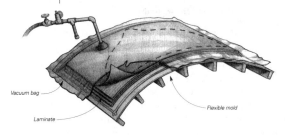

Vacuum bag

Laminate

Flexible mold

5. Flexible molds

After a wet laminate is placed flat on a flexible mold, that mold can be bent to a simple curved shape. The dashed outline of a curved transom is shown on this laminate.

The mold must be able to withstand a vacuum of 2 or 3 psi. I've found a particularly good bag for such an operation to be a "Space Saver" clothes storage bag fitted with a valve that allows a vacuum to be sealed indefinitely. The wet laminate is placed inside the bag along with soft, open cell foam and release fabric, and the bag is then closed with the plastic snap seal. A Shop-Vac hose is placed over the one-way valve attached to the bag and the air evacuated.

The foam, along with the laminate, squeezes together under the 3–5 psi of the typical Shop-Vac. The crushed foam stores energy and slowly relaxes as air leaks in, but pressure is still on the laminate. After 5–10 minutes the Shop-Vac is kicked on again (via an outlet switch timer), repeating the sequence until the adhesive is cured.

THINGS THAT CAN GO WRONG

The typical empty beer can is, actually, not empty at all. It just doesn't have any beer in it. Instead, it is filled with air, the air pressure within the can being equal to that outside it. An inflated balloon, on the other hand, is a nonpermeable bag filled with air that is at a pressure greater than atmospheric. If both the can and the balloon are placed in a vacuum bag and the air evacuated, what would happen and why it would happen are important concepts for successful vacuum bagging. The can would crush, but the balloon would survive and remain inflated (although it would be smaller than before).

Trapped voids

The reason for breather cloth is to promote equal evacuation of the air. If it were not present, the bag would seal itself against the laminate and you'd end up with a series of balloon-like bubbles. Thus, there would be no evenly distributed pressure to force the laminates together, and you would probably end up with no interlaminate adhesion.

Solid or nonporous sheet material, such as wood veneer, may need to be perforated to allow air and excess resin to escape. In a flat or concave mold, the laminates might seal themselves around their edges when vacuum is applied, trapping air and resin beneath them. Air entrapment is less of a problem in convex molds where the center portions of the laminates will contact the mold first and allow air and resin to bleed out around the edges as the vacuum increases.

Bridging

Narrow molds, deep molds, or molds with sharp inside corners can create a problem called bridging (Figure 8). Bridging occurs when any of the laminates or vacuum bagging materials are too short for the mold or too stiff to drape completely into a narrow part of the mold or into a sharp inside corner. The vacuum bag may be cut too short and will "bridge" across a narrow part of the mold when the vacuum is applied, or, a wood veneer may not bend enough to contact the inside of a small radius in a mold. The result of bridging is a void in the laminate.

There are several ways bridging can be avoided. Cut all of the laminate and vacuum bagging material large enough to drape into all parts of the mold. When plating laminate into the mold, push each layer right against the mold. Pound rigid wood veneer into tight inside corners with a padded block as the vacuum is applied. Place overlapping joints of the laminate and vacuum bag material (except for the vacuum bag itself) at the inside corner. This allows the ends of the material to slide into the corner as the vacuum is applied.

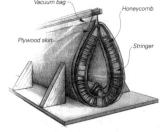

Vacuum bag

Honeycomb

Plywood skin

Stringer

6. Free-form

A wing mast can be preassembled and laminated free-form.

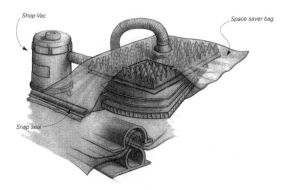

Shop-Vac

Space saver bag

Snap seal

7. Shop-Vac bagging

A low-pressure mold, employing a Shop-Vac as a vacuum source, can be used to clamp a canoe deck or to bond decorative veneer to small items.

When forming the vacuum bag and sealing it, introduce plenty of excess material with large pleats. More is better than too little.

Trapped mold

I have a friend who had a lovely cold-molded wooden dinghy hull and decided to use it as a vacuum-bagging mold. He sealed the boat's gunwale to a flat table. The laminates were applied to the mold, as were the various vacuum bagging materials, and the vacuum bag was then sealed to the table. What's wrong with this approach? Almost nothing, except that when a vacuum was drawn, the beautiful hull-cum-mold crushed like an empty beer can. Some holes drilled through the table, to allow air-pressure equalization, would have prevented this disaster. The only other approach would have been to make the mold able to withstand the immense pressures exerted.

Not airtight

I know of another project where particle board was used for a mold surface because it was cheap and available. As sealant wouldn't adhere to the particle board, mosquito screen molding was used to seal the bag. A tool was used to push the bead into the receiving channel. Great idea. But when a vacuum was pulled, nothing happened. The builder determined that his sealing approach was the culprit, yet a stethoscope revealed no audible leaks. The problem was actually the particle board; it allowed air to pass through it. The leak was so widespread that no sound was detectable. We simply coated the particle board with two coats of epoxy to make it airtight, and it then worked fine.

We learned an ancillary lesson; a stethoscope works great for locating minor leaks—those the size of a nail hole. Major holes, on the other hand, make no noise. If you're reusing your vacuum bag, which is a valid thing to do, mark all penetrations for manifold and gauges with a permanent marker so they can be scaled or reused (otherwise, these large holes would be difficult to locate via sound or sight). If a tear occurs, simply circle in with mastic and cover it with a piece of bag material.

Working time

A boatbuilding company I know began its first vacuum bagging job, which involved a lot of area and complicated assembly. It was thought out in great detail, but the excitement got out of hand, and before they knew it people were mixing glue and spreading it on the pieces. Some were using faster-curing epoxy than others; dirt got into the sealant compromising the seal, and by the time the vacuum was applied, parts of the laminate were already curing and had to be scrapped.

When beginning vacuum bagging, start small. Keep track of time. The time spanning the moment the first person mixes epoxy to the time when the vacuum has been applied must be kept in mind. Always lean toward a slower-curing hardener. Work clean. When you are committed to a big job, do a dry run.

Used with care, the techniques I have described will produce clean, light, stiff, fatigue-resistant hulls and components.

8. Bridging

A vacuum bag can "bridge" across a corner or narrow part of a mold (left) and produce a void in the laminate. Introducing excess bag material with large pleats (right) will solve the problem.

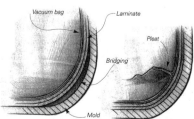

Vacuum bag — *Laminate*

Pleat

Bridging

Mold

SHARPENING TOOLS

Sharp hand and power tools are essential to happy woodworking, whether you're building a boat or anything else. I never thought I had the time to sharpen power tools or even handsaws and am indeed fortunate to have found a really competent mechanic for this work. He has been at his trade for over two decades and takes pride in his work.

Many, many years ago I assisted a boat carpenter on weekends. One time I watched as he set up a long, wide mahogany board, marked where he wanted to cut, picked up his handsaw, made three or four strokes, put down the saw, and set the plank back in the rack. Then he set up his rig for filing handsaw teeth by hand and proceeded to tune up his saw before returning to the project. I had nothing but admiration for this craftsman.

The pages of tool catalogs offer numerous choices of oilstones and waterstones. (See Sources for names and addresses.) I think the Japanese waterstones are superior to the others, and I have tried most kinds, starting with a Carborundum oilstone too many years ago to remember. Japanese waterstones are meant to be used wet, so they are best kept submerged at all times.

Because honing does not use its entire surface, the stone eventually becomes hollow, and the Japanese waterstone is the easiest kind to flatten. This can be done by rubbing two stones together, checking flatness with the base of a try square. Patience is required. Other types of stones are just about hopeless when hollowed— they can be used to hone narrow edges, but are no good for tools like plane irons and chisels.

In catalogs offering honing stones and slips (these are used to hone and deburr gouges and edges with complex shapes), you will also find a large selection of honing guides.

The chances are that brand-new chisels and plane irons have not been fully honed (sharpened), so this must be done before use. Then, as a tool is used, rehoning is usually sufficient to bring the edge up to par unless it has been allowed to become really dull or has been nicked. When this happens it is time to resort to a power grinder. There are two options: one, to use a typical bench grinder, preferably slow speed, which produces a hollow surface on the bevel of a chisel or plane iron and thus reduces the amount of honing time; or two, to use one of the Japanese slow-speed water-cooled machines, which grind on the side of a horizontal abrasive wheel. The latter machines are expensive.

The first sharpening after grinding does away with the roughness and forms a slight wire edge on the back side of the blade. This wire edge, which is easily felt, must be removed by rubbing the flat side of the plane iron or chisel back and forth on the stone. Then honing proceeds as always: Place the beveled edge *flat* on the near end of the stone and push it away from you while carefully holding the bevel angle. Don't rock the tool! Do all the honing on the push stroke and keep the face of the stone *wet*. Looking at a honed edge head-on, you should see no flats along the edge. When there are none, the edge is sharp.

Not only are flat honing stones best, but so are flat plane bottoms, or soles if you prefer. As purchased they are not always perfect; they should be flattened either with a honing stone or by rubbing the plane on a sheet of very fine emery cloth placed on a perfectly flat surface, say a bench saw table. Once more, patience is a must, and don't leave the plane iron in place while flattening the bottom.

There are a number of books about tool sharpening in the tool catalogs, but I suggest for starters you add just one to your library: *Sharpening Basics,* by Patrick Spielman. If this whets your appetite, another excellent book, which consists of twenty-nine articles written by hands-on craftsmen, is *Fine Woodworking on Planes and Chisels.* (See "Recommended Reading" for more information.)

SOURCES

BOATBUILDING PLANS, PATTERNS, AND HULL KITS

There are many more sources for plans, patterns, and kits than those in the following list. Names and addresses can be found in advertisements in the periodicals listed in "Recommended Reading."

Adirondack Museum, Blue Mountain Lake, NY 12812. Plans for the popular Rushton 11' "Wee Lassie" canoe, three other Rushton small craft, a 15'9" Lake George rowing boat, and the 17'9" St. Lawrence skiff "Annie." http://www .adkmuseum.org/

Aladdin Products, Inc., d/b/a Monfort Associates, 50 Haskell Road, Westport, ME 04578. Plans and construction kits for unique ultralightweight small rowing and sailing hulls 8 to 18 feet long, to be built by the Geodesic Airolite method. Kits include all unique materials, such as Kevlar, adhesives, and Dacron fabrics. Design portfolio available. http://gaboats.com/

Atkin & Company, Box 3005A, Noroton, CT 06820. Catalog of 300 small-craft designs of every description, produced by the well-known Bill Atkin and his son John. http://www .atkinboatplans.com/

Bateau, 1360 SW Old Dixie, Ste 103, Vero Beach, FL 32962. Small boats, sailboats, powerboats, and houseboats. http://www.bateau.com/

Brewer Yacht Designs, Ltd., 1825 Evergreen Drive, Agassiz, BC Canada V0M 1A3. Descriptive list of over 80 designs, data sheets, and sail and arrangements plans for catboats, sloops, ketches, cutters, schooners, yawls, cruisers, trawlers, and powerboats from 18 to 68 feet. http://www .tedbrewer.com/

Brooks Boats Designs, 831 Reach Road, West Brooklin, ME 04616. Plans for the Somes Sound 12½ and many more. http://www .brooksboatsdesigns@gmail.com

Cape Fear Museum, 814 Market Street, Wilmington, NC 28401. Plans for popular 18', 20', or 22' Simmons outboard-powered skiffs. www.capefearmuseum.com/ or http://www .simmonsseaskiff.com/

Cutts & Case, P.O. Box 9, Oxford, MD 21654. Cutts offers a book explaining in detail his patented method for building a smooth, lightweight double-planked hull. http://www.cuttsandcase. com/

Devlin Designing Boat Builders, 2424 Gravelly Beach Loop NW, Olympia, WA 98502. Catalog includes plans for 75 simple boats, from a 7'6" dinghy to a 40' schooner, a duck boat, and classic power cruisers. http://www.devlinboat.com/

Duck Trap Woodworking (Walter J. Simmons), P.O. Box 88, Lincolnville Beach, ME 04849. Plans for traditional wooden small craft, such as canoes, wherries, dinghies, tenders, skiffs, and rowboats, all of proven ability; also plans for making oars. http://www.duck-trap.com/

Glen-L.com, 9152 Rosecrans, Bellflower, CA 90706. Boat plans, patterns, and kits for the amateur boatbuilder; 300 plans available. http:// www.glen-l.com/ or http://www.boatdesigns .com/

Hankinson Associates. Designs by Ken Hankinson are now available exclusively through Glen-L. com. Includes the Hankinson Barrelback, power cats, tugs, runabouts, drift boats, cuddies, cruisers, sailboats, sport boats, and others. http://www.boatdesigns.com/

D. N. Hylan Boatbuilders. 53 Benjamin River Drive, Brooklin, ME 04616. Stock plans for *Siri*, Herreshoff's *Coquina*, *Beach Pea*, and several powerboats. http://www.dhylanboats.com/

Mystic Seaport Museum, 50 Greenmanville Avenue, Mystic, CT 06355. Archive of over 100,000 historic ship plans. http://library. mysticseaport.org/collections/spwatercraft .cfm/

The Newfound Woodworks, Inc., 67 Danforth Brook Road, Bristol, NH 03222. Canoe, kayak, and rowing boat kits and plans. http://www .newfound.com/

Northwoods Canoe Company, 336 Range Road, Atkinson, ME 04426. Canoe plans. http://www .wooden-canoes.com/index.htm

Norwalk Island Sharpies, P.O. Box 843, Mt. Barker, South Australia 5251. Plans for shallow-draft beach cruisers 18 to 43 feet long. Website describes the six models. http://www.nisboats .com/

Oughtred, Iain, Struan Cottage, Bernisdale, Isle of Skye IV51 9NS, Scotland. Profusely and beautifully illustrated plans for rowing/ sailing craft from 6'8" to 22'2" in length. Glued-lap clinker plywood planking is stressed, but traditional methods are also applicable. Catalog is out of print but may be available as of Fall 2010. http://jordanboats .co.uk/JB/iain_oughtred.htm or http://www .woodenboatstore.com/

H. H. ("Dynamite") Payson & Company, Pleasant Beach Road, South Thomaston, ME 04858. Catalog of 31 designs. Study packet available on how to build "instant" small craft—row, power, and sail—designed by Phil Bolger. No lofting or building jig required. http://www .instantboats.com/

Roberts, Bruce, P.O. Box 1086, Severna Park, MD 21146. Book of designs for over 250 sailboats and powerboats. Hulls of steel, fiberglass, aluminum alloy, wood epoxy, C-Flex, and Airex core. Roberts can furnish full-size patterns or kits for many of the designs. http://www.bruceroberts. com/public/HTML/BOAT-PLANS.com

Sintes Fiberglass Designs, Inc., 1425 Sylvia Avenue, Metairie, LA 70124. Powerboat plans for amateur and professional builders. Video available. http://www.sintesfiberglass.com/

Stimson Marine, Inc., 261 River Road, Boothbay, ME 04537. Offers plans for a 19' Ocean Pointer outboard and an 11' Sea Urchin sailing skiff, also 12' swallow sailing wherry, and spoondrift 17' or 18' sea kayak skin-on-frame boats. http:// www.by-the-sea.com/stimsonmarine/

WoodenBoat Publications, Naskeag Road, Box 78, Brooklin, ME 04616. Numerous plans are available through the Woodenboat Store. http:// www.woodenboatstore.com/

TOOLS AND GENERAL HARDWARE

Adjustable Clamp Company, 404 North Armour Street, Chicago, IL 60642. Manufacturer of a complete line of clamps under the "Jorgensen," "Pony," and "Adjustable" brand names. Catalog shows many types of clamps beyond those typically displayed in stores. http://www .adjustableclamp.com/

Albert Constantine & Sons, Inc., 2050 Eastchester Road, Bronx, NY 10461, and Constantine's Wood Center, 1040 E. Oakland Park Boulevard, Ft. Lauderdale, FL 33334. An old company that sells tools, including taper-point drills for wood-screw holes and Japanese hand saws, chisels, planes, and waterstones; also carries finishing materials, interior joinerwork hardware, and abrasives. http://www.constantines.com/

Attwood Marine Products, 1016 N. Monroe Street, Lowell, MI 49331. http://www.attwoodmarine .com/

Duck Trap Woodworking (Walter J. Simmons), P.O. Box 88, Lincolnville Beach, ME 04849. Makes and sells a one-of-a-kind boatbuilder's bevel. http://www.duck-trap.com/

Fein Power Tools, Inc., 1030 Alcon Street, Pittsburgh, PA 15220. Carries a line of German power tools recently introduced in the United States. A list of dealers is available. http:// www.fein.de/corp/us/en/custom/index.html

W. L. Fuller, Inc., 7 Cypress Street, Warwick, RI 02888. Countersinks, counterbores, plug cutters, tapered drills. http://www.wlfuller.com/

Garrett Wade Co., Inc., 5389 East Provident Drive, Cincinnati, OH 45246. Extremely complete selection of hardware and tools, including a large variety of Japanese hand tools, in a catalog too good to ever throw away. http://www .garrettwade.com/

Highland Woodworking, 1045 N. Highland Avenue NE, Atlanta, GA 30306. Wide selection of woodworking tools (power and hand), books, and supplies. Also Japanese tools including waterstones and slipstones, honing guide, chisels, handsaws, scooping-type wooden block plane for concave surfaces, feather files, and two sizes of long-handled slicks. http://www .highlandwoodworking.com/

Hood Yacht Systems, 7712 Cheri Court, Tampa, FL 33634. http://www.hoodyachtsystems.com/

Japan Woodworker, 1731 Clement Avenue, Alameda, CA 94501. http://www .japanwoodworker.com/

Laguna Tools, 17101 Murphy Avenue, Irvine, CA 92614. http://www.lagunatools.com/

Lee Valley Tools Ltd., P.O. Box 1780, Ogdensburg, NY 13669-6780. Imports and sells the enxó hand adze. http://www.leevalley.com/us/

Lie-Nielsen Toolworks, 264 Stirling Road, Warren, ME 04864. http://www.lie-nielsen.com/

Marine Hardware, 14560 NE 91st Street, Redmond, WA 98052 or 5 Aviator Way, Ormond Beach, FL 32174. http://marinehardware.com/

MLCS Ltd., P.O. Box 165, Huntingdon Valley, PA 19006-0165. Huge selection of router bits and cove and bead bits for edging ¼" strip planking. http://www.mlcswoodworking.com/

Oliver Carbine Products, Inc., 7445 Mayer Road, Cottrellville, MI 48039. Maker of the Karbide Kutzall line of cutting tools, which have patented "structured carbide" teeth that don't heat up or clog in use. The tools are available from a number of the catalogs on this list. http://www.olivercorp.com/

Olson Saw Company, 16 Stony Hill Road, Bethel, CT 06801. Manufacturer of bandsaw blades

and scroll blades, available online. http://www
.olsonsaw.net/

Perko, Inc., 16490 NW 13th Avenue, Miami, FL
33169. Manufacturer of a complete line of
marine hardware, including navigation lights.
http://www.perko.com/

Sears Holding Corporation, 3333 Beverly Road,
Hoffman Estates, IL 60179. The "Power and
Hand Tools" catalog, available in the hardware
department of Sears retail stores, offers
woodworking and metalworking tools, electric
motors, and just about everything else. http://
www.craftsman.com/

Wetzler Clamp Company, Route 611, Box 175, Mt.
Bethel, PA 18343. Producers of a complete line
of clamps. http://www.wetzler.com/

Wood Carvers Supply, Inc., P.O. Box 7500,
Englewood, FL 34295-7500. Cutting tools. http://
www.woodcarverssupply.com/

Woodcraft, 1177 Rosemar Road, P.O. Box 1686,
Parkersburg, WV 26102-1686. Well-illustrated
catalog includes Japanese chisels, handsaws,
waterstones, and slipstones. This outfit can
supply just about everything you need, by mail
or online. They also have 80 stores nationwide.
http://www.woodcraft.com/

WoodenBoat Store, P.O. Box 78, Naskeag Road,
Brooklin, ME 04616. Bits, hand drills, chisels,
mallets, hammers, carving tools, knives, tool
sets, and more. http://www.woodenboatstore
.com/

Woodworker's Supply, Inc., 1108 North Glenn
Road, Casper, WY 82601. Also locations in
Graham, NC, and Albuquerque, NM. http://
woodworker.com/

BRONZE MARINE HARDWARE

Starting about 1970, some sizes of deck fittings and similar gear were no longer made by the large marine hardware manufacturers in the United States, presumably due to reduced sales. There seems to be no shortage, though, of inferior die-cast, pot-metal fittings and black cleats and the like, which some think good-looking on boats of peculiar shapes. Take heart: there are still a few firms that make traditional hardware. Here are some that might have the gear you seek.

ABI Industries, distributed by SailboatStuff. http://
www.sailboatstuff.com/co_abi.html/

Bristol Bronze, P.O. Box 101, Tiverton, RI 02878.
Specializes in reproductions of Herreshoff
Manufacturing Company hardware. http://www
.bristolbronze.com/

Buck-Algonquin, 370 North Main Street, Smyrna,
DE 19977-1911. http://www.buckalgonquin
.com/

Chatfield Marine, 9 Porana Road, Glenfield, P.O.
Box 100-164, NSMC, Auckland 0745, New
Zealand. http://www.chatfieldmarine.com/

EdsonAnbar Foundry, 146 Duchaine Boulevard,
New Bedford, MA 02745. One of the world's
largest producers of sailboat steerers; catalog
is practically a design handbook. http://www
.edsonfoundry.com/

Fraser Bronze Foundry, 5625 48th Drive NE, Suites
D & E, Marysville, WA 98270. Large assortment
of products related to fishing and boating. http://
www.fraserbronze.com/

J. M. Reineck & Son, 9 Willow Street, Hull, MA
02045-1121. Manufacturers of classic bronze
yacht blocks. http://www.bronzeblocks.com/

Lewmar, Cumbrae House, 15 Carlton Court,
Glasgow, Lanarkshire G5 9JP, Scotland.
Brand names include Simpson Lawrence,
Navtec, Titan, and Whitlock. Windlasses,
genuine CQR "plow" anchors, and other
products made in Scotland.

Marine Associates, 1651 Hanley Road, Hudson,
WI 54018. Makers of single-arm and v-propeller
shaft struts, rudder ports, tiller arms, shaft logs,
and stuffing boxes. http://www.marineassociates.
com/

Marine Hardware, 14560 NE 91st Street, Redmond,
WA 98052 or 5 Aviator Way, Ormond Beach, FL
32174. http://marinehardware.com/

New Found Metals, Inc., 240 West Airport
Road, Port Townsend, WA 98368. http://www
.newfoundmetals.com/

Pert Lowell Co., Inc., Lane's End, Newbury, MA
01951. Classic bronze hardware. http://www
.pertlowell.com/

Port Townsend Foundry, 251 Otto Street,
Port Townsend, WA 98368. Makers of all
sorts of marine hardware. http://www
.porttownsendfoundry.com/marine.htm/

Spartan Marine Hardware, 340 Robinhood Road,
Gerogetown, ME 04548. Manufacturer of bronze
and stainless steel hardware. Also carries
fiberglass tubing. http://spartanmarine.com/

BOATBUILDING LUMBER, PLYWOOD, AND RELATED PRODUCTS

Fortunately, the problem of finding good boatbuilding wood has been reduced somewhat by suppliers named herein who sell specifically (but not exclusively) to boatbuilders, and by the advertisements published in periodicals such as *WoodenBoat*, *Professional BoatBuilder*, *National Fisherman*, *Good Old Boat*, *Small Craft Advisor*, and *Messing About in Boats*. WoodenBoat's *Boatbuilding Woods: A Directory of Suppliers* remains a useful though aging source in 2011. This section also contains sources for moisture meters and other wood-related items.

Also of interest is the Forestry Stewardship Council
(www.fsc.org) and reforestteak.com/

Aircraft Spruce and Specialty Company, 225
Airport Circle, Corona, CA 92882 and 452
Dividend Drive, Peachtree City, GA 30269. Sitka
spruce. http://www.aircraftspruce.com/

Allied Veneer Co., 14711 Artesia Boulevard, La
Mirada, CA 90638. Marine plywood including
Joubert Okoume, Hydrotek, and Aquatek
marine. http://alliedveneer.com/

Almquist Lumber Company, 5301 Boyd
Road, Arcata, CA 95521. Boat woods and
marine plywoods including white oak,
Douglas fir, Port Orford cedar, ipe, African
mahogany, purpleheart, and teak. http://www
.almquistlumber.com/boatwoods.html/

APA—The Engineered Wood Association, 7011
S. 19th Street, Tacoma, WA 98466-5333. http://
www.apawood.org/

Boulter Plywood Corporation, 24 Broadway,
Somerville, MA 02145. Teak, ash, khaya African
mahogany, Philippine mahogany, sapele African
ribbon stripe, Spanish cedar, western red cedar,
white oak, Douglas fir, and premium vertical-

grain Sitka spruce spar stock. http://www
.boulterplywood.com/

Causeway Lumber Company, 2601 South Andrews
Avenue, Ft. Lauderdale, FL 33316. Lumber and
millwork. http://www.causewaylumber.com/

M(aurice). L. Condon Company, Inc., 250 Ferris
Avenue, White Plains, NY 10603. Mast- and
spar-grade Sitka spruce, Philippine and African
mahogany, white cedar, oak, teak, cypress,
Douglas fir, and lignum vitae. http://www
.condonlumber.net/

Albert Constantine & Sons, Inc., 2050 Eastchester
Road, Bronx, NY 10461, and Constantine's
Wood Center, 1040 E. Oakland Park Boulevard,
Ft. Lauderdale, FL 33334. Sells a meter that
determines the moisture content of wood. http://
www.constantines.com/

Dean Hardwoods, Inc., 9244 Industrial Boulevard
NE, Leland, NC 28451. Teak, mahogany, and
vertical-grain decking in lengths up to 20 feet.
http://www.deanwood.com/

Edensaw Woods Ltd., 211 Seton Road, Port
Townsend, WA 98368. Stocks a large range of
plywood for the marine industry including a
Lloyd's of London-rated European-style multi-
layered Okoume marine plywood. http://www
.edensaw.com/

Florida Cypress Wood Products, 1226 Wigmore
Street, Jacksonville, FL 32206. All grades of
cypress, wholesale and retail. http://www
.floridacypress.com/

GE Sensing & Inspection Technologies,
manufacturer of Protimeter Moisture Meters. A
moisture meter for both wood and composite
materials—it works on wet surfaces and does
not require removal of coatings. http://www
.gesensing.com/protimeterproducts/

General Hardwoods and Marine Millwork, Inc.,
2619 Southwest 2nd Avenue, Ft. Lauderdale, FL
33315. http://www.genhardwoods.com/

Genwove U.S. Ltd., 100 Plyler Road, Indian Trail,
NC 28079. http://www.gwv.com/

Harbor Sales Company, 100 Harbor Court,
Sudlersville, MD 21668. Teak, cedar, Douglas fir,
mahogany, and marine-grade plywood. http://
www.harborsales.net/

Logan Lumber Company, 1635 Tappan Boulevard,
Tampa, FL 33619. http://www.loganlumber.com/

Maine Coast Lumber, 17 White Birch Lane, York,
ME 03909. Marine plywoods including sapele-
African mahogany, African okoume, marine
meranti; type 1 glue layups including exterior
okoume, ribbon striped sapele, teak, marine
fir, Honduras mahogany, and luan. http://www
.mainecoastlumber.com/

McEwen Lumber Company, a division of Hood
Industries, 3160 West 45th Street, Jacksonville,
FL 32209 and 12 other locations. Teak, Honduras
mahogany, and many other species. http://www
.hoodindustries.com/

Medley Hardwoods, 7182 Northwest 77th Terrace,
Miami, FL 33136. http://medleyhardwoodsinc
.com/

Merritt Marine Supply, 2621 NE 4th Avenue,
Pompano Beach, FL 33064. Marine plywood.
http://www.merrittsupply.com/

Northwoods Canoe Company, 336 Range Road,
Atkinson, ME 04426. Canoe plans. Canoe-
building material including white cedar; also a
VHS video made in its shop that covers wood
bending, selection and preparation of wood,
and construction of a steam box. http://www
.wooden-canoes.com/index.htm/

Nyle Dry Kiln Systems, 72 Center Street, Brewer,
ME 04412. http://www.nyle.com/

A. E. Sampson & Son, 171 Camden Road, Warren,
ME 04864. Douglas fir, hickory, oak, poplar,
walnut, pine, Jabota (Brazilian cherry), and
European steamed beech. Maine species: ash,
eastern white pine, Norway pine, hard maple,
soft maple, yellow birch, red birch, and cherry.
http://www.aesampsonandson.com/

Shell Lumber Company, 2733 SW 27th Avenue, Miami, FL 33133. http://www.shelllumber.com/Shell_Lumber.html/

Fred Tebb and Sons, Inc., 1906 Marc Street, Tacoma, WA 98421, 253 272-4107. Sitka spruce specialists: wet or dry, rough or planed, various grades. craigleverson@yahoo.com/

Westergard Boatyard, Nova Scotia, Canada. Hackmatack knees. http://www.westergardboatyard.ca/index.html/

West Wind Hardwoods, Inc., #5-10189 McDonald Park Road, Sidney, BC Canada V8L-5X5; 1-800-667-2275. Domestic, European, and Asian marine plywoods. http://www.westwindhardwood.com/

Wicks Aircraft Supply, 410 Pine Street, Highland, IL 62249. Sitka spruce. http://www.wicksaircraft.com/

Wooden Boat Shop, 6569 Gracely Drive, P.O. Box 33013, Cincinnati, OH 45233. Marine plywood. http://www.woodenboatshop.com/

Yukon Lumber Company, 520 West 22nd Street, Norfolk, VA 23517. http://www.yukonlumber.com/

FIBERGLASS AND OTHER HULL MATERIALS

3A Composites, 108 Fairway Court, Northvale, NJ 07647. Manufacturer of Baltek plywood and Airex core materials. http://www.3acomposites.com/

Defender Industries, Inc., 42 Great Neck Road, Waterford, CT 06385. Complete online catalog, including synthetic fabrics and resins. http://www.defender.com/

DIAB Inc., 315 Seahawk Drive, DeSoto, TX 75115. Manufacturer of Divinycell and Klegecell. http://www.diabgroup.com/

Fiberglass Coatings, Inc., 4301A 34th Street N, St. Petersburg, FL 33714. Extensive line of synthetic fabrics and resins. http://www.fgci.com/

Fiberglass Supply, 11824 Water Tank Road, Burlington, WA 98233. http://www.fiberglasssupply.com/

Merritt Marine Supply, 2621 NE 4th Avenue, Pompano Beach, FL 33064. Fiberglass products and marine plywood. http://www.merrittsupply.com/

Seemann Composites, Inc., 12481 Glascock Drive, Gulfport, MS 39503. Manufacturer of C-Flex fiberglass. http://seemanncomposites.com/cflex.html/

METAL AND PLASTIC FASTENERS

Anchor Staple & Nail Company, 28 Blanchard Place, Wakefield, RI 02879. http://www.anchorssn.com/

Chesapeake Marine Fasteners, P.O. Box 6691, 110 Compromise Street, Annapolis, MD 21401. http://www.chesfast.com/

Duck Trap Woodworking (Walter J. Simmons), P.O. Box 88, Lincolnville Beach, ME 04849. Copper clench nails, square-shank boat nails. http://www.duck-trap.com/

W. L. Fuller, Inc., 7 Cypress Street, Warwick, RI 02888. http://www.wlfuller.com/

Hamilton Marine, 155 East Main Street, Searsport, ME 04974. http://www.hamiltonmarine.com/

Jamestown Distributors, 17 Peckham Drive, Bristol, RI 02809. All types of marine fasteners. http://www.jamestowndistributors.com/

McFeely's Square Drive Screws, Lynchburg, VA 24506. Complete line of square-drive screws in most sizes, types, and materials of interest to boatbuilders, including silicon bronze and three grades of passivated stainless steels. The silicon bronze screws are available in two types: boatbuilding with cut threads and full-body-diameter shank, and marine grade with rolled threads and reduced-diameter shanks. http://www.mcfeelys.com/

Metric & Multistandard Components Corporation, 120 Old Saw Mill River Road, Hawthorne, NY 10532. Metric fasteners of all types. http://www.metricmcc.com/

Northwoods Canoe Company, 336 Range Road, Atkinson, ME 04426. Canoe-builders' tack fasteners and other canoe hardware. http://www.wooden-canoes.com/index.htm/

Pacific Fasteners U.S., Inc., 18866 72nd Avenue South, Kent, WA 98032. Online catalog. http://www.pacificfasteners.com/

Small Parts, Inc., 13980 NW 58th Court, Miami Lakes, FL 33014-0650. Gauges for identifying metric fasteners for replacement. http://www.smallparts.com/

Strawberry Banke, Inc., 14 Hancock Street, Portsmouth, NH 03801. Copper clench nails. http://www.strawberybanke.org/

Tremont Nail Company, 457 School Street, Mansfield, MA 02048. Oldest U.S. manufacturer of hot-dipped galvanized boat nails. http://www.tremontnail.com/

Woodworking and Faering Designs, P.O. Box 322, East Middlebury, VT 05740. http://www.faeringdesigninc.com/

ADHESIVES

Aircraft Spruce and Specialty Company, 225 Airport Circle, Corona, CA 92882 and 452 Dividend Drive, Peachtree City, GA 30269. Glues. http://www.aircraftspruce.com/

Fiberglass Coatings, Inc., 4301A 34th Street N, St. Petersburg, FL 33714. Epoxy adhesives. http://www.fgci.com/

Glen-L.com, 9152 Rosecrans, Bellflower, CA 90706. Poxy-Grip epoxy. http://www.glen-l.com/

Gougeon Brothers, Inc., P.O. Box 908, Bay City, MI 48707. Formulates and manufactures WEST System and PRO-SET marine-grade epoxies used around the world in boatbuilding and boat repair. http://www.westsystem.com/ss/ or http://www.prosetepoxy.com/

Industrial Plastics & Paints, 150-12571 Bridgeport Road, Richmond, BC, Canada V6V 2N5. G2 and Cold Cure epoxies. http://www.ippnet.com/

Interplastic Corporation, Commercial Resins Division, 1225 Willow Lake Boulevard, St. Paul, MN 55110-5145. Vinylester and specialty resins. http://www.interplastic.com/

Jamestown Distributors, 17 Peckham Drive, Bristol, RI 02809. http://www.jamestowndistributors.com/

System Three Resins, 3500 West Valley Highway North, Suite 105, Auburn, WA 98001-2436. System Three epoxy tolerates low temperature and high humidity; stocked by a number of marine supply stores, or available direct. http://www.systemthree.com/

Wicks Aircraft Supply, 410 Pine Street, Highland, IL 62249. Epoxies. http://www.wicksaircraft.com/

ALTERNATIVE MATERIALS FOR INTERIOR JOINERWORK

King Plastic Corporation, 1100 N Toledo Blade Boulevard, North Port, FL 34288-8694. Makers of polymer sheets. http://www.kingplastic.com/

Spartech, 120 South Central Avenue, Suite 1700, Clayton, MO 63105-1705. VinylAlloy and FloorLite. http://www.spartech.com/

DECKING MATERIALS

Elsro, Inc., 114 37th Street, Evans, CO 80620. Marine deck planks. http://www.elsroinc.com/marine-deck-plank/

MarQuipt, Inc., 3100 Southwest Tenth Street, Pompano Beach, FL 33069. http://www.marquipt.com/

Nuteak Decking Inc., 3732 SW 30th Avenue, Hollywood, FL 33312. Synthetic teak. http://www.nuteak.com/

Sani-Tred, P.O. Box 1037, Plymouth, IN 46563. Marine deck coverings. http://www.sanitred.com/BoatRepair.htm/

Teakdecking Systems, 7061 15th Street East, Sarasota, FL 34243. Prefabricated teak decking. http://www.teakdecking.com/

DECK AND COMPANIONWAY HATCHES

Atkins & Hoyle Ltd., 180 Kimmetts Side Road, RR7, Napanee, ON K7R 3L2 Canada. http://www.atkinshoyle.com/

Bomar, Inc., P.O. Box 120, Charlestown, NH 03603. http://www.pompanette.com/bomar/

Diamond Sea Glaze, 26995 Gloucester Way, Langley, BC, Canada V4W 3Y3. http://www.diamondseaglaze.com/

Freeman Marine Equipment, Inc., 28336 Hunter Creek Road, Gold Beach, OR 97444. http://www.freemanmarine.com/

Hood Yacht Systems, 7712 Cheri Court, Tampa, FL 33634. http://www.hoodyachtsystems.com/

Innovative Product Solutions, 2710 N John Young Parkway, Kissimmee, FL 34741. http://www.gotohmg.com/

NONWOOD WINDOW FRAMES, RUB RAILS, ETC.

Barbour Plastics, Inc., 101 North Montello Street, Brockton, MA 02305. Rubrails, dock bumpers, et cetera. http://www.barbourcorp.com/

Go Industries, 20331 Lake Forest Drive, Unit C14, El Toro, CA 92630. http://www.goindustries.com/

Ray, Alan C. Aluminum, vinyl, and steel rubrails. http://www.rubrails.com/ or call 1-877-287-6707 for pricing

TACO Metals, 50 NE 179th Street, Miami, FL 33162 and 3 other locations in MA, FL, and TN. http://www.tacomarine.com/

WINDOWS

American Marine, 1790 SW 13th Court, Pompano Beach, FL 33069. http://www.americanmarine.com/

B & J Aluminum Windows, 1308 Coteau Holmes Road, St. Martinville, LA 70582. Heavy-duty metal windows. http://www.boatwindows.biz/

Beclawat Manufacturing Inc., 90 Hanna Court South, Belleville, ON K8P 5H2 Canada. http://www.beclawat.com/

Freeman Marine Equipment, Inc., 28336 Hunter Creek Road, Gold Beach, OR 97444. http://www.freemanmarine.com/

Motion Windows, a division of Peninsula Glass, 6005 NE 121st Avenue, Vancouver, WA 98682. http://www.motionwindows.com/

U.S.A. Marine Windows and Doors Mfg. Inc., 5937 RavensWood Road, Bay-H6, Dania Beach, FL 33312. http://www.usamarinewindows.com/

Waterway Systems, 7010 28th Street, Ct E, C&E Unit 5, Sarasota, FL 34243. http://www.waterwaysystems.com/

DRAWER SLIDE PARTS

Blum Inc., 7733 Old Plank Road, Stanley, NC 28164. http://www.blum.com/us/

Bold Hardware Co., 4200 82nd Street, Suite J, Sacramento, CA 95826. http://www.drawerslides.com/

Grace Manufacturing, Inc., P.O. Box 856, Warsaw, IN 46581-0856. http://www.grace-mfg.com/

NONCORROSIVE LOCKS

Northeast Lock Corp., 48 Oak Street, Clifton, NJ 07014. http://www.northeastlock.com/marinelocks.html/

Phoenix Lock Company, 1220 American Boulevard, West Chester, PA 19380. http://www.phoenixlock.com/

CANING SUPPLIES

Albert Constantine & Sons, Inc., 2050 Eastchester Road, Bronx, NY 10461, and Constantine's Wood Center, 1040 E. Oakland Park Boulevard, Ft. Lauderdale, FL 33334. http://www.constantines.com/

Woodworker's Supply, Inc., 1108 North Glenn Road, Casper, WY 82601. Also locations in Graham, NC, and Albuquerque, NM. http://woodworker.com/

READYMADE WOODWORK

H & L Marine Woodwork, Inc., 2965 East Harcourt Street, Compton, CA 90221. 323-636-1718.

Maine Mystique, P.O. Box 1358, Windham, ME 04062. http://www.mainemystique.com/

Maritime Services Corporation, 3457 Guignard Drive, Hood River, OR 97031. http://www.mscor.com/

S & P Custom, Inc., 575 45th Avenue S, St. Petersburg, FL 33705. http://www.teakmarinewoodwork.com/

Teak Isle Manufacturing, Inc., 401 Capitol Court, Ocoee, FL 34761. http://www.teakisle.com/

Wilson & Hayes Marine Furnishings, 1601 Eastlake Avenue E,, Seattle, WA 98201. http://www.wilson-and-hayes.com/

Woodworker's Supply, Inc., 1108 North Glenn Road, Casper, WY 82601. Also locations in Graham, NC, and Albuquerque, NM. http://woodworker.com/

ABRASIVES

Albert Constantine & Sons, Inc., 2050 Eastchester Road, Bronx, NY 10461, and Constantine's Wood Center, 1040 E. Oakland Park Boulevard, Ft. Lauderdale, FL 33334. http://www.constantines.com/

Maverick Abrasives, 1030 North Batavia Street, Unit B, Orange, CA 92867. http://www.maverickabrasives.com/

Red Hill Corporation, 1540 Biglerville Road, Gettysburg, PA 17325. http://www.supergrit.com/

Woodworker's Supply, Inc., 1108 North Glenn Road, Casper, WY 82601. Also locations in Graham, NC, and Albuquerque, NM. http://woodworker.com/

ONE-OFF OR PRODUCTION CASTINGS OF LEAD

Great Lakes Castings, 800 North Washington Avenue, Ludington, MI 49431. http://www.greatlakescastings.com/

Mars Metal, 4140 Morris Drive, Burlington, ON, Canada L7L 5L6. http://www.marsmetal.com/

Mayco Industries, Inc., 18 West Oxmoor Road, Birmingham, AL 35209. http://www.maycoindustries.com/

ALUMINUM ALLOY SPARS

Dwyer Aluminum Mast Company, 2 Commerce Drive, North Branford, CT 06471. http://www.dwyermast.com/

Hall Spars & Rigging, 33 Broadcommon Road, Bristol, RI 02829. http://www.hallspars.com/

Kenyon Spars, distributed by Rig-Rite, Inc. 401-739-1140. http://www.RigRite.com/

Schaefer Spars, distributed by Rig-Rite, Inc. 401-739-1140. http://www.RigRite.com/

Taco Metals, 50 NE 179th Street, Miami, FL 33162 and 3 other locations in MA, FL, and TN. http://www.tacomarine.com/

Zephyr Spars, Division of Cape Cod Shipbuilding Company, 7 Narrows Road, P.O. Box 152, Wareham, MA 02571.

WOODEN SPARS

Grays Harbor Historical Seaport Authority (The Spar Shop), 712 Hagara Street, Aberdeen, Washington 98520. http://www.thesparshop.org/

Pleasant Bay Boat and Spar Company, LLC, 80 Rayber Road, Orleans, MA 02653. http://www.pleasantbayboatandspar.com/

Shaw & Tenney, 20 Water Street, Orono, ME 04473. http://www.shawandtenney.com/

WOODEN YACHT BLOCKS

Conrad Blocks, 28 Hume Street, Woodend, Queensland, Australia. Traditional wooden shelled blocks for all types of boats. http://www.conradblocks.com/

Dauphinee, A. & Sons Ltd., P.O. Box 115, Lunenberg, Nova Scotia B0J 2CO.902-634-8460.

Ording Blockmakers, Operetteweg 38, 1323 VA Almere, Holland. Wooden blocks, hardware, masts, spars, et cetera. http://www.ording-blokken.nl/eng/

Pert Lowell Co., Inc., Lane's End, Newbury, MA 01951. Wooden cleats, belaying pins, plus mast hoops and parrel beads for gaff-rig buffs. http://www.pertlowell.com/

Wooden Boat Fittings, 43 Fincham Crescent, Wanniassa, ACT 20903, Australia. http://www.woodenboatfittings.com.au/

CAST BRONZE RUDDERS

Buck-Algonquin, 370 North Main Street, Smyrna, DE 19977-1911. http://www.buckalgonquin.com/

Edson International, 146 Duchaine Boulevard, New Bedford, MA 02745. One of the world's largest producers of sailboat steerers; catalog is practically a design handbook. http://www.edsonintl.com/

Glenwood Marine Equipment, 1627 West El Segundo Boulevard, Cardena, CA 09249. http://www.glenwoodmarine.net/Catalog.htm/

Marine Associates, 1651 Hanley Road, Hudson, WI 54018. Makers of single-arm and v-propeller shaft struts, rudder ports, tiller arms, shaft logs, and stuffing boxes. http://www.marineassociates.com/

Marine Hardware, 14560 NE 91st Street, Redmond, WA 98052 or 5 Aviator Way, Ormond Beach, FL 32174. http://marinehardware.com/

HYDRAULIC STEERING COMPONENTS

Autonav Marine Systems, Inc., 55A Clipper Street, Coquitlam, BC, Canada V3K6X2. http://www.autonav.com/

Hynautic—see Telefex

Jastram Engineering, Ltd., 135 West Riverside Drive, North Vancouver, BC, Canada V7H1T6. http://www.jastram.com/

Kobelt Manufacturing Ltd., 8238 129th Street, Surrey, BC, Canada V3W 0A6. http://www.kobelt.com/product-steering.php/

Latham Marine, Inc., 280 SW 32 Court, Fort Lauderdale, FL 33315 http://www.lathammarine.com/

Parker Oildyne Division, 5520 North Highway 169, New Hope, MN. http://www.parker.com/

Teleflex, Inc., 1 Sierra Place, Litchfield, IL 62056. http://www.teleflexmarine.com/

Uflex USA, Inc., 6442 Parkland Drive, Sarasota, FL 34243. http://uflexusa.ultraflexgroup.com

Wagner Engineering Ltd., 135 West Riverside Drive, North Vancouver, BC, Canada V7H 1T6. http://www.wagnerengineering.ca/enter.htm

ENGINE CONTROLS

Autonav Marine Systems, Inc., 55A Clipper Street, Coquitlam, BC, Canada V3K6X2. http://www.autonav.com/

Control Masters, Inc., 14603 Beach Boulevard, Suite 600, Jacksonville, FL 32250. http://www.controlmastersinc.com/

Edson International, 146 Duchaine Boulevard, New Bedford, MA 02745. One of the world's largest producers of sailboat steerers; catalog is practically a design handbook. http://www.edsonintl.com/

Jastram Engineering, Ltd., 135 West Riverside Drive, North Vancouver, BC, Canada V7H1T6. http://www.jastram.com/

Kobelt Manufacturing Ltd., 8238 129th Street, Surrey, BC, Canada V3W 0A6. http://www.kobelt.com/product-steering.php/

Latham Marine, Inc., 280 SW 32 Court, Fort Lauderdale, FL 33315. http://www.lathammarine.com/

Mathers Marine, Inc., 806 Sundown Lane, Camano Island, WA 98282. http://www.mathersmarineinc.com/

Teleflex, Inc., 1 Sierra Place, Litchfield, IL 62056. http://www.teleflexmarine.com/

CIRCUIT BREAKER PANELS

Blue Seas Systems, 425 Sequoia Drive, Bellingham, WA 98226. http://bluesea.com/

Cole Hersee Company, 20 Old Colony Avenue, Boston, MA 02127-2467. http://www.colehersee.com/

Newmar, P.O. Box 1306, Newport Beach, CA 92663. http://www.newmarpower.com/

Paneltronics, 11960 NW 87th Court, Hialeah, FL 33016. http://www.paneltronics.com/

Sea-Dog Line Corporation, P.O. Box 479, Everett, WA 98206. http://www.sea-dog.com/

OARS, PADDLES, OARLOCKS

Barkley Sound Marine, 3073 Vanhorne Road, Qualicum Beach, BC, Canada V9K 1X3. http://barkleysoundoar.com/

Caviness Woodworking, Inc., 200 North Aycock Avenue, Calhoun City, MS. http://www.cavinesspaddles.com/

Duck Trap Woodworking (Walter J. Simmons), P.O. Box 88, Lincolnville Beach, ME 04849. Plans for making oars. http://www.duck-trap.com/

Northwoods Canoe Company, 336 Range Road, Atkinson, ME 04426. Canoe plans. and oars. http://www.wooden-canoes.com/index.htm

NRS, 2009 S Main Street, Moscow, ID 83843. http://www.nrsweb.com/

Sea-Dog Line Corporation, P.O. Box 479, Everett, WA 98206. http://www.sea-dog.com/

Shaw & Tenney, 20 Water Street, Orono, ME 04473. http://www.shawandtenney.com/

SIGNMAKER'S SUPPLIES

Blick Art Materials, P.O. Box 1267, Galesburg, IL 61402-1267. http://www.dickblick.com/

Sign Supply Factory, 18090 Collins Avenue, #163, Miami, FL 33160. http://signsupplyfactory.com/

Wensco, 5760 Safety Drive NE, Belmont, MI 49306. http://www.wensco.com/

WOODCARVERS

Allanson, Brian, Allanson Signs, 22 Park Heights Avenue, Dover, NJ 07801. http://www.carvedsigns.us/

Drew Averette Creative Carving, 1730 Youngs Avenue, Southhold, NY 11971. http://www.drewscreativecarving.com/

Kukstis Woodcarving, 95R Front Street, Scituate Harbor, MA 02066. http://www.kukstis.com/

Lonborg Woodcarving, 568 Plymouth Street, Halifax, MA 02338. http://www.lonborgwoodcarving.com/

Nantucket Carving and Folk Art, 167 Orange Street, Nantucket, MA 02584. http://www.nantucketcarvingandfolkart.com/

Pearson, Adam, adampearson1@hotmail.com. http://www.adampearsoncarvings.com/

Uranker, J. P., Box 1393, 179 County Road, Oak Bluffs, MA 02557. http://www.jpuwoodcarver.com/

Yankee WoodCarvers, 1151 Washington Street, Braintree, MA 02184. http://yankeewoodcarvers.com/

DAVITS

Atkins & Hoyle Ltd., 180 Kimmetts Side Road, RR7, Napanee, ON K7R 3L2 Canada. http://www.atkinshoyle.com/Davit Master, 5560 Ulmerton Road, Clearwater, FL 33760. http://www.davitmaster.com/

Edson International, 146 Duchaine Boulevard, New Bedford, MA 02745. One of the world's largest producers of sailboat steerers; catalog is practically a design handbook. http://www.edsonintl.com/

Hurley Davits, Hurley Marine Inc., 1125 Lake Shore Drive, Escanaba, MI 49829. http://www.hurleymarine.com/

MarQuipt, Inc., 3100 Southwest Tenth Street, Pompano Beach, FL 33069. http://www.marquipt.com/

PipeWelders Custom Marine, 2965 State Road 84, Fort Lauderdale, FL 33312-4823. http://www.pipewelders.com/

Sea Wise Marine, Inc., 7228 Progress Way, #13, Delta, BC V4G 1H2, Canada. http://www.seawisedavits.com/

WATER TRAP VENT/DORADES

Hood Yacht Systems, 7712 Cheri Court, Tampa, FL 33634. http://www.hoodyachtsystems.com/

Nicro Marine, Marineco Electrical Group, N85 W12545 Westbrook Crossing, Menomonee Falls, WI 53051. http://www.marinco.com/brand/nicro/

Plastimo USA, 7455 16th Street East, Suite 107, Sarasota, FL 34243. http://www.plastimousa.com/

PROPELLER SHAFT SEAL

Norscot Propeller Shaft Seal, 15026 Densmore Avenue, Shoreline, WA 98133. http://www.ibsenco.com/Norscot/norscothome.htm/

Pacific Marine and Industrial, P.O. Box 70520, Richmond, CA 94807-0520. http://www.pacificmarine.net/

Tides Marine, 3251 SW 13th Drive, Suite A, Deerfield Beach, FL 33442. http://www.tidesmarine.com/

PLUMBING (HEADS)

Airhead Toilet, P.O. Box 5, Mt. Vernon, OH 43050. Composting toilets. http://www.airheadtoilet.com/

Domestic Sanitation Corporation, 13128 State Route 266, P.O. Box 38, Big Prairie, OH 44611. Maker of SeaLand and VacuFlush toilets. http://www.sealandtechnology.com/

Headhunter, 3380 SW 11th Avenue, Fort Lauderdale, FL 33315. http://www.headhunterinc.com

Jabsco, division of ITT Flow Control, 1 Kondelin Road, Cape Ann Industrial Park, Gloucester, MA 01930. http://www.ittflowcontrol.com/

Thetford Corporation, P.O. Box 1285, 7101 Jackson Road, Ann Arbor, MI 48103. http://www.thetford.com/

TANKS

Atlantic Coastal Welding, 16 Butler Boulevard, Bayville, NJ 08721. Custom tanks. http://www.speedytanks.com/

Florida Marine Tanks, Inc., 120 Peter Grill Road, Henderson, NC 27536. Custom tanks. http://www.floridamarinetanks.com/

Headhunter, 3380 SW 11th Avenue, Fort Lauderdale, FL 33315. http://www.headhunterinc.com/

Luther's Welding, 500 Wood Street, Bristol, RI 02809. Custom tanks. http://www.lutherswelding.com/

Moeller Marine Products, 801 North Spring Street, Sparta, TN 38583. Stock and custom tanks. http://www.moellermarine.com/

Ocean Link, Inc., 3 Maritime Drive, Suite 6, Portsmouth, RI 02871. http://www.oceanlinkinc.com/

Tempo Products Company Inc., 6200 Cochran Drive, Solon, OH 44139. http://www.tempoproducts.com/2004/bd_fuel_tanks1.html/

Vetus America, 7251 National Drive, Parkway Industrial Center, Hanover, MD 21076. Stock nonmetallic tanks. http://www.vetus.nl/us/index.php/

BRASS THREADED ROD

Metal by the Foot, Inc., 3600 East Truman Road, Kansas City, MO 64127. http://www.metalbythefoot.com/

The Nutty Company, Inc., 135 Main Street, Derby, CT 06418. http://www.nutty.com/

Small Parts, Inc., P.O. Box 4650, Miami Lakes, FL 33014-0650. http://www.smallparts.com/

PAINTBRUSHES

Elder & Jenks, Inc., 148 East 5th Street, Bayonne, NJ 07002. http://www.elderandjenks.com/

Epifanes North America Inc., 70 Water Street, Thomaston, ME 04861. http://www.epifanes.com/

Hamilton Marine, 155 East Main Street, Searsport, ME 04974. Badger and badger-type brushes. http://www.hamiltonmarine.com/

West Marine (home office), 500 Westridge Drive, Watsonville, CA 95076. http://www.westmarine.com/

WoodenBoat Store, P.O. Box 78, Naskeag Road, Brooklin, ME 04616. http://www.woodenboatstore.com/

Wooster Brush Company, P.O. Box 6010, 604 Madison Avenue, Wooster, OH 44691. http://www.woosterbrush.com/

PAINT AND OTHER COATINGS

Epifanes North America Inc., 70 Water Street, Thomaston, ME 04861. http://www.epifanes.com/

International Paint Company, 6001 Antoine Drive, Houston, TX 77091. http://www.international-marine.com/

Pettit Paint Company, 36 Pine Street, Rockaway, NJ 07366. http://www.pettitpaint.com

Progress Paint, 300 Envoy Circle, Suite 302, Louisville, KY 40299. http://www.progresspaint.com/

Rodda Paint Co., 6107 N Marine Drive, Portland, OR 97203. http://www.roddapaint.com/

COMPUTER LOFTING SERVICES

Aerohydro, Inc., P.O. Box 684, 54 Herrick Road, Southwest Harbor, ME 04679. http://www.aerohydro.com/

Corvus Boats, Watford, Ontario, Canada. 519-318-9330. http://www.corvusboats.ca/

Elliott Bay Design Group, LLC, 5305 Shilshole Avenue NW, Suite 100, Seattle, WA 98107 and One Canal Place, 365 Canal Street, Suite 1550, New Orleans, LA 70130. http://www.ebdg.com/

Ralph W. Stanley, Inc., 298 Seawall Road, Ocean House, Building 7, Southwest Harbor, ME 04679. http://www.ralphstanleyboats.com/

Sintes Fiberglass Designs, Inc., 1425 Sylvia Avenue, Metairie, LA 70005. http://www.sintesfiberglass.com/

RESPIRATORS

Aearo Company, 5457 West 79th Street, Indianapolis, IN 46268. http://www.aearo.com/

Draeger Safety Inc., 101 Technology Drive, Pittsburgh, PA 15275. http://www.draeger.com/

3M Occupational Health & Safety Products Division, 3M Center, St. Paul, MN 55133. http://www.mmm.com/occsafety/

SAFETY INFORMATION

Also check "Recommended Reading" for the names of some safety publications.

American Boat and Yacht Council, 613 Third Street, Suite 10, Annapolis, MD 21403. http://www.abycinc.org/

National Fire Protection Association, 1 Batterymarch Park, Quincy, MA 02169-7471. http://www.nfpa.org/

Occupational Safety and Health Administration (OSHA), U.S. Department of Labor, 200 Constitution Avenue NW, Washington, DC 20210. Occupational Safety and Health Administration

Underwriter's Laboratories, Inc., 2600 NW Lake Road, Camas, WA 98607-8542. http://www.ul.com/

U.S. Coast Guard, Office of Boating Safety, 2100 Second Street SW, Stop 7581, Washington, DC 20593. http://www.uscgboating.org/

RECOMMENDED READING

Visit www.internationalmarine.com for the world's largest source of nautical ebooks.

BOOKS, EBOOKS, AND PAMPHLETS

Atkin, Gavin. *Ultrasimple Boatbuilding: 15 Boats You Can Build In a Weekend*, Camden, ME: International Marine Publishing, 2008.

Bingham, Fred P. *Boat Joinery and Cabinetmaking Simplified*. Camden, ME: International Marine Publishing, 1993.

Bolger, Philip. *Boats with an Open Mind*. Camden, ME: International Marine Publishing, 1994.

Brewer, Ted. *Understanding Boat Design*, 4th ed. Camden, ME: International Marine Publishing, 1993.

Brooks, John, and Ruth Ann Hill. *How to Build Glued-Lapstrake Wooden Boats*. Brooklin, ME: WoodenBoat Publications, 2004.

Brotherton, Miner and Sherman, Ed. *The Twelve-Volt Bible for Boats*, 2nd ed. Camden, ME: International Marine Publishing, 2004.

Buehler, George. *Buehler's Backyard Boatbuilding*. Camden, ME: International Marine Publishing, 1990.

Burke, John. *Pete Culler on Wooden Boats*, Camden, ME: International Marine Publishing, 2008.

Calder, Nigel. *Boatowner's Mechanical and Electrical Systems*, 3rd ed. Camden, ME: International Marine Publishing, 2005.

———. *Diesel Engine Care & Repair*. Camden, ME: International Marine Publishing, 2007.

Casey, Don. *Don Casey's Complete Illustrated Maintenance Manual*. Camden, ME: International Marine Publishing, 2005.

———.*Sailboat Hull and Deck Repair*. Camden, ME: International Marine Publishing, 2005.

———.*Sailboat Refinishing*. Camden, ME: International Marine Publishing, 2005.

———.*This Old Boat*, 2nd ed. Camden, ME: International Marine Publishing, 2009.

Chapelle, Howard I. *Boatbuilding*. New York, NY: W. W. Norton, 1994.

Colvin, Thomas E. *Steel Boatbuilding: From Plans to Launching*. Easton, MD: Tiller Publishing, 1996.

Culler, R. D. *Skiffs and Schooners*. Camden, ME: International Marine Publishing, 1990.

Devlin, Samual. *Devlin's Boat Building: How to Build Any Boat the Stitch-and-Glue Way*. Camden, ME: International Marine Publishing, 1995.

Dierking, Gary. *Building Outrigger Sailing Canoes*. Camden, ME: International Marine Publishing, 2007.

Doane, Charles. *The Modern Cruising Sailboat*. Camden, ME: International Marine Publishing, 2009.

The Epoxy Book. Auburn, WA: System Three Resins, Inc., 2009.

Forest Products Laboratory, USDA Forest Service. *The Encyclopedia of Wood*, rev. ed. Reprint of the 1987 revised edition of "Wood Handbook: Wood as an Engineering Material," issued by the U.S. Government Printing Office, 1987. New York: Sterling Publishing Company, Inc., 1999.

Gardner, John. *The Dory Book*. Mystic, CT: Mystic Seaport Museum, Inc., 1987.

———. *Building Classic Small Craft*. Camden, ME: International Marine Publishing, 2003.

———. *More Building Classic Small Craft: How to Build 23 Traditional Boats*. Camden, ME: International Marine Publishing, 1990.

Gerr, Dave. *Boat Mechanical Systems Handbook*. Camden, ME: International Marine Publishing, 2009.

———.*The Elements of Boat Strength*. Camden, ME: International Marine Publishing, 1999.

———.*The Nature of Boats: Insights and Esoterica for the Nautically Obsessed*. Camden, ME: International Marine Publishing, 1995.

———.*The Propeller Handbook*. Camden, ME: International Marine Publishing, 2002.

The Gougeon Brothers on Boat Construction. Bay City, MI: Gougeon Brothers, Inc., 2005.

Hankinson, Ken. *Fiberglass Boat Building for Amateurs*. Bellflower, CA: Glen-L Marine Designs, 1982.

———. *How to Build Fiberglass Boats*, 2nd ed. Bellflower, CA: Glen-L Marine Designs, 1986.

Hanna, Jay. *The Shipcarver's Handbook*. Brooklin, ME: WoodenBoat Publications, 1988.

Herreshoff, L. Francis. *Sensible Cruising Designs*. Camden, ME: International Marine Publishing, 1991.

Hill, Tom. *Ultralight Boatbuilding*. Camden, ME: International Marine Publishing, 1987.

Kulczycki, Chris. *Stitch-and-Glue Boatbuilding*. Camden, ME: International Marine Publishing, 2004.

Lowell, Royal. *Boatbuilding Down East: How Lobsterboats Are Built*. Brooklin, ME: WoodenBoat Publications, 2002.

McIntosh, David ("Bud") C. *How to Build a Wooden Boat*. Brooklin, ME: WoodenBoat Books, 1987.

Michalak, Jim. *Boatbuilding for Beginners*. Halcottsville, NY: Breakaway Books, 2002.

Moores, T., and M. Mohr. *Canoecraft: Woodstrip Construction*. Buffalo, NY, and Ontario, Canada: Firefly Books, Ltd., 2000.

Oughtred, Iain. *Clinker Plywood Boatbuilding Manual*. Brooklin, ME: WoodenBoat Publications, 2000.

Parker, Reuel B. *The New Cold-Molded Boatbuilding: From Lofting to Launching*. Brooklin, ME: WoodenBoat Publications, 2005.

———. *The Sharpie Book*. Brooklin, ME: WoodenBoat Publications.

Payson, Harold H. *Build the Instant Catboat*. Camden, ME: International Marine Publishing, 1987.

———. *Build the New Instant Boats*. Camden, ME: International Marine Publishing, 1987.

———. *Instant Boatbuilding with Dynamite Payson*. Camden, ME: International Marine Publishing, 2007.

Pierce, Cecil E. *Fifty Years a Planemaker and User*. Monmouth, ME: Monmouth Press, 1992.

Pollard, Stephen. *Boatbuilding with Aluminum*. Camden, ME: International Marine Publishing, 2006.

Rabl, S. S. *Boatbuilding in Your Own Backyard*. Centreville, MD: Cornell Maritime Press, 1958.

———. *Ship and Aircraft Fairing and Development*. Centreville, MD: Cornell Maritime Press, 1985.

Rizzetta, Sam. *Canoe and Kayak Building the Light and Easy Way*. Camden, ME: International Marine Publishing, 2009.

Rössel, Greg. *The Boatbuilder's Apprentice*. Camden, ME: International Marine Publishing, 2007.

———.*Building Small Boats*. Brooklin, ME: Wooden Boat Books, 1998.

Rules for Building and Classing Reinforced Plastic Vessels. American Bureau of Shipping, 1978.

Schade, Nick. *Building Strip-planked Boats*. Camden, ME: International Marine Publishing, 2009.

Simmons, Walter J. *Finishing*. Lincolnville, ME: Duck Trap Woodworking, 1984.

———. *Lapstrake Boatbuilding*. Lincolnville, ME: Duck Trap Woodworking, 1983.

Spielman, Patrick. New *Router Handbook*. New York: Sterling Publishing Company, 1993.

———.*Router Basics*. New York: Sterling Publishing Company, 1990.

———. *Sharpening Basics*. New York: Sterling Publishing Company, 1991.

Trefethen, Jim. *Wooden Boat Renovation: New Life for Old Boats Using Modern Methods*. Camden, ME: International Marine Publishing, 1993.

Vaitses, Allan H. *Boatbuilding One-Off in Fiberglass*. Camden, ME: International Marine Publishing, 1984.

———. *Covering Wooden Boats with Fiberglass*. Camden, ME: International Marine Publishing, 1989.

———. *The Fiberglass Boat Repair Manual*. Camden, ME: International Marine Publishing, 1988.

———. *Lofting*. Camden, ME: International Marine Publishing, 1987. (out of print)

Witt, Glen L. *Boat Building with Plywood*, 3rd ed. Bellflower, CA: Glen-L Marine Designs, 1989.

Wittman, Rebecca. *Brightwork: The Art of Finishing Wood*. Camden, ME: International Marine Publishing, 2006.

WoodenBoat Books. *Fifty Wooden Boats: A Catalog of Building Plans*. Brooklin, ME: WoodenBoat Publications, 1984.

———. *Forty Wooden Boats: A Third Catalog of Building Plans*. Brooklin, ME: WoodenBoat Publications, 1995.

———. *Thirty Wooden Boats: A Second Catalog of Building Plans*. Brooklin, ME: WoodenBoat Publications, 1988.

BOATBUILDING PERIODICALS

Good Old Boat, 7340 Niagara Ln. N. Maple Grove, MN 55311-2655. http://www.goodoldboat.com/

Messing Around in Boats, 29 Burley Street, Wenham, MA 01984. http://www.messingaboutinboats .com/

Professional Boatbuilder, P.O. Box 78, 41 WoodenBoat Lane, Brooklin, ME 04616-0078. http://www.proboat.com

Small Craft Advisor, P.O. Box 1343, Port Townsend, WA 98368. http://www .smallcraftadvisor.com/

WoodenBoat, P.O. Box 78, Brooklin, ME 04616. http://wwww.woodenboat.com/

INDEX

Numbers in **bold** refer to pages with illustrations.